"*The Political Economy of Plea Bargaining* offers a wide-ranging exploration of the history and development of the dominant dispute-resolution mechanism in US criminal law. Drawing on an eclectic mix of history, social and critical theory, political philosophy, constitutional jurisprudence, and personal reflection, the author powerfully demonstrates how procedural efficiency and an anti-democratic impulse to maintain social control over marginal populations have displaced the long-standing American commitment to trial by jury. This timely work brings a unique critical-theoretic lens to the current debate and should prompt new misgivings about the plea-bargaining paradigm."

Russell D. Covey, *Law Professor and Co-Chair of the ABA Plea Bargaining Task Force*

"This fresh, insightful, and wide-ranging work explores – and explodes – a leading cause of contemporary injustice – plea bargaining. Drawing on various disciplines and legal doctrine, Professor Schehr powerfully deconstructs the flawed rationales for extinguishing the fundamental right to jury trial, and catalogues the resulting catastrophic damage to US law and society."

Jack Chin, *Professor of Law, and Director of Clinical Legal Education, UC Davis School of Law*

"This captivating exploration delves into the origins and evolution of plea bargaining as a legal instrument of social control in capitalist America. Drawing on interdisciplinary scholarship from Law, Political Economy, and Sociology, this must-read book offers a unique perspective on the anti-democratic nature of plea bargaining, its role within capitalist systems, and the injustices it perpetuates."

Geert Dhondt, *Associate Professor of Economics, John Jay College of Criminal Justice, The City University of New York*

THE POLITICAL ECONOMY OF PLEA BARGAINING

The Political Economy of Plea Bargaining provides the political, economic, and cultural context for understanding the evolution of plea bargaining as a juridical technology implemented to ensure the efficient administration of violations of criminal law.

Across two parts, this book contends that the confluence of political, economic, and cultural factors necessary to enhance the legal preservation of the slave system and white supremacy spatiotemporally coincided with burgeoning Northern industrial capitalism and the liberty of contract doctrine, and that each was contextualized within hegemonic liberal republican ideology out of which grew the implementation of an efficient technology of juridical control achieving normative legal status – plea bargaining. It argues that, as with their predecessors, contemporary actors operating within the criminal legal system and who are responsible for administering plea bargaining are perpetuating a system reproducing a steering mechanism that historically constitutes a through line from Reconstruction to the present day. Following Von Mises, these actors serve as useful innocents, modern-day confused and misguided sympathizers. They are juridical actors who inherited and are perpetuating a system of conflict resolution that serves to maintain a form of social control uniquely situated to historically relevant political, economic, and cultural power in the United States.

The Political Economy of Plea Bargaining will be important reading for legal and social science academics researching and practicing within the field of criminal law and procedure. It will also act as a valuable guide to the debates surrounding plea bargaining for students with a keen interest in criminal law.

Robert Schehr is a Professor in the Department of Criminology and Criminal Justice at Northern Arizona University, USA. His research expertise and publications focus on wrongful conviction, the political economy of law and order, and the jurisprudence of plea bargaining. He is an international speaker on the topic of wrongful conviction. Professor Schehr received a PhD in Sociology from Purdue University in 1991, completed a post-doctoral fellowship at the University of Georgia, and has held positions at Colgate University and the University of Illinois at Springfield. Dr Schehr has been a United States Fulbright Scholar, during which he taught at both Griffith College Law School and Trinity College Law School, Ireland. In May of 2022, Dr Schehr completed a Master's in the Study of Law at Yale Law School.

Directions and Developments in Criminal Justice and Law

https://www.routledge.com/Directions-and-Developments-in-Criminal-Justice-and-Law/book-series/DDCJL

The ways in which crime is constructed in society is of time-honored interest to criminologists across the globe. The ever-changing landscape of what is criminal and what is not affects scholars and policymakers in their approach to the body of law defining prohibited conduct, how that law evolves, and the modes by which it is administered. Rule of law cannot exist without a transparent legal system, strong enforcement structures, and an independent judiciary to protect against the arbitrary use of power. Critical consideration of the mechanisms through which societies attempt to make the rule of law a reality is essential to understanding and developing effectual criminal justice systems. The *Directions and Developments in Criminal Justice and Law* series offers the best research on criminal justice and law around the world, offering original insights on a broadly defined range of socio-legal topics in law, criminal procedure, courts, justice, legislation, and jurisprudence. With an eye toward using innovative and advanced methodologies, series monographs offer solid social science scholarship illuminating issues and trends in law, crime, and justice. Books in this series will appeal to criminologists, sociologists, and other social scientists, as well as policymakers, legal researchers, and practitioners.

Revisiting Juvenile Justice in India
A Study on Juvenile Justice (Care and Protection of Children) Act, 2015
Atul Jaybhaye

Racial and Prejudicial Stereotyping by Police
Its Impact on Investigative Interviewing and the Outcomes of Criminal Investigations
Rashid Minhas

Prisoners' Vote
A Multidisciplinary and Comparative Perspective
Martine Evans and Jérôme Thomas

A Children's Rights Assessment of Juvenile Detention in Australia
Anita Mackay

The Political Economy of Plea Bargaining
Robert Schehr

THE POLITICAL ECONOMY OF PLEA BARGAINING

Robert Schehr

Routledge
Taylor & Francis Group
LONDON AND NEW YORK

Designed cover image: The Star Chamber, circa 1800 (Photo by Universal History Archive/ Getty Images)

First published 2025
by Routledge
4 Park Square, Milton Park, Abingdon, Oxon OX14 4RN

and by Routledge
605 Third Avenue, New York, NY 10158

Routledge is an imprint of the Taylor & Francis Group, an informa business

British Library Cataloguing-in-Publication Data
A catalogue record for this book is available from the British Library

ISBN: 9781032472133 (hbk)
ISBN: 9781032472157 (pbk)
ISBN: 9781003385103 (ebk)

DOI: 10.4324/9781003385103

Typeset in Sabon
by Deanta Global Publishing Services, Chennai, India

This book is dedicated to my academic mentors who blessed me with the love of knowledge, the requirement to take intellectual risks, and the tireless pursuit of justice. Each of you gently, patiently, but sternly guided me along the path to a life of intellectual gratification. I am forever indebted to each of you. And while there are too many of you to name here, I do wish to list a few who are foundational to my intellectual growth: Dr George Manning, Dr Larry Golden, Dr Robert Sipe, Dr Hugh Harris, and Dr Proshanta Nandi. Each of you recognized something in me that I did not see in myself. You embraced me, educated me, and launched me into the world of academia, my home. I love each of you, and I owe you more gratitude than these words can supply.

CONTENTS

PREFACE

With all that is happening in the United States and globally, why would a prospective reader want to spend their valuable time reading about the political economy of plea bargaining? After all, there can be no greater buzz-kill than reading, "The Political Economy of..." well, anything. Admittedly, I have selected a book title that is about as exciting as hearing Ben Stein repeatedly say, "Bueller, Bueller, Bueller."[1]

As this book makes clear, constituted as a legal technology implemented for the efficient administration of justice, plea bargaining signifies a threat to American democracy. At present, there are many threats to what we in the United States have for generations considered normative legal-rational behavior. For the reasons that I have reserved for presentation in this book, plea bargaining towers like an Egyptian pyramid relative to existing threats because: a) over the course of two centuries it has realized normative legal status; b) between 95 and 97 percent of all felony criminal cases are disposed of via the plea; c) it places all significant power in the executive branch in the person of the prosecutor; d) it has usurped the Article III §2 and the Sixth Amendment's trial by jury mandate when liberty interests are at stake; e) it has fallaciously embraced *contract law* to evade the constitutional trial by jury mandate; f) it is premised upon Federal Rule 11 of the Federal Rules of Criminal Procedure where its knowing/intelligent and voluntary prongs justify the plea practice, and where its "factual basis" criteria for engaging in plea negotiations is an empty signifier; and g) it facilitates coercion by confronting a defendant with harsher punishment if convicted at trial in order to induce a plea bargain.

Writing a book that applies political economic analysis to anything requires a commitment to pursuing many theoretical and conceptual rabbit holes. The analysis must be historical in nature, theoretically and conceptually sophisticated, empirically sound, and it must provide readers with a thorough account of each argument made. That is what I have attempted to do in the pages of *The Political Economy of Plea Bargaining*. Before we commence Chapter 1, I think that it would be useful for me to provide readers with a sort of roadmap to the argument that they will encounter. Sometimes having a view from 30,000 feet that provides a macro-level overview of the argument to be made helps to contextualize theoretical, conceptual, and empirical minutiae. In the pages that follow, I will be taking readers on a rhizomatic journey over many centuries in order to provide the necessary political, economic, and cultural context to consider the evolution and purpose of the plea. But I promise that if readers commit to the trip, it will be worth their while.

How I Will Proceed

In the first chapter, I introduce the Federal Rules of Criminal Procedure Rule 11 that guides plea bargaining practices, plea bargaining procedure, the rolc of the legislature in promoting the plea, United States Supreme Court plea case law, a brief history of the appearance of the plea in the United States, and plea bargaining's "innocence problem."

In Chapter 2, I piece together what I believe to be the institutional predicates to the practice that we refer to as plea bargaining. Identification of the *precise* moment that plea bargaining arrived as a procedural technology, and was institutionally recognized as such, is hard to identify largely because it is multicausal. Among the many historical movements that may have culminated in the plea are: a) the growing consolidation and professional authority of lawyers; b) the growing disenchantment with the trial by jury; c) the emergence of the liberty of contract doctrine and its emphasis upon the "freedom to work"; d) the re-emergence in the South during Reconstruction of attempts to re-enslave freed men and women, and perhaps most controversially; e) fear amongst judges, prosecutors, and defense attorneys in the South of mob lynchings which led to rapid case disposition.

Chapter 3 applies Chapter 2's accounting of conciliation courts to the 19th-century Freedmen's Bureau practices. Conciliation courts occupied a central role during Reconstruction and existed mostly in the 15 former slave states, and as I demonstrate, they provide unique insight into the comingling tension between conciliation and adversarialism. Conciliation courts were created as part of the newly formed Freedmen's Bureau, also known as the Bureau of Refugees, Freedmen, and Abandoned Lands. Bureau-operated conciliation court practices began to resemble contemporary plea bargaining through the administrative power of Bureau agents. Agents adjudicated disputes in a manner that was often unique to the jurisdiction and the agent involved, but with a specific emphasis on the introduction and reproduction of dominant cultural values.

Chapter 4 proceeds with reference to contemporary challenges confronting the republic, a discussion of the historical understanding of the inalienability and indefeasibility of rights, a brief history of the jury trial, and an introduction to natural law principles. I conclude the chapter, and the first part of the book with an introduction to the centrality of rights in a republic.

Part II of *The Political Economy of Plea Bargaining* begins with Chapter 5. Chapters 5, 6, and 7 signify the core political economy sections of the book. In Chapter 5, I focus upon the evolution of the liberty of contract doctrine as it appears in the United States, beginning in the early 19th century. That doctrine, which contemporary economists claim is long deceased, continues to inform the collective imaginary of neoliberal economists and conservative politicians. But more importantly, it is the liberty of contract doctrine, a doctrine that frames *Homo sapiens* as *Homo economicus*, supported by United States Supreme Court opinions, that establishes the normative ideological frame contextualizing plea bargaining.

The "free labor" ideology that emerged during the mid-19th century demonstrated both a philosophical commitment to privileging human agency and an ideological justification for the pursuit of political, economic, and cultural self-interest. Serving as the Archimedean core, Article I §10, cl. 1, also known as the "Contract Clause" of the United States Constitution, the United States Supreme Court further developed the essentializing power constituting the individual right to contract through its 19th and early 20th-century common law opinions. This important juridical and cultural emphasis upon *Homo sapiens* as *Homo economicus* that provided the hegemonic context necessary to argue, as it did in *Brady v. United States* and the other relevant 1970s plea cases discussed in Chapter 1, that an indicted felony criminal defendant may, if they choose (autonomy), abdicate their constitutionally protected Fifth and Sixth Amendment trial rights in exchange for a sentencing reduction.

It is in Chapter 6 where I briefly return to the liberty of contract doctrine to explore the two principal ideological and political assumptions guiding it: individual autonomy and efficiency. Next, I discuss the application of conventional contract law to plea bargaining by exploring concerns relating to improperly obtained assent. Finally, I introduce my argument that plea bargaining signifies the confluence of conventional contract law with contracts of adhesion.

Chapter 7 will require the reader to commit to a complex presentation of governmentality, the state, and civil society-lifeworld. The reader will be exposed to the following important context: 1) understanding how the intersectionality of politics, economics, and culture produces and reproduces the spatio-temporal dominance of power blocs; 2) understanding the always fluid, never sedimented, complex of interests producing power blocs, each vying for political, economic, and cultural superiority in a discursive milieu that reproduces dominant cultural norms and values; 3) understanding that power contains both positive and negative (i.e., repressive) elements; 4) understanding that the development and manifestation of "the state" has occurred over millennia and produced regionally unique spatio-temporal forms; 5) understanding that "governmentality" and "the state" are grammatically and practically disparate since "governmentality" refers to a *process*, while "the state" refers to a *system-reproducing steering institution*; "governmentality" is a verb, and "the state" is a noun, and 6) understanding that theoretical models that occlude the inclusion of civil society-lifeworld neglect perhaps the most vital location of lived experience. I begin with a discussion of Michel Foucault's articulation of governmentality, the *process* that facilitates the implementation of state power. Once established, I move to locate the act of governmentality within an analysis of state theory, especially as presented by Bob Jessop. Missing from nearly all liberal and even neo-Marxist political economic accounts of the state and economy, but most especially in the neotenic law and political economy scholarship, is the conceptualization of civil society-lifeworld.

Having made reference to it throughout the book, in Chapter 8 I introduce the unconstitutional conditions doctrine and apply it to plea bargaining. The unconstitutional conditions doctrine stands for the principle that the federal government may not condition the receipt of a government benefit upon the relinquishment of constitutional rights. It is my contention that plea bargaining signifies an unconstitutional condition (abdication of Fifth and Sixth Amendment rights) placed upon a benefit (charge and sentence reduction).

I conclude my argument with Chapter 9, where I assert that the plea emerged in the United States alongside growing industrialization, that it was an outgrowth of equity and conciliation model courts, the professionalization and increasing influence of lawyers, and the need to maintain social control over marginal populations in both the North and the South. I present evidence that the historical reference to police powers was narrowed in the middle of the 19th century with the increasing influence of the state and its facilitation of the growth of industrialization and the influence of corporate power. The most important claim I make in this book is that plea bargaining is a threat to democracy.

Love

I draw this Preface to a close by saying that in two ways this book is a labor of love. It is a labor of love in the first instance because the ideas presented here represent more than 30 years of painstaking study. But it is love as I mean it in the second instance with which I wish to conclude these remarks.

This book, like my work generally, is driven by love, a powerfully animating impulse to enhance the quality of life for all living beings. As with most of us, I suppose, it's not readily apparent to us how our commitments and obligations evolved and grew over time to constitute our intellectual and behavioral habits. But what I know is that I have reached a point in my life where I have come to understand that the dialectical force of love is an imperative, perhaps even a categorical imperative, for all life on the planet to thrive as an alternative to the neoliberal social Darwinism characteristic of the capitalist mode of production. To that end, and in the spirit of poet Wendell Berry, I no longer speak of "justice" since the concept has been appropriated by all actors to claim legitimacy for their actions. What is "just" to me may not be "just" to you. Rather, I challenge myself and my students to create a criminal legal system model that is premised upon love.

Wendell Berry has always been one of my most valued poets. While a few generations older than me, he grew up in Kentucky not too far from where I did in Cincinnati, Ohio. In his most recent book, *The Need To Be Whole: Patriotism and the History of Prejudice*,[2] Berry applies his poetic scalpel to contemporary manifestations of prejudice in the United States. Like my critique in this book, Berry argues that the absence of a commitment to a community of care, brought about by the ruthless competition for scarce and low-wage work, has generated the following circumstance:

> Thus a fundamental relationship and obligation is broken by the now generally accepted "realism" and "necessity" of economic competition, which necessarily brings us to our present condition: a public consisting of dismembered families and communities and the virtually deserted economic landscapes of our country.[3]

Berry continues this thread with reference to Paul Tenny, a journalist who wrote that for the most part the common has devolved to "a collection of unrelated individuals whose interactions are mediated through various shallow and transactional mechanisms, where common ground with a neighbor can only, at best, be found in the most banal of trivialities."[4] But what if, Berry wonders, rather than a culture that appears to endlessly promote fear of the other by openly celebrating the "deadly sins" of Biblical reference, we change course: "What would happen to our economy if the marketers and advertisers shifted their appeal from anger, covetousness, envy, gluttony, lust, pride, and sloth to justice, prudence, fortitude, temperance, faith, hope, and love."[5] Wendell Berry is a white Southern Christian poet from Kentucky. He is a "working man's" poet. Much like Walt Whitman, he is a man of the people. His references to Christian teachings signify the source of his moral core. So, while he clearly contextualizes his analysis of contemporary United States within his own cultural capital and habitus, his larger point is agnostic.

As I indicated above, while the concept of "justice" may be amorphous, the concept of "love" is not. I challenge the readers of this book the same way that I challenge my students, to develop a criminal legal system model premised upon love. What would such a system look like if it were premised upon Biblical admonishments to "love thy neighbor,"[6] and to "love thy enemy"?[7] How would it operate? What would its rules of criminal procedure be? And so on. It is with love as our guiding spirit that I welcome all readers to join me on what promises to be a most compelling, challenging, and rewarding journey.

Robert Schehr
July 17, 2024

Notes

1 From the film Ferris Bueller's Day Off.
2 Wendell Berry. The Need To Be Whole: Patriotism and the History of Prejudice. New York: Shoemaker and Co. (2022).
3 Id at 144.
4 Tenny cited in Berry. Id at 147.
5 Id at 148.
6 Mark 12:31 "The second is this, 'You shall love your neighbor as yourself.' There is no other commandment greater than these."
7 Mathew 5:43–44. 43 "Ye have heard that it hath been said, Thou shalt love thy neighbor, and hate thy enemy." 44 "But I say unto you, Love your enemies, bless them that curse you, do good to them that hate you, and pray for them which despitefully use you, and persecute you."

ACKNOWLEDGEMENTS

As this book is the culmination of more than 30 years of academic study, there is a long list of people who are deserving of recognition. I wish to extend my deepest gratitude to Dr Raymond Michalowski, Professor Jack Chin, Professor Russell Covey, Dr Paul Lenze, Dr Andrew Bisto, Judge Jed Rakoff, Professor Stephen Bright, my Yale Law School professors John Fabian Witt, Amy Kapczynski, Julie Suk, Stephen Carter, Justin Driver, Tracey Meares, and James Q. Whitman, my comrade in all things LPE Daniel Quintanilla, and my Northern Arizona University students. Each of you to varying degrees has contributed to the strengths of my work. Any errors or omissions are my own.

Most of all, I wish to acknowledge my partner, Lynn, who has spent a lifetime with me beginning as an undergraduate as I sought to explore whatever intellectual skills I possessed. She has pulled up roots, vicariously suffered the fear that comes with writer's block, and the euphoria when shards of light expose a mystery. She has supported a mature academic's desire to attend Yale Law School at the age of 60. In the end, it is Lynn who has enabled me to develop into the kind of person and academic that I am today. She has kept me grounded and focused, and she has always provided me with the space necessary to explore. Lynn Spence is, and always has been, the source of a deep well of love and care for me, for our children, and for all who know her. This book could not have appeared without the four decades of her sweet love for me.

ACKNOWLEDGMENTS

PART I

1

THE PLEA

Why should Americans care about plea bargaining? Despite the more visible attempts by the framers of the United States Constitution, subsequent Congresses, and the United States Supreme Court to protect a defendant's substantive and procedural rights upon accusation of the commission of a felony (typically the Fourth, Fifth, Sixth, Eighth, and Fourteenth Amendments), Americans assert their right to trial in only three to five percent of cases. This is true at both the state and federal levels. What that means is that most of our vigorously debated and righteously protected rights meant to serve as a counterweight to the exercise of state power simply do not apply to the vast majority of felony criminal defendants. Before going further, I think that it is beneficial to be reminded of the stages of criminal procedure leading from arrest to sentencing. The criminal legal system operates according to the following linear process:

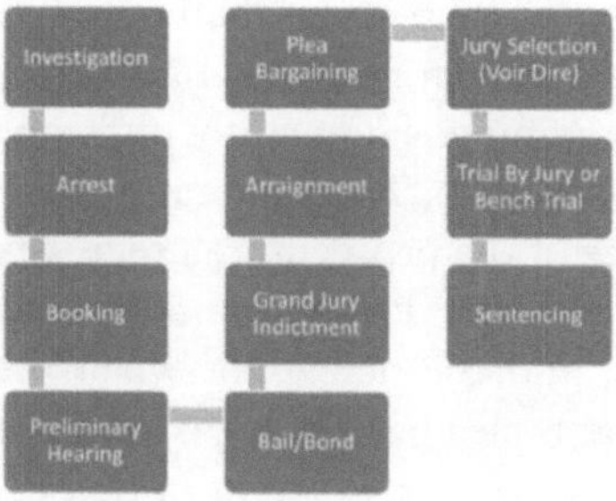

When a criminal defendant has been indicted by a grand jury, at their arraignment they must enter a plea of either "guilty" or "not guilty." Following arraignment, and assuming a "guilty" plea has been entered by

DOI: 10.4324/9781003385103-2

the defendant, prosecutors commence the plea negotiation process. What that means is that an indicted criminal defendant who pleads "not guilty" will assert their right to trial cloaked with all of their constitutional rights protections, or they will plead "guilty," whereby the prosecutor and the defendant will commence negotiation relating to charge and sentencing reductions. The negotiated or plea bargained sentence represents a "downward departure" from what the defendant would have confronted had they taken their chances at trial and were convicted and sentenced under mandatory maximum state sentencing statutes. For example, in the state of Arizona, a defendant charged with second-degree murder may be sentenced to between a minimum of ten and a maximum of 22 years in prison, with the presumptive sentence being 16 years.[1] A prosecutor who extends a plea bargain that includes a ten-year sentence has offered the defendant a 12-year downward departure from the maximum sentence possible. It is important to note here that considerable scholarly attention has been directed at the effect of a defendant's race/ethnicity upon the quality of plea agreements. In general, and holding other variables constant (e.g., prior records, age, gender), white defendants receive statistically significantly better (meaning lighter) charge and sentencing bargains than non-white defendants.[2]

As a consequence of the acceptance of a guilty plea, the defendant immediately abdicates their Fifth and Sixth Amendment rights protections. Between 95 and 97 percent of felony criminal defendants engage in plea bargaining. As such, it is the plea process, rather than the more dramatic trial, on which we should be focusing our critical lens since the plea is nearly all that encompasses the administration of justice in the United States.

Plea bargaining is a legal technology implemented for the purpose of expediency (there is little to no discovery), predictability of outcome (there is a guaranteed conviction), and efficient application of resources (rapid resolution of cases saves money on costly discovery and trials). At issue is more than simply a matter of criminal case adjudication, which, as I indicated, accounts for between 95 and 97 percent of all criminal cases in both the state and federal systems. As a system-reproducing steering mechanism,[3] it is my contention that plea bargaining is inherently undemocratic and has no place in a republican system of justice. This is because plea bargaining places sole authority in the province of the prosecutor, a regressive move comparable to a contemporary Star Chamber.[4] Plea bargaining arguably benefits prosecutors, defense attorneys, and the defendant when the bargain is especially favorable. Most important, plea bargaining is *monolithic* in the sense that all power resides with the prosecutor, *efficient* in that cases move quickly from indictment to conviction,[5] *private* as they are conducted outside the purview of the public, *adversarial*, and *far less expensive* than pursuing trial. With the plea, prosecutors are assured a conviction, and defendants receive less punishment than if they were convicted at trial (the trial tax). Contemporary plea law is governed by a number of important Supreme Court cases to be discussed below,[6] as well as Federal Rules of Criminal Procedure, Rule 11.[7] Case law and statute adhere to constitutional separation of powers by prohibiting judges from knowing anything about the case file or the machinations manifesting in the plea bargain itself. Only prosecutors and defense attorneys will know the case. For their part, judges serve to make the plea process constitutional by holding a plea colloquy in open court. During that colloquy, the judge must ascertain whether the defendant entering the plea fully understands the charges, the proposed sentence, and the rights being waived.[8] This is considered the *knowing* or *intelligent* aspect of the plea.

Next, the judge must establish verbally from the defendant in open court that she has not been coerced into the plea, but rather is fully accepting responsibility for the charges brought by *voluntarily* entering into it.[9] The last responsibility the judge possesses is to issue a sentence. The judge may accept the recommendation of the prosecutor, or she may deviate depending upon the relevant sentencing range for the offense.

As I have previously argued, as interpreted by the Court, the knowing and voluntary criteria are woefully inadequate to provide constitutional comfort or in any way serve as assurance that the process as administered is a fair and just one.[10]

Plea agreements are negotiated between a relatively powerless criminal defense attorney and a prosecutor shielded from the watchful eye of journalists and the public, with the prosecutor serving as judge and jury. Federal Rules of Criminal Procedure, Rule 11(a)(3) Determining the Factual Basis for a Plea states that, "Before entering judgment on a guilty plea, the court must determine that there is a factual basis for the plea."[11] What is important to note here is that: a) judges have no authority to consider the "factual basis" upon which a plea has been struck, thereby removing independent judicial oversight; b) no one really knows what a "factual basis" means as it relates to a quantum of evidence necessary to establish guilt (most plea files include little more than a police report and a pre-sentencing report); c) plea prosecutions follow indictment typically by a grand jury where the standard of proof to indict is *probable cause*; d) grand jury indictments are virtually assured since the procedure is non-adversarial, prosecutors may permit the use of hearsay evidence, and if one grand jury decides not to indict, a prosecutor may simply empanel a new one until finding one that will; and e) presence of a criminal defense attorney during plea negotiations is meaningful, but it's hard to know how much since it is unlikely that they will know much about the defendant or the case prior to entering the plea,[12] and since they are part of a courtroom working group[13] that requires that same defense attorney to interact daily with the same prosecutor and the same judge to procure the best possible outcome for their clients. It is this level of undemocratic procedural opacity, rhetorically fashioned as efficient case management beneficial to the state and defendants alike, that generates the most pernicious aspect of plea procedure – *felony convictions are predicated upon the second lowest standard of proof – probable cause.*[14] The probable cause standard of proof requires a grand jury to determine whether: a) the government has presented the evidence necessary to convince the grand jury that a crime has been committed, and b) the government has properly charged the responsible party.

In reading this, a practiced attorney might raise one or both eyebrows depending upon their level of confusion or skepticism. That is, it is uncommon among criminal legal practitioners (or legal scholars, for that matter) to speak to a "standard of proof" required for indictment as being relevant to the plea, and most certainly to the assertion that the 19th and early 20th-century transition from jury trials to pleas was (and is) in any way a systemic abuse of power. But in my estimation, when prosecutors commence plea negotiations following the presentation of scant evidence before a grand jury where the standard of proof necessary to return a true bill indictment is probable cause, and when probable cause signifies the second lowest standard of proof (just above reasonable suspicion), one that is premised upon a non-adversarial procedure that almost inevitably produces indictments, to move from there to the plea negotiation leading to an agreed-upon sentence not only violates the exalted status held by the proof beyond a reasonable doubt standard for conviction at trial, but as this book will demonstrate, it signifies an imbalanced and unchecked executive branch power that, as I argue, is a threat to American democracy.

The Hidden Role of the Legislature

One of the persistent challenges confronted by legal scholars and practitioners seeking to address the ubiquity and constitutionality of the plea appears in the following well-rehearsed claim:

> There are too many criminal cases being processed in the states. If every defendant chose to assert their constitutional right under Article III §2 to a trial by a jury of peers the system would collapse since there are far too few resources including courts, judges, prosecutors, defense attorneys, private investigators, and the fiscal wherewithal to effectively accommodate them.

This is a red herring. In fact, the argument made by those who, even reluctantly, support the preservation of the plea, when confronted with challenges that raise constitutional and justice-related concerns, shrug and contend that the system "is what it is," and that we simply have to accept the plea as an efficient and pragmatic administration of justice. As this book will make clear, this is a circular argument. It is the legislatures of each state that construct criminal sentencing guidelines. To that end, states' general assemblies play a pivotal role in pushing defendants toward the plea. This is true because the states have created draconian sentencing guidelines constituted by severe mandatory minimum and maximum ranges for years to be spent in prison. Defendants confronting a mandatory maximum if convicted at trial will be induced to accept a plea bargain since the downward departure from the mandatory maximum will often be significant. It is in this way that the legislature creates a dynamic that predictably leads to the plea. In addition, legislatures are the political body that *creates* crimes. That is, until a behavior is officially designated as a violation of criminal law, that behavior is not criminal. However, once a legislature passes a statute designating a behavior a crime, hydraulic pressure is placed upon criminal legal system actors downstream, requiring police to arrest suspects for violations of criminal acts, investigate those cases, and share those cases with prosecutors for possible litigation. In short, it is the naming of behaviors as crimes that generates the flood of possible cases that must be managed by the criminal legal system. It is in at least these two ways – creation of draconian sentencing ranges and the naming of behaviors as crimes now ensconced in state law – that locates the legislature of each state as a central agent generating the plea.

So, to claim, as virtually every prosecutor and defense attorney whom I have queried about the plea has, that the criminal legal system is too unwieldy as it is deluged with too many cases, signifies a *circular argument* because the problem is created by the legislature itself. Circular arguments signify a fallacy of reasoning or argumentation.[15] Circular reasoning is known as "question begging." As is the case with system justifications for plea bargaining, self-dependent justifications lead to fallacious arguments where "the evidence [in this case, high caseloads] presupposes the truth of the claim it is trying to support [i.e., the system needs plea bargaining to manage high caseloads]."[16] To summarize, the problem of plea bargaining manifests the pressure accruing from excessive caseloads, thereby requiring a legal technology capable of efficiently disposing of cases. As I have demonstrated, for system actors to justify the probity of the plea as a necessary palliative to heavy caseloads ignores the role played by the legislature in creating the caseload dynamic in the first instance. It is in this way that prosecutors, defense attorneys, and judges each engage in circular reasoning since "the evidence presupposes the truth of the claim that it is trying to support."

More categories of crime are created that place downward hydraulic pressure upon the police, prosecutors, defense attorneys, and courts to administer them. Defendants, for their part, are confronted with a devil's bargain. Either they take their chance at trial where, if convicted, they will spend significantly greater time in prison due to legislatively enacted sentencing ranges, or accept the downward departure from the maximum trial sentence, the plea. This is what is known as the "trial tax." Defendants are "taxed," i.e., punished, for asserting their right to trial by risking excessive punishment. Criminal legal system actors respond as if the caseload issue appeared from whole cloth. It didn't. It was and continues to emanate from a state actor. The syllogism, then, is something like this: through its authority over criminalization of behavior and the setting of sentencing ranges, legislatures create the dynamic leading to the proliferation of the plea. Hydraulic pressure is placed upon criminal legal system actors who contend that there are too many cases and far too limited resources for each defendant to assert their right to trial by jury. Therefore, we must adopt a more efficient and pragmatic technology to administer justice – the plea. Two immediate responses are possible. First, the legislature can decriminalize acts currently considered criminal. This is especially relevant to marijuana possession and distribution, which account for a significant proportion of state prison populations. Second, by significantly reducing mandatory sentencing regimes, the legislature can revisit sentencing ranges to encourage defendants to consider going to trial without fear of a trial tax. In sum, the problem of the plea has partly emerged from and been sustained by the legislative branch of state government.

In the sections that follow, I will sketch out what I perceive to be the fundamental historical, political, and economic frames used to justify the plea, followed by my own critique of the commodification of rights. Part II will provide an overview of the law pertaining to plea bargaining.

Constitutional Confusion

The final paragraph of Article III §2 of the United States Constitution provides the following language:

> The trial of all Crimes, except in Cases of Impeachment, *shall be by Jury*; and such Trial shall be held in the State where the said Crimes shall have been committed; but when not committed within any State, the Trial shall be at such Place or Places as the Congress may by Law have directed.[17]

This constitutional language was adopted in May of 1787. However, four years later, when the Sixth Amendment was ratified in 1791, the simple addition of one word in the text of what otherwise was substantively identical to Article III §2 provided a doctrinal pathway to the contemporary plea.

> In all criminal prosecutions, the accused shall *enjoy* the right to a speedy and public trial, by an impartial jury of the state and district wherein the crime shall have been committed, which district shall have been

> previously ascertained by law, and to be informed of the nature and cause of the accusation; to be confronted with the witnesses against him; to have compulsory process for obtaining witnesses in his favor, and to have the assistance of counsel for his defense.[18]

For reasons that are, to my knowledge, lost to history, Madison both expanded the reach of the right to include "all criminal prosecutions" (not just the "*trial* of all crimes"), but more importantly, he added the word "enjoy." This will become an important moment in the discursive history of Sixth Amendment doctrine, especially as it pertains to plea bargaining, as the Sixth Amendment language (like much of what appears in the Constitution) seems to be pulling in opposite directions. Madison's editorial change to the opening sentence of Article III §2 to include "all criminal prosecutions" would cover the breadth and depth of contemporary criminal legal adjudication, whereas the original Article III language includes the limiting noun "trial" as in, "The trial of all crimes…." Crucially, Madison's more expansive language captures *all manner of prosecution where there are liberty interests at stake*. But then he adds the word "enjoy" to the sentence: "In all criminal prosecutions, the accused shall *enjoy* the right to a speedy and public trial" In the hands of future Supreme Court justices, this will prove to be an important semantic opening to relax the Article III §2 mandate "shall" with the more permissive verb, "enjoy." As it pertains to the constitutionality of plea bargaining, the Supreme Court's interpretive battle regarding the right to a jury trial commences with two late 19th-century opinions authored by Justice Harlan.

In my previously published article, "The Emperor's New Clothes: Intellectual Dishonesty and the Unconstitutionality of Plea Bargaining,"[19] I emphasize the juxtaposition of Justice Harlan's 1884 *Hopt v. Utah* opinion and his 1898 *Thompson v. Utah* opinion,[20] with the 1930 case called *Patton v. United States*.[21] In each case, Justice Harlan rejects the constitutionality of criminal convictions where a jury of fewer than 12 casts a guilty verdict. Harlan does so by emphasizing the Article III §2 language. Harlan's *Hopt* opinion establishes salient points apropos of the plea: (1) that rights are cultural artifacts that are not solely the possession of discrete individuals; and (2) the inalienability of rights means that, while they cannot be *taken* away, they also cannot be freely *given* away.[22] Harlan makes this emphasis clear in *Thompson*:

> The [pro-waiver] argument necessarily proceeds upon the ground that [the defendant] alone is concerned as to the mode by which he may be deprived of his life or liberty, and that the chief object of the prosecution is to punish him for the crime charged. … [However,] [t]he public has an interest in his life and liberty. … *That which the law makes essential*

> *in proceedings involving the deprivation of life and liberty cannot be dispensed with or affected by the consent of the accused, much less by his mere failure, when on trial and in custody, to object to unauthorized methods.*[23]

Just 31 years later in the case of *Patton v. United States*[24] Justice Sutherland upended the *Thompson* opinion with reference to what he considered to be the more *permissive* language provided by the Sixth Amendment to the Constitution, given its invocation to "enjoy" the right. For the majority in *Patton*, this meant that the Sixth Amendment right to trial by jury was to be more flexibly interpreted than the Article III language permitted. Moreover, argued Justice Sutherland, since the Sixth Amendment was temporally more recently adopted by Congress, it must have been what the framers intended the language to mean. At issue in *Patton* was the question of the constitutionality of waiving trial rights. In the specific case, defendant Patton was convicted of attempting to bribe a federal prohibition agent. For most of the trial, a jury of 12 was assembled as is required by the Constitution. However, well into the presentation of facts, one of the 12 jurors became seriously ill and had to be relieved of their jury duty. The trial judge queried both the state and defense as to whether they wished to continue with the trial now having only 11 jurors. Without the consent of each party, the judge would be forced to declare a mistrial. Both Patton and the state agreed to continue with the case, and Patton was convicted by the remaining 11 jurors. The question put to the Supreme Court in the *Patton* case was the following:

> After the commencement of a trial in a federal court before a jury of 12 men upon an indictment charging a crime, punishment for which may involve a penitentiary sentence, if one juror becomes incapacitated and unable to further proceed with his work as a juror, can defendant or defendants and the government through its official representative in charge of the case consent to the trial proceeding to a finality with 11 jurors, and can defendant or defendants thus waive the right to a trial and verdict by a constitutional jury of 12 men?[25]

So, while the *Patton* case did not specifically raise the question of plea bargaining, focusing instead upon the numerical composition of the jury, at bottom was the question of *the waiveability of constitutional rights.* Justice Sutherland and the unanimous majority did raise the specter of plea bargaining. The italicized portions of each paragraph below are my own.

> All will doubtless agree, at least the unquestioned authority is that way, that these protective provisions of the Constitution are not so imperative that an accused shall be tried by jury *when he desires to plead guilty*; or

> that his trial, in the event of trial, shall be held invalid for want of due process of law, based upon the ground that he was not confronted with his witnesses when he had waived that constitutional right and consented to the use of depositions.[26]
>
> It surely cannot be true that the public is interested in the protection of an accused in proportion to the magnitude of his offending-that its solicitude goes out to the great offender but not to the small-that there is a difference in point of sacredness between constitutional rights when asserted by one charged with a grave crime and when asserted by one charged with a lesser one. *Hence, when it is held in Schick v. U. S., 195 U. S. 65, 24 S. Ct. 826, 49 L. Ed. 99, 1 Ann. Cas. 585, that in trials for the lowest grades of offenses the accused may waive, not only the continued presence of the full number of jurors required to make up a jury, but the right to trial by jury, the only possible conclusion is that the purely theoretical element of public concern, as potential to override the accused's own free choice and render him effectually unfree even before conviction and sentence, cannot be regarded as in reality much of a factor in any case.*[27]
>
> A defendant is supposed to understand his rights, and may be aided, if he so desires, by counsel to advise him. *There are many legal provisions for his security and benefit which he may dispense with absolutely*, as, for instance, his right to plead guilty and submit to sentence without any trial whatsoever.[28]

As it pertains to plea bargaining, *Patton* was the camel's nose under the tent, for it weakened adherence to the necessity of trials under conditions where liberty was at stake.[29] Forty years after the *Patton* opinion, the Supreme Court formally took up the specific question pertaining to the constitutionality of plea bargaining in the 1970 case *Brady v. United States.*[30] The *Thompson* and *Patton* opinions signify a massive clash of values as the United States retreats from its Jeffersonian and Jacksonian commitment to Enlightenment-inspired liberty protections, especially as it relates to the trial by jury (discussed in Chapter 4), which, it must be added, were written in the spirit of preserving *individual autonomy* as against the intruding power of the state, in order to develop a due process system that found its legitimacy through Supreme Court validation of the efficiency of prosecution. The Supreme Court's *Patton* and *Brady* opinions constructed and greased the plea assembly line.

Plea Case Law

Writing in dissent in *Lafler v. Cooper,*[31] Justice Antonin Scalia said that the United States Supreme Court has "elevated plea bargaining from a necessary evil to a constitutional entitlement." It is hard to disagree. I will not present every plea case addressed since the 1930 *Patton* opinion. Rather, I will focus my attention upon the most important decisions constitutionalizing the plea emerging during the decade of the 1970s. I will also present a few cases that appear in the 21st century that announce important procedural changes to the plea.

It was during the 1970s that the United States Supreme Court embarked upon its efforts to constitutionally legitimate the plea bargaining adjudication practice. The cases that I will briefly present here for context are: *Brady v. United States*, 397 US 742 (1970), *North Carolina v. Alford*, 400 US 25 (1970), *Parker v. North Carolina*, 397 US 790 (1970), *Santobello v. New York*, 404 US 257 (1971), *Chaffin v. Synchcombe*, 412 US 17 (1973), *Bordenkircher v. Hayes*, 434 US 357 (1978), and *Corbitt v. New Jersey*, 439 US 212 (1978). In the 21st century, the Supreme Court decided the important cases, *United States v. Ruiz* (2002) and *Lafler v. Cooper* (2012), and *Missouri v. Frye* (2012).

Before consideration of *Brady v. United States*, the first case to constitutionalize the plea, we must consider the Supreme Court's holdings in *United States v. Jackson*[32] and *Boykin v. Alabama*.[33] Prior to the 1970 *Brady* opinion, the Court had taken a skeptical view of plea bargaining, especially in those circumstances where a defendant was confronted with the threat of a death sentence if convicted at trial as a tool to manipulate the defendant's procedural decision to plea bargain or assert their right to trial. At issue in *Jackson* was the recently adopted federal statute, 18 USC §1201(a), which provided one of two options for defendants confronting a serious felony charge of kidnapping – either they risk their chances at trial where, if convicted, they may be sentenced to death, or accept a plea deal where the punishment would be life in prison. The question presented before the Court in *Jackson* was whether it was constitutionally permissible to threaten a defendant with harsher punishment, in the extant case with death, in order to encourage the defendant to engage in plea bargaining where they will receive a reduced sentence (e.g., life in prison). Upon deciding the unconstitutionality of what were clearly considered to be coercive threats meant to deter the assertion of a constitutional right (what I will address in the final chapter as the unconstitutional conditions doctrine), the Court's majority held that, "The evil in the federal statute is not that it necessarily coerces guilty pleas and jury waivers but simply that it needlessly encourages them."[34] At issue for the Court was a centuries-long concern over the voluntariness prong of the plea. Had prosecutors created an adjudication process that overbore the will of defendants, thereby removing any pretense to voluntary decision-making? Once again, in *Boykin v. Alabama*, the Court would revisit that question.

Boykin is important for two reasons. First, because it directly confronted the voluntariness question, and second, because it established the language that would, five years later, constitute the 1974 Federal Rules of Criminal Procedure, Rule 11, the federal rule that guides the plea bargaining procedure. Specifically, the Court held that "A plea of guilty is more than a confession which admits that the accused did various acts; it is itself a conviction; nothing remains but to give judgment and determine punishment."[35] Once more, as they had in *Jackson*, in *Boykin* the majority of the Court expressed its concern over plea bargaining as a normative criminal legal procedure, drawing specific attention to whether defendants are capable of voluntarily committing to the abdication of their Fifth and Sixth Amendment rights protections.

For most of the late 19th and 20th centuries (until 1970 and the *Brady v. United States* opinion discussed below), the United States Supreme Court expressed pointed concern over the likelihood of *coerced confessions* generating guilty pleas. The Court found precedent for its first case addressing pleas as confessions, *Hallinger v. Davis*,[36] in the 1793 English court opinion in *Rex v. Warickshall*.[37] In *Hallinger* the Court held that so long as plea bargains were voluntary, they were considered non-coercive and therefore constitutional admissions of guilt. Since a defendant's admission of guilt pursuant to a plea was perceived as being no different from any other confession, the Court declined to identify a bright line rule that specifically would apply to plea bargains. The continued concern from the Court about the voluntariness of confessions generated two additional 19th-century cases of note – *The Whiskey Cases* and *Bram v. United States*. In *The Whiskey Cases*,[38] a prosecutor rather than a judge or governor appears for the first time as the central figure representing the state in a criminal case before the Supreme Court as the progenitor of a plea agreement. The Court reversed the guilty plea agreements which came with an offer of immunity (typically the sole power of the governor) arguing prosecutorial overreach. In *Bram*,[39] the Court overturned Bram's plea-induced conviction due to concerns over voluntariness. Here, the Court held that the prosecutor's use of coercion, threats of violence, and promises of benefits used to induce the plea were unconstitutional violations of the defendant's Fifth Amendment rights.

The 20th century produced eight opinions between 1927 and 1970 that demonstrate the Supreme Court's continued concern over plea bargaining's voluntariness problem. The cases originate in 1927 with *Kercheval v. United States*.[40] The Court follows *Kercheval* with opinions challenging prosecutorial authority and raising serious doubts over whether voluntariness was truly procured prior to entering a plea agreement. The remaining seven cases are: *Walker v. Johnston*,[41] *Waley v. Johnston*,[42] *Shelton v. United States*,[43] *Machibroda v. United States*,[44] *United States v. Jackson*,[45] *Boykin v. Alabama*,[46] and *McCarthy v. United States*.[47]

While there is clear case law pointing to the Supreme Court's late 19th and early to mid-20th century concern over whether the plea overbore the will of defendants, thereby raising doubt as to the voluntariness of the plea bargain, the Court's naivete, as expressed in *Boykin* concerning the sociological and psychological complexities associated with human decision-making, led to a far too simplistic set of criteria for determining the knowing and voluntary criteria that would, in 1974, constitute the language establishing Federal Rules of Criminal Procedure, Rule 11. This would be the last time that the Supreme Court would render an opinion about the constitutionality of the plea that demonstrated a set of principled concerns relating to voluntariness. Beginning with *Brady v. United States* in 1970, the Court would embark upon a common law trajectory that would firmly ensconce plea bargaining as the normative legal technology for the resolution of felony criminal cases.

In June 1969, Chief Justice Earl Warren retired and was replaced by Warren Burger. This proved to be a significant change in Court personnel, as the Burger Court was far more supportive of plea bargaining than its predecessor Court had been. The Court heard oral arguments in *Brady v. United States* in November 1969, and it delivered its opinion in May 1970. As with *Jackson*, the Court was confronted with a kidnapping case in which the trial court had threatened execution if convicted at trial. Brady accepted the plea and was sentenced to 50 years in prison. He then filed a federal habeas appeal in the United States District Court in New Mexico, claiming that his plea had been coerced due to the threat of execution if he had exercised his right to trial and was convicted. Unlike the *Jackson* Court, however, the Court in *Brady* found no constitutional violation consistent with overbearing the defendant's will. Rather, the *Brady* Court applied an entirely novel justification for the constitutionality of the plea – contract law. The justification proceeded from the assumption that since the defendant was provided with counsel as guided by the Sixth Amendment, the defendant would be provided with the necessary procedural protection to satisfy the "knowing" portion of the "knowing and voluntary" prongs. In keeping with rhetorical notions of subject autonomy (that we will see were predicated upon *Homo economicus* and the establishment of subjects as "free" within the discourse of the liberty of contract doctrine), that is, that each defendant should be valued for their individual ability to make reasonable decisions, the Court held that plea bargains were no different from entering any other contract (a topic explored in Chapters 5 and 6). In fact, the Court lauded the plea as a legal technology that benefited defendants and as such was in no way involuntary: "We decline to hold, however, that a guilty plea is compelled or invalid under the Fifth Amendment whenever motivated by a defendant's desire to accept the certainty or probability of a lesser penalty rather than face a wider range of possibilities extending from acquittal to conviction and a higher penalty authorized by law for the crime charged."[48] Consistent with contract law, the Court held that "plea-bargaining flows from the mutuality of advantage to defendants and prosecutors."[49] Finally, and with attention to the efficiency promised by way of the plea procedure, the Court claimed that "For a defendant who sees slight possibility of acquittal, the advantages of pleading guilty and limiting the probability of penalty are obvious – his exposure is reduced, the correctional processes can begin immediately, and the practical burdens of trial are eliminated."[50] To sum, in stark contrast to its predecessor Court's case law, the *Brady* majority established the constitutionality of the plea premised upon the *voluntary* negotiation of a *contract* between a prosecutor and a defendant, a contract that would provide for a downward departure in sentencing from the prospective sentence if convicted at trial.

The question of voluntariness would appear in two early 1970s cases – *North Carolina v. Alford* and *Parker v. North Carolina*. In *Alford*, the Court held that a defendant who accepted a plea to second-degree murder in order to avoid the risk of conviction at trial where the maximum sentence was the death penalty (the trial tax), and where the defendant maintained their innocence, raised serious questions about voluntariness. Since the defendant, Alford, refused to confess, his case was unique relative to plea bargains that generate an admission of guilt. The Court held that a defendant who raises an *Alford* plea may continue to claim innocence, while the state may claim guilt, but the outcome of the plea means that the defendant will be released from prison. In *Parker v. North Carolina*, however, the Court majority tips its hand and affirms its commitment to the constitutionality of the plea so long as the prosecutor meets the knowing and voluntary prongs. As with *Alford*, in *Parker* a 15-year-old African American male was charged with rape and burglary and faced the death penalty if he exercised his right to trial and was convicted. Parker accepted a plea. On appeal, however, Parker argued that his guilty plea was the result of coercion because the threat of death if convicted at trial was a threat used to induce his plea (the trial tax). The Court upheld the constitutionality of Parker's plea. Delivering the opinion of the Court, Justice White held that,

> On the basis of the record in this case, petitioner's guilty plea was voluntary.
>
> (a) An otherwise valid plea *is not involuntary* because induced by a defendant's desire to limit the possible maximum penalty to less than that authorized if there is a jury trial (my emphasis).

The following cases round out the decade of the 1970s and secure the constitutionality of the plea: *Santobello v. New York*,[51] *Chaffin v. Synchcome*,[52] *Corbitt v. New Jersey*,[53] and *Bordenkircher v. Hayes*.[54] In *Santobello*, the Supreme Court held that: a) prosecutors must honor their plea agreements, and b) plea bargaining is now an essential part of the criminal legal system. In *Chaffin*, the Court affirmed its prior judgments in *Brady*, *Alford*, and

Parker that threats made by a judge or prosecutor regarding harsher punishment if a defendant exercised their right to trial and was found guilty did not violate a defendant's Fifth or Sixth Amendment rights. The *Chaffin* majority notes that,

> Although every such circumstance [of plea bargaining] has a discouraging effect on the defendant's assertion of his trial rights, the imposition of these difficult choices was upheld as an inevitable attribute of any legitimate system which tolerates and encourages the negotiation of pleas.[55]

The Court continues by arguing consistent with Justice Sutherland in his *Patton* opinion that,

> The criminal process like the rest of the legal system, is replete with situations requiring "the making of difficult judgments" as to which course to follow .... Although a defendant may have a right, even of constitutional dimensions, to follow whatever course he chooses, the Constitution does not, by that token, always forbid requiring him to choose.[56]

As I will demonstrate in Chapter 4, this view is at odds with English common law, the laws of the colonies, and the law as established in Article III §2, and the Fifth, Sixth, and Seventh Amendments of the United States Constitution.

The final two cases of note originating in the 1970s are *Corbitt v. New Jersey* and *Bordenkircher v. Hayes*, each of which addressed the threat of excessive punishment as coercion. The Court held in *Corbitt* that judicial or prosecutorial threats of excessive punishment if convicted at trial would not violate a defendant's Fifth, Sixth, or Fourteenth Amendments. Similarly, in *Bordenkircher* the Court's majority sustained the probity of the plea bargain even when prosecutors threatened significant charge and sentencing enhancements should the defendant reject a plea offer. Defendant Hayes was charged with forgery for which he faced between two and ten years in prison. The prosecutor offered Hayes a plea deal that would sentence him to five years in prison. Had Bordenkircher rejected the plea offer, the prosecutor threatened him with a habitual offender charge enhancement that would carry a life sentence if convicted at trial. In a 5–4 opinion with Justices Burger, Stewart, White, Rehnquist, and Stevens writing in the majority, the Court appeared to throw its collective hands in the air as it concluded, "Whatever might be the situation in an ideal world, the fact is that the guilty plea and the often concomitant plea bargain are important components of this country's criminal justice system."[57] In short, the Court is saying that this is the way that we do things now; plea bargaining is the norm and we cannot act in a way that would disrupt its usefulness to prosecutors. In another part of the Court's majority opinion, the Court clearly establishes its framing of the plea as consistent with contract law: "To punish a person because he has done what the law plainly allows him to do is a due process violation of the most basic sort .... But in the "give-and-take" of plea bargaining there is no such element of punishment or retaliation so long as the accused is free to accept or reject the prosecution's offer."[58] And finally, revealing the obvious, the Court says the quiet part out loud: "It follows that, by tolerating and encouraging the negotiation of pleas, this Court has necessarily accepted as constitutionally legitimate the simple reality that the prosecutor's interest at the bargaining table is to persuade the defendant to forego his right to plead not guilty."[59] Whether persuasion is different from coercion is a matter of some dispute.[60] What is not in dispute is that the Supreme Court had, by the end of the decade, firmly ensconced plea bargaining as constitutional.

Three Supreme Court cases from the 21st century are worthy of consideration: *United States v. Ruiz*,[61] *Lafler v. Cooper*,[62] and *Missouri v. Frye*.[63] The first case is *United States v. Ruiz*. As it relates to the theme of this book – plea bargaining signifies an unconstitutional threat to democracy – with *Brady*, the *Ruiz* case is perhaps most important. In *Ruiz*, the Court held that,

> The Constitution does not require the Government to disclose material impeachment evidence prior to entering a plea agreement with a criminal defendant. Although the Fifth and Sixth Amendments provide, as part of the Constitution's "fair trial" guarantee, that defendants have the right to receive exculpatory impeachment material from prosecutors, see, e.g., *Brady* v. *Maryland*, 373 U. S. 83, 87, a defendant who pleads guilty forgoes a fair trial as well as various other accompanying constitutional guarantees, *Boykin* v. *Alabama*, 395 U. S. 238, 243.[64]

Novice students of the criminal legal system are likely aware of the Supreme Court opinion in the case *Brady v. Maryland*. At issue in that *Brady* case was whether, as part of the pre-*trial* discovery process, defendants have a constitutional right to inculpatory and exculpatory material evidence known to the prosecutor. The 7–2 *Brady* majority held that *withheld evidence violates the due process clause of the Fourteenth Amendment*. But as *Ruiz* makes clear, *Brady v. Maryland does not apply to plea bargains* because, as *Boykin* affirmed, a defendant relinquishes their Fifth and Sixth Amendment rights upon their agreement to plead, including their right to confront their accusers (Sixth Amendment). As such, the normal rules of criminal trial procedure, rules that have evolved over centuries to ensure procedural fairness, do not apply to the plea. What this means in practice is that prosecutors *may withhold exculpatory impeachment evidence* without violating the due process clause of the Fourteenth Amendment. In legally withholding potentially exculpatory evidence, the absence of which may influence a defendant's decision to plead, prosecutors assume far too much power. Without a thorough discovery record, a defendant is flying blind. As will become clearer in Chapter 6, a lack of transparency leading to information imbalances between the prosecutor and defendant signifies a violation of contract law (the law guiding pleas) as it represents what is called *improperly obtained assent*.

Finally, in the 42 years since its holding in *Brady*, the Supreme Court had not addressed the question of whether criminal defendants engaging in plea bargaining retain the right to competent counsel. The Sixth Amendment right to appointed counsel for cases going to trial was affirmed in the 1963 case, *Gideon v. Wainwright*.[65] Since plea bargaining signifies an adversarial proceeding, defendants who plead retain their right to counsel. The right to *competent trial counsel* emerged with the Court's 1984 *Strickland v. Washington*[66] opinion. In two opinions announced on the same day in March of 2012, the question put before the Court was *whether the right to competent counsel inures to criminal defendants who plea bargain*. On March 21, 2012, the Supreme Court delivered two opinions, *Lafler v. Cooper* and *Missouri v. Frye*, each affirming a defendant's right to competent defense counsel.

Winship and *Brady*

The irony of the Supreme Court's plea jurisprudence can be found in its artfully reasoned expression of the proof beyond a reasonable doubt standard for felony convictions in the 1970 case *In re Winship*,[67] while only five weeks later holding in *Brady v. United States*[68] that even when there are liberty interests at stake, a defendant may "bargain away" their guaranteed rights protections (Fifth and Sixth Amendments), including in those circumstances when the state was threatening the defendant with the death penalty if convicted at trial.[69]

Hidden from view was the reasoning by contract law applied by the majority that usurped Fifth[70] and Sixth[71] Amendment constitutional due process protections in service of the *efficiency of prosecution*. This is important because a defendant who pleads will relinquish the right prohibiting compelled self-incrimination (Fifth Amendment), the right to trial (Sixth Amendment), the right to confront witnesses (Sixth Amendment), and the right to compulsory process for obtaining witnesses in one's favor (Sixth Amendment). Finally, a defendant who accepts a guilty plea will also waive non-jurisdictional defects committed by the government prior to the entry of the plea. Non-jurisdictional defects may include illegal search and seizure, coerced confessions, improper grand jury selection, denial of a right to a speedy trial, entrapment, sufficiency of evidence, prosecutorial defects, and relevant statutory claims. For example, in *Menna v. New York*,[72] the United

States Supreme Court noted that because a guilty plea is an admission of the facts alleged, it removes the issue of factual guilt from the case and "simply renders irrelevant those constitutional violations not logically inconsistent with [i.e., consistent with] the valid establishment of factual guilt and which do not stand in the way of conviction, if factual guilt is validly established."[73]

Justice Brennan's five-member majority opinion in *Winship*, however, articulated a commitment to the proof beyond a reasonable doubt standard for criminal cases, given the potential for loss of liberty and reputation.

> The reasonable doubt standard plays a vital role in the American scheme of criminal procedure. It is a prime instrument for reducing the risk of convictions resting on factual error. The standard provides concrete substance for the presumption of innocence – that bedrock "axiomatic and elementary" principle whose "enforcement lies at the foundation of the administration of our criminal law." *Coffin v. United States, supra,* at 156 U.S. 453. As the dissenters in the New York Court of Appeals observed, and we agree, "a person accused of a crime ... would be at a severe disadvantage, a disadvantage amounting to a lack of fundamental fairness, *if he could be adjudged guilty and imprisoned for years on the strength of the same evidence as would suffice in a civil case.*" 24 N.E.2d at 205, 247 N.E.2d at 259.[74]

Despite the majority's contention that the presumption of innocence is "axiomatic and elementary,"[75] and its emphasis upon a standard of proof higher than what exists in the civil system (preponderance of the evidence), just five weeks later the Court's majority in *Brady* approved of an adjudication procedure that includes a standard of proof *far below* what is required in civil cases by committing to a criminal legal system where the standard of proof is *probable cause.* Adjudication of plea bargaining commences upon indictment, most often by a grand jury, when a defendant is confronted with a two-pronged procedural pathway – plead not guilty and go to trial, or plead guilty and commence charge and sentencing bargaining. Between 95 and 97 percent of all felony convictions in the United States are procured via the plea.[76] That means that the criminal legal system is comfortable doing precisely the opposite of what the *Winship* Court demanded when there are liberty interests at stake, settling instead for an adjudication process that is premised upon a scant evidentiary record and mandatory relinquishment of Fifth and Sixth Amendment rights protections.

Two opinions separated by a few short weeks in the spring of 1970 produced procedural whiplash. *In re Winship* articulated a standard of proof beyond a reasonable doubt for all cases where liberty interests were at stake, but the standard announced in *Winship* would only apply to three to five percent of cases where the defendant exercised their right to trial. Meanwhile,

Brady v. United States removed constitutional due process protections in the name of efficiency and voluntariness (autonomy) by invoking contract law and a defendant's right to bargain with prosecutors for charge and sentence reductions.

Scholarly Evidence of Plea Practice

Consider the famous 19th-century case *Plessy v. Ferguson*.[77] The record indicates that Homer Plessy was offered two guilty pleas, one of which he accepted. The Supreme Court opinion in *Plessy v. Ferguson* was rendered in 1896. Plessy's original trial took place in 1892.[78] Much like Rosa Parks and the 1955 Montgomery, Alabama bus boycott, Homer Plessy's case was intentionally designed to expose a matter of unconstitutional law. The *Comite des Citoyens*, a Creole organization located in Louisiana, sought to bring a case to the United States Supreme Court to overturn the state's 1890 Separate Car Act.[79] Originally, the *Comite* identified Daniel Desdunes as the person who would intentionally violate the new law, be arrested for violating it, and proceed to trial with the backing of *Comite*-compensated attorneys. Before the case could be prosecuted against Desdunes, however, another organization operating within Louisiana had beaten the *Comite* to the appellate punch. Relying upon the Commerce Clause and United States Supreme Court precedent, in that case, *Abbot v. Hicks*,[80] the Louisiana Supreme Court held that *interstate* travel *could not* be obstructed. Upon the *Abbot* opinion, District Court Judge John H. Ferguson dismissed Desdunes's case as the issues had become moot. The *Comite* needed a new case with a specific focus on *intrastate* travel.

Homer Plessy was arrested for violating the state's Separate Car Act when he purchased his ticket on June 7, 1892. His first-class ticket would take him from New Orleans to Covington, Louisiana. Plessy had no intention of actually traveling on the train to Covington. Rather, the idea was to have him purchase the ticket and take his seat. He would predictably be arrested. Prior to his 1892 trial, Judge Ferguson "ordered Plessy *to plead to the facts in the information*. As directed by counsel, Plessy refused to plead to the facts."[81] The judge continued by explaining that if he was convicted at trial, Plessy faced a fine or imprisonment or both. In 1896, the United States Supreme Court remanded Plessy's case back to Louisiana to determine Plessy's race for purposes of the extant case. Was Homer Plessy white or black? The Criminal Court of New Orleans once again offered Plessy the opportunity to plead guilty rather than pursue his case at trial. This time, he took it. On January 11, 1897, Homer Plessy pled guilty and paid a $25 fine.[82] These two events, the original trial and the remand, provide evidence that Plessy was offered two opportunities to avoid trial by accepting a guilty plea and paying a fine. The years were 1892 and 1897.

In their widely celebrated 1922 investigation into criminal procedure in Cleveland, Ohio, Roscoe Pound and Felix Frankfurter note that:

> The statutes of Ohio do not expressly provide for the acceptance, in felony cases, of a plea of guilt of a lesser offense than that charged and, consequently, do not regulate the procedure. *In actual practice the court accepts the request of the prosecutor for permission to accept such plea and is necessarily dependent on the prosecutor's statement justifying that course.*[83]

Despite its being published during the early 20th century, I cite this passage for two reasons. First, the authors make it clear that while Ohio law did not explicitly permit plea bargaining, the practice occurred nonetheless, an indication of how difficult it is for legal historians and social scientists to capture a clear expression of actual day-to-day practices occurring prior to the early 20th century. What Pound and Frankfurter alerted us to in their Cleveland Foundation research is that the law on the books is not necessarily the law in practice.

My second reason for including the Pound and Frankfurter data is that they serve as a clear temporal moment when plea bargaining appears without references to leniency, equity, or conciliation courts of justice. Still, it remains unclear precisely when the plea emerged as a standalone procedure culturally understood as such.

In his 1929 publication called "Notes on Judicial Organization and Procedure," Walter F. Dodd of Yale University surveyed state criminal justice commission data. Like Pound and Frankfurter before him, Dodd was able to identify the practice of the plea occurring this time in 1926 in Minnesota.[84] In 1933, Newman F. Baker identified the practice of plea bargaining as commonplace. His article, "Initiating Prosecution," addressed the matter of pleading to lesser offenses as occupying a central place with regard to dispute resolution. In fact, echoing many of the concerns raised by contemporary plea bargain scholars, Baker says the following about the decision to prosecute:

> How much more significant would it be to have figures on the situations arising behind closed doors in the prosecutor's office! Court statistics are enlightening to such an extent that it is now almost commonplace to designate the prosecutor as the most powerful official in local government. If we had some means of checking decisions of the prosecutor when the question 'to prosecute or not to prosecute?' arises, such figures would go much farther to substantiate such a statement. Nowhere is it more apparent that our government is a government of men, not of laws. Nowhere do the very human elements of dishonesty, ambition, greed, lust for power, laziness, or bigotry have more room for development.[85]

Given what legal and social science scholars have discerned in the latter 20th and early 21st centuries with regard to prosecutorial power and concerns over transparency, Baker's revelatory insight published in 1933 is suggestive of a practice that had been functionally well established in previous decades. Included in Baker's assessment of prosecutorial authority is his awareness that prosecutorial legitimacy resounded in conviction rates: "A prosecutor must create a 'record' of convictions if he rates as a success and, unfortunately, this record often is developed by trials of minor offenses and pleas of guilty."[86] A negotiated guilty plea might include the defendant agreeing to leave town not to return. So long as the prosecutor was amenable to the defendant's offer, the plea was sealed. The punishment: leave town.[87] Moreover, "A high percentage of pleas of guilty is necessary if the prosecutor intends to make a good record."[88] And now sounding very much like their late 20th-century legal and social science descendants, "The prosecutor should be a good bargainer and if he is skillful at that he can render good service to the State in saving time and money avoiding trial … During the day's work of the busy prosecutor usually appear several situations which require plain ordinary trading ability." And as Walter Dodd's research revealed ten years earlier, Baker states more clearly that, "The crime surveys have made reference to the 'startling percentage' of cases in which the plea of guilty is to an offense of lesser gravity than the original charge and how often we find that the reduction is from a grave felony to a misdemeanor."[89]

In 1931, the Wickersham Commission Report[90] affirmed concerns over plea bargaining that had been raised in the preceding decade by state crime commission reporting. But unlike those earlier state commission studies, the Wickersham Commission directly addressed the question of plea bargaining. Under the section called "Prosecutor's Bargaining," the commissioners included a major heading: "ACCEPTANCE OF PLEA OF LESSER OFFENSE – PROSECUTOR'S BARGAINING FOR DISPOSITION."[91] As with Dodd and Baker, the Wickersham report affirms that "Reference has been made to the startlingly large percentage of cases in which this plea is to an offense of lesser gravity than the original charge, in a very considerable percentage of the cases the reduction being from a felony to a misdemeanor."[92] There are many other fascinating aspects to the Wickersham report, but one that provides us with some clarity regarding the reason for the opaqueness of the plea process is indicated by the fact that "pleas to a lesser offense and acceptance thereof sometimes occur in the court of preliminary examination and sometimes in the general trial court."[93] That is, unlike contemporary practice where defendants typically meet with prosecutors at the county attorney's office, given the availability of the practice along with judicial authority, a plea could be rendered at trial court as well. But what becomes clear in the Commission Report is the now prominent role played by prosecutors as opposed to judges as would have been the case prior to the mid-19th century.

> Though the court has theoretically and by statute the power to refuse to accept such pleas, the court, in actuality, is so dependent for information upon the prosecutor, and the later results of the case, if the plea be refused, are so dependent upon the prosecutor, that the prosecutor, rather than the court, is, under existing conditions and procedure, the more influential in regard to such pleas.[94]

Wickersham Commission investigators identified the institutional centralization of prosecutorial power that had accrued over the previous 60 years or so beginning in 1865. As the Commission clearly understood, prosecutors had nearly sole authority to determine whether, when, and how justice would be administered.

For good measure, the Wickersham Commission Report provides extensive data regarding all aspects of criminal prosecution and conviction in its "Statistical Analysis – Criminal Cases" portion of the Report.[95] Happily the data provided include the prevalence of plea bargaining across jurisdictions in the United States. For example, in Milwaukee County from 1919 to 1928, guilt established "On plea of guilty" ranged from 625 convictions in 1919 to a high of 1,051 in 1927.[96] In 1924, Hennepin County, Minnesota, the home of Minneapolis, registered 414 guilty plea convictions.[97] In Cincinnati, Ohio, the two years encompassing 1925–1926 witnessed 16 percent of criminal case dispositions resolved via the plea.[98] Finally, for 1928, the Federal District Court of the Northern District of Ohio reported that 99 percent of criminal convictions were the product of guilty pleas (274 out of 278 cases).[99] By way of reminder, the Wickersham Commission Report was published in 1931. It seems likely, given the references made to sedimented prosecutorial power, that the practice of pleading to lesser charges to obtain a reduced sentence and certain conviction had been firmly established during the first two decades of the 20th century. The Wickersham Commission Report emphasizes this point with a major heading: ACCEPTANCE OF PLEA OF LESSER OFFENSE – PROSECUTORS BARGAINING FOR DISPOSITION. Here, the Commission is referring to charge and sentencing reductions in exchange for prosecution at trial.

The first three decades of the 20th century, assessment of criminal procedure establishes what by then appears to have been a ubiquitous practice of plea bargaining. That said, there are precious little data relating to procedure as it pertains to the plea for the period of my analysis – 1865–1900. Initially, the 1890 Census of the United States presented some optimism with regard to the existence of plea bargaining; after all, it was titled: CRIME, PAUPERISM, AND BENEVOLENCE – PART 1.[100] While the census data are thorough in their demographic identification of crimes, age, gender, ethnicity, region, and the like, there is no mention that I can find of pleading to lesser charges. The absence of a specific reference to pleas does not mean, however, that the practice of pleading was non-existent. As Vogel and Fisher's work makes clear, there was a practice of charge and sentence bargaining in Boston at least that can be identified as early as the 1830s and 1840s. So, it is quite likely that the practice was taking place in jurisdictions across the country.[101]

One possible source signifying the application of a more flexible criminal procedure may be found in state prosecutions of "bastardy."[102] Inherited from English Common Law and adopted by many of the colonies and subsequently the states, bastardy laws addressed the breach of promise to marry. These laws

> rested their opinion on a new reading of the judicial obligation to protect the public welfare by claiming that the only obvious effect must be to induce persons to execute their contracts of marriage, where seductions have ensued from them, for fear of being compelled to answer in damages for the pain and ignominy which the breach of such contracts would bring upon the victims of their lust and fraud.[103]

The gist of this statement is clear: any male who engages in sexual intercourse with a woman who becomes pregnant, and who pledges marriage to that woman, is bound by law to act upon that promise. Failing to do so resulted in a "breach of promise," a violation of a contractual agreement.

By the mid-19th century, it is historically interesting to notice the cultural transitions taking place regarding the power to control criminal procedure, a manifestation of Article III constitutional power.[104] Judges began applying their authority to the policing of new societal commitments to gendered sexual identity, as well as the patriarchal commitment to de-sexing women by emphasizing their Victorian wholesomeness. According to Grossberg:

> Judges assumed their new roles in ways that were more varied than those presented in legal historiography. In domestic relations they became a kind of state patriarch ... The designation 'judicial patriarchy' indicates that part of the consciousness of these men, and part of their power, stemmed from the ability of judges to divide the world into various categories and assume different poses in each; these ranged from patriarch to promoter, to policeman.[105]

Following the framers' granting of coequal power to the judiciary, judges in the United States assumed power that had not been previously realized in England. This power included judicial review, but equally important was the now greater freedom for judges to establish policy through their written legal opinions. And, "Judicial power grew further as early nineteenth century legislatures gradually relinquished authority over private legislation such as corporate charters and divorce, professionals dedicated to common law supremacy ousted lay judges, *and judges wrested control of trials from juries*."[106] There's a lot to unpack in that statement, but two points are immediately relevant. First, with the growing strength of the judiciary came an increasing emphasis on positive law in the administration of justice. Second, and equally important, is the extent to which judges assumed multiple dispute-resolution roles. For example, procedural flexibility (what Vogel referred to as *episodic leniency*) enabled judges to fit charges and sentences in accordance with their role as community patriarchs. This occurred throughout the 19th century as judges began to "paper over inconsistent state laws with a rule that accepted their continued existence but provided a mechanism for resolving individual problems. The new doctrine thus accepted the legitimacy of state domestic relations jurisdiction and yet constituted an attempt to create a national common law by balancing centralism and localism."[107] Significantly, judges during this period began "elevating individual rights over regulatory acts, relying on persuasion rather than compulsion in the regulation of legal behavior, and creating flexible doctrines dependent on judicial discretion."[108] The flexibility pertaining to judicial discretion could, in bastardy cases, be used to resolve breaches of promise simply by offering the offending male the opportunity to "do the right thing" by keeping the promise that was made to marry. That is, the judge provided the offending male with one of two choices ("trial tax"): either he could uphold his promise to marry his now pregnant female friend, in which case no charges would be brought, or he could refuse to honor the promise that he made, in which case he would be charged and prosecuted at trial.[109] The resulting resolution to the problem of bastardy reinforced patriarchal cultural norms and protected the state from having to raise a neglected child, but it did so in a way that avoided the time and expense of trial. It is my contention that through the application of judicial discretion, a judge presenting a male offender with the "offer" to marry or face trial was engaging in plea bargaining.

Plea Bargaining's Innocence Problem

In this final section of Chapter 1, I want to very briefly turn my attention to the documented number of felony cases where a defendant was actually innocent yet accepted a plea bargain, leading to often severe sentences. Since 1989, 915 wrongful convictions have occurred as a result of a guilty plea.[110] According to the National Registry of Exonerations, of the 3,368 wrongful convictions documented since 1989, 27 *percent are cases where an actually innocent defendant accepted a guilty plea* rather than asserting their right to trial. To be "actually innocent" means that a defendant had absolutely nothing whatsoever to do with the commission of the alleged crime.

Typically, defendants who are actually innocent yet plead guilty find that their decision was affected by a number of factors, including failure to meet the knowing and voluntary standard discussed earlier, as well as the presence of the trial tax. In this section, I want to emphasize two additional reasons why an actually innocent defendant would plead guilty to a crime they did not commit: a) the existence of any prior criminal record, and b) the defendant's "perceived stereotypicality."

If a defendant has a prior record, even a juvenile record, they may be confronted with the possibility that their prior convictions will be introduced at trial as a way to frame them before a jury as possessing the type of character likely to have led them to commit the presently charged crime. Determination as to whether and under what circumstances a defendant's priors are introduced before a jury will follow a pre-trial evidentiary hearing initiated by a motion to the court filed by the prosecutor. That hearing will include the prosecutor who wishes to present prior convictions as part of their case in chief, defense attorneys who will likely argue that prior convictions are too prejudicial to the defendant and should in no way be presented to the jury, and the judge who will determine the outcome of the prosecutor's motion. Depending upon the specific request, the judge may consider the following Federal Rules of Evidence (FRE): Rule 401 (Test for Relevant Evidence), Rule 403 (Excluding Relevant Evidence for Prejudice, Confusion, Waste of Time, or Other Reasons), Rule 404 (Character Evidence; Other Crimes, Wrongs, or Acts), Rule 405 (Methods For Proving Character), Rule 608 (A Witness's Character for Truthfulness or Untruthfulness), and Rule 609 (Impeachment By Evidence of a Criminal Conviction). Most often, what will be at stake is a battle between the defense attorney, who will raise FRE Rule 403 as a way to construct a firewall separating prior criminal convictions from the currently adjudicated case. The reason for this is that jurors may be persuaded that if a defendant had spent time in prison for one felony, they are *the kind of person* who would have committed the currently charged felony, thereby enhancing the likelihood of conviction.

For their part, prosecutors have numerous tools provided by the FRE that can enable them to overcome Rule 403 objections. For example, character evidence is the purpose of Rule 404. Rule 404(a)(1) *prohibits* the introduction of character evidence by a prosecutor where the prosecutor attempts to identify a specific character trait as consistent with the kind of person who would have committed the charged crime. However, Rule 404(b)(2) provides an exception to 404(a)(1). That exception, which means that a defendant's character traits may be introduced at trial, includes the following language: "Permitted Uses. This evidence may be admissible for another purpose, such as proving motive, opportunity, intent, preparation, plan, knowledge, identity, absence of mistake, or lack of accident."[111] Given the breadth of this list of the elements of a crime, it's not hard to see how the state can overcome Rule

403 and 404(a)(1) concerns for prejudice. FRE Rule 609 speaks specifically to the introduction of prior criminal convictions at trial as a way to confront a witness's character and commitment to truthfulness. Prior criminal convictions may be presented to a jury: a) if a defendant was convicted of a felony punishable by more than one year in prison, b) if a defendant serves as a witness, and c) if the probative value of the evidence outweighs its prejudicial effect to the defendant.[112]

Each defendant will be confronted with the reality of the FRE upon consideration of exercising their right to trial or accepting a plea. Since there is no way to know in advance of a plea decision what the outcome of pre-trial evidentiary hearings might reveal (after all, we are not going to trial so there will be no pre-trial evidentiary hearing), a defendant with prior felony convictions and time spent in prison must thoughtfully weigh: a) the likelihood that character evidence may be introduced as an exception to FRE 403 and 404(a)(1), b) the likelihood of testifying as a witness on their own behalf (not likely), and c) whether the state can convince a judge that the probative weight of the evidence outweighs a defendant's right to avoid the introduction of prejudicial evidence. For prosecutors, a victory relating to the introduction of character evidence before a jury would likely generate a serious imbalance in favor of the state's case leading to conviction. In all likelihood, a defendant will be made aware of the FRE by defense counsel before committing to a decision as to whether to plea, since the FRE signifies a serious obstacle to prevailing at trial.

One other important consideration for criminal defendants considering whether to exercise their right to trial pertains to the "perceived stereotypicality" of the defendant. In 1985, Bodenhausen and Wyer published their research establishing the prevalence of stereotypes as a common heuristic drawn upon by jurors when deliberating over defendant culpability.[113] In a persuasive publication addressing the effects of the perceived stereotypicality of a black defendant upon a jury's likelihood to convict at trial, especially when the victim was white, Eberhardt et al. (2004) conclude that, "We argue that only in death-eligible cases involving White victims – cases in which race is most salient – will Black defendants' physical traits function as a significant determination of deathworthiness."[114] A similar finding was published by Smalarz et al. (2018),[115] who assessed the prevalence of perceived stereotypical criminal traits on mock jurors considering whether defendants were coerced into confessions. Findings indicate that jurors were influenced by a defendant's criminal stereotypes when deciding whether a confession was voluntary or coerced. Dushiyanthini et al. (2023), published a fascinating study addressing whether defendants with stereotypically black names like "Jamal" receive disparate treatment from jurors at sentencing when compared with more stereotypically white names, like "James." Their results provide statistically significant evidence that stereotypically black names produce longer sentences than those perceived by jurors to be more "white."[116]

While only a superficial slice of the published evidence, it is clear that jurors make decisions (often unconsciously) about guilt and appropriate sentences premised upon defendant stereotypes. Criminal defense attorneys know this from experience if not from their time in law school researching the topic, and they will consider perceived defendant stereotypicality and its prospective effect upon jury deliberation when advising their clients as to whether to plead or assert their right to trial.

One final point as it relates to jury bias is relevant to the advice provided by criminal defense attorneys to defendants considering the plea. Simply put, jurors are human beings who arrive at the courthouse as complex subjects constituted by the quality of their brains and their diverse experiences. What seems to coalesce jurors, however, is their commitment to declare guilt "after a detective referred the case to the district attorney and when he was formally charged and thus a criminal defendant."[117] That is, jurors presume that upon indictment by a grand jury the defendant is likely to be guilty of the crimes alleged. In their 2022 publication, Lee J. Curley, James Munro, and Itiel Dror identify three types of bias that constitute jurors' pre-trial assumptions about guilt – pre-trial bias, cognitive bias, and bias from external legal factors (e.g., legal experts).[118]

The combination of the quite reasonable presumption made by jurors that a criminal defendant is likely to be guilty as charged (after all, why are we here?) with the perceived stereotypicality of defendants increases the likelihood of conviction at trial. Criminal defendants may be deterred from considering a not guilty plea for these reasons alone.

***

In this chapter, we have covered significant ground. We have learned about Federal Rule 11 and plea bargaining procedures, the role of the legislature in promoting the plea, plea case law, a brief history of the appearance of the plea in the United States, and plea bargaining's innocence problem. In the next chapter, I will introduce what I perceive to be an important historical moment of coalescence between equity and conciliation courts with the American commitment to adversarialism that may have provided the institutional framework for the adoption of the plea.

Notes

1 The presumptive sentence is the sentence defendants most commonly receive for the charged offense.

2 Carlos Beredo. Criminalizing Race: Racial Disparities in Plea-Bargaining. 59 B.C. L. Rev. 1187 (2018), John A. Humphrey and Timothy J. Fogarty. Race and Plea Bargained Outcomes: A Research Note. Social Forces 66(1)

(1987): 176–182; Brian D. Johnson and Rebecca Richardson. Race and Plea Bargaining. In Vanessa A. Edkins and Allison D. Redlich (eds), A System of Pleas: Social Science's Contributions to the Real Legal System. London: Oxford University Press, 2019; Besiki Luka Kutateladze, Nancy R. Andiloro, and Brian D. Johnson. Opening Pandora's Box: How Does Defendant Race Influence Plea Bargaining? Justice Quarterly 33(3) (2016): 398–426.

3 Bob Jessop. The State: Past, Present, Future. London: Polity Press (2016); Rene B. Bertramsen, Jens Peter Frolund Thomsen, and Jacob Torfing. State, Economy, and Society. London: Unwin-Hyman (1991). Jessop's novel creation of the theory of the strategic-relation approach (SRA) "widens its [theory of the state] focus, so as to capture not just the state apparatus but the exercise and effects of state power as a contingent expression of a changing balance of forces that seek to advance their respective interests inside, through, and against the state system" (Jessop at 54). The theory of state strategic selection generally flows from Jessop's "strategic-relational" analysis of the state (pp. 53–58), and it refers to the contingent nature of the power of state actors to assess dysfunction within various vectors (e.g., economy, education, media, law, religion, politics) and target those vectors for specific intervention necessary to promote dominant cultural values and systemic order.

4 John Langbein. Torture and Plea Bargaining. 46, 1, U of Chi. L. Rev., 3 (1978).

5 Robert Schehr. Standard of Proof, Presumption of Innocence, and Plea Bargaining: How Wrongful Conviction Data Exposes Inadequate Pre-Trial Criminal Procedure. 54 C. W. L. Rev. 1, 51 (2018).

6 See *Brady*, 397 US 742; *North Carolina v. Alford*, 400 US 25 (1970); *Parker v. North Carolina*, 397 US 790 (1970); *Santobello v. New York*, 404 US 257 (1971); *Chaffin v. Synchcombe*, 412 US 17 (1973); *Bordenkircher v. Hayes*, 434 US 357 (1978); *Corbitt v. New Jersey*, 439 US 212 (1978).

7 https://www.law.cornell.edu/rules/frcrmp/rule_11

8 Defendants who plead guilty must abdicate their Fifth and Sixth Amendment rights.

9 Rule 11 language pertaining to the voluntary requirement for plea bargaining. *(2) Ensuring That a Plea Is Voluntary*. Before accepting a plea of guilty or *nolo contendere*, the court must address the defendant personally in open court and determine that the plea is voluntary and did not result from force, threats, or promises (other than promises in a plea agreement).

10 Robert Schehr and Chelsea French. Mental Competency Law and Plea Bargaining: A Neurophenomenological Critique. 79, Alb. L. Rev. 3 (2016): 1091–1182.

11 https://www.law.cornell.edu/rules/frcrmp/rule_11

12 https://www.americanbar.org/content/dam/aba/administrative/legal_aid_indigent_defendants/ls_sclaid_louisiana_project_report.pdf; Albert Alschuler. The Defense Attorney's Role in Plea Bargaining. 84 Y. L. J. 6, 1179 (1975); Stephen Bright. The Failure to Achieve Fairness: Race and Poverty Continue to Influence Who Dies. 11 J. Con. L. 1, 23 (2008).

13 Christi Metcalfe. The Role of Courtroom Working Groups in Felony Case Dispositions: An Analysis of Workgroup Familiarity and Similarity. 50, L &. Soc. R., 3, 637 (2016).

14 Robert Schehr. Standard of Proof, Presumption of Innocence, and Plea Bargaining: How Wrongful Conviction Data Exposes Inadequate Pre-trial Criminal Procedure. 54, 1, Cal. W. L. Rev., 51 (2018).

15 Ulrike Hahn. The Problem of Circularity in Evidence, Argument, and Explanation. Perspectives on Psychological Science, 6(2): 172–182 (2011).

16 Id at 172.

17 The Constitution of the United States of America. New York: Barnes and Noble (2005): 27. My emphasis.
18 Id at 39 (My emphasis).
19 Robert Schehr, The Emperor's New Clothes: Intellectual Dishonesty and the Unconstitutionality of Plea Bargaining, 2Tex. A&M L. Rev.385 (2015):33.
20 170 U.S. 343 (1898).
21 281 U.S. 276 (1930).
22 This is referred to as the doctrine of unconstitutional conditions.
23 *Thompson*, 170 US at 354.
24 281 US 276 (1930) (*Patton*).
25 *Patton v. United States* 281 US 276 (1930): 4.
26 Id at 32.
27 Id at 76.
28 Id at 78.
29 The Seventh Amendment to the United States Constitution equally provides for trial by juries in matters of private law. "In Suits at common law, where the value in controversy shall exceed twenty dollars, the right to trial by jury shall be preserved, and no fact tried by a jury shall be otherwise reexamined in any Court of the United States, than according to the rules of the common law." As with criminal jury trials, Federal Rules of Civil Procedure (FRCP) and United States Supreme Court case law have generated unevenness as it pertains to the right to trial by jury. Consider FRCP 56 Summary Judgment, and *Celotex Corp. v. Catrett*, 477 US 317 (1986) and *Anderson v. Liberty Lobby, Inc.*, 477 US 242 (1986) by way of example.
30 397 US 742 (1970).
31 132 Sup. Ct at 1397 (2012).
32 390 US 570 (1968).
33 395 US 238 (1968).
34 Supra 32 at 583.
35 Supra 33 at 242.
36 *146 US 314 (1893).*
37 168 Eng. Rep. 234 (1783).
38 99 US 594 (1878).
39 168 US 532 (1897).
40 274 US 220 (1927).
41 312 US 275 (1941).
42 316 US 101 (1942).
43 356 US 26 (1958).
44 368 US 487 (1962).
45 390 US 570 (1968).
46 395 US238 (1969).
47 394 US 459 (1969).
48 *Brady v. United States*, 397 US at 751.
49 Id at 752.
50 Id at 758.
51 404 US 257 (1971).
52 412 US 17 (1973).
53 439 US 212 (1978).
54 434 US 357 (1978).
55 Supra 52 at 31.
56 Supra 52 at 32.
57 Supra 54 at 361.
58 Supra 54 at 363.

59 Supra 54 at 364.
60 See, for example, Kenneth W. Simons. Offers, Threats, and Unconstitutional Conditions. 26 San Diego L. Rev., 289 (1989).
61 536 US 622 (2002).
62 566 US 156 (2012).
63 566 US 134 (2012).
64 Supra 61 at 623.
65 372 US 335 (1963).
66 466 US 668 (1984).
67 397 US 358 (1970).
68 397 U.S. 742 (1970)
69 *In re Winship* was decided on March 31, 1970, while *Brady v. United States* was decided on May 4, 1970. *Brady v. United States* uprooted *United States v. Jackson* 390 US 570 (1968) which held that threatening a defendant with execution if convicted at trial presented an "impermissible burden upon the exercise of a constitutional right." 390 US at 572.
70 No person shall be held to answer for a capital, or otherwise infamous crime, unless on a presentment or indictment of a Grand Jury, except in cases arising in the land or naval forces, or in the Militia, when in actual service in time of War or public danger; nor shall any person be subject for the same offense to be twice put in jeopardy of life or limb; nor shall be compelled in any criminal case to be a witness against himself, nor be deprived of life, liberty, or property, without due process of law; nor shall private property be taken for public use, without just compensation.
71 In all criminal prosecutions, the accused shall enjoy the right to a speedy and public trial, by an impartial jury of the State and district wherein the crime shall have been committed, which district shall have been previously ascertained by law, and to be informed of the nature and cause of the accusation; to be confronted with the witnesses against him; to have compulsory process for obtaining witnesses in his favor; and to have the Assistance of Counsel for his defense.
72 423 US 61 (1975) (*Menna v. New York*).
73 Id.
74 Supra 18 at 397. My emphasis.
75 In *Bell v. Wolfish*, 441 US 520 (1979) the Supreme Court addressed the question pertaining to the moment that the presumption of innocence "attaches" and, in doing so, deviated from long-standing Court precedent. At issue in that case was whether pre-trial detention conditions violated the presumption of innocence. In a majority opinion authored by Justice Rehnquist, the Court held that the presumption of innocence attaches at trial.
76 *Lafler v. Cooper*, 566 US (2012), *Missouri v. Frye*, 566 US (2012). *Lafler* and *Frye* were decided on the same day, March 21, 2012.
77 163 US 537 (1896).
78 *State v. Plessy*, No. 19, 117 (Criminal District Court, Parish of Orleans 1892).
79 http://projects.leadr.msu.edu/makingmodernus/exhibits/show/plessy-v--ferguson-1896/louisiana-separate-car-act--18
80 11 So.74, 76 (La. 1892).
81 Thomas J. Davis. More Than Segregation, Racial Identity: The Neglected Question In *Plessy v. Ferguson*. 10 Wash. & Lee Race & Ethnic Anc. L. J. 1 (2004) at 27. My emphasis.
82 https://64parishes.org/entry/plessy-v-ferguson
83 Roscoe Pound and Felix Frankfurter. Criminal Justice in Cleveland. Reports of the Cleveland Foundation Survey of the Administration of Justice in Cleveland, Ohio. The Cleveland Foundation. 1922: 181. My emphasis.

84 Walter F. Dodd. Notes on Judicial Organization and Procedure. 21 Am. Pol. Sci. Rev. 949. 1929: 949. ("Whenever a plea of guilty is accepted for an offense less than that charged, a written record of the reasons must be made").
85 Newman F. Baker. The Prosecutor: Initiation of Procedure. 23 J. Crim. L. and Criminology, 5, 770, 1933: 771.
86 Id at 775.
87 Id at 775.
88 Id at 786.
89 Id at 788.
90 The National Commission on Law Observance and Enforcement was established by President Herbert Hoover on May 20, 1929. The Commission was orchestrated by former United States Attorney General George W. Wickersham.
91 Id at 95.
92 Id at 95.
93 Id at 95.
94 Id at 96.
95 Readers may be interested in procuring pages 201–221 of the Statistical Analysis – Criminal Cases data as it clearly identifies the existence of guilty pleas and criminal convictions.
96 Supra 90 at 201.
97 Supra 90 at 201.
98 Supra 90 at 206.
99 Supra 90 at 213.
100 Department of the Interior, Census Office. Report on Crime, Pauperism, and Benevolence in the United States at the Eleventh Census: 1890. Washington, D.C.: Government Printing Office. 1896.
101 I did review previous and subsequent census reports, but none provided the specific emphasis upon crime and punishment that came to define the 1890 census. In his critique of Vogel and those like myself who frame plea bargaining within the context of political economy, Fisher argues that there is little evidence that the public knew anything about plea bargaining during the 19th century, thereby suggesting that there was no cultural milieu within which to discuss or debate the importance of the practice. See Fischer, supra 14 at 144–151.
102 My thanks to Dr Paul Finkelman, President of Gratz College, for pointing me in the direction of bastardy laws.
103 Michael Grossberg. Crossing Boundaries: Nineteenth-Century Domestic Relations Law and the Merger of Family and Legal History. 10, Am. B. Found. Res. J. 4 (1985): 810.
104 https://www.law.cornell.edu/constitution/articleiii
105 Supra 103 at 818.
106 Supra 103 at 818.
107 Supra 103 at 822.
108 Supra 103 at 822.
109 Of course, contemporary practices would forbid any involvement in deal-making on behalf of judges for the purpose of the plea as they are bound by the Federal Rules of Criminal Procedure Rule 11.
110 National Registry of Exonerations. Site visited on September 7, 2023. https://www.law.umich.edu/special/exoneration/Pages/detaillist.aspx
111 https://www.law.cornell.edu/rules/fre/rule_404
112 https://www.law.cornell.edu/rules/fre/rule_609
113 G.V. Bodenhausen and R.S. Wyer. Effects of Stereotypes in Decision Making and Information-Processing Strategies. Journal of Personality and Social Psychology, 48(2) (1985): 267–282.

114 Jennifer L. Eberhardt, Paul G. Davies, Valerie J. Purdie-Vaughns, and Sheri Lynn Johnson. Looking Deathworthy: Perceived Stereotypicality of Black Defendants Predicts Capital-Sentencing Outcomes. Cornell Law Faculty Publications, Paper 41 (2004): 383.
115 Laura Smalarz, Stephanie Madon, and Anna Turosak. Defendant Stereotypicality Moderates the Effect of Confession Evidence on Judgments of Guilt. Law and Human Behavior, 42(4) (2018): 355.
116 Kenthirarajah Dushiyanthini, Nicholas P. Camp, Gregory M. Walton, Aaron C. Kay, and Geoffrey L. Cohen. Does "Jamal" Receive a Harsher Sentence Than "James"? First Name Bias in the Criminal Sentencing of Black Men. Law and Human Behavior, 47(1) (2023): 169–181.
117 Nicholas Scurich and Richard S. John. Jurors' Presumption of Innocence. Journal of Legal Studies, 46(1) (2017): 187.
118 Lee J. Curley, James Munro, and Itiel E. Dror. Cognitive and Human Factors in Legal Layperson Decision Making: Sources of Bias In Juror Decision Making. Medicine, Science and the Law, 62(3) (2022): 206–215.

References

Albert Alschuler. The Defense Attorney's Role in Plea Bargaining. 84(6) *Y. L. J.*, 1179 (1975)

Newman F. Baker. The Prosecutor: Initiation of Procedure. 23(5) *J. Crim. L. and Criminology*, 770 (1933)

Carlos Beredo. Criminalizing Race: Racial Disparities in Plea-Bargaining. 59 *B.C. L. Rev.*, 1187 (2018)

Rene B. Bertramsen, Jens Peter Frolund Thomsen, and Jacob Torfing. *State, Economy, and Society*. London: Unwin-Hyman (1991)

G.V. Bodenhausen and R.S. Wyer. Effects of Stereotypes in Decision Making and Information-Processing Strategies. 48(2) *J. Pers. Soc. Psychol.*, (1985)

Stephen Bright. The Failure to Achieve Fairness: Race and Poverty Continue to Influence Who Dies. 11(1) *J. Con. L.*, 23 (2008)

Lee J. Curley, James Munro, and Itiel E. Dror. Cognitive and Human Factors in Legal Layperson Decision Making: Sources of Bias In Juror Decision Making. 62(3) *Med. Sci. Law.*, 206–215 (2022)

Thomas J. Davis. More Than Segregation, Racial Identity: The Neglected Question In Plessy v. Ferguson. 10 *Wash. & Lee Race & Ethnic Anc. L. J.*, 1 (2004)

Department of the Interior, Census Office. Report On Crime, Pauperism, and Benevolence in the United States at the Eleventh Census: 1890. Washington, DC: Government Printing Office (1896)

Walter F. Dodd. Notes on Judicial Organization and Procedure. 21 *Am. Pol. Scie. Rev.*, 949 (1929)

Kenthirarajah Dushiyanthini, Nicholas P. Camp, Gregory M. Walton Aaron C. Kay, and Geoffrey L. Cohen. Does "Jamal" Receive a Harsher Sentence Than "James"? First Name Bias in the Criminal Sentencing of Black Men. 47(1) *Law & Hum. Behav.*, 169–181 (2023)

Jennifer L. Eberhardt, Paul G. Davies, Valerie J. Purdie-Vaughns, and Sheri Lynn Johnson. Looking Deathworthy: Perceived Stereotypicality of Black Defendants Predicts Capital-Sentencing Outcomes. Cornell Law Faculty Publications. Paper 41 383 (2004)

Michael Grossberg. Crossing Boundaries: Nineteenth-Century Domestic Relations Law and the Merger of Family and Legal History. 10 *Am. B. Found. Res. J.*, 4 (1985)
Ulrike Hahn. The Problem of Circularity in Evidence, Argument, and Explanation. 6(2) *Perspect. Psychol. Sci.,* 172–182 (2011)
John A. Humphrey and Timothy J. Fogarty. Race and Plea Bargained Outcomes: A Research Note. 66(1) *Soc. Forces.,* 176–182 (1987)
Bob Jessop. *The State: Past, Present, Future.* London: Polity Press (2016)
Brian D. Johnson and Rebecca Richardson. Race and Plea Bargaining. In Vanessa A. Edkins and Allison D. Redlich (eds.) *A System of Pleas: Social Science's Contributions to the Real Legal System.* London: Oxford University Press (2019)
Besiki Luka Kutateladze, Nancy R. Andiloro, and Brian D. Johnson. Opening Pandora's Box: How Does Defendant Race Influence Plea Bargaining? 33(3) *Justice Quarterly,* 398–426 (2016)
John Langbein. Torture and Plea Bargaining. 46(1) *U of Chi. L. Rev.*, 3 (1978)
Christi Metcalfe. The Role of Courtroom Working Groups in Felony Case Dispositions: An Analysis of Workgroup Familiarity and Similarity. 50(3) *L & Soc. R.*, 637 (2016)
Roscoe Pound and Felix Frankfurter. Criminal Justice in Cleveland. Reports of the Cleveland Foundation Survey of the Administration of Justice in Cleveland, Ohio. The Cleveland Foundation (1922)
Robert Schehr. The Emperor's New Clothes: Intellectual Dishonesty and the Unconstitutionality of Plea Bargaining. 2(3) *Tex. A&M L. Rev.*, 385 (2015)
Robert Schehr. Standard of Proof, Presumption of Innocence, and Plea Bargaining: How Wrongful Conviction Data Exposes Inadequate Pre-Trial Criminal Procedure. 54(1) *C. W. L. Rev.*, 51 (2018)
Robert Schehr and Chelsea French. Mental Competency Law and Plea Bargaining: A Neurophenomenological Critique. 79(3) *Alb. L. Rev.*, 1091–1118 (2016)
Nicholas Scurich and Richard S. John. Jurors Presumption of Innocence. 46(1) *J. Leg. Stud.*, (2017).
Kenneth W. Simons. Offers, Threats, and Unconstitutional Conditions. 26 *San Diego L. Rev.*, 289 (1989)
Laura Smalarz, Stephanie Madon, and Anna Turosak. Defendant Stereotypicality Moderates the Effect of Confession Evidence on Judgments of Guilt. 42(4) *Law & Hum. Behav.*, 355 (2018)
The National Commission on Law Observance and Enforcement was established by President Herbert Hoover on May 20, 1929.

Cases

Brady v. United States, 397 US 742 (1970).
North Carolina v. Alford, 400 US 25 (1970).
Parker v. North Carolina, 397 US 790 (1970).
Santobello v. New York, 404 US 257 (1971).
Chaffin v. Synchcombe, 412 US 17 (1973).
Bordenkircher v. Hayes, 434 US 357 (1978).
Corbitt v. New Jersey, 439 US 212 (1978).
Lafler v. Cooper, 566 US (2012).
Patton v. United States, 281 US 276 (1930).
Brady v. United States, 397 US (1970).
Missouri v. Frye, 566 US (2012).

2

COURTS OF EQUITY AND CONCILIATION

In this chapter I attempt to piece together what I believe to be the institutional predicates to the practice that we refer to as plea bargaining. Since we have already discussed plea bargaining generally, this section will not address the contemporary practice beyond references by juxtaposition with historical court practices. Rather, it will explore what I believe are two procedural paths that converged within the uniquely American system of criminal justice.

Before I proceed, a few caveats are in order. First, I am not a historian by training; I am a sociologist. Historical analysis is not unknown to sociology, and it represents a significant aspect of my training in political economy. Second, the argument that I present here is ripe for debate as the evidence that exists with regard to actual court practices across the United States, especially prior to the 20th century, is scant. Where evidence does exist, it is often incomplete, or the language and data-gathering practices (where they existed) were unique to the time and location. This is important because, while I contend that the evidence that I present here is powerful, maybe even convincing with regard to the emergence of the plea in the United States, there are gaps in my argument. For example, there is evidence for the existence of each of the types of courts (equity and conciliation) referenced in this section, the regions in which they were most commonly applied, and in some jurisdictions quite detailed information about cases, such as Boston.[1] Identification of the *precise* moment that plea bargaining arrived as a procedural technology, and was institutionally recognized as such, is hard to identify largely because it is multicausal. Among the many historical movements that may have culminated in the plea are: a) the growing consolidation and professional authority of lawyers, b) the growing disenchantment with the

DOI: 10.4324/9781003385103-3

trial by jury, c) the emergence of the liberty of contract doctrine and its emphasis upon the "freedom to work," d) the re-emergence in the South during Reconstruction of attempts to re-enslave freed men and women, and perhaps most controversially, e) fear amongst judges, prosecutors, and defense attorneys in the South of mob lynchings which led to rapid case disposition. These themes signify the core argument of this book.

A recently authored article by William Ortman[2] suggests that there have been three prominent explanations regarding the origin of the plea: caseload pressure, trial complexity, and increased professionalization of police and prosecutors. First, following George Fisher, plea bargaining appeared as a legal technology necessary to manage ever-increasing caseloads. Important here is the fact that by 1850, *criminal* caseloads appear to have leveled off, while civil caseloads rose dramatically with the growing corporate claims made relative to the increasing dominance of capitalism. The second claim regarding the origin of the plea Ortman associates with the work of John Langbein. Specifically, it was Langbein's assertion that beginning in the middle of the 19th century, American trial practice had been overcome with procedural rules. As Ortman explains, prior to the adoption of more exacting procedural rules beginning in the latter third of the 19th century, trials were dramatically different from those we experience today. According to Langbein, there was no "extended voir dire, exclusionary rules and other evidentiary barriers, motions designed to provoke and preserve issues for appeal, maneuvers and speeches of counsel."[3] With increasing procedural complexity, trials became more expensive, more time-consuming, and less comprehensible to non-lawyers. For adherents to the "trial complexity" argument for the origination of the plea, it is no surprise that with plea bargaining in the ascendency, when juxtaposed to the more modern trial procedures, pleas held the benefit of efficiently disposing of cases. The third argument identified by Ortman with regard to the origins of the plea associates the practice with the increasing professionalization of police and prosecutors.[4] Here, it is the work of Lawrence Friedman and Robert Percival who contend that with enhanced police and prosecutor investigation skills, trials were no longer necessary since police and prosecutors would clearly identify the proper suspect. Citing Friedman and Percival, "Defendants charged by these professional crime fighters were 'obviously guilty,' so '[w]hy go through the long, expensive process' in court."[5] It is quite likely that it was some combination of each of the three historical processes identified by Ortman that assisted the growth of pleas.

What these three explanations for the origin of the plea – caseload, trial complexity, and increasing professionalization of police and prosecutors – reveal is descriptive insight akin to the parable of the blind man and the elephant. Depending upon one's attention to the matter, there are different aspects or component parts that definitely do constitute aspects of the whole. However, what appears to be missing is a theoretical and conceptual model of the emergence of the plea that contextualizes caseloads, trial complexity, professionalization of police and prosecutors, growing skepticism relating to the competency of jurors to manage complex positive law, and the re-emergence in the South of attempts to enhance social control over freed men and women, within the broader political, economic, and cultural attention to preservation of wealth and power, especially as capitalists, politicians, and the Supreme Court embraced the liberty of contract doctrine as the master narrative guiding dominant cultural expressions of freedom.

The work of Mary Vogel's political economic analysis signifies a fourth research pathway toward understanding the plea, and one that I find particularly compelling. It is Vogel's contention that the 19th century emerges as a period of massive political, economic, and cultural transformation in the United States.[6] George Fisher indicates that the practice is well established in Middlesex County, Massachusetts in the late 18th century.[7] These cases constituted liquor violations, as well as felony and misdemeanor cases.[8] Mary Vogel produces evidence that plea bargaining commenced in Boston during the 1830s and 1840s largely as a procedural attempt to maintain social order.[9] Vogel contends that by the middle of the 19th century "plea bargaining was already in place," and "trials become more complex."[10] And while I have not seen reference to this mid-century period as one that may be described as a "paradigm shift" in the way that our 20th-century minds might have understood it, my reading of the 1865–1900 timeframe signifies precisely that. Vogel agrees, arguing that previous attempts to understand the origins of the plea failed to acknowledge the extent to which the practice is uniquely American and suited to our own "changes in social context, events, and culture that shaped how those in the courtroom perceived and pursued their interests."[11] For the courts, this was challenging since it is difficult at any time to determine while in the maelstrom of the moment whether something new is on the horizon, and whether that new legal artifact has come to establish a place of normativity in practice.

The most controversial proposition that I will make as it relates to the proliferation of plea bargaining stems from research conducted by Michael Klarman.[12] While Klarman limits his analysis to criminal trials, it is my argument that the rationale for the plea bargain, especially in the South, has everything to do with the local court's interest in rapid case disposition. This became an urgent matter during Reconstruction when, upon arrest for a violent crime, blacks and Jews were far too frequently victimized by mob violence leading to lynchings before case facts had been thoroughly presented to a court. The response from criminal legal system actors was to expedite trials in order to ameliorate the concerns of the mob by demonstrating that the court and the rule of law would properly function to administer justice. According to Klarman, "Arkansas adopted a law designed to prevent lynchings by providing for special court terms within ten days in cases of rape or other crimes likely to arouse community passions."[13] Across the South, convictions were assured since "[P]rosecutors urged juries to convict in order to reward mobs for good behavior and thus encourage future restraint."[14] While Klarman's focus is on serious felonies adjudicated at trial, given the rationale for rapid case disposition to avoid lynchings, it makes sense to consider that same impetus as driving the efficient and rapid case disposition characteristic of the plea. But as I indicated, this is purely conjecture on my part as I have not, as yet, been able to generate the evidence necessary to make this link with objective data. My reason for including Klarman's insight here is to raise for consideration and future research the possibility that judges and prosecutors may have found the opacity and certainty accompanying the plea bargain to be particularly tempting as a way to avoid the publicity and violence that marked trials as theatrical events leading to the death of defendants at the hands of the mob.

It certainly appears that the juridical system apparatuses, for a host of reasons largely having to do with the growing status of the legal profession (especially prosecutors and judges), and its concomitant role in legitimizing the inevitability of capitalism and its detritus, are coalescing into what we recognize today as our adversarial system of due process. Still, it's impossible to judge one's own historical moment with clarity, and the United States Supreme Court has admitted as much.

In 1923, the United States Supreme Court held in *Frye v. United States*[15] that "Just when a scientific principle or discovery crosses the line between the experimental and demonstrable stages is difficult to define. Somewhere in this twilight zone, the evidential force of the principle must be recognized"[16] What will soon be apparent is that the "twilight zone" I will be assessing pertains largely to the 1865 to 1900 time frame. It was during this period when, in both the North and the South, considerable jurisprudential experimentation was taking place, but for somewhat unique historical reasons in each case. As I will attempt to demonstrate with brief reference to Vogel, followed by my own contribution to the "emergence of pleas question," plea bargaining in America has its roots in Europe, but its manifestation in the United States was uniquely an American product.

To begin, I would like to provide a contextual schema to guide my argument. The American justice system is largely the product of the combination of English Common Law, Equity Courts, Conciliation Courts, and our unique contribution to adversarial due process. It is my contention that while the quasi-inquisitorial practices outlined below amounted to transplanted *civil* procedure (not criminal), their ubiquity and efficiency were adopted by criminal law practitioners. A similar contemporary example might be found in *Daubert v. Merrell Dow Pharmaceuticals*, a civil case decided in 1993 that in time was interpreted for application to criminal cases where the question relating to the admission of expert witness testimony has increasingly raised serious structural concerns over the admission of "junk science."[17] The Daubert Standard, in either strict or modified form, has largely replaced the 1923 *Frye*[18] Standard for the admission of expert witness testimony in criminal cases.[19] My point here is simply to emphasize that while equity and conciliation courts originated as civil courts in Europe, as they gained popularity in the United States and were met with adversarialism, they transmogrified into the criminal case arena.

In the diagram below, I sketch out what my research reveals to be historical correlates affecting the adoption of plea bargaining. We begin with two predominant and antithetical approaches, English Common Law and Quasi-Inquisitorial courts. On the left side of the chart runs the historical pathway from Common Law to America's commitment to adversarialism, and finally to the adaptation of the plea within adversarial due process. On the right side of the chart lies quasi-inquisitorial procedure that historically originates in Rome with civil courts of equity. Later, in the 19th century and largely inspired by the 18th-century social theorist Jeremy Bentham,[20] Americans adopted courts of conciliation.

It is my contention that plea bargaining is a byproduct of both equity and conciliation court practices, principles, and culture (especially the Freedmen's Bureau, as we will see in Chapter 3) where, following Max Weber and Jurgen Habermas, a sociological analysis such as the one I present in this book would ask: "What actually happens in a group owing to the probability that persons engaged in social action [*Gemeinshaftshandeln*] ... subjectively consider certain norms as valid and practically act according to them, in other words, orient their own conduct towards these norms."[21] Furthermore, Habermas reveals that,

> the conditions for the ideal validity assumed with the belief in legitimacy constitute necessary, even if not sufficient, conditions for the social validity of a legal order. This is because legal orders are "legitimate orders" that, *although certainly not fitting ideas seamlessly together with interests, do interpret interests through ideas, thereby making reasons and validity claims factually effective.*[22]

The italicized portion of the previous sentence will prove fundamental to my contention that, while a clear exposition of the precise moment when plea bargaining appears may be difficult, what is apparent from the literature is recognition that the "legal order" operating in the mid to late 19th century attempted to manifest its interests in social control through the prevailing ideas relating to equity, conciliation, adversarialism, and positive law. In so doing, and now following Weber, a concurrent emergence of new norms appears to legitimate the quasi-inquisitorial administration of justice, albeit as administered through newly emerging prosecutorial power. This is an important caveat since, *although certainly not fitting ideas seamlessly together with interests* (an extremely difficult task given the paucity of available evidence), what does appear is the *idea* of more efficient case disposition.

Much like today, quasi-inquisitorial practices operated alongside common law trials (e.g., alternative dispute resolution, drug courts, mental health courts). Beginning during Reconstruction, as Americans became more committed to adversarialism largely due to the professionalization of lawyers and the legal profession, those quasi-inquisitorial practices were appropriated by judicial actors, imbued with adversarial due process, and repackaged for a system premised upon positive law. That the United States operated its legal system by way of adversarial process was well known. In fact, adversarialism and American civil and criminal procedure are nearly synonymous. However, and this is the point of the schema that I employ below, while the caricature of American jurisprudence is one exclusively predicated upon adversarialism, what we now know is that there was an equally legitimate and robust function for judicial flexibility within quasi-inquisitorial modes of due process. Each system of adjudication operated simultaneously within jurisdictions.

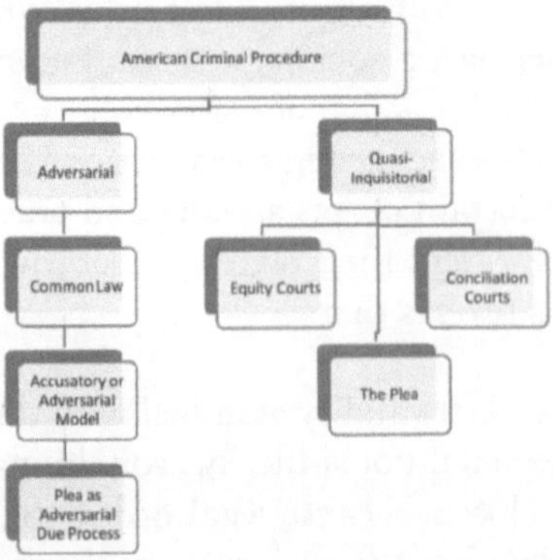

In this chapter, I introduce both courts of equity and conciliation courts as institutionally relevant to the establishment of plea bargaining. Admittedly, this argument is conjectural as it is premised upon my interpretation of the confluence of historical events that may have significantly influenced criminal case adjudication procedures as it evolved from English and French civil procedures and, as I attempt to demonstrate, combined with common law criminal procedures to manifest as an expedient legal technology for resolving felony criminal disputes.

Equity courts trace their origin to ancient Rome. Conciliation courts first appeared to emerge in the United States during the early 19th century. Each of these institutions exists within the juridical and political milieu carefully addressed by Vogel, and they emerge within the context of her articulation of "episodic leniency." Emerging as a byproduct of judicial power in the new American state, plea bargaining hypothetically manifested as a quasi-inquisitorial way for judges to manage political, economic, and cultural unrest by relying upon their knowledge of the English application of leniency. According to Vogel, the practice was "episodic" in that it was not something that could be relied upon with any predictability, but when it was applied, it meant "frequent but irregular pardons and grants of clemency."[23]

Equity Courts

The framers were well aware of the courts of equity as they had existed from the time of ancient Rome. Alexander Hamilton made reference to equity courts in Federalist LXXX, where he acknowledges the ubiquity of the practice by saying,

> It has also been asked, what need of the word "equity"? What equitable causes can grow out of the Constitution and laws of the United States? There is hardly a subject of litigation between individuals which may not involve those ingredients *of fraud, accident, trust, or hardship*, which would render the matter an object of equitable rather than legal jurisdiction, as the distinction is known and established in several of the states.[24]

Hamilton affirms the parallel existence of 18th-century equity courts with common law courts of justice. It is his contention that, "It is the peculiar province, for instance, of a court of equity to relieve against what are called *hard bargains*."[25] In fact, Hamilton claims that, "it would be impossible for the federal judicatories to do justice without an equitable as well as legal jurisdiction."[26] That said, he was cognizant that there were states where the practice of equity was unknown, and where his principled preference for equity jurisprudence was not as warmly received.

Aristotle contended that equity was a corrective to the law when the law failed to properly address specific case matters, or when it was unreasonable. Aristotle's support for equity courts was later realized in Rome, where "In Roman jurisprudence we may see many traces of this doctrine, applied to the purposes of supplying the defects of the customary law, as well as to correct and measure the interpretation of the written and positive code."[27] Put another way, for Aristotle, equity courts served as "a source of judicial power whereby in particular cases in which justice would be lost by too close an adherence to the letter of the law, the positive law could be bent and softened as necessary."[28] Most important was that Roman law mandated that justice was to be administered in an open dialogical forum. It was to be transparent, *res publica*, a public event.[29]

Among the most articulate and steadfast supporters of the existence and expansion of equity courts in the United States was Supreme Court Justice Joseph Story. McDowell says that Justice Story "was, in sum, the last major defender of the original understanding of Equity as it had been transmitted from Aristotle to Blackstone."[30]

Story contends that one of the principal roles of the Roman Praetor was the "application of equity, as contradistinguished from mere law."[31] Praetors followed their conscience to guide them through "the interpretation and limitation of the words of positive or written laws: by construing them, not according to the letter, but according to the reason and spirit of them."[32] Equity was understood by Justice Blackstone to mean "a method of interpreting laws by the reason of them." In a lengthier exposition, Justice Blackstone goes further by contending that: "Equity, in its true and genuine meaning, is the soul and spirit of all law; positive law is construed, and rational law is made by it. In this, equity is synonymous with justice; in that, to the true and sound interpretation of the rule."[33] Justice Story follows Blackstone's definition by suggesting that "equity must have a place in every rational system of jurisprudence, if not in name, at least in substance."[34] The most prevalent explanation for the practice of equity can be found in the lack of specificity constituting law. That is, no body of law applied *strictum jus* can possibly attend to all manifestations of human behavior. In order to promote justice, a Praetor must interpret the textual meaning of the law. The Praetor must then interpret statutory language in such a way as to promote the *intent* of the law. It is this practice of interpreting the textual meaning of statutes that required what Story called "equitable interpretation," where "it is the administration of equity, as contradistinguished from a strict adherence to the mere letter of the law."[35] A legal system that acknowledges equity does so as a way to "temper and mitigate the rigour of the law," whereby, "equity is a rightwiseness, that considerith all the particular circumstances of the deed, which is also tempered with the sweetness of mercy."[36] For St Germain: "Equity is that which is commonly called equal, just, and good; and is a mitigation or moderation of the common law, in some circumstances, either of the matter, person, or time; and often it dispenseth with the law itself."[37]

Justice Story's lengthy and thorough accounting of the origins of equity courts in Rome moves on to discover a similar commitment to equity in the works of Pufendorf (1632–1694) and Grotius (1583–1645). In fact, Story contends that it is they who announce the presence of an English court of equity that was premised upon Roman law. That is, it is clear from the record that by the 17th century, English law provided for *episodic leniency* to operate parallel to common law. Sir Henry Finch (1558–1625), the influential predecessor to Justice Blackstone,[38] makes reference to equity in his 17th-century publication, *Nomotexnia*,[39] a book committed to synthesizing

English common law. In it, Finch suggests that "the nature of equity is to amplify, enlarge, and add to the letter of the law."[40] For his part, Justice Blackstone explained that English courts of equity were designed "to abate the rigour of the common law."[41]

One of the prevailing concerns registered by legal scholars was that regardless of whether a case was prosecuted at common law or presented to quasi-inquisitorial equity courts, *judges must adhere to the written law. Aequitas sequitur legum* (Equity (fairness) follows the law). The cases that were most commonly brought before the court of equity were fraud, accident, and trust.[42] The informality of equity justice by no means eliminated adherence to statutory or legal authority; rather, equity was a normative part of the administration of justice. According to McDowell, "Equity was a part of the broader Common Law which itself was a reflection of the natural law and a system of rights and obligations dictated by natural justice."[43] Justice Story puts it this way: "It is the duty of every court of justice, whether of law or of equity, to consult the intention of the legislature. And, in the discharge of this duty a court of equity is not invested with a larger or more liberal discretion than a court of law."[44] Still, there were other influential jurists writing in the 18th century who viewed equity courts as an institutional remedy for failures at common law. The most often cited 18th-century court case to reference equity was *Dudley v. Dudley*.[45] In *Dudley*, Sir John Trevor summarizes equity this way:

> Now, equity is no part of the law, but a moral virtue, which qualifies, moderates, and reforms the rigour, hardness, and edge of the law, and is a universal truth. It does also assist the law, where it is defective and weak in the constitution (which is the life of the law), and defends the law from crafty evasions, delusions, and mere subtleties, invented and contrived to evade and elude the common law, whereby such as have undoubted right are made remediless. And thus is the office of equity to protect and support the common law from shifts and contrivances against the justice of the law. Equity, therefore, does not destroy law, nor create it, but assists it.[46]

Justice Story was unnerved by Trevor's recitation about the rather ubiquitous power of equity as a legal technology used at times to usurp common law authority in the name of justice (so too was Blackstone, as we will see), and the reasons are precisely those that have come to define scholarly and practitioner concerns over contemporary plea bargaining. This is important so I'll share it as it was written. According to Justice Story, Trevor's explication of equity "would be the most gigantic in its sway and the most formidable instrument of *arbitrary power* that could well be devised. It would literally place the whole rights and property of the community under the *arbitrary will of the judge*, acting, if you please, *arbitro boni judicis* (disposal good judge), and, it may be, *ex aequo et bono* (according to the right and the good, or according to equity and conscience), according to his own notions and conscience, but still acting with a despotic and sovereign authority.[47] At this point, I would request that the reader substitute "judge" with "prosecutor" and re-read Justice Story's claim. A temporally relevant political, economic, and cultural shift from England to the United States would render judges virtually powerless with regard to administering equity. This was especially the case beginning during Reconstruction and for the decades to follow into the early 20th century when the power of prosecutors was elevated beyond that of judges. Still, what we gather from Trevor's justification for equity in *Dudley* is awareness of a dispute resolution technology operating parallel to common law, and as a less formal mechanism than common law, to promote just outcomes. While inquisitorial systems were designed to adjudicate criminal cases, and equity courts civil ones, it appears that equity justice as it was practiced in England shared significant characteristics of those inquisitorial systems. Equity judges met with disputants in secret, maintained written as opposed to oral proceedings, and differed with regard to the procurement of discovery material.[48] It is in that way that equity courts practiced a quasi-inquisitorial adjudication. However, with powerful judges at the helm, critics could easily imagine usurpation of equity justice to the whim of local culture, habit, power, and, in the end, to the character of the judge. Blackstone cautions the same. According to him, "if a court of equity in England did really act, as many ingenious writers have supposed it (from theory) to do, it would rise above all law, either common or statute, and be a most arbitrary legislator in every particular case."[49] It is my contention that Blackstone's prescient cautionary concern expresses precisely what becomes of equity as it is practiced in the United States. That is, courts of equity, combined with conciliation courts, transmogrify into the ubiquitous practice of plea bargaining and with precisely the same concern – that "it would rise above all law," and that it would "be a most arbitrary legislator in every particular case." All that is necessary to do is to insert the prosecutor and remove the judge as the United States' expression of the Praetor. In his role as prosecutor (there were no female judges or lawyers), and by way of the application of episodic leniency: a) the administration of justice could operate parallel to criminal and civil trials, b) prosecutors would be sworn to administer justice through the application of legal statute and case law, and c) there would be no public oversight of equity case administration.

To sum up, equity jurisprudence originated in Rome and made its way to England through Roman conquest. By the 14th century, equity courts had formed. From there, equity courts played a significant role in the administration of justice. Equity courts helped to compensate for the shortcomings of common law by encouraging local dispute resolution. Equity courts were administered by judges who had extraordinary power to render opinions consistent with county community and legal standards. They were not permitted to operate *outside* of the common law to apply, say, magical or superstitious thinking to addressing interpersonal conflict. What equity courts did was introduce episodic leniency as a parallel mechanism of due process to avoid the time and expense of trial while softening the rough edges of common law. Resolutions made by judges were consistent with written law. In that way, the procedure avoided being *extrajudicial.* This is important because extrajudicial jurisprudence had largely been rendered obsolete by the 16th and 17th centuries, to be replaced with a rational written system of common laws. Two adjudication systems operated simultaneously within the same jurisdiction – common law and courts of equity. Most important for Justice Story, "He saw equity not as a mere set of procedural remedies but as a system of jurisprudence, an auxiliary to the strict law," that would, if properly administered alongside common law, recover and preserve "the ethical and moral basis of the law."[50]

As we will see, equity courts shared much in common with the French *bureaux de conciliation* (conciliation courts), especially their emphasis upon the introduction of "simple justice" as an institutional mechanism designed to expand access to the courts for working people, and to generate solutions to problems consistent with local norms.

Conciliation Courts

The history of conciliation courts in the United States comports with its growing presence in Europe, especially in France, Germany, and Denmark. Conciliation courts in the United States were premised upon the French *bureaux de conciliation.* According to Kessler, by the middle of the 19th century, Americans had started openly discussing the adoption of conciliation courts as a way to "promote the amicable, extralegal settlement of disputes."[51] Conciliation courts, like equity courts, were "staffed by lay judges, who lacked formal legal training and were selected by those whose disputes they were responsible for solving."[52] It was the stated purpose of conciliation courts to eliminate the trappings of common law procedure by attempting to find an equitable outcome for disputing parties. Interestingly, by the middle of the 19th century, there is growing concern among the legal profession that the public was losing its patience with the formality, time delay, and expense of trials, in addition to the growing unrest in the country that accompanied increasing urbanization and industrialization in the North, and slavery and later Reconstruction in the South. As such, the notion that conciliation courts should be adopted in the United States was seriously considered. And while conciliation courts may at first blush appear to be similar to contemporary alternative dispute resolution (ADR), given its stated flexibility and conviviality, nothing could be further from the truth. The principal claim made in this book is that contemporary plea bargaining is a synthetic byproduct of *both* equity and conciliation courts. My schema indicates that the confluence of equity and conciliation, when combined with a uniquely American investment in adversarialism, is one of the historical factors that led to the common practice of the plea. The presumption is that until equity and conciliation met adversarialism, the former two were perceived as a kinder, gentler, more equitable dispute-resolution practice mediated by a grandfatherly judge whose sole purpose was facilitating resolution to conflict consistent with local norms. In actuality, argues Kessler, conciliation "exhibits little concern for whether the resolution ultimately reached promotes the interests that the parties themselves recognize (and embrace) as their own."[53] At the core of conciliation was power. The institutional practice was designed to "encourage deference to social superiors (i.e., the judge), rather than individual autonomy," where "conciliation is thus conducted by a third party who is not a mere neutral, but instead a recognized figure of authority within the community."[54]

This is an important point as it pertains to the evolution of equity and conciliation toward plea bargaining. As Kessler points out, judges, at the time the most revered among judicial practitioners, while appearing to play the role of an unbiased member of the community, were actually serving to impose a specific kind of authority (recall the judge's role regarding bastardy cases). The point that I will make as it pertains to judicial authority, especially as we enter the latter decades of the 19th century, is that it gives way to prosecutorial authority. In that way, the prosecutor, and not the judge, will soon serve to facilitate "conciliation-like" dispute resolution, but within the criminal case context.

For Bentham, who wrote extensively about conciliation courts in France, Denmark, and Germany, conciliation courts introduced a legal technology to more efficiently dispose of cases. Bentham was a powerful advocate for an administration of justice that was less formal and intimidating than it had been in the past. For example, he proposed substituting the word "court" with "judicatory" as a way to symbolically supplant the power of judges and the crown. Bentham also proposed that all adjudication proceedings occur orally before a judge.[55] It was Bentham's view that "publicity, 'underwritten by simplicity', would be the 'main security against misdecision and non-decision'."[56] However, his enthusiasm for conciliation courts was primarily directed at the resolution of family disputes. This is an important caveat as we will see. Bentham's articulation of conciliation as a more transparent and simplified administration of justice would later be adopted by the original Commissioner of the Freedman's Bureau (see Chapter 3), Major General Oliver Otis Howard, as what he called "simple justice."

In Denmark, for example, Bentham remarked that conciliation courts "obtained such general credit, that more causes were brought before them, than before all the regular tribunals together."[57] So impressed was Bentham with the fact that conciliation courts disposed of between "two-thirds to three-fourths" of all cases, and that they freed disputants from the time, expense, and confusion of trial courts, that in his opinion justice would now be more readily available to common people. Sounding like a contemporary legal or social science commentator, Bentham's criticism of 18th-century criminal trial procedures included its "enormous amount of the mass factitious delay, expense, and vexation."[58] Still, Bentham presented a series of cautions with regard to adopting conciliation courts. His most prescient concern related to the opaquely distributed power of the justice of the peace or local judge presiding over a form of private justice well outside of public scrutiny. This was (and is) a matter of great seriousness since private meetings between disputants, held only in the presence of the judge, who would apply *common sense* within a context of natural law decision-making to generate an equitable resolution, meant for Bentham that judges would aver based largely upon their own biases. The result? According to Kessler, Bentham concluded that "the importation of such domestic procedure into the public domain threatened and undermined the rule of law."[59] Judges who would not be viewed as *neutral* arbiters of law threatened the *legitimacy of law*. Resnik cites the insightful William Twining and his interpretation of Bentham's view of conciliation as grudgingly supportive. That is, while conciliation may be a proper mechanism for family dispute resolution as a way to avoid "ill-will," Bentham advocated "rectitude of decision, that is, a strict adherence to justice under the law, and thus accorded only a grudging place to compromise."[60] Engaging in opaque conciliation procedures may lead a judge "to permit 'partiality' for one side to provide that party a partial victory [...] under the pretext of conciliation. As a consequence, in some instances, settlements could be 'repugnant to' and a 'denial of' justice."[61] This is precisely the concern that emerges in the mid to late 20th century with regard to plea bargaining. Plea bargains are made in secret. Federal Rules of Criminal Procedure, Rule 11, establish the terrain of plea bargains to be entirely the purview of prosecutors (it is no longer judges) who must establish that a "factual basis" exists for a case to be pled.[62] While criminal defendants currently do possess the right to legal representation during the plea process,[63] as was also the case beginning in the late 19th century, the procedural advantage structurally bends to the state. Of course, at the time that Bentham was writing, it was judges who were of greatest concern. But as we have seen, beginning in the middle of the 19th century the lawyers' guild in the United States grew significantly in its prosecutorial power.[64] So, Bentham's admonition that the power imbalance inherent in the conciliation model could generate "partial justice" by tipping the scales of justice this way or that in accordance with personal bias, resonates as so much more of a clarion call now than it did even then. For now, the "interest" represented by the prosecutor is no longer a matter of local squabbles, but rather, transparently that of state power.

What emerges as the practice of plea bargaining in the late 19th century is the confluence of conciliation's informality, privacy, cost-efficiency, unilateral power (now the prosecutor), and procedural efficiency (ease of resolution), with the application of positive law. In short, the American adaptation to Bentham's concerns over the promiscuousness of conciliation courts was remedied in the United States by the encroaching power of prosecutors, whose recognition of the *power* and *efficiency* provided by conciliation needed only to be met with the professionalization of lawyers, a commitment to neutrality, and the systemic legitimacy offered through the application of positive law. Still, Bentham goes further in his critique of conciliation in a way that anticipated the coming concern over plea bargaining. Specifically, when a defendant pleads guilty in the United States, they abdicate their Fifth and Sixth Amendment rights protections as part of the bargain. Depending upon jurisdiction, additional plea waivers of rights also apply. And to the question: what would move a person to abdicate their rights? Bentham responded: omnipresent and disproportionate power.[65] Once again I request that the reader substitute references to judges with those of prosecutors when considering Bentham's concerns, now with direct reference to *bargaining*: "In the system of conciliation, the equality [that reigns at law] is destroyed; it establishes between the two parties a kind of auction where each bargains on his own behalf, but where all the advantage lies with the one who is more tenacious, more greedy [*avide*]."[66] As the American states deliberated over the adoption of conciliation courts, they had omnipresent the concerns raised by Bentham, none more so than concern over an authoritarian usurpation of power by judges and prosecutors. Kessler explains:

> Just as Bentham came to reject conciliation courts (in all non-familial matters), so too did the various American states that considered adopting such institutions, and for precisely the same reasons – namely, concern that these courts encouraged a discretionary exercise of authority that would reinforce power differentials and subvert the rule of law.[67]

The influence of Bentham on 19th-century English jurisprudence was important, especially for Lord Henry Brougham (1778–1868). Chancellor Brougham enthusiastically adopted Bentham's recitation of the advantages flowing from the adoption of the French *court de conciliation*, but, claims Kessler, without the caution leveled by Bentham against its adoption for anything but family disputes. What Lord Brougham articulates as his vision for England, concerning the adoption of the *court de conciliation*, would meet with contemporary understanding as an explanation for the adoption of plea bargaining. For example, in the middle of the 19th century, Lord Brougham advocated for a kind of procedure that would be more widely available to common people, not solely the wealthy. He found in the *court de conciliation* just the procedure that would be flexible enough to achieve those ends. The *court de conciliation* would be characterized by simplified procedure and significantly reduced costs, each a characteristic of the plea. With due recognition of Bentham's concern over the abdication of rights for those petitioners pursuing dispute resolution through conciliation, Lord Brougham assured the English that all that is necessary to make certain that disputants' rights would be protected is to assure that engagement at the *court de conciliation* was purely *voluntary*, and that once decided, each party would adhere to the court's decision.[68] As it anticipates the evolution of plea bargaining, Lord Brougham's advocacy of a quasi-inquisitorial due process included: 1) expediency, 2) cost efficiency, 3) colloquial administration of justice, and 4) a requirement that the procedure be entered into voluntarily. The only rationale missing from Lord Brougham's commitment to the *court de conciliation* that would be commonplace today is the "knowing and intelligent" component of Federal Rules of Criminal Procedure, Rule 11, as well as the right to legal representation (which would have been at the time a seeming contradiction since the idea was to make the conciliation process as non-adversarial as possible).

Significant is the fact that Lord Brougham's publications regarding the law in general, as well as his advocacy for the adoption of *courts de conciliation*, were well known and distributed in the United States. And while equity and conciliation courts were in operation in the United States, what at first emerged as a way to facilitate a less intimidating, less formal administration of justice became during the mid-19th century an institutional technology used to hold off the growing power and influence of lawyers who were principally committed to formal-rational positive law as administered at trial. Americans were generally supportive of *courts de conciliation* and for the reasons previously stated – they were less intimidating, locally administered efforts at peacemaking that proved far less costly and generated far fewer opportunities for community disruption. Following Kessler, "Advocates of conciliation courts viewed conflict, and thus litigation, as an evil to be avoided at all costs – one that would necessarily tend towards social collapse and disharmony."[69] The stage had been set for two powerful legal institutional technologies on a collision course – *court de conciliation*, and adversarialism. But the fear of despotism emerging out of a flexible mode of dispute resolution, conducted in private, with no necessary adherence to law, led even supporters of conciliation to raise serious concerns. Kessler contends that while there were certainly internal US debates over whether and how to administer conciliation, the debate was mired in anti-European sentiment overall.

"The lawyers are coming." Boden writes that by the 18th century in the United States, the legal profession began to find its foundation. This occurred "first in the middle colonies, then in the South and in New England."[70] By the early 19th century, the nascent American lawyers' guild commenced consolidating its power over all procedural debates that took place in the states. Later in the 19th century, James Willard Hurst cites Edward G. Ryan stating in 1873 "that every lawyer in his law office is effectually a judge, and that more matters are adjudicated in lawyers' offices than ever reach the courts."[71] It is Hurst's assessment that from 1800 until the 1870s, there was no organized legal bar to speak of. In fact, prior to the 1870s, lawyers learned their profession through apprenticeship. The first law degree was issued in 1793 by the College of William and Mary. Harvard Law School, the oldest continuing law school in the United States, was founded in 1817.[72]

If conciliation courts were to coexist alongside trial-based adjudication, lawyers must be permitted to play a role. Why? Because, as Bentham warned, the laxity and privacy of conciliation practice meant that it would be too tempting for local justices of the peace or judges to eschew the application of positive law, thereby rendering the administration of justice idiosyncratic. The debate is clearly presented in the state of New York, where New York City attorney Henry Nicholl, moves the ball ever closer to formal plea bargaining in practice. Nicholl offers two specific reasons for the inclusion of lawyers during conciliation: 1) because "the people had confidence in them," lawyers would assure the proper *legal* outcome in conciliation disputes, thereby enhancing legal-rational authority and legitimacy, and 2) that lawyers would care more about "enforcement of the letter of the law than on promoting equitable outcome."[73]

With the increasing statewide power of lawyers' guilds to articulate and advance statutory criminal procedure, compromises were made that: a) permitted the continued operation of conciliation, while b) reconceiving the practice to now require the inclusion of formal legal representation and decision-making. As such, the transition during the middle of the 19th century in the United States with regard to *courts de conciliation* led to the manifestation of a hybrid quasi-inquisitorial criminal procedure that increasingly would be characterized by the presence of lawyers trained in positive law to properly administer justice within an adversarial system. Ultimately, the state of New York did adopt a compromise hybrid system that emphasized a "lawyer-based and rule-bound" system of justice that would be predicated on the defendant's *voluntary* commitment to it.

To sum up, conciliation courts initially signified a more colloquial administration of justice that was less rule-bound, less formal, less expensive, and yet more efficient with regard to dispute resolution and the maintenance of community stability.[74] By the middle of the 19th century, however, powerful lawyer guilds organized to effect significant changes to the original conciliation model. These lawyers, especially in New York where we have a record of such proceedings, pressured the New York state legislature to either eliminate conciliation courts entirely or provide for a hybrid model that would include them (the lawyers). The New York state legislature accommodated the state's attorneys and established a bastardized version of conciliation as part of its 1850 draft of the Field Code.[75] Most important, conciliation would now be facilitated by trained lawyers who would administer justice, not necessarily as a commitment to maintaining local habitus, but rather, enhancing the dramatic power of their profession (and by extension the encroaching power of the state) through application of positive law. Resnik puts it this way:

> Through case management, judicial efforts at settlement and mandatory ADR in or through courts, devolution to administrative agencies, and *enforcement of waivers of rights to trial*, the framework of "due process procedure" with its independent judges and open courts, is being replaced by what can fairly be called "*contract procedure*."[76]

After all, plea bargaining is guided not by criminal law, but rather, by *contract law*.[77]

***

In this chapter, we covered evidence relating to the ubiquity of the plea from the late 19th through the early 20th century. It is my contention that equity and conciliation procedures played a significant role as existing legal norms that were usurped by ever-empowered prosecutors and that led to establishing criminal plea practices. In the next chapter, I will introduce the prevalence of plea bargaining as an important aspect of dispute resolution for the Freedmen's Bureau.

Notes

1 See Mary Vogel. Coercion to Compromise. London, Oxford University Press (2007) and George Fisher. Plea Bargaining's Triumph. Stanford University Press (2003). Data supporting the arguments made by both Fisher and Vogel relies extensively upon the city of Boston, especially during the early 19th century.
2 William Ortman. When Plea Bargaining Became Normal. 100, Boston UL Rev., 1437 (2020)
3 Cited in Ortman. Id at 6.
4 Id at 6
5 Id at 6

6 Sven Beckert and Seth Rockman (eds). Slavery's Capitalism: A New History of American Economic Development. Philadelphia, PA: Pennsylvania University Press (2016); Gordon Wood. The *Idea of America*. New York: Penguin Press (2011); Matthew Stewart. Nature's God: The Heretical Origins of the American Republic. London: Norton Press (2014); Bernard Bailyn. The Ideological Origins of the American Revolution. Cambridge, MA: Harvard University Press (2017).
7 George Fisher. Plea Bargaining's Triumph. Stanford University Press (2003). Fisher's work emphasizes the "caseload pressure" argument. He is mentioned here for his contribution to the origin of the plea as represented by his analysis of the city of Boston.
8 Id at 22.
9 Supra 1 at 8.
10 Supra 1 at 12.
11 Supra 1 at 13.
12 Michael Klarman. From Jim Crow to Civil Rights: The Supreme Court and the Struggle for Racial Equality. London: Oxford University Press (2004).
13 Id at 119.
14 Id at 119.
15 293 F. 1013 (D.C. Cir. 1923).
16 Id (*Frye v. United States*).
17 509 US 579 (1993).
18 *Frye v. United States*, 293 F. 1013 (DC Cir. 1923).
19 https://www.expertinstitute.com/resources/insights/daubert-versus-frye-a-national-look-at-expert-evidentiary-standards/
20 Jeremy Bentham. A Treatise on Judicial Evidence. Andesite Press (2015); Jeremy Bentham. The Works of Jeremy Bentham. Wentworth Press (2019).
21 Max Weber cited in Jurgen Habermas. Between Facts and Norms: Contributions to a Discourse Theory of Law and Democracy. Cambridge, MA: The MIT Press, (1998): 70.
22 Jurgen Habermas. Between Facts and Norms: Contributions to a Discourse Theory of Law and Democracy. Cambridge, MA: The MIT Press, (1998): 70. (My emphasis).
23 Supra 1 at 7.
24 Alexander Hamilton. Federalist LXXX. New York: Penguin (1987): 448–449.
25 Id at 449. My emphasis.
26 Id.
27 Joseph Story. Commentaries on Equity Jurisprudence. London: Street and Maxwell (1920): 3.
28 Gary L. McDowell. Joseph Story's "Science" of Equity. Supreme Court Review, Vol. 1979 (1979): 158.
29 Judith Resnik. The Democracy in Courts: Jeremy Bentham, "Publicity," and the Privatization of Process in the Twenty-First Century. NoFo 10 (2013): 79.
30 Supra 28 at 172.
31 Supra 27 at 4.
32 Supra 27 at 5.
33 Supra 27 at 5.
34 Supra 27 at 5.
35 Supra 27 at 6.
36 Story citing to St. Germain. Supra 27 at 7.
37 Id at 7 (Story).
38 Wilfrid Priest. The Dialectical Origins of Finch's *Law*. 36, Cambridge L. J. 2 (1977): 326–352.
39 http://lawlibrary.wm.edu/wythepedia/library/FinchNomotexnia1613.pdf.

40 Supra 27 at 8.
41 Supra 27 at 9.
42 Supra 27 at 82.
43 Supra 28 at 163.
44 Supra 27 at 10.
45 (1705) Prec Ch 241; 24 ER 118.
46 Supra 27 at 11.
47 Supra 27 at 13. My emphasis.
48 Amalia D. Kessler. Inventing American Exceptionalism. New Haven, CT: Yale University Press (2017): 5.
49 Supra 27 at 13.
50 Supra 28 at 172.
51 Amalia D. Kessler. Deciding Against Conciliation: The Nineteenth-Century Rejection of a European Transplant and the Rise of a Distinctively American Ideal of Adversarial Adjudication. Theoretical Inquiries In Law, 10 (2) (2009): 426.
52 Id at 426.
53 Id at 428.
54 Id at 428.
55 Supra 29 at 82.
56 Supra 29 at 83.
57 Supra 51 at 436..
58 Supra 51 at 437..
59 Supra 51 at 438.
60 Supra 29 at 83.
61 Supra 29 at 83.
62 https://www.law.cornell.edu/rules/frcrmp/rule_11; section (b)(3).
63 Id (Federal Rule 11).
64 This is not surprising since the United States was engulfed in systemically challenging social problems that included, but wasn't limited to, managing dislocation caused by the Civil War, emancipation of freed men and women, the massive growth of major urban cities, and the intensification of immigration. The result was increasing state and federal legislation, thereby enhancing the role played by lawyers.
65 Supra 51 at 441.
66 Supra 51 at 441.
67 Supra 51 at 442.
68 Supra 51 at 444.
69 Supra 51 at 454.
70 Robert F. Boden. The Colonial Bar and the American Revolution. 60 Marquette L. Rev. 1 (1976): 2.
71 James Willard Hurst. Lawyers in American Society 1750–1966. 50 Marquette L. Rev. 4 (1967): 598–599.
72 For additional analysis of the evolution and impact of the legal profession in the 19th century, see, for example: Rachel F. Moran,. The Three Ages of Modern American Lawyering and the Current Crisis in the Legal Profession and Legal Education. 58 Santa Clara L. Rev. 453 (2019); M.H. Hoeflich, Ethics and the "Root of All Evil" in Nineteenth Century American Law Practice. 7 St. Mary's J. Legal Mal. & Ethics 160 (2017).
73 Supra 51 at 462.
74 In a way, we have returned to the early conciliation court practice (e.g., small claims court).
75 Code of Civil Procedure, 641–642 (title VII, section 1523).

76 Supra 51 at 110 (Resnik). My emphasis. I have made a similar argument that plea bargaining is not guided by criminal procedure, but rather, it is premised upon contract law. See Robert Schehr. The Emperor's New Clothes: Intellectual Dishonesty and the Unconstitutionality of Plea Bargaining. 2 Tex. A&M 3 (2015).

77 See Schehr, Id at 7.

References

Bernard Bailyn. *The Ideological Origins of the American Revolution*. Cambridge, MA: Harvard University Press (2017)

Sven Beckert and Seth Rockman (eds.). *Slavery's Capitalism: A New History of American Economic Development*. Philadelphia, PA: Pennsylvania University Press (2016)

Jeremy Bentham. *A Treatise on Judicial Evidence*. Wolcott, New York: Andesite Press (2015)

Jeremy Bentham. *The Works of Jeremy Bentham*. Wentworth Press (2019)

Robert F. Boden. The Colonial Bar and the American Revolution. 60(1) *Marquette L. Rev.*, 2 (1976)

George Fisher. *Plea Bargaining's Triumph*. Stanford: Stanford University Press (2003)

Jurgen Habermas. *Between Facts and Norms: Contributions to a Discourse Theory of Law and Democracy*. Cambridge, MA: The MIT Press (1998)

Alexander Hamilton. *Federalist LXXX*. New York: Penguin (1987): 448–449

M.H. Hoeflich. Ethics and the "Root of All Evil" in Nineteenth Century American Law Practice. 7 *St. Mary's J. Legal Mal. & Ethics* 160 (2017)

James Willard Hurst. Lawyers in American Society 1750–1966. 50(4) *Marquette L. Rev.*, 598–599 (1967)

Amalia D. Kessler. Deciding Against Conciliation: The Nineteenth-Century Rejection of a European Transplant and the Rise of a Distinctively American Ideal of Adversarial Adjudication. 10(2) *Theoretical Inquiries In Law*, 426 (2009)

Amalia D. Kessler. *Inventing American Exceptionalism*. New Haven, CT: Yale University Press (2017)

Michael Klarman. *From Jim Crow to Civil Rights: The Supreme Court and the Struggle for Racial Equality*. London: Oxford University Press (2004)

Gary L. McDowell. Joseph Story's "Science" of Equity. 1979 *Supreme Court Review*, 158 (1979)

Rachel F. Moran. The Three Ages of Modern American Lawyering and the Current Crisis in the Legal Profession and Legal Education. 58 *Santa Clara L. Rev.*, 453 (2019)

William Ortman. When Plea Bargaining Became Normal. 100 *Boston U. L. Rev.*, 1437 (2020)

Wilfrid Priest. The Dialectical Origins of Finch's *Law*. 36(2) *Cambridge L. J.*, 326–352 (1977)

Judith Resnik. The Democracy in Courts: Jeremy Bentham, 'Publicity', and the Privatization of Process in the Twenty-First Century. NoFo 10 (2013)

Mathew Stewart. *Nature's God: The Heretical Origins of The American Republic*. London: Norton Press (2014)

Joseph Story. *Commentaries on Equity Jurisprudence*. London: Street and Maxwell (1920)

Mary Vogel. *Coercion To Compromise*. London: Oxford University Press (2007)

Gordon Wood. *The Idea of America*. New York: Penguin Press (2011)

3
THE FREEDMEN'S BUREAU

Conciliation courts occupied a central role during Reconstruction and existed mostly in the 15 former slave states, and as I hope to demonstrate, they provide unique insight into the comingling tension between conciliation and adversarialism.[1] Conciliation courts were created as part of the newly formed Freedmen's Bureau, also known as the Bureau of Refugees, Freedmen, and Abandoned Lands.[2] Section 2 of the Act stipulates that,

> The supervision and care of said bureau shall extend to all loyal refugees and freedmen, so far as the same shall be necessary to enable them as speedily as practicable to become self-supporting citizens of the United States, and to aid them in making the freedom conferred by proclamation of the commander-in-chief, by emancipation under the laws of States, and by constitutional amendment, available to them and beneficial to the republic.[3]

For the purposes of this chapter, it is Section 14 of the Act that contains the most relevant language:

> And be it further enacted, That in every State or district where the ordinary course of judicial proceedings has been interrupted by the rebellion, and until the same shall be fully restored, and in every State or district whose constitutional relations to the government have been restored in such relations, and shall be duly represented in the Congress of the United States, the right to make and enforce contracts, to sue, be parties, and give evidence … and to have full and equal benefit of all laws and proceedings concerning personal liberty, personal security,

DOI: 10.4324/9781003385103-4

> and the acquisition, enjoyment, and disposition of estate, real and personal, including the constitutional right to bear arms, shall be secured to and enjoyed by all the citizens of such State or district without respect to race, or color, or previous condition of slavery ... The President shall, through the commissioner and the officers of the bureau, and under such rules and regulations as the President, through the Secretary of War, shall prescribe, extend military protection and have military jurisdiction over all cases and questions concerning the free enjoyment of such immunities and rights, and no penalty or punishment for any violation of law shall be imposed or permitted because of race or color, or previous condition of slavery, other or greater than the penalty or punishment to which white persons may be liable by law for the like offence.[4]

The person designated commissioner to administer the Freedmen's Bureau's conciliation court experiment was Civil War hero and Union Major General, Oliver Otis Howard.[5]

The Freedmen's Bureau was created as a way to facilitate the *assimilation* of freed black men and women into their new roles as citizens. As Kessler reveals, "Former slaves had to be taught to view themselves 'as men from whom, in their new character of freedmen, self-reliance and self-support are demanded'."[6] This occurred in many ways, but by far one of the most important was through the creation of conciliation courts. Conciliation courts were administered by associate commissioners who were white former members of the Union military. Associate commissioners were non-lawyers adjudicating disputes largely, though not exclusively, between freed black men and women and regional whites, and by monitoring the actions of local Southern courts and their racist administration of justice.[7] Kaczorowski claims that Southern state legislatures acted to protect local judges who refused to prosecute cases against white defendants when the victims were black by appropriating state funds to "pay the legal expenses of local judges who were prosecuted in federal courts for violations of the Civil Rights Act."[8] In fact, while critics of the efficacy of Bureau courts claimed that across the South they were mostly ineffectual, that was typically due to state and local political machinations rather than the structure or intent of the Bureau and its agents. Pressure from the Johnson administration to minimize usurpation of local juridical practices by encouraging Bureau accommodation to them led Bureau agents to act "circumspectly even when state laws, such as the black codes, discriminated on their face."[9] Southern opposition to the imposition of the 1866 Civil Rights Act, coupled with a friendly advocate in the White House, generated a paradox when it came to the implementation of Howard's vision of the conciliation court model since Bureau courts were not welcome in the South.

In his 1865 statement identifying the purpose of conciliation courts, Howard reports that, "assistant commissioners were to adjudicate, either themselves or through officers of their appointment, all difficulties arising between negroes themselves, or between negroes and whites or Indians."[10] Typically, conciliation courts were comprised of a three-judge panel of local citizens representing different interests in the case at hand. Major General Davis Tillson, assistant commissioner for the state of Georgia, shared the following directive with his officers and agents of the Bureau: "Remember that it is the chief object of the bureau to do *simple justice* to all parties, white or black."[11]

In general, according to Kessler, and with due recognition that there were deviations across the Freedmen's Bureau jurisdictions regarding the precise application of conciliation practices, there were commonalities. For example, all conciliation courts were operated by lay judges who had no legal training whatsoever. Rather, like the judges appointed by English courts of equity, they were selected from among the community for their moral and ethical quality and their public reputations. Lay judges were not formally trained in law, so they often didn't apply it to conflict resolution situations. Rather, they were to rely upon their respected judgment as to the best outcome for the grieving parties, and for the community generally, perceiving their role as one that would encourage reconciliation rather than the more adversarial trial-based due process. Bureau courts most often addressed misdemeanor cases (e.g., petty theft, disobedience, breach of the peace, and cruelty and abuse of freed black men and women), leaving felony prosecution to military courts of justice. Bureau courts prosecuted private individuals by assuming jurisdiction whenever local courts of justice failed to protect the rights of freed men and women. For example, "Bureau agents and tribunals assumed primary jurisdiction and law enforcement functions such as investigating alleged crime, making arrests, trying and, upon conviction, sentencing criminals."[12] According to Kaczorowski, the list of crimes addressed in his research of the Bureau conciliation courts included murder, manslaughter, assault, theft, and involuntary servitude.[13] Typically, however, it appears that while arrests could be made by Bureau agents in felony cases, because of the seriousness of the offenses and their lack of training in the law, those cases would be handed off to local authorities for prosecution.[14] Christopher Bean has generated perhaps the most thorough data documenting cases and dispositions with a specific emphasis upon a two-month time frame in the Texas Bureau courts. In 1866 there were 6,794 court cases addressed by the Bureau. Subdistricts typically generated 100–500 cases. Those cases ranged from bestiality to assault. Bean indicates that case dispositions fell favorably upon plaintiffs 41.6 percent of the time, and they were predicated upon the introduction of evidence. Most of these cases, 69 percent, involved a black plaintiff and a white defendant.[15]

Bureau-operated conciliation court practices began to resemble contemporary plea bargaining through the administrative power of Bureau agents. In their contemporaneous assessment of the Freedmen's Bureau, R. Sutton, D.F. Murphy, and James J. Murphy, editors of *The Reporter*,[16] a 19th-century Washington DC periodical that produced commentary on United States Supreme Court opinions and Congressional matters, raised precisely this concern in their February 26, 1866 edition. Specifically, the editors raised concerns about the linguistic ambiguity pertaining to phrases in the Act like, "the deprivation of any civil right secured to white persons." What, they wondered, did that mean? Ambiguity, they argued, generated far too much flexibility for local Bureau commissioners to interpret the law and punishment in accordance with their own biases.

> The agent in one State may construe it to mean one thing, and the agent in another State another thing. It is broad and comprehensive – "the deprivation of any civil right secured to white persons." That act of deprivation is the crime that is to be punished ... It is not a military court, because among military men the highest honor is observed; no sides are taken, but they stand upon the highest pledge of honor to do justice as between one military man and another. But here is a court, not military in its character not examining into a military, but a civil offense – the refusal to recognize a civil right; and that trial is had before this irresponsible officer and no appeal is allowed. None of the proceedings are defined. What evidence shall be required to convict, what means of procuring witnesses, and how the sentence is to be executed, are all left to the discretion of the Department.[17]

The editors of *The Reporter* were far from completing their criticism of this newly created "government within a government." In this same edition, the editors claim that the Freedmen's Bureau, as constituted, would lead to government oppression of the people.

> In times of peace, in communities that are quiet and orderly and obedient to law, it is proposed to establish a government not responsible to the people, the officers of which are not selected by the people, the officers of which need not be of the people governed – a government more cruel, more despotic, more dangerous to the liberties of the people than that against which our forefathers fought in the Revolution. *There is nothing that these men may not do, under this bill, to oppress the people.*[18]

Agents adjudicated disputes in a manner that was often unique to the jurisdiction and the agent involved, but with a specific emphasis on the introduction and reproduction of dominant cultural values. This practice is widely known today as local county attorneys (or in some places, district attorneys) are elected officials who campaign for office by announcing specific prosecutorial priorities of interest to the communities they serve. When it comes to administering pleas, there is precious little light separating them from Bureau actions. (This, of course, is similar to the concerns we learned about regarding equity judges, but with Bureau courts, the focus was *not* on deciding cases consistent with local cultural norms but rather, with a federal commitment to the implementation of positive law through the administration of the 1866 Civil Rights Act.) In fact, it wasn't the issues raised by plaintiffs that predicted the outcome of a dispute, but rather, who the actual Bureau agent was. With the introduction of federal civil and criminal law to the administration of Bureau conciliation courts, agents began to resemble more closely prosecutors in contemporary plea bargaining since Bureau agents were free to administer the law as they saw fit. Like contemporary prosecutors, Bureau agents were free to consider a plaintiff's claims, or not, bring charges, or not. They took evidence. They would determine the outcome of the case internally and without public transparency. Finally, participation in the conciliation court was free, and cases could be dispensed with quickly. Generals Steedman and Fullerton were assigned responsibility for reporting upon "the Condition of the Freedmen's Bureau in the Southern States."[19] In their May 8, 1866 report to O.O. Howard concerning the state of Virginia, Steedman and Fullerton provide two clear examples of what was by then common knowledge – the idiosyncratic application of Bureau rules and state laws constituted the day-to-day operation of the Bureau. The first major heading in their report reads: "EVERYTHING DEPENDS UPON THE AGENTS." Under a separate heading called: SPECIMEN OF THE DECISIONS OF THE BUREAU, Steedman and Fullerton provide the following example of idiosyncratic quasi-inquisitorial decision-making on behalf of a Bureau agent.

> As an evidence of the manner in which this arbitrary power is exercised, we would state that an agent of the Bureau, presiding in a freedmen's court in Accomac county, decided a question of title to land as follows: A colored man, who was freed twenty years ago by his master, and who was permitted through the kindness of the master to make his home on the plantation wherever he choose, set up a claim to ten acres thereof around a cabin in which he had lived for ten years. The agent decided that the colored man had acquired title to the ten acres by adverse possession, and forbade the owners of the plantation from bringing the question again before his court, or any other court, on pain of punishment.[20]

The general continues with another example of ad hoc Bureau agent decision-making:

> These agents exert the widest latitude in the exercise of their judicial functions, trying questions involving title to real estate, contracts, crimes, and even actions affecting the marital relation. We witnessed the trial of a divorce case before the sub-agent at Charlottesville. The trial lasted about ten minutes, and resulted in a divorce decree.[21]

And still, there's one more example from Steedman and Fullerton's reporting, this time from North Carolina, that demonstrates the fact that Bureau agents were operating throughout the South as prosecutor, judge, and jury. The principal actors were Rev. Horace James, superintendent of the Bureau for the district, James's clerk, Boyden, and the freedman.

> The freedman was accused of stealing provisions from the store of Colonel Whittlesey and Mr. James, was arrested, tried, and convicted by Mr. James as agent of the Bureau, and was sentenced to dig ditches on their plantation. While working out this sentence he ran away, and was pursued by James and his clerk, Boyden, who arrived at the bank of the river while the freedman was attempting to cross in a canoe. Boyden ordered him to return, telling him that if he did not he would shoot, and the freedmen disregarding the order, Boyden fired. Boyden states himself that he thinks he hit him.[22]

Not to put too fine a point on it, but James, an alleged victim of theft from his co-owned store and the superintendent for the Bureau in his region, acted more in line with vigilante "justice" than anything approximating adherence to the rule of law. To sum up, the reporting from Generals Steedman and Fullerton signifies the ad hoc administration of justice exhibited by Bureau agents in the South.

Each of these characteristics of conciliation courts mirrors plea bargaining practices, and Bureau agents, despite not being lawyers, implemented a due process of case resolution that closely approximates the behaviors of contemporary prosecutors. During floor debate over proposed Amendments to the Act, Representatives Davis (in opposition to the Act) and Speaker of the House Trumbell (supporter of the Act) engaged in spirited argument over the apparent unrestricted power of Bureau agents when administering justice. According to coverage of the exchange found in the March 5, 1866 edition of *The Reporter*, Rep. Davis

> inquired if this bill does not vest judicial powers in the assistant commissioners and the agents under it; and whether it was in the competence of Congress by the passage of law to confer a part of the judicial power of the Government upon such officers? These assistant commissioners and agents take jurisdiction of all contests between the freed negro and the man that hires him.[23]

Speaker Trumbell replied that bureau agents and courts will only reside in those locations where civil unrest persisted, and where municipal and state courts were dysfunctional. Still unconvinced, Rep. Davis further exclaimed that the

> employees, agents, and officers of this bureau were not part of the army. The bill makes them civil officers, and it invests them with judicial powers and judicial functions, and with the faculty of passing judgment and executing that judgement between the citizens of the United States. The bill authorizes the President of the United States to protect the assistant commissioners and agents in the exercise of these judicial functions in passing and enforcing their judgments. It was dangerous that any branch of the magistracy – judges, assistant commissioners under the Freedmen's Bureau, or agents – that are invested with judicial powers and with the function to pass in judgment upon the rights of citizens, should have the power to invoke the military to uphold their unconstitutional and usurped authority.[24]

The proposed amendments to the Freedmen's Bureau Act were each unceremoniously defeated and by relatively wide margins. Rep. Davis's amendment, for example, received 8 yeas and 31 nays.[25] Despite losing the floor vote, Rep. Davis's objections, much like those of the editors at *The Reporter*, raise serious concerns with regard to the equitable administration of justice throughout the 15 former slave states due to what appeared to many as indiscriminate applications of juridical power infused with the imprimatur of federal power. It seems that a more transparent expression of hegemonic state power would be hard to find, and recognition of it is precisely what Vogel attempted to explicate in her prescient analysis of plea bargaining and political, economic, and cultural upheaval.[26] Regardless of the political motivations behind objections to the Freedmen's Bureau Act, the arguments presented by Rep. Davis and others signify transparent recognition of the hegemonic state power underlying attempts to administer justice, especially in the South.

Assistant Commissioners' Reports to O.O. Howard

On March 19, 1866, Secretary of War Edwin Stanton, submitted a comprehensive 418-page report (from here on, the "Report") on behalf of the Freedmen's Bureau to the House of Representatives.[27] The Report was authored by Freedmen's Bureau Commissioner O.O. Howard and covered a nearly two-year time frame beginning in 1865 and concluding in March 1866.[28] Howard's Bureau report is comprehensive in that it addresses all manner of responsibilities pertaining to the role of the Freedmen's Bureau as implemented in North Carolina, Louisiana, Alabama, Tennessee, Missouri, Florida, South Carolina, Virginia, Texas, Mississippi, and Kentucky. What I will emphasize in this chapter, however, is the application of due process through conciliation courts. One final caveat is in order. In the sections that follow, I have included direct citations of letters sent to Bureau Commissioner O.O. Howard. These letters signify formal correspondence between regional assistant commissioners and Howard, so it would have been well understood that Howard might share the information provided with the House of Representatives as part of his reporting responsibilities. This is significant because the information provided reveals all manner of attempts made by assistant commissioners and other Bureau agents to interrupt and repair long-standing hatred between whites and freed men and women. While that, in and of itself, is rudimentary, what is revealed by these men in field offices across the South is the depth of depravity visited upon freed men and women, as well as the quasi-inquisitorial and idiosyncratic means for addressing it. Given the extraordinary earnestness exemplified by regional Bureau agents in their correspondence with Commissioner Howard, one has to believe that the activities taking place on the ground were probably even more ad hoc and consistent with the conciliation court model than what is presented in Howard's Report to Secretary of War Stanton.

Archival Correspondence

There is no way to know what is in a man's heart. That being the case, legal historians have to rely upon the published record in order to infer by way of empathy what the assistant Bureau commissioners were confronting as they took up residence across the former slave states to implement the Freedmen's Bureau mission. In addition to being unwelcome in the South generally, these assistant commissioners and field-level Bureau agents were confronted with massive social problems that required immediate attention. Since my focus in this chapter is on the implementation of conciliation court practices leading to plea bargaining, I have limited my discussion of the Report to matters associated with it.

To provide context, I am including only one detailed explication of the violence ravaged upon freed men and women by white people. There are two reasons for this. First, the example provided below captures much of what was occurring throughout the South. Second, and as important to me, is to avoid a certain pornographic devolution into the horrific details of violence, especially since that sort of documentary evidence is not the primary purpose of this chapter. Rest assured, for readers interested in levels of detail from across the South as it relates to violence perpetrated against freed men and women, there exists multiple detailed deposition-based evidence in the Report.

Unspeakable Inhumanity: Violence Directed at Freed Men and Women in Kentucky

In Kentucky, P. Bonesteel, the special inspector for both Kentucky and Tennessee, generated a horrific account of the treatment of freed men and women. For a period of one month, Bonesteel interviewed and took depositions from freed men and women under oath to discern their condition. What he found shook him. For, as he revealed in his report to Commissioner Howard, "In some counties, there are organized bands of men called 'rangers,' 'moderators,' 'nigger killers,' who have driven the freedmen entirely out of certain sections, and begin at last to threaten and intimidate Union white men."[29]

> An examination of this sworn evidence on the abstracts made therefrom will reveal to you sixty cases of outrage in a limited district and period, unparalleled in their atrocity and fiendishness; cruelties for which in no instance, as developed by the testimony, is there the least shadow of excuse or palliation.[30]

Bonesteel documents the following abuses:

> I have classified these outrages as follows: Twenty-three cases of severe and inhuman beating and whipping of men; four of beating and shooting; two of robbing and shooting; three of robbing; five men shot and killed; two shot and wounded; four beaten to death; one beaten and roasted; three women assaulted and ravished; four women beaten; two women tied up and whipped until insensible; two men and their families beaten and driven from their homes, and their property destroyed; two instances of burning of dwellings, and one of the inmates shot.
>
> On the night of the 16th of February, 1866, a gang of white men, residents of Bath county, entered the house of Joseph Balls, a person who had been a freedman for several years, humble and inoffensive and much respected, the owner of forty acres of land, and beat and most terribly mangled him; his body was burst open, his intestines protruding. He lingered two days in agony and died. At the same time they set upon another old colored man named Thackel, who was at the house of Balls, beating him for some time, putting out an eye, and then very deliberately placed him over the fire, roasting him first upon one side and then upon the other.
>
> Upon the same night, and as is presumed, by a portion of the same gang, an attack was made upon the house of Pate Burns, about four miles from the residence of Balls. Burns was a most exemplary man, and a preacher of the Gospel. They robbed him of his bacon, clothing, and money, shot him in the head, severely wounding him, and then in his

> presence ravished his wife. Two other persons who were at the house of Burns at this time were severely beaten, and one of them shot in the head. Two of the offenders were arrested by the agent of the Freedmen's Bureau of Bath county, and while removing them for safe-keeping to a military camp a writ of habeas corpus was issued by Judge Apperson, of Montgomery county, and the men discharged and set at liberty, he holding that the Freedmen's Bureau has no legal existence in Kentucky, and that the writ of habeas corpus is not suspended in this State.[31]

Bonesteel's depositions, taken over a one-month period, reveal the depths of human depravity. What is clear from Bonesteel's recitation is his absolute horror at what he had found. When confronted with the kind of hatred, violence, and lack of justice he witnessed in Kentucky, Bonesteel, like many other regional commissioners, manifested a zeal that was at once a very human response to pain and a firm institutional commitment to the Bureau's stated purpose. Bureau agents, when confronted with the reality of racist violence on the ground, turned to the institutional power of conciliation courts to render judgment and issue punishment. This thread should be clear as we proceed.

The Assistant Commissioners' Reports

In North Carolina, commissioners were instructed by E. Whittlesey, Colonel and Assistant Bureau Commissioner, that, among other things,

> It will be the duty of all officers of this bureau ... To protect freedmen from injustice ... Arrests should not be made until careful inquiry has furnished ground for a belief that wrong has been done. This preliminary investigation may be and made by [sic] requesting the parties between whom difficulties have arisen to meet the officer of this bureau. *In ordinary cases an explanation and settlement may be effected at once.* But in cases of violence and personal assault, a requisition should be made upon the district or post commander in accordance with General Order 102, Adjutant General's War Office, War Department, Washington, May 31, 1865 for a sufficient military force to arrest the alleged criminal, in order that he may be brought before a proper court for trial. Civil courts, before which the testimony of colored witnesses is not admitted, are not competent, under existing regulations, to try any case in which the interests of freedmen are involved The jurisdiction of such courts will not be recognized by officers of this bureau Circular No. 5, War Department, Bureau of Refugee, Freedmen, & c., May 30, 1865, approved by the President of the United States, June 2, 1865, is the authority upon which the above instructions are founded.[32]

I have italicized the one sentence that speaks to "simple justice" as advocated by Commissioner Howard. Whittlesey also provides North Carolina commissioners with four responsibilities as it pertains to administering justice:

1. This bureau being in the War Department, its officers and agents are subject to military jurisdiction, and all their decisions and acts are subject to review by the general commanding the department.
2. In all cases of difficulty between freedmen, or between freedmen and whites, officers of this bureau have authority to summon the parties before them for examination, and upon their refusal to appear may request the nearest district or post commander to arrest him.
3. After careful investigation, officers of this bureau may punish offenders guilty of light offences by fines, not exceeding one hundred dollars ($100), or by imprisonment, not exceeding thirty (30) days. Cases of grave crime, where there seems to be clear evidences of guilt, will be reported to the district commander, with the charges preferred and the names of witnesses.
4. When practicable, officers of this bureau will associate with them one or two citizens of each county, acceptable to both classes, in their respective districts, to assist in the adjudication of difficulties arising therein.

What appears clear from the substance *lacking* in these four points is the power of Bureau commissioners to decide cases with no oversight, and no right to appeal the decision. The power to assess claims, hear evidence, produce charges, and, in the case of "light offenses," administer punishment, opaquely takes place contrary to the grand *res publica* articulated by Aristotle and Bentham. Moreover, even under circumstances of serious and violent crime, the Bureau commissioner had the power to submit to the district commander a list of witnesses as well as a proposed set of charges. In Tennessee, Brigadier General and Associate Commissioner Clinton B. Fisk makes it clear to new Bureau agents the following: "In all cases where the civil officers decline such adjudication (that is, when local municipal or state authorities refuse to administer justice to freed men and women) *you will become the administrator of justice*, and in your proceedings will be governed by the laws of the State in which you reside, except so far as those laws make a distinction on account of color."[33] Arkansas presented a unique model. There, Assistant Commissioner and Brigadier General J.W. Sprague appointed civilian superintendents to serve in the capacity of Bureau agents.[34] Like Tennessee, and in keeping with the Bureau's mission, these newly appointed civilian agents "are empowered to administer justice in the cases above referred to, and they will be governed by the laws now in force in Arkansas, except so far as these laws make a distinction on account of color."[35] In South Carolina, freed men and women who were "wronged" should approach the Bureau where the dispute may be settled by three "impartial friends of both parties." Specifically, "[I]n cases of difficulty between white men and yourselves, you should appeal to one of the agents of this bureau in your vicinity, who may appoint one referee, the other party one, and you should appoint a third, and the decision of the majority should be considered final."[36] In Virginia, Major General Commanding Alfred H. Terry reports the placement of Captain Moses Stevens at the Norfolk headquarters of the Bureau. Terry instructs Moses to do the following: "He [Moses] will adjudicate all cases in which the penalty does not exceed a fine of one hundred dollars or imprisonment at hard labor for thirty (30) days. All other cases will be referred by him to a commission appointed by the military commandant of the sub district."[37] Circular No. 7, emanating from the Vicksburg, Mississippi field office, expresses in more colloquial language the power of the Bureau agents to resolve violations of civil law.

> II. By the proclamation of the President, sanctioned by Congress, the colored people are free. The result of the war, in which so many colored men have taken an honorable part, confirms their freedom. If in any place they are still held and treated as slaves, it is an outrage. To prevent such a wrong, and *to secure to them protection*, the Bureau of Freedmen has been established, and its officers placed throughout the district. *All colored people have a right and are invited to go to these officers for advice and protection whenever they think themselves wronged.* The officers ask for the confidence of the colored people. *Whenever the State laws and courts do not do justice to the colored man, by refusing the testimony of colored witnesses, or in any other way, the freed people must apply to the nearest officer of the bureau; he will tell what is to be done in each case.*
>
> The freedmen must not attempt to take the law into their own hands, or to right themselves by any kind of violence, carrying off property, or the like. White men will sometimes trespass upon a black man's rights or commit acts of personal violence, and then try to shield themselves under the plea that there is nothing but negro testimony against them. *The officers of the bureau have power to take up all such cases, and to admit the negro testimony, and the colored people must seek their remedy by going to these officers.*

This Circular was issued on July 29, 1865, by Lieutenant Stuart Eldridge. I have italicized those phrases in the preceding two paragraphs that clearly signify the power of Bureau agents to alone bring about the resolution to all manner of personal grievances arising from conflicts between freed men and women and white residents of Mississippi. Also, from Mississippi comes a direct reference to *the use of civilian lawyers* to assist with cases. *Please place a pin in that one.*

III. It is of the highest consequence, however, that on account of the ignorance and poverty of the freed people, they be assisted in presenting their causes in the courts, advised as to their rights and the proper modes of maintaining them before the tribunals, *and even aided with professional counsel when justice can in no other way be secured.* Sub - commissioners are directed, therefore, as next *friends of the freedmen*, to appear, or secure the services of an attorney, in the courts of Mississippi, whenever called on to do so; to give them suitable counsel and instruction, and, if necessary to the ends of justice, material aid.

IV. They will inform themselves as to the merits of causes thus brought to their notice, and *advise parties who need it as to the best modes of procedure*, and *dissuade them from useless litigation* of wrong or frivolous cases. They will see that *witnesses are suitably instructed in the nature, obligations and responsibilities of the oath, that guards the purity of the witness stand, in order that they may not ignorantly expose themselves to the crime and peril of giving false testimony.*[38]

Once again, I have italicized those phrases in the two paragraphs that speak first with regard to the practice of bringing local attorneys into the litigation process, as well as providing legal guidance pertaining to procedure, case frivolity, and witness preparation. Each of the Bureau agent activities mentioned here resembles those of a practicing attorney. Indeed, there's even reference to "witness coaching" in preparation for providing sworn testimony.

For his part, Brevet Major J.K. Stone took a far more cautious approach to administering cases in South Carolina: "I discourage litigation, the tendency being to widen the breach between whites and blacks. It is one of the unpardonable sins for a 'nigger' to complain to the 'Yankees,' and terrible threats are muttered against him. The people are poor, and can ill afford to pay costs."[39] Stone's account in South Carolina differs widely from his Virginia counterpart, First Lieutenant M.S. Hopkins:

February 28, 1866. Sir: I have the honor to report, in compliance with circular No. 6, from your office, dated January 31, 1866, requiring report of condition of freedmen's affairs, & c., that there is a good understanding between whites and blacks generally, but the feeling of the blacks is that of distrust of the whites, and that of the whites is "you are my niggers by right; you ought to be my slaves, and then you would be happy; but see what a condition you are in now. You have no master to look after you, & c., & c. But if these d -d Yankees ever leave us, we will see what will then be." The blacks look to us to protect them from outrage, and are industrious, contented, and self- supporting. The whites fear us and hurrah for the "President's policy, which, they say, will restore them 'as

> they were' and 'leave them to manage the nigger,' instead of us, who don't understand him." I have no particular suggestions to make.[40]

Desperation and a powerful sense of responsibility for attending to the needs of freed men and women were generally commonplace in these reports. Hopkins's statement comports with that of First Lieutenant W.G. Roberts from King George County, Virginia. Roberts states: "The blacks all appear to be quiet and orderly, and I am happy to be able to say that I seldom hear of any difficulties between the two races. There has been only one case during the month just past, come to my knowledge, where a black person was assaulted by a white person, and in that case *the white man was brought before the freedmen's court at this place and promptly punished*."[41] While caution is advised when attempting to understand precisely what was meant by statements like the one that I italicized above, the assertion made by Roberts makes it clear that: a) he was alerted to an assault upon a freed man, b) he had the alleged assailant arrested and brought before the Freedmen's Bureau court, where he c) deduced guilt and d) rendered punishment. (Sadly, there's nothing more in the record to discern whether each party presented witnesses, or whether other forms of evidence had been taken into consideration.)

After revealing a lengthy list of abuses directed at freed men and women in Kentucky and Tennessee (for which there exists documentation in the Report),[42] and in what reads like a breathless grasping at straws, Brevet Major General Clinton B. Fisk concludes his report to Bureau Commissioner O.O. Howard this way:

> While I remain in this position I desire the power to protect the poor, the weak, and the ignorant, who confidently look to this bureau for the protection which the State, made rich by their unrequited toil, yet fails to afford them.[43]

Advocacy. Like Fisk, that's what most of the Bureau commissioners I have read in this report had committed their lives to. And while laudable in many respects, their free expressions of support for due process as directed at freed men and women also enabled them to play loose with the law and procedure. Consider the request made by Brevet Major General and Assistant Commissioner Wager Swayne in December of 1865. Swayne's jurisdiction included Mobile, Alabama. Desperate to quell marauding violence directed at freed men and women, Swayne requested the authority to issue "rewards" for information and capture of those suspected of engaging in regional acts of race-based terror.

> Several cases of outrages have come to my knowledge, perpetrated by men in disguise, and in the night. I have thought much how to correct

> this evil, and I am disposed to try the means used elsewhere to stimulate justice, i.e, *rewards*. Thus, with your approval, I should like to advertise pretty widely that *I will give a reward of $1,000 for the apprehension and conviction of the parties who, in Mobile; have burned three churches within six months*. And there are two other cases in other parts of the State where smaller rewards would answer an excellent purpose. People would at least be careful of new crimes. As I said, uses for money multiply. I do not want to be extravagant, yet I feel bound to make to you suggestions which I think for the good of the work.[44]

One month later, in his January 1866 report to O.O. Howard, Swayne, sounding even more exasperated than in his December correspondence, reveals his desire to bring the full weight of the United States military to prosecute a local Alabama militia that had arisen to terrorize freed men and women:

> Two men were arrested near here one day last week, who were robbing and disarming negroes upon the highway. The arrests were made by the provost marshal's forces. The men represented themselves as in the military service, and acting by my order. They afterwards stated, what was probably true, that they belonged to the Macon county militia. I have procured a military commission, and shall proceed to try them, making the first charge the unlawful assumption of authority. A habeas corpus will be issued out and taken to the President. *I am sorry to give you this trouble, but I must enforce upon this people my original proposition, that if they don't do justice, it will be done for them*. And it is further desired to convince the local militia that stealing clothing, pistols, and money, under guise of "disarming the negroes," or stealing pistols only, is robbery, and will be so dealt with, according to the means we have. There must be "no distinction of color" in the right to carry arms, any more than in any other right. When the writ of habeas corpus is served, a special communication will be forwarded for presentation to the officer to whom the prisoner's application is referred.

I cite Swayne's reports to Howard to emphasize a few important points. It is clear that he has been emotionally and professionally moved by the Bureau's mission and purpose. It appears that he will use all available resources (and some that he is requesting) to disrupt white violence directed at freed men and women. But it also appears that Swayne has prejudged the events about which he has secondary knowledge to the point of sending the military to arrest and bring forth members of the accused Alabama militia. I could locate no record as to whether prosecutions were forthcoming in any of these cases. What appears to be clear, however, is the bias constituting commissioners' commitment to the Bureau mission of protecting freed men and women. That is, rather than serving as a local neutral arbiter of disputes and acting consistent with due process, Bureau commissioners actively intervened in cases to administer what they perceived to be a just result. And, of course, Swayne is no exception. On December 26, 1865, Georgia commissioner, Davis Tillson, wrote to O.O. Howard:

> I have no doubt the passage of the act admitting the testimony of negroes in the courts of this State will be followed by a demand upon the President to withdraw martial law from the State and turn over all offenders to the civil courts for trial; such a proceeding would, in my opinion, be exceedingly unwise and in the highest degree prejudicial to the best interests of the State, and especially of the freed people. *I have no hope or belief whatever that justice would be done the freed people by the civil authorities, in the present temper of the people of this State. An improvement, however, in the disposition and tone of the people is observable, and sooner or later, with kind and skillful management on the part of officers of the bureau, the administration of justice may be safely left with them.*[45]

At the end of January 1866, Tillson generated another impassioned plea for support of freed men and women as they confronted the impossibility of receiving justice in civil court.

> In almost every case, as heretofore reported, the withdrawal of troops has been followed by outrages on the freed people; their school-houses have been burned, their teachers driven off or threatened with death, and the freed people by fraud, and even by violence, made to enter into unjust and fraudulent contracts. The responsible and educated classes are ashamed of these outrages, and loudly and justly claim that they should not all be judged by the people who are mean and cruel enough to practice these wrongs; but the convictions of the former never take form in action – seldom in a manly, open protest. It requires the most careful nursing and culture to keep alive even a show of justice towards the freed people.[46]

Assistant commissioner of South Carolina, R. Saxton, revealed precisely the kind of idiosyncratic administration of justice through conciliation courts that initially drew the ire of Bentham and the opponents of the Act:

> Fully conscious of the importance of maintaining friendly relations with former masters, I have been scrupulously careful to be just to them, and not to exercise any authority not clearly set forth in my instructions. *I have only asked simple justice for those committed defenceless to my care, contented oftentimes not even to secure this, carrying the olive*

> *branch where conviction would have declared for the sword of justice.* I have not always been met in the same spirit. The hard lesson which the former slaveholder has to be taught, to treat those he owned as freemen, and to deal justly with them, is not to be learned in a day. It is, however, being learned as rapidly, perhaps, as could be expected.[47]

It is this kind of flexibility with regard to case adjudication that makes the conciliation model one that may produce "simple justice," in that Saxton has clearly deduced from experience that the success of the Bureau and the future peace realized by freed men and women depend upon his capacity to understand local culture and work within it. On the other hand, Saxton also reveals the kind of prosecutorial discretion most often found in plea bargaining cases. Deciding whether, when, whom, and with what to charge an accused is here, and in each of the previously cited examples, simply a matter of who the Bureau agent was. Finally, I include one more example of the kind of judicial flexibility that existed as part of the Freedmen's Bureau's quasi-inquisitorial conciliation process. Here, we read from the report of J.S. Fullerton, commissioner responsible for overseeing Bureau activities in Louisiana. Midway through this paragraph, Fullerton articulates the "elephant in the room," what up to this point has been intuited but not specifically stated – *Bureau agent advocacy for freed men and women.* I have italicized the language in the paragraph below:

> The next step taken by me was to direct that no more arrests be made by the officers of the bureau and to abolish these tribunals of special jurisdiction known as freedmen's courts. I thought it better that in cases where arrest were necessary the officers of the bureau should call on the military officers in the vicinity to take cognizance of the matter. By so doing justice would be equally obtained, and a disagreeable feature removed from the bureau. *There are men in the bureau whose prejudices in favor of the black race go so far that they can hear only one side of a complaint, and whose zeal leads them, in many instances, to use the power of arrest that had been committed to them to the great detriment not only of the white man, but also of the black.* Whenever a wrong is done the white man, the result is to create in his breast a proportionate hatred of, or enmity towards, the blacks. These officers escaped all ill effects of such action, except personal abuse, but the black man suffers otherwise.[48]

Smithsonian Institute Archive Data

In addition to the Report cited at length above, I have culled data from the Smithsonian Institute that pertains to the practice of conciliation in the state of North Carolina. The Smithsonian has preserved scattered and often piecemeal correspondence between state Bureau commissioners and local agents prosecuting cases. Still, the correspondence provides insight into Bureau case management practices. For example, references to the kind of procedural flexibility offered by Bureau agents to local dispute resolution appear in letters of correspondence from the Beaufort, North Carolina field office. In this letter, the agent administering the Beaufort Bureau office shares with his supervisor his disposition of cases:

> Crime, I am happy to say has not been prevalent in this Sub District. The complaints of freedmen were generally against their employers for wages, my practice has been when a freedman, brought a bill against his employer to endorce [sic] on it requesting him to settle it, or, Report at my office giving from 3 to 10 days according to the distance the parties lived from my office ... The parties would invariably settle the accounts in my office of this number were 27. There were 2 cases of assault by whites on blacks. I find the parties and gave half the fine to the freedman, the other to the Bureau.[49]

While difficult to locate, direct references to pleas of guilt were also registered in the North Carolina Bureau records. In the Records Relating to Court Cases, Case Files Relating to the Administration of Justice 1, appears the following entry:

> This case divides mainly into two parts. The first is for Assault and Battery upon Daniel Bagley (Freedman). To this charge the Defendant now pleads guilty but that it was done without criminal intent and in discharge of duty as Master of the Apprentice.

Citizens George Rudd ("Carrying deadly weapons") and Thomas Harley ("Carrying deadly weapons") each accepted a Bureau-negotiated guilty plea.[50] By far, the most prolific references to guilty pleas that I can find in the North Carolina Smithsonian record apply to men serving in the military. Three cases located in the March 1865–July 1868 North Carolina Assistant Commissioner, Issuances, General Orders cite guilty pleas from Corporal James F. Dampman of the Sixth Infantry ("Drunkenness on duty"), Private John Richardson of the Sixth Infantry ("Absence without leave,") and Private Michael Moran of the Fourth Infantry ("Desertion").[51] The record from the North Carolina Bureau indicates that: a) caseload volume differed widely across the state, b) cases were disposed of privately by Bureau agents, and c) Bureau agents offered defendants the opportunity to plead guilty thereby adopting charge and sentencing reductions.

In Texas, Bureau courts addressed the following categories of cases: contract violations, wages, denial of parental rights, property disputes, and minor threats and assaults. Together, these categories of cases amounted to 91 percent of the overall conciliation court proceedings.[52]

Once again, the Bureau intervened in such cases when local jurisdictions failed to. In a March 30, 1865, policy directive issued by Commissioner Howard, he explains when and why the Bureau courts would intervene to seek local justice:

> Those in places where there is an interruption of civil law, or in which local courts, by reason of old codes ... disregard the negro's right to justice before the law to adjudicate ... all difficulties arising between negroes themselves or between negroes and whites or Indians, except those in military service ... and not taken cognizance of by other tribunals, civil or military, of the United States.[53]

According to Rapport,

> it is probably fair to suggest that these men – untrained in the law and not obliged to issue written opinions – felt little obsession about the force of precedent or the importance of judicial rationality. Their conception of justice implied evenhandedness tempered by leniency and guided by a commitment to free labor and familial unity.[54]

It was the Bureau conciliation courts that attempted to address violations of freed women's and men's rights through the application of Northern paternalism. Insofar as Bureau agents were committed to protecting the rights of freed slaves, they did so consistent with a system reproducing commitment to instilling "northern white notions of free labor and domesticity."[55] As revealed by the following quote, Freedmen's Bureau agents approached their responsibilities with a mixture of civil rights zealotry and Northern white bourgeois family values:

> Freedmen, as this federal official explained, "need to be encouraged, to have their manhood appealed to. They need to have praise judiciously mixed with blame." They must 'be protected in their rights as well as punished for their misdeeds, to be instructed in their duties and treated as men with immortal souls rather than as beasts of burden or machines for pulling cotton.[56]

Important for Bureau agents was a firm belief that "emancipation had brought, at the very least, government protection for the rights to self-ownership, to movement, to the fruit of one's labor, and to lawful marriage and familial relations."[57] In North Carolina, Captain James, the Assistant Bureau Commissioner, provides insight into the concerns, experiences, and practices of the Bureau. I cite Capt. James's letter in full because it captures the commitment and the challenges confronting Bureau agents. You will also see that near the end of the letter Capt. James references an assistant Bureau agent who was able to dispose of "180 complaints in a single day."

> Regarding this Bureau as the appointed instrument for redeeming the solemn pledge of the nation through its Chief Magistrate, to secure the rights of freedmen, *I have made every effort to protect them from wrongs.* All officers of the Bureau were directed in accordance with your Circular No. 5 to investigate these difficulties between the two classes, to settle them by counsel and arbitration if possible, to punish light offenses by fines or otherwise, and to report more serious cases of crimes to the Military Authorities for trial. *The exact number of "Cases" heard could not be given. They have been so numerous that no complete record could be kept. One officer reported that he had heard and disposed of as many as 180 complaints in a single day.*[58]

Only lasting four years, the Freedmen's Bureau Courts signified a short-lived experiment for quasi-inquisitorial conciliation efforts in the South. Its limited tenure was largely due to the 1866 United States Supreme Court opinion in *Ex parte Milligan*,[59] and the passage of the Fourteenth Amendment in 1868. In *Milligan*, the Court held that wherever there existed a locally functioning system of courts where due process was available to residents, conciliation courts were unnecessary and unconstitutional since they would be viewed as extrajudicial. Following the Court's opinion in *Milligan*, President Andrew Johnson withdrew federal support for the Freedmen's Bureau's conciliation courts. While critics of Bureau courts cited their conservative commitment to assimilating freed men and women into what was considered Northern white bourgeois cultural arrangements (especially regarding familial relationships), "These men, as 'judge and jury,' achieved the best that they could be expected at the time. They walked a thin line, balancing the wishes of their superiors (in Galveston, New Orleans, and Washington), the country's uneasiness with actions threatening federalism, and the nation's hesitancy to try civilians in military courts."[60]

Conclusion to Equity and Conciliation Courts

In Chapter 2, and here in Chapter 3, I contend that institutional practices characteristic of both equity and conciliation are recognizable today as part of plea practice. These characteristics include: (1) private case disposition (until the plea colloquy, which is *pro forma*), (2) cost-efficiency, (3) the unilateral power of the prosecutor, and (4) procedural efficiency. We should also reference Bentham's powerful admonition that conciliation would permit "partiality" to one side or the other where settlements would be "repugnant to" and a "denial of" justice. Since it is now the prosecutor with whom negotiations are made, and since the prosecutor represents local political interests as well as those of the state more generally, it is in this sense that plea bargaining as conciliation may not generate justice for victims of crime, just as Bentham warned.

Contemporary plea bargaining is guided by Federal Rules of Criminal Procedure, Rule 11. The Rule guides plea procedure insofar as it addresses the prosecutorial authority to plead whenever there is a factual basis to do so, and where the defendant knowingly and voluntarily agrees to it. As an indication of the historical transformation that took place beginning in the middle of the 19th century, it is now entirely the prosecutor's ambit of power that is of utmost concern. Stipulated in Rule 11 is a separation of powers that prohibits judges from intruding upon executive branch authority to charge and prosecute crimes. Judicial authority is limited to: a) determining the constitutionality of the plea by attempting to discern in open court whether the defendant knowingly and voluntarily agreed to the bargain (the plea colloquy is the only time when the plea bargaining process appears in public, but with none of the "horse trading" that takes place during plea negotiations), and b) issuing a sentence.

Plea bargaining as it is practiced today has its origins in the quasi-inquisitorial equity and conciliation courts. As these two procedures coexisted alongside adversarial due process directed at trials, and as their popularity grew with regard to the ease of case disposition (most spectacularly as manifested in the Freedmen's Bureau, where one North Carolina Bureau agent managed 180 case dispositions in one day), and as lawyers grew in stature, adversarialism was introduced to the quasi-inquisitorial adjudication models. What each of the two court systems provided was judicial flexibility, episodic leniency, and simple justice. Each of the court models early on relied upon lay judges, the legitimacy of whose decisions would rest upon their stature within respective communities. Over time, especially as we consider the Freedmen's Bureau, concerns fell far more frequently upon the desire for administration of social control through enhanced hegemonic state power.

I ask the reader to consider the following three issues: 1) "conciliation is conducted by a third party who is not a mere neutral, but instead a recognized figure of authority within the community," 2) that lawyers care more about "enforcement of the letter of the law than on promoting equitable outcomes," and 3) Mississippi's active recruitment of local lawyers to administer justice consistent with the Bureau's commitment to conciliation.

With regard to (1) above, equity and conciliation transmogrified into the plea upon the addition of adversarialism and positive law through the person of the prosecutor. As the chief law enforcement agents within locales, county attorneys are elected officials who carry significant political and cultural weight within their respective communities. In this case, the "non-neutral" quality of prosecutors is obvious given their personal political biases and their adherence to the rule of law. The latter, of course, serves to preserve dominant cultural expressions of order. This point is related to the second, where in (2) above it is clear that the purpose of equity and conciliation was to adhere closely to state power through the adoption of positive law. This is clearly stated in the 1931 Wickersham Commission Report: "the prosecutor, rather than the court, is, under existing conditions and procedure, the more influential in regard to such pleas."[61] Finally, the third matter requiring attention is identification from the records in Mississippi that the Assistant Commissioner of the Bureau approved the hiring of local attorneys to administer Bureau conciliation simple justice. This is important as I have been arguing that the existence of the conciliation model was well known to local authorities. That we have a record of lay attorneys now properly embedded within the Bureau, and that there does not appear to be any hesitation whatsoever from the Assistant Commissioner upon announcing said program to O.O. Howard, one may assume that such a practice was in operation in other jurisdictions as well. That said, I could not locate any specific reference to lay attorneys in the Record outside the state of Mississippi.

Beginning in the middle of the 19th century, American criminal procedure became increasingly adversarial. In addition to public trials, which lawyers in America preferred as a way to demonstrate their oratory skills, there existed quasi-inquisitorial practices that operated parallel to trials. The New York Bar made the practice of conciliation adversarial in nature by successfully gaining a concession from the New York General Assembly to permit Bar-trained lawyers to engage in it. In my estimation, this is one example from the historical record that provides clear insight into the hegemonic aspect of plea bargaining as social control. Conciliation would be permitted to coexist alongside formal trial-based due process, but only insofar as Bar-certified attorneys would take over the practice. The second jarring example of the confluence of equity, conciliation, and adversarialism appeared in the short-lived but extremely impactful Freedmen's Bureau courts.

Over time, with the increasing power of lawyers, and with due recognition of the benefits afforded to prosecutors and local and state politicians, plea bargaining emerged out of equity and conciliation but with a far more legal-rational constitution. Just as their predecessors with the Freedmen's Bureau courts, prosecutors would determine whether to charge, who to charge, what to charge defendants with, and they proposed the sentence.

Predicated upon both equity and conciliation court models and cultures, we adopted a system of plea bargaining that today adjudicates between 95 and 97 percent of all felony cases in the United States.[62] Our institutional adaptation of equity and conciliation to adversarialism and positive law appears to have generated precisely the apocalyptic failure that

Bentham anticipated and warned about. Namely, that "he who says conciliation [*accommodement*] says, in other terms, partial denial of justice" due to the abdication of rights protections.[63] Or Justice Story's caution that the introduction of a flexible system of adjudication "would be the most gigantic in its sway and the most formidable instrument of arbitrary power that could well be devised."[64] In the early 19th century, Justice Story was writing that "arbitrary power" resided with a judge. Today, that power is exercised by prosecutors, and with precisely the same caution attached. Blackstone, it will be recalled, anticipated Justice Story when he said that, "if a [equity] court of England did really act ... it would rise above all law, either common or statute, and be a most arbitrary legislator in every particular case."[65] As it pertained to conciliation courts, we learned from Kessler that the institutional practice was designed to "encourage deference to social superiors, rather than individual autonomy," where "conciliation is thus conducted by a third party who is not a mere neutral."[66] Bentham warned that adoption of the conciliation court model for any but familial disputes "threatened and undermined the rule of law."[67] Since conciliation judges (and now prosecutors) would not be viewed as neutral arbiters of the law, the institutional commitment to conciliation would generate excesses that would delegitimate law. Finally, what are we to make of the serious objections that were raised prior to passage of the Freedmen's Bureau Act from Rep. Davis, and from the editors at *The Reporter*, each of whom raised the specter of oppressive state power being used under the disguise of benevolence.

In the end, it was the quasi-inquisitorial nature of equity and conciliation that rendered the practice appealing to lawyers. With the addition of positive law to the disposition of cases, lawyers would now benefit from the principal characteristics of those early experiments with equity and conciliation courts to more efficiently achieve the state's interest in maintaining social control by way of simplified due process leading to certain conviction. Enhanced conviction rates favored the career aspirations of prosecutors and judges since those rates were, and still are, used to rationalize the quality and efficiency of local county attorneys' offices with regard to case prosecution. As a result, say those prosecutors, our communities are safer. Vote for me.

Federal Rule 11 statutorily codified centuries-old criminal procedures that were originally designed to be less threatening because they intentionally did not operate through a legal-rational application of law, precisely as a way to maintain community stability in non-adversarial settings. In so doing, contemporary plea bargaining has usurped the trial in the United States as the most efficacious criminal procedure available to prosecutors to guarantee a guilty verdict.

***

Having provided some historical analysis of plea bargaining in the previous three chapters, in the final chapter of Part I, I introduce the history and practice of trial by jury. This is important since the historical record relating to the trial by jury, both in England and in the United States, provides context for understanding the role that it played as a public check on legislative, executive, and judicial power.

Notes

1 https://law.marquette.edu/facultyblog/2012/12/before-there-were-red-and-blue-states-there-were-free-states-and-slave-states/comment-page-1/
2 *An Act to establish a Bureau for the Relief of Freedmen and Refugees, and for other Purposes.* "July 16, 1866. Be it enacted by the Senate and House of Representatives of the United States of America in Congress assembled, that the act to establish a bureau for the relief of freedmen and refugees, approved March third, eighteen hundred and sixty-five, shall continue in force for the term of two years from and after the passage of this act."
3 Id at 174.
4 Id at 176–177.
5 Howard most notably served as the founder, namesake, and president of Howard University from 1869 to 1874.
6 Amalia Kessler. The Freedmen's Bureau Exception: The Triumph of Due (Adversarial) Process and the Dawn of Jim Crow. In Supra 16 at 263 (Kessler, 2017).
7 Robert J. Kaczorowski. The Freedmen's Bureau and Civil Rights Enforcement, 1866–1868. In The Politics of Judicial Interpretation: The Federal Courts, Department of Justice, and Civil Rights, 1866–1876. Fordham University Press (2005): 22. ("Local peace officers usually failed to bring terrorists to justice, either because of fear for their personal safety or because of their support for the terrorists. Sheriffs refused to arrest suspects, judges refused to try defendants, and juries refused to convict them." (22))
8 Id at 23. Reference is to the 1866 Civil Rights Act. "The Civil Rights Act of 1866, which declared that all people born in the United States were U.S. citizens and had certain inalienable rights, including the right to make contracts, to own property, to sue in court, and to enjoy the full protection of federal law. The act gave the U.S. district courts exclusive jurisdiction over criminal cases related to violations of the act, and concurrent jurisdiction, along with the U.S. circuit courts, of all civil and criminal cases affecting those who were unable to enforce in state court the rights guaranteed by the act." https://www.fjc.gov/history/timeline/civil-rights-act-1866
9 Id at 30.
10 Supra 6 at 280 (Kessler 2017).
11 Sara Rapport. The Freedmen's Bureau as a Legal Agent for Black Men and Women in Georgia: 1865–1868. 73, The Georgia Historical Quarterly, 1 (Spring 1989): 47, note 68.
12 Supra 7 at 32.
13 Supra 7 at 32.
14 Mary Farmer-Kaiser. Strict Justice for Every Man, Woman, and Child": Gender, Justice, and the Freedmen's Bureau. In Freedwomen and the Freedmen's Bureau: Race, Gender, and Public Policy in the Age of Emancipation. Fordham University Press (2010): 144.

15 Christopher Bean. Bureau Expansion, Bureau Courts, and the Black Code: The J.B. Kiddoo Era, Summer 1866–November 1866. In Too Great a Burden to Bear: The Struggle and Failure of the Freedmen's Bureau in Texas. Fordham University Press (2016): 70.
16 The Reporter: A Periodical Devoted to Religion, Law, Legislation, and Public Events. Washington D.C., February 26, Volume II (1866).
17 Id at 11.
18 Supra 130 at 11 (My emphasis).
19 The Freedmen's Bureau Reports of Generals Steelman and Fullerton on the Condition of the Freedmen's Bureau in the Southern States. Wilmington, NC, May 8, 1866.
20 Id at 2.
21 Id at 2.
22 Id at 4.
23 The Reporter. Volume II, March 5, 1866: 4.
24 Id at 4.
25 Id at 4.
26 My application of hegemony is predicated upon the work of Italian theorist, Antonio Gramsci. Hegemony, as I interpret it here, is rule by consent, backed up by the threat of coercion. See Antonio Gramsci. Selections from the Prison Notebooks. International Publishers Co; Reprint, 1989 edition.
27 https://babel.hathitrust.org/cgi/pt?id=uc1.aa0014725683&view=plaintext&seq=1. Please note that the page numbers referenced to the Report are those provided by the digitized Hathitrust webpage, not to the Report itself.
28 Washington, March 19, 1866. Sir: In obedience to your indorsement upon the resolution of the House of Representatives, of date March 8, 1866, requesting that the Secretary of War be directed to communicate to the House all orders issued by the Commissioner and assistant commissioners of the Freedmen's Bureau, and such other information not heretofore communicated as may be in possession of the bureau. I have the honor to transmit herewith the following papers:
No. 1. Files of orders and circulars of assistant commissioners.
No. 2. Files of Bureau of Refugees, Freedmen, and Abandoned Lands, War Department No. 3. Report of tour of inspection of Kentucky, by Mr. P. Bonesteel.
No. 4. Report of bureau affairs in Edgefield District, South Carolina.
No. 5. Report of General Fisk, relative to Tennessee and Kentucky, and bill relative to negro testimony.
No. 6. Report of General Sprague, relative to Arkansas.
No. 7. Letter of General Tillson, Georgia, concerning Sea Island.
No. 8. Reports of sub-assistants of affairs in Virginia.
I am, sir, very respectfully,
O.O. HOWARD,
Major General, Commissioner.
Hon. Edwin M. STANTON,
Secretary of War.
29 Id at 210.
30 Id at 209.
31 Id at 209.
32 Id at 12.
33 Id at 54 (my emphasis).
34 It may be recalled that this was precisely the concern raised by House of Representatives member Davis, and was one of the principal issues raised in his amendment to the Freedmen's Bureau Act.

35 Supra 28 at 85.
36 Supra 28 at 100.
37 Supra 28 at 135.
38 Supra 28 at 181.
39 Supra 28 at 229.
40 Supra 28 at 232.
41 Supra 28 at 233.
42 An example of the kind of reporting taking place across jurisdictions can be found in this report made by the North Carolina Commissioner, E. Whittlesey, Colonel and Assistant Commissioner:
During the quarter, thirty-seven (37) cases of violent assault upon freedmen, or other criminal acts, have been reported to the military authorities for trial, or such action as might be deemed proper. Of these thirty-seven cases, the only ones brought to trial, so far as this bureau has information, are those of "Isaac and Wiley, freedmen, of the town of Salisbury, Rowan county", on the charge of "larceny," of which they were found "not guilty," and discharged. Several cases reported during the previous quarter have been tried; among them are:

1. Emanuel Baxter, (colored): "Assault with intent to commit rape." Not guilty. 2. John W. Gorman, (white): "Assault and battery."
2. "Assault and battery." Guilty; fined $50, and imprisoned thirty days. Fine remitted by reviewing officer.
3. Stephen C. Lee, (white): "Murder." Found guilty, and sentenced to be hung. Sentence remitted by reviewing officer on the ground that malice was not proved.
4. Joseph Corpening, (white): "Assault with intent to kill." Found guilty of "shooting with intent to maim." Sentence: five hundred dollars fine and ninety days' imprisonment.
5. George A. Pitts, J. A. Propst , William Ristler, Alfred Sitaker, Thomas Williford, Gibson Kline, and Dwight Russell (white): "Riot and assault and battery." Pitts, Propst, Ristler, Williford, and Sitaker found guilty, fined, and imprisoned; Kline and Russell acquitted.
6. Shock, (colored): "Rape on colored girl." Finding, guilty; sentenced to be hung. Sentence mitigated to one year's hard labor.
7. Monroe Davis, (white): "Riot and assault and battery." Guilty, and imprisoned for four months.
8. Privates Bloom, Shannon, and Lims , 128th Indiana volunteers: "Assault upon freedmen," & c. Guilty, and sentenced to loss of six months' pay.
9. Henry Brown (colored): "Theft." Guilty, and imprisoned two months.
10. Guión Earp, (white): "Maltreatment of freedman, and assault and battery." Guilty; sentenced to hard labor on the public works for two years.

Some of the cases reported during the last quarter are as follows: 1. Willis P. Moore, charged with the murder of a colored man. 2. Reddick Kearney and others, Pitt county. Riot and murder of two freed
3. Magistrates of Brunswick County sentenced two colored men to be sold into servitude for five years. This case was acted upon promptly by General Crook, and the freedmen were released.

43 Supra 28 at 247.
44 Supra 28 at 304.
45 Supra 28 at 322.
46 Supra 28 at 336.
47 Supra 28 at 378.
48 Supra 28 at 406.

49 North Carolina Field Offices, Subordinate Field Offices: Beaufort, Letters Sent, Volume 1 (70), January 1866–August 1867).
50 Id (North Carolina Field Offices, Subordinate Field Offices: Beaufort, Letters Sent, Volume 1 (70), January 1866–August 1867).
51 Id. North Carolina Field Offices, Subordinate Field Offices: Beaufort, Letters Sent, Volume 1 (70), January 1866–August 1867).
52 Supra 15 at 72.
53 Supra 14.
54 Supra 14 at 48.
55 Supra 14 at 142.
56 Supra 14 at 142.
57 Supra 14 at 144.
58 Report of Captain James. North Carolina Assistant Commissioner, Letters Sent, Vol. 1 (7), July 4, 1865–July 13, 1867. Smithsonian Institution Transcription Center, Freedmen's Bureau.
59 71 US 2 (1866) (*Ex parte Milligan*).
60 Supra 15 at 79.
61 The National Commission on Law Observance and Enforcement (Wickersham Commission). May 20, 1929: 96.
62 *Lafler v. Cooper*, 566 US 156 (2012), *Missouri v. Frye* – 566 US 134, 132 S. Ct. 1399 (2012).
63 Amalia D. Kessler. Deciding Against Conciliation: The Nineteenth-Century Rejection of a European Transplant and the Rise of a Distinctively American Ideal of Adversarial Adjudication. Theoretical Inquiries in Law, 10 (2) (2009): 441.
64 Joseph Story. Commentaries on Equity Jurisprudence. London: Street and Maxwell (1920): 13.
65 Id at 80.
66 Supra 63 at 428.
67 Supra 63 at 438.

References

Christopher Bean. Bureau Expansion, Bureau Courts, and the Black Code: The J.B. Kiddoo Era, Summer 1866–Novermber 1866. In *Too Great A Burden to Bear: The Strugggle and Failure of the Freedmen's Bureau in Texas*. Fordham University Press (2016): 70

Mary Farmer-Kaiser. Strict Justice for Every Man, Woman, and Child: Gender, Justice, and the Freedmen's Bureau. In *Freedwomen and the Freedmen's Bureau: Race, Gender, and Public Policy in the Age of Emancipation*. Fordham University Press (2010): 144

Robert J. Kaczorowski. The Freedmen's Bureau and Civil Rights Enforcement, 1866–1868. In *The Politics of Judicial Interpretation: The Federal Courts, Department of Justice, and Civil Rights, 1866–1876*. Fordham University Press (2005): 22

Amalia Kessler. The Freedmen's Bureau Exception: The Triumph of Due (Adversarial) Process and the Dawn of Jim Crow. at 263 (2017)

Sara Rapport. The Freedmen's Bureau as a Legal Agent for Black Men and Women in Georgia: 1865–1868. 73(1) *The Georgia Historical Quarterly*, 47, note 68 (Spring 1989)

The Reporter: A Periodical Devoted to Religion, Law, Legislation, and Public Events. Washington, DC, February 26, Volume II (1866)

4

TRIAL BY JURY

Natural Law and the Problem of Inalienable Rights

The United States is confronting an authoritarian threat to popular sovereignty. The threat emanates from the contemporary Republican Party, reconstituted as the MAGA movement by former president and current Republican Party candidate for president in the 2024 election, Donald Trump, as well as from the far-right supermajority of the United States Supreme Court. Construction of the right-wing supermajority on the Court first began during the Obama administration with an ideologically motivated political move made by United States Senate President Mitch McConnell. It was McConnell who, despite his constitutionally prescribed duty to hold hearings on Supreme Court nominees emanating from the president of the United States, refused to hold *any* hearings to fill the Supreme Court vacancy left by Justice Antonin Scalia's death. There is no ambiguity in the Constitution's language. Article II, §2 is known as the Appointments Clause:

> He shall have Power, by and with the Advice and Consent of the Senate, to make Treaties, provided two thirds of the Senators present concur; and he shall nominate, and by and with the Advice and Consent of the Senate, shall appoint Ambassadors, other public Ministers and Consuls, Judges of the supreme Court, and all other Officers of the United States, whose Appointments are not herein otherwise provided for, and which shall be established by Law: but the Congress may by Law vest the Appointment of such inferior Officers, as they think proper, in the President alone, in the Courts of Law, or in the Heads of Departments.[1]

In violation of the Constitution, that vacancy was held by the Senate for the next president to fill – Donald Trump. During his four-year term as president,

DOI: 10.4324/9781003385103-5

Trump filled three vacancies with far-right justices – Neil Gorsuch, Amy Coney Barrett, and Brett Kavanaugh.

It is precisely the kind of threats against democracy currently presented by Trump, the Republican Party, and the United States Supreme Court that led the English, North American colonists, and the framers of the American Constitution to elevate the jury trial to essential status. Before I take up the historical understanding of the perceived role of the jury as a check on legislative, executive, and judicial authority, and because history has a way of repeating itself, if imperfectly, I begin below with a brief discussion of contemporary challenges confronting the rule of law in the United States (including the plea), and that, at least in my view, signify tangible threats to the republic. As my presentation of the history of the trial by jury in England and the United States makes clear, the institution was viewed as a way for the people to directly confront abuses of power by the legislative, executive, and judicial branches, abuses that in their current manifestation are threatening American democracy.

This chapter proceeds with reference to contemporary challenges confronting the republic, a discussion of the historical understanding of the inalienability and indefeasibility of rights, a brief history of the jury trial, and an introduction to natural law principles. I conclude the chapter with an introduction to the centrality of rights in a republic.

Contemporary Concerns about the Executive, Legislative, and Judicial Branches

During the four years of his presidency (2016–2020), Donald Trump routinely denigrated and sought to delegitimize the rule of law, prosecutors, judges, the Federal Bureau of Investigation, the Department of Justice, the Department of Homeland Security, the Centers for Disease Control, and perhaps most insidiously, American people who volunteered as election poll workers, and anyone else who attempted to hold him accountable.[2] Trump continued to deny the outcome of the 2020 election, fomented an attempted insurrection, attempted to strongarm state election officials into changing the outcome of the 2020 presidential vote in the battleground states of Georgia, Arizona, Michigan, Pennsylvania, New Mexico, and Wisconsin, expressed fondness for white supremacists and autocrats, and has been indicted in two separate cases – one for retention of classified documents, and the other for conspiracy to defraud the United States government in an attempt to disrupt the peaceful transfer of power, and conspiracy against rights (i.e., Trump's attempt to disenfranchise all voters who supported Joe Biden).[3] In June 2023, and straight from an autocrat's playbook, Trump declared that if re-elected to the presidency he would use his executive authority to prosecute the current president, Joe Biden: "I will appoint a real special prosecutor to go after the most corrupt president in the history of the United States of America, Joe Biden, and the entire Biden crime family."[4] More recently, Trump announced his interest in being a "dictator on day one," and he, and members of the Republican Party, have publicly stated their interest in "retaliation" being directed at current and former members of the Biden administration, and the Department of Justice, among others.[5]

Autocratic predilections have the former president and current candidate for president in the Republican Party, Donald J. Trump, seemingly in the firm grasp of both the civil and criminal legal systems.

In a New York civil suit, on May 9, 2023, Donald Trump was *found liable for sexually abusing and defaming E. Jean Carroll.* In the same month, on May 30, 2024, Trump was once again found guilty, this time in a New York *criminal* court. Following four weeks of testimony from 22 witnesses, a Manhattan jury found Trump guilty on 34 felony counts that fell into three categories: 1) invoices for legal services, 2) checks paid for legal services, and 3) ledger entries for legal expenses.[6] How is it that these state-level violations of civil law rose to the level of criminal indictments? Because the fraudulent process that was materially established at trial, and that Trump was a central figure in planning and carrying out, was set in motion as a way to keep from the American people Trump's extramarital relationships with two women – Karen McDougal and Stormy Daniels – just weeks before the 2016 presidential election. Trump is scheduled for sentencing on July 11, 2024.

The remaining three cases pending against Trump are: 1) *State of Georgia v. Donald John Trump et al.*,[7] 2) *United States v. Donald J. Trump*,[8] and 3) *United States of America v. Donald J. Trump et al.*[9] At the time of writing, the United States Supreme Court has placed the two federal cases on hold while it attempts to decide whether, acting in his capacity as president of the United States, Donald Trump has absolute immunity from criminal prosecution.[10][11]

Trump's brazen disregard for the rule of law has unleashed a powerful threat to the republic, as the Republican Party at both the state and federal levels is complicit in his destabilizing rhetoric and actions.

As I demonstrated in Chapter 1, the Supreme Court has played a significant role in the story of plea bargaining. I share with Professor Chemerinsky the view that it should be the role of the Court to uphold Constitutional principles "against the will of the majority."[12] That said, I also share Professor Chemerinsky's incredulity when considering how well the Court has played that role.

> My disappointment in the Court is both historical and contemporary. One need only look at the Court's decisions from the past few years – preventing employment discrimination suits and class actions against

> the largest corporations, keeping those injured by misconduct of generic drugmakers (sic) from having any recovery, denying remedies to those unjustly convicted and detained – to see what has historically been true: the Supreme Court usually sides with big business and government power and fails to protect people's rights.[13]

In addition to the examples provided above by Professor Chemerinsky,[14] I would like to emphasize two areas of Supreme Court jurisprudence that speak to a reversal of well-established statute and constitutional law. The first example relates to the Court's attack on voting rights. The second example shines a light on the Court's conservative ideologues (Justices Roberts, Alito, Thomas, Gorsuch, Kavanaugh, and Coney Barrett) and their extraordinary move to declare the constitutional right to abortion a nullity. I begin with voting rights.

The United States Supreme Court's Republican-appointed justices initiated their attack on voting rights beginning in 2013 with the *Shelby County v. Holder*[15] opinion written by Chief Justice John Roberts, a holding that gutted Section 4 of the 1965 Voting Rights Act's preclearance requirement.[16] In 2021, Justice Samuel Alito wrote the majority opinion *Brnovich v. Democratic National Committee*,[17] a holding that severely weakened Section 2 of the Voting Rights Act. With regard to voting rights, the United States is on the verge of returning to the state of apartheid that existed prior to the passage of the 1964 Civil Rights Act and the 1965 Voting Rights Act. This has historical origins. In 1866, Congress passed the Civil Rights Act as an attempt to provide civil rights protections to freed men and women. The Act also sought to circumvent the United States Supreme Court's *Dred Scott* opinion. However, the Act failed to provide the protection necessary to firmly establish freed men and women as citizens constituting suffrage rights, as states began passing what at first were known as the Black Codes and later would become Jim Crow laws. Suffrage rights for black Americans would await the 1965 Voting Rights Act. The 2013 *Shelby* opinion and the 2021 *Brnovich* opinion provide the statutory space necessary to place the United States squarely in the pre-1964 period of Jim Crow.

Strangely, however, the United States Supreme Court held in three important voting rights cases, each decided in the summer of 2023, that gerrymandering in both Alabama[18] and Louisiana[19] is in violation of §2 of the Voting Rights Act. Importantly, these were 5–4 opinions with the reliably conservative members of the Court writing in dissent (Thomas, Gorsuch, Barrett, and Alito). The most potentially devastating of the voting rights cases before the Court in the 2022–2023 term originated in North Carolina. In *Moore v. Harper*[20] the Court held by a 7–2 majority in an opinion written by Chief Justice Roberts that the fictional "independent state legislature theory" (it is *not* a theory) applied by the Republican Party in North Carolina, an idea that if adopted and applied to state elections would eliminate state or federal judicial review of legislative enactments affecting voting rights, was impermissibly broad, and would have potentially devastating effects on the checks and balances vital to a republic. The two dissenters in the *Moore* case were Justices Thomas and Gorsuch. Given Chief Justice Roberts's history regarding voting rights legislation, these opinions come as something of a (happy) surprise and a relief to voting rights advocates. Is it possible that, given the majority of the nation's response to the Court's *Dobbs* opinion, discussed below, as well as ongoing concerns over the Justices' ethics and integrity,[21] that the Chief Justice understood the weight of the challenge before the Court regarding the Court's legitimacy and moved to correct its steamrolling toward the total elimination of the Voting Rights Act? Sure it is. After all, the Court was preparing to eliminate 45 years of affirmative action law,[22] as well as provide a constitutional right for private businesses to discriminate against those they do not like.[23] Finally, the 2022–2023 term witnessed the Court's aggressive intrusion upon Congress's legislative authority by defanging the 1972 Clean Water Act,[24] and by curtailing the power of the Secretary of Education to permit the elimination of student loan debt.[25] Each of these opinions signifies a direct conservative attack upon the administrative state.

Perhaps the most politically, economically, and culturally destabilizing opinion (possibly in the history of the Court) emerging from the Court is its June 24, 2022 opinion in *Dobbs v. Jackson Women's Health Organization.*[26] The opinion, authored by Justice Alito, ended 50 years of the constitutionally protected right to abortion originating in *Roe v. Wade*,[27] and affirmed in *Planned Parenthood of Southeastern Pennsylvania v. Casey.*[28] This is the first time in American history that a constitutional right has been rescinded. I wish to draw attention to two of the most significant aspects of the *Dobbs* opinion – the Court's questioning of the legitimacy of substantive due process rights located in the Fourteenth Amendment's preservation of life, liberty, and property with equal protection under due process of law,[29] and the level of scrutiny applied to consideration of the right of a woman to lawfully exercise her right to procure abortion services.

Justice Alito's justification for overturning *Roe v. Wade* in the *Dobbs* opinion rejects the application of the Fourteenth Amendment's privileges or immunities, equal protection, and due process clauses as applied to the creation and preservation of civil rights legislation. The rights that Americans have procured through the application of the Fourteenth Amendment are called *substantive due process* rights. Substantive due process rights are those unenumerated rights (rights that are not mentioned in the Constitution or the Bill of Rights) that the Court has held may be inferred from the text of the Fourteenth Amendment's privileges or immunities, due process, and equal protection clauses. In taking this position, the conservative members of the United States Supreme Court make a claim to originalism, the approach to the interpretation of the Constitution that limits its application solely to those fundamental rights explicitly stated or implied in the text of the Constitution. As it relates to the *Dobbs* opinion, since there is neither mention of a right to abortion nor a right to bodily integrity in the text of the Constitution, *Roe v. Wade* was bad law and had to be overturned. At this point, one might wonder why the Court would react that way since the Fourteenth Amendment clearly *implies* a right to bodily integrity (right to life and liberty) and specifically pertains to equal protection of the laws. For Justice Alito and the conservative members of the Court, however, the only Constitutional Amendments that are worthy of citation are those constituting the Bill of Rights.[30] Consider here the language used by Justice Thomas in his concurring opinion:

> Because the Court properly applies our substantive due process precedents to reject the fabrication of a constitutional right to abortion, and because this case does not present the opportunity to reject substantive due process entirely, I join the Court's opinion. But, in future cases, we should "follow the text of the Constitution, which sets forth certain substantive rights that cannot be taken away, and adds, beyond that, a right to due process when life, liberty, or property are taken away." [This reference is to the Fifth Amendment. Similar language appears in the Fourteenth Amendment which incorporated the Fifth Amendment against the states.] *Carlton*, 512 U.S. at 42 (opinion of Scalia, J.). Substantive due process conflicts with that textual command and has harmed our country in many ways. Accordingly, we should eliminate it from our jurisprudence at the earliest opportunity.[31]

Continuing with Justice Thomas's concurring opinion in the *Dobbs* case, application of the principle articulated in *Dobbs* relating to the Fourteenth Amendment's equal protection and due process clauses means that the right of Americans to procure contraception (*Griswold v. Connecticut*),[32] engage in same-sex sexual relations (*Lawrence v. Texas*),[33] and the right to same-sex marriage (*Obergefell v. Hodges*)[34] should each come under Supreme Court scrutiny.[35] One might also easily imagine that given the logic of Justice Thomas's concurrence and Justice Alito's opinion, each challenging the legitimacy of substantive due process rights located in the Fourteenth Amendment, the right to interracial marriage (*Loving v. Virginia*)[36] could also be in jeopardy. Finally, in two days in June 2023, the Supreme Court managed to overturn 45 years of precedent[37] permitting consideration of race as a factor in college and university admissions decisions, as well as providing Christian evangelicals with the right to discriminate against those who offend them.[38] These important constitutional provisions sought, in one instance to remedy centuries of institutional discrimination directed at non-white people, while in the other to provide constitutional protection to a protected class prone to discrimination – the LGBTQ community. This current highly politicized version of the United States Supreme Court has eliminated any pretense to adhering to precedent or even to "evolving standards of decency" in the service of conservative Christian white evangelicals.

In his valuable contribution to our understanding of who we are as Americans and how we came to believe in ourselves consistent with the narrative presented by the Declaration of Independence and the Constitution, Kermit Roosevelt juxtaposes each of those documents with the period of Radical Reconstruction and the Reconstruction Congress's passage of the Fourteenth Amendment.[39] Rather than the usual list of valorized framers (e.g., Jefferson, Madison, Hamilton, Franklin, Adams, Monroe, Jay), Roosevelt offers a different set of American politicians and activists who set the nation on a course of redemption premised upon principles of equality (e.g., Abraham Lincoln, the Republican Congress, Thaddeus Stevens, Charles Sumner, and John Bingham). The Radical Republican Congress and its abolitionist supporters (e.g., Frederick Douglass and Prince Hall) were able to generate a document that stipulated, in a way that neither the Declaration nor the Constitution had, a commitment to the preservation of life, liberty, and property with equal protection and due process of law. Only with the passage of the Fourteenth Amendment did those principles become a part of the Constitution.[40] For Roosevelt, the Fourteenth Amendment "fundamentally restructured American society" because it "provides textual confirmation of rupture in our constitutional history."[41] When we consider the Roberts Court opinions, but most especially the *Dobbs, 303 Creative*, and *Fair Admissions* cases, it is clear that the Court has engineered a juridical reversal of the Reconstruction era's commitment to the Fourteenth Amendment, once again dialectically positioning Americans in a battle over who we were at our founding and who we are now. I accept Roosevelt's contention that, "We are not Founding America, and we are not the heirs of that first Republic, either. We are the heirs of the people who destroyed it. We are Reconstruction America."[42] However, the "We" is currently under significant threat from the Nine.[43]

To summarize, the current Court's *Dobbs* opinion (and *Fair Admissions*, and *303 Creative*) has potentially far greater reach than declaring unconstitutional a woman's right to procure an abortion. Rather, by grounding its argument in originalism, it neglects the powerful language constituting the Fourteenth Amendment's life, liberty, and property clause, its privileges or immunities clause, and its equal protection and due process clauses. Each of these clauses has been essential to enhancing the quality of life for Americans as it has, among other rights, provided for the right to interracial marriage, contraception, gay marriage, and consensual adult sex. If Justices Alito and Thomas get their way, identification of and constitutional support for unenumerated substantive rights under the Fourteenth Amendment will disappear. To paraphrase Justice Thomas, the harm that has been caused to our country has manifested with the *Dobbs* opinion and may soon affect many other civil liberties currently protected by the Fourteenth Amendment.

The second issue of concern raised by the *Dobbs* opinion pertains to the level of scrutiny the Court applied to its deliberation over the constitutionality of *Roe*. Levels of scrutiny are very important to understand because they affect the quantum of proof necessary to establish the constitutionality of existing law. There are three levels or tiers of scrutiny – strict, intermediate, and rational basis. The most robust and most difficult level of scrutiny to overcome is strict scrutiny. Strict scrutiny is applied by the Supreme Court whenever there is an equal protection or due process challenge to a law that protects what the Court has determined to be a "protected class" (e.g., race, alienage), as well as what the Court has determined to be fundamental rights (e.g., speech, voting rights, right to travel, right to privacy). Under strict scrutiny, a law will be upheld if it is necessary to achieve a *compelling government purpose*. So long as the law in question has been determined to have met a compelling government purpose, it has met the strict scrutiny test. Perhaps most importantly, under strict scrutiny, the government or petitioners have the burden of proof should they advocate for the removal of a constitutional right, especially those affecting protected classes, as with strict (and intermediate) scrutiny.

The second level of scrutiny is intermediate. Intermediate scrutiny requires a law to be *substantially related* to an important government purpose. Gender discrimination requires intermediate scrutiny, and once again it is the government that must demonstrate that a law passes the substantially related test.

The final level of scrutiny is the lowest, rational basis. Here, the question of the constitutionality of laws is returned to the states to be considered through the application of state police powers. That is, if a state legislature declares a law unconstitutional, it may do so by answering whether there is a *rational basis* for that action. Here, a law will be upheld if it is rationally related to a legitimate government purpose. Most important, unlike the previous two higher levels of scrutiny requiring those challenging the constitutionality of laws to meet the burden of the compelling and substantially related tests, under rational basis review it is the citizens who are affected by the laws that must argue for their retention. States justify rational basis review through the application of their state police powers. An oddly worded doctrine that has nothing to do with the way that we colloquially refer to law enforcement, police powers refer to a state's responsibility to see to it that any federal or state legislation is consistent with the promotion and maintenance of the health, safety, morals, and general welfare of the public.[44]

Let us return now to the *Dobbs* opinion.Rather than applying the intermediate standard of scrutiny to a case relating to gender, a standard that would require petitioners wishing to remove a constitutional right to demonstrate a "substantial government interest," Justice Alito applied the lowest standard of proof to justify his opinion – rational basis. In so doing, Justice Alito returned to the states the decision as to whether abortion services should be provided to its residents. The rational basis test places the power to eliminate the right squarely in states' general assemblies consistent with their respective police powers. So, rather than forcing the state to meet the higher standard of scrutiny to remove a right – intermediate – Justice Alito places the burden upon the subjects of the state (women who require abortion services) to argue for *preservation* of the right. The Court's incorrect and troubling application of rational basis over intermediate scrutiny shifts power away from constitutional protection of a woman's right to choose, including its emphasis upon there being a substantial relationship to a government purpose, returning the decision to the states' general assemblies. This has placed women in need of abortion services in states primarily controlled by Republicans in dire circumstances across the nation.[45]

It is my contention that the United States of America is confronting creeping destabilization of its criminal, legal, and voting systems from a political party, its former leader and current presidential nominee, and a Supreme Court that has demonstrated a commitment to flaunt legal precedent to nullify constitutional rights (abortion and affirmative action), and to the point of an attempted coup instigated by the former president to disrupt the peaceful transfer of power (January 6, 2021). This kind of behavior was well known to our English and American ancestors who had mostly only experienced monarchs and church-affiliated authoritarians (Pope Innocent III (1161–1216)[46] comes immediately to mind) who harshly, unfairly, and opaquely distributed justice. Their response was to establish the public trial by jury as the most essential mechanism to confront lawlessness and abuses of power.

Why does this matter? Systemic legitimacy depends upon a properly functioning legal-rational criminal legal system.[47] Jurgen Habermas provides a succinct explanation of the requirements for legal-rational authority by combining his work with that of sociologist Max Weber. Since system legitimacy (Habermas uses "legitimation") is paramount to the smooth functioning of social systems, it is worth taking a moment to extend our understanding of it. I cite here a lengthy but relevant passage from Habermas.

> Because the reproduction of class societies is based on the privileged appropriation of socially produced wealth, all such societies must resolve the problem of distributing the surplus social product inequitably and yet legitimately. They do so by means of structural force, that is, by fixing in

> a system of observed norms the asymmetrical distribution of legitimate chances to satisfy needs. The factual recognition of such norms does not, of course, rest solely on belief in their legitimacy by those affected. It is also based on fear of, and submission to, indirectly threatened sanctions, as well as simple compliance engendered by the individual's perception of his own powerlessness and the lack of alternatives open to him.[48]

In order for systems to be legitimate, they must appear to be driven by rational authority. For Weber, rational authority must meet two conditions: "(a) the normative order must be established positively; and (b) those legally associated must believe in its legality, that is, in the formally correct procedure for the creation and application of laws."[49] But is it necessary that a criminal legal system be a *moral* system in order to maintain system legitimacy? For natural law theorists, the answer is, "Yes." In order for a juridical system of laws to be accepted by the people as just and thereby legitimate, the law and its administration must equally be driven by considerations of morality.

Surely Professor Fuller, then, must be correct when he says, "some minimum adherence to legal morality is essential for the practical efficacy of law," and with regard to systemic legitimacy under circumstances of a ubiquitous normative criminal legal system, "There is no recognition [by legal positivists] that there may be a continued public acceptance of a single source of legal power and yet that power may be so ineptly or corruptly exercised that an effective legal system is not achieved,"[50] leading to a kind of system instability that Habermas called a *legitimation crisis*.[51] This is a subject that will be explored more fully when discussing governmentality, but for now, it is Professor Fuller's association of legal morality with legal positivism that exposes the ramifications of flawed, immoral, and unjust actions flowing from the Republican Party, the former president, and a United States Supreme Court that, it appears, has claimed authority over public policy.[52] The ramifications of a legitimacy crisis generated by the criminal legal system are beginning to be realized in public opinion polls, and a general sense among the majority of Americans that the Supreme Court is a *political* and not a *judicial* actor.[53]

As we commence our brief excursus into the origins of the trial by jury, especially the passion with which it was defended as a juridic technology capable of inhibiting the worst impulses of powerful prosecutors, judges, and legislators, please continue to keep in mind that our time may not in any meaningful way be different from what confronted our ancestors.

How Did We Get Here?

The political, economic, and cultural evolution from colonial America to the United States of America was generated by the historical confluence of natural law principles and English constitutionalism. As we will see, natural law principles provided the ideological framework for the adoption of positive English common law and its emphasis on rights. The Declaration of Independence (1776) appeared nearly 500 years after William of Ockham (1287–1347) first introduced the idea of subjective rights. Originating with Roman law, in the 17th century references to the inalienability of rights (what the framers referred to as "unalienable" rights) can be found in the writings of English philosophers, as well as the French Huguenots. According to Edelstein, "During the eighteenth century, it was not uncommon for philosophers, such as Francis Hutcheson, and theologians, such as Richard Fiddes, to refer to our 'unalienable rights' or 'the natural and inalienable rights of mankind'."[54] Later, we will be introduced to the physiocrats as they articulated the synthesis between natural rights, the inalienability of rights, the individualization of rights, and the liberty of contract as it manifests in the United States. Edelstein argues that until around 1750 there was little talk of subjective rights in France, but *by* 1750 French philosophers such as Voltaire, Rousseau, and Diderot were each dedicating their attention to justifications for a regime of individual rights protections. Along with the writings of John Locke (which appear to have had little influence upon late 17th- or early 18th-century French thinking), Thomas Jefferson would have at his disposal a prestigious epistemological heritage to draw from when it came to writing the American Declaration of Independence.

The second paragraph of the Declaration of Independence thunders with the pronouncement: "We hold these *truths* to be *self-evident*, that all Men are created equal, that they are *endowed by their Creator* with certain *unalienable Rights*, that among these are Life, Liberty, and the Pursuit of Happiness."[55] As we have seen, by 1776 Jefferson's pronouncement that life, liberty, and the pursuit of happiness were self-evident truths could lay claim to a long line of English and French philosophers and theologians. His argument that "Men" possessed "unalienable rights" was comfortably consistent with 17th-century French and English political theory. The "truths" to which Jefferson referred flowed from Jefferson and his founding generation's adoption of natural law principles. The first paragraph of the Declaration of Independence makes this clear:

> When in the Course of human Events, it becomes necessary for one People to dissolve the Political Bands which have connected them with another, and to assume among the *Powers of the Earth*, the separate and equal station to which the *Laws of Nature* and of *Nature's God* entitle them, a decent Respect to the Opinions of Mankind requires that they should declare the causes which impel them to the Separation.[56]

Colonial Americans were not the primary audience for the Declaration of Independence. Rather, Jefferson's document was a political manifesto meant to generate financial and military support from abroad in anticipation of war with England.[57] At bottom, the Declaration articulated the justification for severance from England and was not an expression of the virtues that would constitute the republic.

Regardless, powerful and historically ubiquitous references to "self-evident truths" and "unalienable rights" remain animating principles of the collective American imagination. It is colloquially understood to mean that once declared, the government of the United States may not take rights away from its citizens; they are unalienable.[58] But what if I also argue that while rights may not be *taken* away, they may equally not be *given* away? That is, generally speaking, rights only retain their efficacy if they are held in common. This idea commences with the Greek philosophers who, according to Fuller, "took it for granted that man as a political animal had to find the good life in a life shared with others."[59] Writing in the 13th century, Thomas Aquinas, perhaps the most influential natural law philosopher, addressed the question of why the people were required to obey the law. Assuming the laws are just, the first reason articulated by Aquinas pertained to a shared *collective consciousness* (what Emile Durkheim would later refer to as the "conscience collective") that would manifest around normative adherence to law in the service of moral action. The second point made by Aquinas emphasizes the relationship between law and the common good, where "A just law is one which is consistent with the requirements of natural law – that is, it is 'ordered to the common good'."[60] And furthermore, "Law is nothing else than an ordinance of reason for the common good, promulgated by him who has the care of the community."[61]

In his powerful defense of natural law, Professor Finnis makes the following argument with regard to the prevailing principles guiding natural law jurisprudence:

> For those [natural law] principles justify the exercise of authority in community. They require, too, that that authority be exercised, in most circumstances, according to the manner conveniently labeled the Rule of Law, and with due respect for human rights which embody the requirements of justice, and for the purpose of promoting a common good in which such respect for rights is a component.[62]

David Brooke contends that Finnis's natural law articulation of the purpose of law is a more historically contemporary aspiration that "refers to an ideal potential use of law to unlock and promote the common good of society subject to law."[63]

So, while the state through its various agents may not withdraw a right that has been awarded to all citizens of the United States (and non-citizens under the Fourteenth Amendment), the companion principle is the acknowledgment that citizens, by virtue of their being self-same as *Homo sapiens*, are also *constituted* by those rights protections; they signify our collective political, economic, and cultural DNA. Following Bailyn, and consistent with natural law jurisprudence (especially Aquinas, Kant, and Finnis), "the *rights* that constitutions existed to protect were understood in the early years of the period ... to be seen as inalienable, indefeasible rights inherent in all people by virtue of their humanity."[64]

To permit individual Americans the "right" to *give away* their rights would, in relatively short order, diminish their efficacy for the common good. If an offer of some benefit made by an agent of the state to a subject leads to the abdication of a right by that subject, the state has successfully commodified that right. The state actor has placed a "price" on a right in exchange for receiving some benefit.

To summarize, we understand that as a general rule the state may not take rights away from us. However, it is my strong contention, one that, as we have seen, is shared by a long line of natural law theorists, that because rights constitute our collective agreement regarding how we organize ourselves in a republic, *we may not abdicate our rights by willingly giving them over to the state, regardless of the offered benefit*. So perhaps at first glance, paradoxically, while subjects *possess* a right, that right does not *belong* to them. This is because a *right* is part of a complex political, economic, and cultural code that provides a community (and a nation) with shared norms and values that are prerequisites to the survival of the republic.[65] James Otis (1725–1783), a Revolution-era attorney and early defender of the Constitution and the Republic, draws a similar conclusion in reference to the slave trade. For Otis, a vocal critic of slavery, especially as it was to manifest in the Constitution, "those who every day barter away other men's liberty will soon care little for their own."[66] Reference here to "bargaining away liberties" is precisely what occurs during a plea bargain – the commodification of rights – an exchange or bargain that produces an offer (from a prosecutor) and a benefit (for the defendant).

In subsequent chapters, I will develop more thoroughly the notion, shared by both liberal economists and Marxist political economists but for significantly different reasons, that it was only under capitalism, where subjects were "free" to contract for labor as they saw fit given their interests, skills, and available work, that "moral and legal duty can reach its full development."[67] Unshackled by previous modes of production that normatively segmented labor and its opportunities for work beyond that of slave, serf, or indentured servant, under the capitalist mode of production white and most Northern black subjects were now able to freely move about seeking the work that most suited them and their needs. It was the ability of subjects to "freely" and privately contract for work that established the notions of exchange and reciprocity far beyond the economic sphere to include the legal sphere. After all, if subjects were the free-thinking, freely acting, reasonable, rational beings promised by the Enlightenment, their inherent autonomy should privilege subjective decision-making about all manner of political, economic, and cultural matters. As we will see, it is precisely this notion of *Homo economicus* (economic man) freely engaging in contractual relationships that frames prosecutors and defendants in a relationship of exchange in the context of the plea.

The commodification of rights appears as a natural outgrowth of what the Marxist political theorist, Evgeny Pashukanis (1891–1937), referred to as the Commodity Exchange Theory of Legal and Moral Duty.[68] For Pashukanis, and for liberal economists, since the foundation of American society was premised upon the capitalist mode of production where liberty of contract and exchange were paramount, that exchange-reciprocity would normatively affect legal and political institutions since "the legal subject is thus the legal counterpart of the agreement."[69]

The normativity of transactional exchange in capitalism is fully present in the transactional nature of legal exchanges. Whether the criminal legal system *ought* to reflect this normativity of exchange is, however, another question entirely. This point was firmly expressed by Justice Harlan when he was confronted with the question in the 1898 case *Thompson v. Utah*[70] – "*Should defendants be procedurally able to waive their right to a trial by jury?*" Consistent with natural law and preservation of the common good, Justice Harlan was emphatic in his objection.

In this chapter, I argue for the historical relevance of the jury trial as a continuation of common law practices that were established in England by the Magna Carta in 1215 and later the English Bill of Rights in 1689. In the American republic, the jury trial was considered so central to the creation and survival of the American republic that it is included in both the Constitution (Article III §2) and the Bill of Rights (Fifth, Sixth, and Seventh Amendments). What we find in both England and the United States (as well as each of the colonial constitutions prior to the Revolutionary War) was a clearly articulated commitment to transparency and fairness in the administration of justice. This was important for a number of reasons, the most obvious of which was that a jury of common people would determine *both law and fact* in any criminal case,[71] thereby serving as a public check on the authority of the state. The second reason that trial by jury was considered imperative was that it was considered to be the most publicly transparent way to educate citizens of the United States on the centrality and legitimacy of the rule of law. Since juries were responsible for deliberating over all manner of civil and criminal cases, merely serving on a jury would enhance one's worldview and understanding of public affairs. Moreover, Amar makes the point that judges would embrace trials as an opportunity to educate jurors, as well as the lay public, on the meaning and purpose of the law. Finally, it can be argued that serving on a jury "was in part an intermediate association designed to educate and socialize its members into virtuous thinking and conduct."[72]

Immediately, it must occur to the curious reader that I have not yet addressed perhaps the most important question relating to the founding generation's commitment to trial by jury in criminal cases: Are there rights, such as those located in Article III §2 of the Constitution, and the Fifth, Sixth, and Seventh Amendments, rights that, in the case of Article III §2 language mandate trial by jury in all criminal proceedings, that are so central to a republic that it cannot endure as a republic without them? For example, is the application of executive prosecutorial power manifest in the ability to charge, indict, prosecute, and convict of such a magnitude of importance that transparency in the application of that power is vital to the legitimacy of the criminal legal system? Asked a bit differently, is it possible for a republic to be true to its promise if the criminal legal system operated in virtual secrecy? Clearly, our English and founding-generation American ancestors were of the belief that there were rights so important that they were considered "unalienable"; the jury trial was one of those rights. It appears that for our ancestors, our republic could not flower under conditions of opaque administration of justice. Transparency in the criminal legal system was imperative.

Beginning with the Magna Carta ("The Great Charter") and ending in 1930 with the *Patton v. United States* case,[73] the trial by a jury of 12 was considered a vital and normative aspect of criminal procedure.[74] For 715 years, our English and American ancestors understood and acted legislatively (i.e., positively) to affirm the centrality of trial by jury. Most important for my purposes is that Justice Sutherland's opinion in the *Patton* case raises the specter of the "waiveability" of rights. That is, in the 81st paragraph of the *Patton* opinion, Justice Sutherland attempts to simultaneously articulate the nation's commitment to trial by jury in criminal cases while claiming that defendants have the *right* to *waive* their jury trial rights:

> Not only must the right of the accused to a trial by a constitutional jury be jealously preserved, but the maintenance of the jury as a fact-finding body in criminal cases is of such importance and has such a place in our traditions, that, before any waiver can become effective, the consent of government counsel and the sanction of the court must be had, in addition to the express and intelligent consent of the defendant.

Important, the concept of waiveability does not appear in the Constitution or the Bill of Rights. But as we saw in Chapter 1, the *Patton* opinion and the language applied by Justice Sutherland to justify the constitutionality of waiving rights will appear in the 1970 case, *Brady v. United States*.[75] It is the Brady case that constitutionalizes plea bargaining procedure.

In the following sections of this chapter, I will introduce the origins of trial by jury, along with its natural law justification. A few questions guide this inquiry. First, why was trial by jury considered so essential in England, the colonies, by both the Federalists and Anti-Federalists, and to the framers of the Constitution? Second, what are rights and why are they important? What is the difference between a right and a privilege? Are there rights so essential to the legitimate functioning of a republic that they may not be waivable? What, if any, are the arguments stemming from a commitment to personal autonomy and efficiency that provide justification for rights waivers? Do rights pertain solely to a subject, or are they held by the people in common, or both? How are they affected by the liberty of contract doctrine? Does the constitutional permission to waive the right to trial by jury through administration of a plea bargain pose a threat to our republic?

As we make our way through these questions, perhaps the reader can consider the magnitude of power constituting prosecutorial authority and whether, as it relates to plea bargains, appropriate checks on that power exist as a procedural matter. It will come as no surprise that, in my estimation appropriate checks on prosecutorial power are far too few and too weak, especially given the constraints imposed by Federal Rule of Criminal Procedure Rule 11, which prohibit judges from knowing the facts of the case under consideration, thereby having to rely solely upon the prosecutor's, and to a lesser extent the defense attorney's, intent.

A Brief History of the Jury Trial

In England, by the 14th century, the practice of a public jury of 12 reaching a unanimous decision regarding matters of *fact and law* had been initiated.[76] In 1606, The Virginia Charter "guaranteed colonists the rights of Englishmen as if they still resided in the mother country. Trial juries in Virginia had a right to decide questions of law."[77] In *Georgia v. Brailsford*,[78] Chief Justice John Jay reminded the jury of the

> good old rule, that on questions of fact, it is the province of the jury, on questions of law, it is the province of the court to decide. But it must be observed that by the same law, which recognizes the reasonable distribution of jurisdiction, you have nevertheless the right to take upon yourselves to judge of both, and to determine the law as well as the fact in controversy.[79]

As long ago as the framing of the Constitution, American legal scholars have referred to the trial by jury as the true "palladium of liberty."[80] In fact, "the popularity of the jury in eighteenth century England, where it was regarded as a check on the manipulation of the law as an instrument of royal despotism, was shared by the colonies with an added patriotic coloration."[81] For Alshuler and Deiss, "The framer's enthusiastic support for the jury stemmed in large measure from the role that juries had played in resisting English authority before the Revolution."[82] Perhaps the watershed moment in awakening colonists to the value of trial by jury was the 1735 prosecution of New York printer John Peter Zenger. According to Alschuler and Deiss, Zenger's paper, *The New York Weekly Journal*, was the first journal of political criticism in America.[83] Despite evidence of his guilt, three grand juries refused to indict Zenger. The essay describing his prosecution was reprinted and circulated as a pamphlet 14 times among the colonies. When discussing the importance of the Zenger pamphlet for the colonists, Alschuler and Deiss argue that "more than any formal law book, it became the American primer on the role and duties of the jury."[84]

Commitment to trial by jury was grounded in the application of natural law's presumption that the people – whose understanding of and inspiration by a "higher law" – would be able to inhibit the application of unjust law in civil and criminal cases. Since the Constitution was perceived to be guided by natural law, a jury acting to oppose the application of a law that it believed was unjust would be acting consistent with the Constitution. Supporters of this view perceived members of the community "as the only sure protection of the natural law standard. The defendant needed protection from the government; and the judge, a member of the establishment, could not be relied on to protect his rights. The jury's closeness to the community made it a more reliable guardian of the defendant's constitutional rights, and surer source of justice."[85] By 1850, voices critical of trial by jury pointed to their habit of acting consistent with regional prejudice and disruptive of the predictability promised by positive law.[86] It is quite possible that the growing disaffection with the jury system that manifested in the late 19th century may have contributed to the expansion of the plea bargain as a way to guarantee certainty of case disposition. Still, from our status as colonial subjects of England, to the crafting of state constitutions, and finally to the language inserted in the Constitution and the Bill of Rights, trial by jury was sacrosanct.

Following the passage of the Stamp Act in 1762, which removed the right to a jury trial placing authority within the admiralty courts, John Adams wrote: "But the most grievous innovation of all, is the alarming extension of the power of courts of admiralty. In these courts, one judge presides alone! No juries have any concern there! The law and the fact are both to be decided by the same judge."[87] In ways that should sound familiar from what was presented in Chapter 1, the removal of juries from the administration of justice to be replaced by a lone judge who determines both law and fact, today, plea bargaining places that same power in the hands of prosecutors. In fact, this was a concern raised by John Tabor Kemp, attorney general of New York, in response to the passage of the Townshend Acts of 1767. Among other things, the Townshend Acts promoted the use of summary judgments from judges in vagrancy cases. That is, consistent with the admiralty courts, for purposes of efficiency and expediency, a judge acting alone without a jury would determine both law and fact, and issue sentence. Kemp acknowledges concern that summary judgments occurring in secret may dilute the application of the public trial by jury, "that Grand Bulwark of our freedom."

> It may not be improper to presume that the whole scope of that act is of a very extraordinary nature and appears upon very little reflection to be destructive of that Grand Bulwark of our Freedom and Safety, the tryal (sic) by Jury, inasmuch as it is calculated to enable magistrates to punish the subject criminally without the judgment of their peers.

It is my contention that plea bargaining signifies a contemporary manifestation of summary judgment.

American revolutionary, Massachusetts politician, and cousin to President John Adams, Samuel Adams (1722–1803) argued that admiralty courts invited a "most violent infraction of the right of trials by jury – a right which this House [Massachusetts legislature], upon the principles of their British ancestors, hold most dear and sacred, it being the only security of the lives, liberties, and properties of his Majesty's subjects here."[88] Levy contends that by the time of the American Revolution, the right to trial by jury was the most common right included in each of the state constitutions, only equaled by religious freedom. In addition, the right to trial by jury was the first right recognized by the framers attending the 1787 Constitutional Convention in Philadelphia.[89]

In 1852, American Lysander Spooner wrote the following in his treatise on the history of trial by jury:

> For more than six-hundred years – that is, since Magna Carta, in 1215 – there has been no clearer principle of English or American Constitutional law, than that, in criminal cases, it is not only the right and duty of juries to judge what are the facts, what is the law, and what was the moral intent of the accused; *but that it is also their right, and their primary and paramount duty, to judge of the justices of the law, and to hold all laws invalid, that are, in their opinion, unjust or oppressive, and all persons guiltless in violating, or resisting the execution of, such laws.*[90]

By the end of the 19th century, however, *American juries would be limited to solely determining matters of fact, with matters of law to be dictated by a judge*.[91] The significance of this move away from common law is expressed by Spooner: "In short, if the jury have no right to judge of the justice of a law of the government, they plainly can do nothing to protect the people against the oppressions of the government; for there are no oppressions which the government may not authorize by law."[92] It was the jury's responsibility to the country to stand stalwart against the power of the state because "In this way, the people at all times, hold their liberties in their own hands, and never surrender them, even for a moment, into the hands of the government."[93] Once again Spooner's exasperated defense of the trial by jury speaks to its central role as a check on government power. Let's take one more look at his justification for the exalted status of the jury.

> Since, then, this forcible resistance to the injustices of the government is the only possible means of preserving liberty, it is indispensable to all *legal* liberty that this *resistance* should be legalized. It is perfectly self-evident that where there is no *legal* right to resist the oppression of the government, there can be no *legal* liberty. And here it is all-important to notice, that, *practically speaking*, there can be no *legal* right to resist the oppressions of the government, unless there be some *legal* tribunal, other than the government, and wholly independent of, and *above*, the government, to judge between the government and those who resist its oppressions; in other words, to judge what laws of the government are to be obeyed, and what may be resisted and held for nought (sic). The only tribunal know to our laws, for this purpose, is a jury.[94]

While seemingly a bit paranoid when read from our contemporary place in history (though, as the opening of this chapter makes clear, not necessarily so), "Amendments V–VIII were centrally concerned with the agency problem – the danger that government officials might attempt to rule in their own self-interest at the expense of their constituents' sentiments and liberty."[95] Writing in agreement with Spooner, Professor Akhil Reed Amar makes the same point, "The dominant strategy to keep agents of the central government under control was to use the populist and local institution of the jury."[96]

The right to trial by jury is mentioned once in the Constitution (Article III §2), and three times in the Bill of Rights – the Fifth Amendment right to grand jury, the Sixth Amendment right to jury trial in criminal cases, and the Seventh Amendment's right to trial in civil cases. It is the only right that appears repeated so often. The most emphatic statement of the right to trial by jury is Article III §2 where it states: "The Trial of all Crimes, except in Cases of Impeachment, *shall* be by jury."[97] The word "shall" expresses a mandate. There is no room in the Article III §2 language for "waiving" the right, nor is there the possibility that the state may proffer some benefit in exchange for the exercise of the right (what I have referred to as the commodification of the right). Addition of the word "enjoy" to the Sixth Amendment led Justice Sutherland, in his 1930 *Patton v. United States* opinion, to the ahistorical and incorrect interpretation of the Sixth Amendment as providing a more "permissive" interpretation of the right. Professor Amar contends that the Supreme Court's holding in the 1888 case, *Callan v. Wilson*, made it clear that the Sixth Amendment language changed nothing regarding the substance or magnitude of Article III. According to Amar, "In *Callan*, decided in 1888, the Court held that the undiminished words of Article III required jury trials in the District of Columbia, even though the Sixth Amendment speaks only of 'States'."[98] As we saw in Chapter 1, it is the *Patton* opinion that significantly altered the Court's historical application of the common law commitment to jury trials. So, what was the primary purpose of the Sixth Amendment if the language of Article III was clear? For Professor Amar, it was to firmly establish vicinage in response to Anti-Federalist concerns. That is, the purpose of the Sixth Amendment was to formally address the question as to *where* criminal prosecutions and jury trials would take place ("by an impartial jury of the *State and district* wherein the crime shall have been committed; the district shall have been previously ascertained by law"). The language of Article III had failed to refer to vicinage, and "many Anti-Federalists wanted an explicit guarantee that juries would be organized around local rather than statewide communities."[99] Why? Because for Anti-Federalists, it was juries, viewed as a corollary to the judiciary, that would, if necessary, serve as a check on judges who failed to appropriately apply the law. Implicit in this assumption was an Anti-Federalist commitment to common people serving to administer the government.[100]

In a similarly robust way, Tocqueville invokes natural law and universal human rights when he says that "A nation resembles a jury entrusted with the task of representing the universal society and of applying justice which is its law."[101] For Tocqueville, the jury signified popular control over the powerful forces, public and private, that might seek to manipulate the levers of power to the advantage of the few.[102] Perhaps as important, service on a jury served a broader public purpose to educate the public about the fair administration of the law to generate a just result.

> The jury, and more especially the civil jury, serves to communicate the spirit of the judges to the minds of all citizens; and this spirit, with the habits which attend it, is the soundest preparation for free institutions. It imbues all classes with a respect for the thing judged and with the notion of right ... It may be regarded as a gratuitous public school, ever open, in which every juror learns his rights.[103]

For its part, the Federalists were equally committed to trial by jury as expressed by Alexander Hamilton in Federalist LXXXIII:

> The friends and adversaries of the plan of the convention, if they agree in nothing else, concur at least in the value they set upon the trial by jury; or if there is any difference between them it consists in this: the former regard it as a valuable *safeguard to liberty*; the latter represent it as the very *palladium* of free government. For my own part, the more the operation of the institution has fallen under my observation, the more reason I have discovered for holding it in high estimation; and it would be altogether superfluous to examine to what extent it deserves to be esteemed useful or essential in a representative republic, or how much more merit it may be entitled to as a defense against the oppressions of an hereditary monarch, than as a barrier to the tyranny of popular magistrates in popular government.[104]

So, to be clear, the redundancy of substance (with the exception of vicinage) existing between Article III §2 and the Sixth Amendment was obvious to the framers and to the United States Supreme Court, that is, until 1930 when Justice Sutherland reinterpreted the Sixth Amendment in the *Patton* case.

The "Vanishing Jury"

By 1850, critics of the trial by jury were numerous and influential. Jurors from across the states were referred to as "miserable wretches," "vagabonds," "idle and dissolute persons," and as "loafers and drunkards" who frequently took bribes (especially in violent felony cases), and who were mostly illiterate.[105] What appears to be happening beginning in the middle of the 19th century was, according to Professor Langbein, a massive clash between common law supporters of the lay jury system and the professionalization of law and legal practitioners who demanded both a stronger commitment to positive law and a greater appreciation of the growing complexity of law, a complexity that would likely supersede the intellectual abilities of most jurors.[106] As the professionalization of the criminal legal system grew in importance politically, economically, and culturally, it became clear that the right of jurors to determine matters of law was unworkable as a matter of pragmatic application of positive law and the certainty of case dispositions. Jury nullification would be seriously hampered as the century came to a close because, "'Jury law' was not book law. Over the course of the nineteenth century, as American society grew more diverse and jury membership more inclusive (and as the legal issues presented to the courts grew more complicated), the belief that jurors' consciences would yield sound, shared, consistent answers to legal questions undoubtedly faded."[107] As the 19th century came to a close it was apparent that, "in a process that had become highly professionalized, it was incongruous to entrust the evaluation of the experts' arguments on technical points to uninformed laymen. The centrality and predictability of the system would suffer if decisions of law were left to the jury."[108] Alschuler and Deiss provide three reasons to explain the steady erosion of support for the jury system – the "declining faith in natural law, the greater diversity of the jury's composition, and the increasing complexity of American life."[109]

Legal historians appear to be in agreement regarding events leading to the erosion of public and professional support for the trial by jury. By the last two decades of the 19th century, a move had been made by legislators, judges, and prosecutors to evade jury trials through the introduction of plea bargains. As I have demonstrated, numerous reports documenting the plea and published at the turn of the 20th century indicate that by the end of the 19th century, state jurisdictions were pleading 90 percent of their cases (Chapter 1).

As I conclude this brief discussion of the right to trial by jury, I want to punctuate the important evidence revealed above, identifying the reasons for the erosion of support for the trial by jury as complementary to my more specific focus on the political economy of plea bargaining. As I attempt to make clear in subsequent chapters, at precisely the time when the nation was committing to the liberty of contract doctrine with its emphasis on efficiency and predictability, legal practitioners who disavowed common law's natural law approach to jury determinations of law and fact exerted their influence over an administration of justice that not only eschewed the practice but initiated a move ever closer to the reintroduction of the Star Chamber. Plea bargains are dominated by prosecutors with virtually no procedural oversight.

Natural Law and the Centrality of Rights

In this final section of Chapter 4, I want to briefly introduce natural law principles in a more formal way to properly contextualize the meaning of rights. This is important because it is my contention that Article III §2, and the Sixth Amendment providing for the right to trial by jury in all criminal cases, signify positive rights that help to ensure transparency in the administration of justice. I also find myself in agreement with our ancestors that trial by jury serves to provide a common law check on executive, legislative, and judicial authority, while serving to educate Americans on the rightful application and centrality of the rule of law in our republic.

Natural Law

Natural law has inspired the juridical organization of Western civilizations at least as far back as ancient Greece. Natural law jurisprudence is guided by the belief that "there are objective moral principles which can be discovered by reason."[110] The presumption is that there are moral truths that transcend time and culture, and it is these truths that *ought* to form the foundation of law. For Professor Finnis, the most recognized 20th-century natural law theorist, the basic forms of good are: life, knowledge, play, aesthetic experience, sociability, practical reasonableness, and religion.[111] Each of these goods can only be realized in "a community of human beings for only in communal life are there conditions for the pursuit of basic goods."[112] Seeking to avoid ancient references to the "will of God," Finnis seeks guidance from Aristotle and Aquinas. For him, "the normative conclusions of natural law are not based on the observation of human or any other nature but rather on a reflective grasp of what is self-evidently good for human beings."[113] Finnis's list of seven goods is, in his view, self-evident goods, goods that are manifested across all cultures.

What follows is a brief introduction to a few of the essential natural law philosophers, namely, Cicero, Aquinas, Locke, Blackstone, Kant, and Finnis. This is by no means presented as exhaustive of the complexity of their work, but rather is provided here solely as a way to realize through their own words the similarity of emphasis upon the categorical imperative (Kant), that just law is moral law, and that all law must be equitably shared by the common in order for human beings to attain Finnis's basic forms of a good life (see above), and for there to be criminal legal systemic legitimacy.

It was the Roman Cicero (106–43 BC), likely influenced by the Stoics, who generated the most widely recognized expression of the principles of natural law.

> True law is right reason in agreement with nature; it is of universal application, unchanging and everlasting; it summons to duty by its commands, and averts from wrongdoing by its prohibitions. And it does not lay its commands or prohibitions upon good men in vain, though neither have any effect on the wicked. It is a sin to try to alter this law, nor is it allowable to attempt to repeal any part of it, and it is impossible to abolish it entirely. We cannot be freed from its obligations by senate or people, and we need not look outside ourselves for an expounder or interpreter of it. And there will not be different laws at Rome and at Athens, or different laws now and in the future, but one eternal and unchangeable law will be valid for all nations and all times, and there will be one master and ruler, that is, God, over us all, for he is the author if this law, its promulgator, and its enforcing judge.[114]

Most relevant in this passage is Cicero's advancement of the morality of law. Since law was inspired by the Gods and comprehensible to *Homo sapiens* through the application of right reason, all unjust laws must in fact not be considered genuine law. This is because "for Cicero moral purpose was an essential feature of law."[115]

The most historically influential of the natural law philosophers is Thomas Aquinas (1225–1274). Unlike Cicero, who expressed a thesis of divine law settled once and for all, Aquinas's articulation of natural law was far more nuanced. For starters, Aquinas understood that there could be a distinction made between the divine and the human as manifested in law. For example, "Aquinas's basic arguments about the nature of law, and about the relation of law with morality, are not dependent on particular views about the sources or substantive content of that morality. If there can be a secular morality antecedent to human laws and concrete institutions, the basic principles of the natural law tradition can be considered even apart from their location within the traditions of Catholic theology."[116] Application of the Thomist expression of natural law to human law requires us to assess the *moral reasons* for adopting and applying that law. This is because "the natural law tradition has always argued that human 'positive' law derives its moral authority [and, I might add, systemic legitimacy] from its derivation from principles of (God-given) natural law."[117] From Aquinas's *Summa Theologica*, we receive the following:

> Thus, ... Law is nothing else than an ordinance of reason for the common good, promulgated by him who has the care of the community.
>
> Just as in the speculative reason, from naturally known indemonstrable principles we draw the conclusions of the various sciences, the knowledge of which is not imparted to us by nature, but acquired by the efforts of reason, so too it is that from the precepts of the natural law, as from common and indemonstrable principles, the human reason needs to proceed to the more particular determination of certain matters. These particular determinations, devised by human reason, are called laws.
>
> The force of a law depends on the extent of its justice. Now in human affairs a thing is said to be just from being right, according to the rule of reason.[118]

It was the "higher law" tradition inspired by John Locke[119] that was influential upon the framers of the Constitution. This higher law tradition, flowing as it does from Aquinas, pressed the importance of moral foundations for just law. In his statement relating to the state of nature, Locke directly references our collective responsibility to each other in preservation of the common good. Like Rousseau, Locke provided a theory of the social contract, one that would preserve personal property rights. As it pertains to our concern in this chapter – whether a subject should be free to relinquish rights – Locke's response oozes with natural law principles consistent with the promotion of moral law.

> But though this be a state of liberty, yet it is not a state of licence (sic): though man in that state have an uncontroulable (sic) liberty to dispose of his person or possessions, yet he has not liberty to destroy himself, or so much as any creature in his possession, but where some nobler use than its bare preservation calls for it. The state of nature has a law of nature to govern it, which obliges every one: and reason, which is that law, teaches all mankind, who will but consult it, that being all equal and independent, not one ought to harm another in his life, health, liberty, or possessions: for men being all the workmanship of one omnipotent, and infinitely wise maker; all the servants of one sovereign master, sent into the world by his order, and about his business; they are his property, whose workmanship they are, made to last during his, not one another's pleasure: and being furnished with like faculties, share all in one community of nature, there cannot be supposed any such subordination among us, that may authorize us to destroy one another, as if we were made for another's uses, as the inferior ranks of creatures are for our's.[120]

From Locke, we are able to discern vaguely referenced natural law principles that influenced the framers of the American Constitution, but not in the way that historians have traditionally interpreted it. Specifically, the framers were far more influenced by Locke's emphasis upon the protection of individual liberty (especially to procure and retain property) and his well-known articulation of the right to rebel against an oppressive sovereign ruler.[121] Locke writes directly about mutual obligation to adhere to natural law through the application of reason. He emphasizes that human beings have no right to extinguish their lives or hurt others since we are all products of the divine, each deserving of respect.[122] Finally, like the Greek and Roman philosophers, and Thomas Aquinas, Locke situates the administration of just law within the context of the common good. Following Edelstein, "Locke offered a way to step back from English constitutionalism and discuss the foundation and origins of all governments. In this regard, while his own account of rights was something of an obstacle, Locke helped the colonists frame their constitutional rights within a broader theory of government."[123]

In addition to an American revisionist interpretation of John Locke's *First and Second Treatises of Government*,[124] English jurist and cataloger of common law, William Blackstone (1723–1780), was familiar to and influential over the founding generation of Americans. Blackstone was committed to the argument that for law to be just, it must be moral. An immoral law was no valid law at all (this view was originally articulated by Augustine). For Blackstone, as with all advocates of natural law, "once it becomes clear that things like constitutions and statutes and regulations and court cases are but the realization of a higher law, then it is a mistake not only when statutes enacted by fallible human beings try to enforce what is not moral, but also when they fail to enforce what *is* moral."[125]

In his *Groundwork of the Metaphysics of Morals*, Immanuel Kant (1724–1804) applies a methodology that identifies three unique historical periods leading to the transition from common cognition to philosophical moral rational cognition.[126] It is in this work that Kant presents us with themes that in time would come to encompass much of the Western consideration of morality and law, especially as applied to the evolution of and support for human rights law.[127] For example, Kant argues that "every human being is an end in himself or herself, not to be used as a mere means by others; that respect for your own humanity finds its fullest expression in respect for that of others; and that morality is freedom, and evil a form of enslavement."[128] For our purposes I wish to emphasize the Kantian commitment to viewing all human beings as ends in themselves, one consistent with natural law principles, that enables states to generate laws consistent with the moral dictates of human thriving. For Kant, "a human being and generally every rational being *exists* as an end in itself, not merely as a means for the discretionary use of this or that will [a critique of utilitarianism], but must in all its actions, whether directed towards itself or also to other rational beings, always be considered at the same time as an end."[129] With regard to the duty to act consistently with the categorical imperative of universal practical reason, Kant declares that consciousness of our collective humanity is antecedent to experience; it is an innate feature of our practical reason.

> the ground of all practical legislation lies *objectively in the rule* and the form of universality, which (according to the first principle) makes it capable of being a law (or perhaps a law of nature), *subjectively*, however, *in the end*; the subject of all ends, however, is every rational being, as an end in itself ...: from this now follows the third principle of the will, as the supreme condition of its harmony with universal practical reason, the idea *of the will of every rational being as a universally legislating will.*[130]

Finally, and with due recognition that this presentation of Kant's theory is woefully simplistic but is presented here for his emphasis upon the collective duty to commit to moral law, Kant argues that a human will "universally legislating through all its maxims" is suited to the categorical imperative so long as

> "it is founded on no interest and can thus alone, among all possible imperatives, be unconditional; or better still, by converting the proposition, if there is a categorical imperative (i.e., a law for every will of a rational being), then it can only command to do everything from the maxim of

> one's will as one that could at the same time have as its object itself as universally legislating.[131]

To summarize, for Kant certain maxims generating freedom may be uncovered through practical reason. Inasmuch as these maxims are fundamental to human beings regardless of their cultural experiences, adhering to legislative initiatives seeking to promote collective well-being is a categorical imperative; a responsibility that each human being has to themselves and to each other. I present Kant's work here because he extends the depth of our understanding of natural law, human will, and duty to obey categorical imperatives given their ubiquitous constitution of the human experience. It is my contention that the trial by jury, commonly held by our English and early colonial American ancestors, appeared as a categorical imperative, a duty of every member of the commons to see to it that laws be properly administered, and that the authority to create and administer law was sufficiently balanced by common law commitments to justice. As the trial by jury was established by no specific private or public interest seeking to gain power for themselves or others like them, but rather, as a procedural check on expressions of irrational authority impeding the realization of freedom, the trial by jury appears to meet Kant's definition of a categorical imperative. Service is to rational universal legislation determined through practical reason and grounded upon a commitment to human will, duty, and mutual respect.

The final natural law theorist that I will present has already been introduced, John Finnis. Originally published in 1979, in *Natural Law & Natural Rights* Finnis articulated a contemporary vision for natural law attorneys and legal scholars. Finnis draws his inspiration from Aristotle and Aquinas, and as such has produced a more nuanced vision of natural law than the caricatures of natural law produced by positive law theorists beginning in the 18th century with Jeremy Bentham's caustic quip that natural law was "nonsense on stilts." As with Aristotle and Aquinas, Finnis contends that human beings possess an innate sense of the common good. In direct response to 20th-century positivists, Finnis argues, consistent with the position I have taken in this book thus far, that

> If one could ever rightly choose a single act which *itself* damages and *itself does* not promote some basic good, then one could rightly choose whole programmes and institutions and enterprises that themselves damage and do not promote basic aspects of human well-being, for the sake of their "net beneficial consequences."[132]

And as if referring directly to the imposition of the plea bargaining procedure,

> It only remains to note that if one thinks that one's rational responsibility to be always doing and pursuing good is satisfied by a commitment to act always for best consequences, one treats every aspect of human personality (and indeed, therefore, treats oneself) as a utensil. One holds oneself ready to do *anything* (and thus makes oneself a tool for all those willing to threaten sufficiently bad consequences if one does not cooperate with them).[133]

Plea bargaining is premised on systemic needs for efficiency and predictability, with the consequence being certainty of conviction. A subject who commits to authoritatively justified yet questionable acts that violate basic human values to promote system stability will, according to Finnis, facilitate locomotion toward the diminution of human rights. This is because justice demands a set of elements crucial to its realization. For Finnis, those elements are: 1) other-directedness, one's relations and dealings with other persons; it is "inter-subjective" or interpersonal; 2) duty of what is owed or due to another, and correspondingly of what that other person has a right to; and 3) equality, proportionality, or *equilibrium* or balance.[134] Finnis concludes his remarks by saying that, "The requirements of justice, then, are the concrete implications of the basic requirement of practical reasonableness that one is to favour and foster the common good of one's communities."[135]

This admittedly brief exploration of natural law principles is meant to provide context for the final section of this chapter, one that I have reserved for discussion until the proper context had been established. At issue in this book is the political economy of plea bargaining. My argument is that the trial by jury signifies a categorical imperative, a legal technology so important to the legitimate functioning of the criminal legal system that without it the republic has returned to the opaque administration of justice that existed prior to its emergence in the 14th century and was the reason for it. As we have seen, the framers considered the right to trial by jury so important that it is the most often presented of the rights in the Constitution and the Bill of Rights, and it was the first right to be agreed upon at the 1787 Constitutional Convention. We have also learned that the idea of unalienable or inalienable rights emerged from natural law principles, principles requiring that all law be moral and attentive to the common good. It is from the philosophical framing of natural law that the idea of rights emerges. This is the issue to which we now turn our attention.

Rights

My purpose in this final section of this chapter is to provide an overview of the evolution of subjective rights in relation to the rights held by the commons as members of civil society. There is a massive literature addressing the origin of rights in the West, especially human rights, so this presentation will only provide a brief summary. That said, it will provide us with the context necessary to consider the relevance of the right to trial by jury as articulated in the Constitution and the Bill of Rights toward the democratic preservation of the republic.

In my research into the origin of rights in the West, I have found that Dan Edelstein's[136] framing of the history of rights is both epistemologically sound and heuristically quite useful. Edelstein identifies three different "rights regimes" emerging by the 16th century – abridgement, transfer, and preservation. Briefly, abridgement theorists argued that in order for human beings to realize some sense of civil order and happiness, they *must abdicate any natural rights* (except for the right to life) to a sovereign leader. Thomas Hobbes (1588–1679), Hugo Grotius (1583–1645), and Samuel von Pufendorf (1632–1694) were abridgement theorists. Theorists advocating for the *transfer of rights* to a sovereign argued, consistent with social contract theory, that in order for freedom to flourish, subjects necessarily had to relinquish *some* of their natural rights in exchange for the preservation of political, economic, and cultural relations that would promote and protect the acquisition and retention of private property and to advance economic exchange relationships more generally. John Locke (1632–1704) and Jean-Jacques Rousseau (1712–1778) were transfer rights theorists.

The last regime identified by Edelstein is the preservation regime. *The preservation regime is the one adopted by the American framers of the Constitution.* William Blackstone (1723–1780), James Otis (1725–1783), and the French physiocrats (18th century) were preservationists.

Preservationism was primarily associated with the writings of the French physiocrats, most importantly, Francois Quesnay (1694–1774). Notably, the physiocrats identified labor as the locus of economic value, especially as it related to agricultural work and the transformation of land into usable goods. Indeed, the Greek word *physiocratie* translates to "government of nature." Physiocratic emphasis on the labor theory of value would influence English economist David Ricardo, who would later serve as the source of Karl Marx's articulation of the theory of value.

Preservation rights theorists argued for the retention of all natural rights inalienably belonging to the individual. They considered most important those rights preserving and protecting private property, religious worship, and speech, each codified in a constitution and enhanced through positive statutory law. Unlike the abridgment and transfer theories, preservationists never advocated for the abdication of their subjective rights to a sovereign, even one ostensibly guided by a social contract, but rather viewed the institutions of the state and the judiciary as necessary for the systemic protection of natural individual rights. This theoretical move enabled preservationists to retain the ideological commitment to republican government by framing it as an affirmative institution necessary for the protection of natural individual liberties. By Edelstein's account, it was the physiocrats who played the most significant role in establishing the preservationist regime, especially their most recognized theorist, Quesnay. Much like Locke, Quesnay held that natural rights, such as the right to individual property, should be constitutionally and statutorily protected. Advancing Quesnay's theoretical argument, unfettered laissez-faire pursuit of subjective interests in procuring and preserving property and other goods was embellished by the editor of the publication *Physiocratie* (1768), Nicolas Baudeau. Framed in the spirit of Quesnay's preservationist theory, Baudeau stresses, "[Y]ou will only reassure men and their moveable assets, by letting them enjoy their natural rights in total safety and complete liberty."[137] In addition to Quesnay and Baudeau, Le Mercier de La Riviere (1719–1792) and the comte de Mirabeau (1715–1789) each articulated physiocratic preservationist arguments but with greater attention to political rights as well as economic ones, especially concerning matters of poor relief. It was Turgot (1727–1781), a preservationist physiocrat, who expressed the view that "society has an obligation to assist those who cannot find employment or are too sick to work," asserting that "the poor have undeniable rights (*des droits incontestables*) on the abundance of the rich."[138] For Turgot, political, economic, and cultural institutions should be designed to enhance individual self-interest in the procurement of private property and distributive political rights. His work is preservationist in that Turgot sought the protection of private property through positive law. In that way, individuals were not required to abdicate or transfer their rights, but rather, those natural rights would now be protected by the rule of law. It is Edelstein's contention that the American Bill of Rights signifies a nod to preservationism, especially from the perspective of Anti-Federalists, to accomplish precisely what Turgot had promised. Finally, writing at the same time as Turgot, the marquis de Condorcet (1743–1794) argued for the promotion of laissez-faire economic policy as consistent with a natural rights preservationist regime. For Condorcet, it was obvious that no sovereign had the authority to strip subjects of their natural rights, nor was it necessary for any subject to prove that their rights were unalienable.[139]

While French physiocrats played a significant role in the growing preservationist narrative, American framers were most favorably influenced by English common law. As the 18th century matured, American authors combined the ideology of natural rights with the positive law Rights of Englishmen. By way of example, we may consider the Preamble to the United States Constitution, written by Gouverneur Morris, as a natural law expression of the *principles* guiding just government in a republic.[140] Those principles would supply the theoretical context for a more specific articulation of rights that appears in both the Constitution and the Bill of Rights. Consistent with the preservationist regime,

> Most American authors did believe that natural rights lay at the origin of their political freedoms, yet when it came to defining these freedoms in practice, they fell back on the 'liberties and privileges' of the English constitution and common law. They adhered, in sum, to the doctrine of natural constitutionalism, a political theory that had first emerged in England during the Civil War and had remained in favor among marginal Protestant groups such as the Quakers and Puritans.[141]

The framers of the Constitution created a hybrid theory of government that preserved the natural law principles inherited from the Greeks, Romans, English, and French, and combined it with natural constitutionalism premised upon English common law. The figure who appears central to the development of a preservationist rights regime in the United States was James Otis. Otis was a powerful defender of individual liberty and natural rights. He was a graduate of Harvard College where he studied law, and he was later elected to the Massachusetts General Court, where he would serve for most of his life. According to Edelstein, Otis delivered a speech related to the defense of Boston merchants opposing English writs of assistance. In attendance for that speech was a young John Adams. Adams, writing many years after hearing Otis's speech, was riveted. Adams stated that "Otis gave a dissertation on the rights of man in a state of nature. He asserted that every man, merely natural, was an independent sovereign, subject to no law, but the law written on his heart ... Otis asserted that these rights were inherent and inalienable ... They never could be surrendered or alienated but by idiots or madmen."[142] For Adams, Otis's speech signified the origin of the new nation: "Here began the revolution in the principles, views, opinions, and feelings of the American people."[143] But as we have seen, none of the principles identified by Otis in his speech were new. References to inalienable natural rights that were protected by a constitution had appeared in England, France, and some colonies (most notably Massachusetts) decades before. Attorney and influential Revolution-era theorist John Dickinson (1732–1808) of Pennsylvania joined Otis in his vehement assertion that no sovereign, regardless of its form, could *give* people rights. Rather, for Dickinson, the rights of Pennsylvanians "are founded on the acknowledged rights of human nature."[144] Dickinson further proclaimed that the Revolution-era writers viewed their rights as innate:

> They are not annexed to us by parchments and seals. They are created in us by the decrees of Providence, which establish the laws of our nature. They are born with us; exist with us; and cannot be taken from us by any human power without taking our lives. In short, they are founded on the immutable maxims of reason and justice.[145]

Joining Otis and Dickinson in his defense of innately possessed natural laws was Alexander Hamilton. Hamilton proclaimed that "the sacred rights of mankind are not to be rummaged from among old parchments or musty records. They are written, as with a sunbeam, in the whole volume of human nature, by the hand of divinity itself, and can never be erased or obscured by mortal power."[146]

In addition to his public political defense of natural rights, Otis was the first person in the colonies to cite William Blackstone's *Analysis of the Laws of England* (1756).[147] Blackstone's publications were widely read and generally valued across the political spectrum in the colonies. His defense of the preservation of natural rights through law makes it clear that "[T]he principle aim of society is to protect individuals in the enjoyment of those absolute rights, which were vested in them by the immutable laws of nature [...] [T]he first and primary end of human laws is to maintain and regulate these *absolute* rights of individuals."[148]

Edelstein reveals that the natural rights appearing in the Declaration of Resolves of the First Continental Congress (1774) were largely cribbed from English constitutionalism, common law, and the English Bill of Rights (1689). Most relevant for our purposes is the Continental Congress's emphatic declaration in the Fifth Resolve: "That the respective colonies are entitled to the common law of England, and more especially to the great and inestimable privilege of *being tried by their peers of the vicinage*."[149] As we have seen, trial by jury was a central focus of both English common law and the laws of civil and criminal procedure adopted in the colonies.

The physiocrats, Otis, Blackstone, Dickinson, and Hamilton signify powerful preservationist voices during the protean stage of American development. To sum up, the United States of America adopted a preservationist rights regime, one that was premised upon the synthesis of natural law with English common law. So far, so good. But what, precisely, *are* rights?

Defining Rights

To begin, we must differentiate private from public law. From the literature referenced thus far, it should be clear that the overriding concern for Enlightenment legal philosophers and theologians was essentializing private subjective rights under law. This was important because the protection of subjective rights under positive law demonstrated the utmost respect for human autonomy, especially as it manifested in the procurement and preservation of private property (Locke's primary concern). And while there is ongoing dispute over whether claims to natural law "rights" antecedent to law are oxymoronic since "rights" have no normative systemic existence without reference to law (e.g., Bentham and Kelson), the idea that human beings as human beings are constituted by pre-juridical "human rights"

(Kant) and that, under the preservationist regime, those rights must be formally acknowledged and protected under the color of law remains powerfully animating. This is because, as New York politician and slave trader, Philip Livingston (1716–1778), claimed, "Legal rights are those rights which we are entitled to by the eternal laws of right reason; they exist independent of positive law, and stand as the measure of its legitimacy."[150] As should be familiar, Livingston's reference to "right reason" conjures up references to Aristotle, Aquinas, and Kant. These more general references to natural law rights signify the framers' acknowledgment that in order for positive law to operate within a natural law framework, a clear statement of what Max Weber called an "ideal type" must be formulated and adopted. What rights, expressed at the most general level, should be adopted by the framers and the nation and that would be expressive of our innate natural law rights? The answer: the right to life, liberty, and property. Once articulated, as in the Preamble to the Constitution, the framers were free to construct positive laws that more specifically led the country toward the realization of the principled ends. It was through the adoption of a constitution, a document that would outline the limits of state power, that public law served to advance the normative interests of the common in civil society.

Consistent with private law, a "right" is a legal technology that in modern legal theory bestows a special status upon individuals, one that enables "one person to impose an obligation upon another person."[151] Importantly, the notion of "personhood" is a legal construct, one that must establish its juridical meaning in opposition to public law and the common good. As Menke makes clear, "the modern form of rights does not exist because there are autonomous subjects, but autonomous subjects exist because the modern form of rights does."[152] Reminiscent of the position I took at the opening of this chapter – while a person is *constituted by* subjective rights, those rights do not *belong* to the subject – Menke elaborates upon this point:

> Subjective rights are modes of authorization that confer normative power. In other words, subjective rights are subjective not because a subject has them, but, precisely to the contrary, because they produce the subject. For to be a subject means precisely to be an authority of capacities and opportunities, an authority of power. Subjective rights are subjective because they subjectify.[153]

While private law has as its modus operandi the equality of individuals engaged in contractual exchanges under the protection of law, public law is guided by constitutional principles addressing concerns of the common good. Here, equality among individuals is not assumed. This distinction is similar to the physiocratic emphasis upon subjective natural rights to private property gained by way of a competitive market, with recognition that economic instability, class position, and the cultural distribution of skills and opportunities will invariably produce significant hardships for many, thereby requiring an ideological and juridical commitment to ameliorating their suffering through public law.

To summarize, the United States of America adopted a synthesis of natural rights and positive law, where natural rights provided the ideological frame through which positive law would operate. While popular understanding situates John Locke as the social contract theorist of greatest influence upon the framers' adoption of a preservationist rights regime, as has been demonstrated, this view is incorrect; Locke articulated a transfer of rights regime. Rather, it was the physiocrats, William Blackstone, James Otis, and John Dickinson, among others, who would provide the foundation for preservationism in the republic. It was Otis, though, who would reframe the framers' understanding of Locke, especially his well-known expression of the right of people to overthrow an oppressive sovereign, that Americans would find most appealing in Locke's theory.

Rights signify an obligation to act. Whether we are discussing private or public law, where rights exist, they do so to provide the subject with juridical protection, protection that is horizontal in the case of private law (contractual relationships between two or more people) and vertical in the case of public law, where there is an acknowledgment that political, economic, and cultural resources are inequitably distributed, and where rights administered through a system of law should be applied to ameliorate that inequity.

***

The right to trial by a jury of 12 commences in the West in 1215 with the Magna Carta ("The Great Charter"). It is premised upon a natural and common law articulation of the sovereignty of the people to check the power of the executive, legislative, and judicial branches of government. Consistent with Kant, I contend that trial by jury, as it appears in Article III §2 of the Constitution, and the Fifth, Sixth, and Seventh Amendments, signifies a categorical imperative grounded in public law that was and remains necessary to protect the people, cloaked with natural rights, from the authoritarian whims of the powerful. Moreover, since natural rights may never be taken from a subject given their origin in human reason and mutual respect, because rights do not belong to the subject (in fact, the subject is constituted by those rights), those public rights necessary to the preservation of liberty for the common in civil society are not commodified personal goods that can be contracted away. Rather, public rights like the right to trial by jury signify an essential element for the preservation and flourishing of our republic under law.

Epilogue

In the opening pages of this chapter, I presented readers with what at the time was the current status of civil and criminal lawsuits facing former president, Donald Trump. In addition, I introduced some of the more serious concerns being raised by legal scholars pertaining to the United States Supreme Court. In this brief Epilogue, I provide an update regarding the legal status of the former president, and I emphasize what is now considered to be perhaps the most unprecedented and dangerous of United States Supreme Court opinions – *Trump v. United States*. Because *Trump v. United States* dramatically changed the legal landscape affecting whether presidents of the United States are immune from criminal prosecution, I begin there.

On July 1, 2024, the United States Supreme Court sent a thunderbolt across the legal canon when it held in *Trump v. United States* that the former president, as well as all subsequent presidents, possess either absolute or presumptive immunity from criminal prosecution for acts committed as part of their official duties. In addition, the Court held that important forms of documentary and electronic evidence (i.e., cell phone, text, email, etc.) may not be used as evidence against a president, nor may prosecutors consider criminal intent. In short, the Court has immunized the office of the president from criminal prosecution, thereby effectively establishing monarchical power. An all-too-strong executive branch was of grave concern during the 1787 Constitutional Convention, when in response to proposals for a unitary executive, Edmund Randolph of Virginia said, "The unitary executive will be the foetus of monarchy."[154]This opinion and its justification are at odds with all prior understanding of Article II powers (the Executive Branch), which until July of 2024 was guided by the prescient Alexander Hamilton's Federalist 69, in which Hamilton says

> The President of the United States would be liable to be impeached, tried, and, upon conviction of treason, bribery, or other high crimes or misdemeanors, removed from office; and would afterwards be liable to prosecution and punishment in the ordinary course of law (my emphasis).[155]

Starting on July 1, 2024, Hamilton and all prior Supreme Court opinions addressing the matter[156] were effectively erased. In the final sentence of her powerful dissent, Justice Sonja Sotomayor wrote the following: "With fear for our democracy, I dissent."[157]

The United States Supreme Court's *Trump v. United States* opinion has introduced unpredictability to the pending cases against the former president. In the federal documents case in Florida, for example, the Supreme Court's immunity decision has led to the dismissal of the entire case on July 15, 2024. Special Prosecutor, Jack Smith, has appealed the decision of the United States District Court judge, Aileen Cannon, to the 11th Circuit

Court of Appeal. At the time of this writing, on November 26, 2024, Trump faces sentencing in the hush money case, where he was found guilty on 34 charges. Two federal cases against Donald Trump remain in flux – the Florida classified documents case, and the January 6, 2021, election interference case. Finally, while the judge in the Georgia election interference case has dismissed some of the original charges, the case remains viable.

Notes

1 https://constitution.congress.gov/browse/essay/artII-S2-C2-3-5/ALDE_00013096/

2 See Special Counsel Robert S. Mueller, III, Report On The Investigation into Russian Interference in the 2016 Presidential Election. United States Department of Justice (March, 2019). See also the Final Report, Select Committee to Investigate January 6th Attack on the United States Capitol. December 22, 2022. 117th Congress Second Session. House Report 117–663. See also What is the Trump Mar-a-Lago case about and why is it significant? https://www.theguardian.com/us-news/2023/jun/08/trump-mar-a-lago-case-explainer; The Georgia Trump election investigation keeps getting bigger. https://www.vox.com/politics/2023/6/4/23748503/georgia-trump-investigation-rico.

3 The *United States of America v. Donald J. Trump*. https://apnews.com/trump-election-2020-indictment.

4 https://www.nytimes.com/2023/06/15/us/politics/trump-indictment-justice-department.html

5 Trump's Vows to Prosecute Rivals Put Rule of Law on the Ballot. New York Times. June 5, 2024: https://www.nytimes.com/2024/06/05/us/trump-retribution-justice.html

6 Ximena Bustillo and Andrea Bernstein. Former President Trump is found guilty in historic New York criminal case. NPR: https://www.npr.org/2024/05/30/nx-s1-4977352/trump-trial-verdict

7 Pertaining to Trump and his allies' attempts to steal votes through direct intervention to pressure Georgia election officials.

8 Special Counsel Jack Smith, has brought four charges directly against Trump: 1) Conspiracy to Defraud the United States, 2) Conspiracy to Obstruct an Official Proceeding, 3) Obstruction of, and Attempt to Obstruct, an Official Proceeding, and 4) Conspiracy of Rights.

9 Donald Trump has been federally indicted on 32 counts of "Willful Retention of National Defense Information," classified documents that Trump hauled with him to Florida following his loss to Biden in the 2020 presidential election. An additional 33rd charge relates to Trump's role in obstructing justice, "Conspiracy to Obstruct Justice."

10 *Trump v. United States*. See Leah Litman. Something's Rotten About the Justices Taking So Long On Trump's Immunity Case. Guest Essay, New York Times, June 19, 2024: https://www.nytimes.com/2024/06/19/opinion/supreme-court-trump-immunity.html

11 By far the most thorough presentation of each of the cases confronting Donald Trump is Melissa Murray & Andrew Weissmann's, The Trump Indictments: The Historical Charging Documents With Commentary. New York: Norton (2024).

12 See David Kaplan. The Most Dangerous Branch: Inside the Supreme Court's Assault on the Constitution. New York: Crown Press (2018); Erwin Chemerinsky. The Case Against the Supreme Court. New York: Penguin (2015).
13 Erwin Chemerinsky. The Case Against the Supreme Court. New York: Penguin Books (2014): 6.
14 The list is long; here are a few recent examples of the Court's genuflection to power: *Janus v. American Federation of State, County and Municipal Employees, Council 31.* 585 US (2018); *Sackett v. Environmental Protection Agency,* 598 US (2023); *Arizona v. Navajo Nation.* 21–1484, 599 US (2023).
15 570 US 529 (2013).
16 Preclearance applied to each of the states that had a history of voter discrimination directed at non-white voters. In 1965, when the Voting Rights Act was passed, the following states required preclearance: Alabama, Georgia, Louisiana, Mississippi, South Carolina, and Virginia. In time, additional states and counties were added to this list as necessary to enhance voter protection laws. Preclearance required those states and counties identified as having a history of violating voting rights to seek approval from the Department of Justice prior to the implementation of any new voting rights restrictions.
17 19–1257, 594 US (2021).
18 *Allen v. Milligan,* 599 US (2023).
19 The Supreme Court let stand the lower court opinion. https://www.politico.com/news/2022/06/28/supreme-court-reinstates-louisiana-house-map-amid-racial-bias-claims-00042924. It requires four justices to agree to hear a case appealed to the Supreme Court. At least four of the current justices, likely the four in dissent in the Alabama case, were willing to challenge §2 of the Voting Rights Act. Chief Justice Roberts served as the swing vote in each case.
20 600 US 2023 (*Moore v. Harper*).
21 https://www.newsweek.com/ethics-scandals-supreme-court-justice-spouses-1797768
22 *Students for Fair Admissions v. President and Fellows of Harvard College.* 20–1199. Citation pending (2023).
23 *303 Creative LLC v. Elenis.* 21–476. Citation pending (2023).
24 *Sackett v. Environmental Protection Agency.* 598 US (2023). The *Sackett* opinion follows the Court's opinion last term in *West Virginia v. Environmental Protection Agency.* 597 US (2022). Here, the Court limited the EPA's authority to regulate carbon emissions.
25 *Biden v. Nebraska.* 600 US (2023).
26 19–1392, 597 US (2022) (*Dobbs*).
27 410 US 113 (1973).
28 505 US 833 (1992).
29 It is Section 1 of the text of the Fourteenth Amendment that applies to our concerns here. Section 1 reads as follows: "All persons born or naturalized in the United States and subject to the jurisdiction thereof, are citizens of the United States and of the State wherein they reside. No state shall make or enforce any law which shall abridge the privileges or immunities of citizens of the United States; nor shall any State deprive any person of life, liberty, or property, without due process of law; nor deny to any person within its jurisdiction the equal protection of the laws."
30 The Bill of Rights contains the first ten Amendments to the Constitution.
31 Justice Clarence Thomas's concurring opinion in *Dobbs.*
32 381 US 479 (1965).
33 539 US 558 (2003).
34 576 US 644 (2015).

35 Supra 26. Justice Thomas concurring.
36 388 US 1 (1967).
37 Supra 23(Students for Fair Admissions). Application of race as a factor in college and university admissions decisions was determined to be constitutional by the United States Supreme Court beginning with *Regents of the University of California v. Bakke*. 438 US 265 (1978). The Bakke opinion was followed by *Grutter v. Bollinger*. 539 US 306 (2003); *Gratz v. Bollinger*. 539 US 244 (2003) in which the Court once again upheld the constitutionality of applying race as a consideration for college and university admissions.
38 Supra 23.
39 Kermit Roosevelt III. The Nation that Never Was: Reconstructing America's Story. Chicago, IL: University of Chicago Press (2022).
40 Id at 210.
41 Id at 160.
42 Id at 167.
43 Reference to the nine members who serve as members of the United States Supreme Court.
44 See *The Slaughter House Cases*, 83 US (16 Wall.) 36 (1863). Justice Miller delivers the opinion of the Court: "Moreover, such regulation is traditional. 'Unwholesome trades, slaughter houses, operations offensive to the senses, the deposit of powder, the application of the steam power to propel cars, the building with combustible materials, and the burial of the dead, may all,' says Chancellor Kent, 'be interdicted by law, in the midst of dense masses of population, on the general and rational principle, that every person ought so to use his property as not to injure his neighbors; and that private interests must be made subservient to the general interests of the community.' This is called the police power .... This power is, and must be from its very nature, incapable of any very exact definition or limitation. Upon it depends the scrutiny of social order, the life and health of the citizen, the comfort of an existence in a thickly populated community, the enjoyment of private and social life, and the beneficial use of property. 'It extends ... to the protection of the lives, limbs, health, comfort, and quiet of all persons, and the protection of all' property within the state, ... and persons and property are subjected to all kinds of restraints and burdens in order to secure the general comfort, health, and property of the State." Cited in Paul Brest, Sanford Levinson, Jack M. Balkin, Akhil Reed Amar, and Reva B. Siegel (eds.). Processes of Constitutional Decision Making: Cases and Materials. New York: Wolters Kluwer (2018): 360–361.
45 Human Rights Watch. Human Rights Crisis: Abortion in the United States after Dobbs. https://www.hrw.org/news/2023/04/18/human-rights-crisis-abortion-united-states-after-dobbs. See also the well-documented and current website devoted to addressing the crisis initiated following the *Dobbs* opinion: Kaiser Family Foundation. Abortion in the United States Dashboard. https://www.kff.org/womens-health-policy/dashboard/abortion-in-the-u-s-dashboard/
46 Pope Innocent III is perhaps the most ironically named of all the popes, since he was responsible for significantly enhancing the murderous Crusades. https://popehistory.com/popes/pope-innocent-iii/
47 Max Weber. Economy and Society. Guenter Roth and Claus Wittich (eds). Berkeley, CA: University of California Press (1978): 215–223. In making this argument, neither Weber nor I contend that this is our *preferred* model. Rather, with Weber, I provide a metatheoretical argument that the instruments of legal-rational power are applied in ways that promote the hegemonic *perception* of reasonableness by establishing, for example, efficiency as a normative aspect of culture.

48 Jurgen Habermas. Legitimation Crisis. Thomas McCarthy (Trans.) Boston, MA: Beacon Press (1975): 96.
49 Id at 98.
50 Lon Fuller. The Morality of Law. New Haven, CT: Yale University Press (1964): 156–157.
51 Jurgen Habermas. Legitimation Crisis. Thomas McCarthy (Trans.) Boston, MA: Beacon Press (1975).
52 Dahlia Lithwick and Mark Joseph Stern. "John Roberts Is Winning. The Rest of Us Are Losing." Slate. July 3, 2023. https://slate.com/news-and-politics/2023/07/supreme-court-john-roberts-winning-americans-losing.html
53 Jeffrey M. Jones. "Confidence in U.S. Supreme Court Sinks to Historic Low." Gallup. June 23, 2022.
54 Dan Edelstein. On the Spirit of Rights. Chicago: University of Chicago Press (2019): 17–18.
55 The Declaration of Independence. In The Constitution of the United States of America with the Declaration of Independence and the Articles of Confederation. New York: Barnes and Nobles (2005): 61 (emphasis added).
56 Id. (Declaration)(emphasis added).
57 Kermit Roosevelt III. The Nation That Never Was: Reconstructing America's Story. Chicago IL: University of Chicago Press (2022).
58 The most notable and recent rejection of the unalienability principle is the United States Supreme Court's holding in *Dobbs v. Jackson Women's Health Organization*, No. 19–1392, 597 U.S. (2022). Originally established in 1973 in the *Roe v. Wade* decision, then reaffirmed in *Planned Parenthood of Southeastern Pennsylvania v. Casey*, 91–744, 505 U.S. 833 (1992), the Supreme Court's Dobbs opinion overturned the right of women to obtain abortion services.
59 Lon Fuller. The Morality of Law. New Haven, CT: Yale University Press (1969): 13.
60 Brian Bix. Jurisprudence: Theory and Context. Durham, NC: Carolina Academic Press (2009): 70.
61 Cited in Frederick Schauer and Walter Sinnott-Armstrong. The Philosophy of Law: Classic and Contemporary Readings. New York: Harcourt Brace (1996): 13.
62 John Finnis. Natural Law and Natural Rights. London: Oxford University Press (2011): 23.
63 David Brooke. Jurisprudence. London: Routledge Q&A Press (2013): 117.
64 Bernard Bailyn. The Ideological origins of the American Revolution. Cambridge, MA: Harvard University Press (2017): 184–185.
65 See Sociologist Emile Durkheim, The Division of Labor in Society. New York: Free Press (1933); Niklas Luhmann, Law as a Social System. Klaus A. Ziegert (trans.), Fatima Kastner, Richard Nobles, David Schiff, and Rosamund Ziegert (eds). London: Oxford University Press (2004).
66 James Otis. Cited in Bernard Bailyn. The Ideological Origins of the American Revolution. Cambridge, MA: Harvard University Press (2017): 237.
67 Lon Fuller. The Morality of Law. New Haven, CT: Yale University Press (1964): 24.
68 Evgeny Pashukanis. The General Theory of Law and Marxism. https://www.marxists.org/archive/pashukanis/1924/law/
69 Lon Fuller. The Morality of Law. New Haven, CT: Yale University Press (1964): 25.
70 170 US 343 (1898).
71 The common law responsibility of juries to find both law and fact was upended in the United States in *Sparf and Hansen v. United States*. 156 US 51 (1895).

Justice Harlan delivered the opinion of the Court, in which he provided a historical assessment of the common law responsibility to judge both law and fact, ultimately deciding that it was right and proper for a judge to explain applicable law, while the jury was to determine the efficacy of facts.

72 Akhil Reed Amar. The Bill of Rights. New Haven, CT: Yale University Press (1998): 93.

73 281 US 276 (1930). The *Patton* case addressed the question as to whether a trial conducted with fewer than 12 jurors met Article III and Sixth Amendment requirements. Justice Sutherland delivered the opinion of the Court and held that: "The solution of the question depends upon the determination whether a trial by less than 12 is an irregularity or a nullity. If the latter be held, no sentence imposed may be sustained, but the contrary is true, if the former and correct conclusion be reached. In the case of misdemeanors, the Superior Court has sustained the sentences where a voluntary waiver appeared. Com. v. Beard, supra. No real justification for a different decision in the case of felonies, not capital, can be supported" (para. 79).

74 Leonard Levy contends that a grand jury of 12 was first assembled under the reign of King Henry II (1154–1189). "The Constitutions of Clarendon in 1164 provided the precedent for turning to twelve men of the countryside for a verdict on a question concerning property rights." Leonard Levy, The Palladium of Justice. Chicago: Ivan R. Dee (1999): 13.

75 397 US 742 (1970).

76 Leonard Levy. The Palladium of Justice: Origins of Trial by Jury. New York: Ivan R. Dee (2000): 73.

77 Leonard Levy. The Palladium of Justice: Origins of Trial by Jury. New York: Ivan R. Dee (2000): 3, 69.

78 3 US 1 (1794).

79 Cited in Leonard Levy, supra 76 at 103.

80 See Alexander Hamilton, Federalist Papers: LXXXIII. "The former [friends of the Constitution] regard it [trial by jury] as a valuable safeguard to liberty; the latter [those opposing the Constitution] represent it as the very palladium of free government" (464). The phrase is attributed to Blackstone's Commentaries.

81 The Yale Law Journal. The Changing Role of the Jury in the Nineteenth Century. 74, 1 (1964): 171.

82 Albert Alschuler and Andrew Deiss. A Brief History of the Criminal Jury in the United States. 61, U. of Chicago Law Review, 3 (1994): 871.

83 Id at 872.

84 Id at 874.

85 Supra 81 at 179.

86 Supra 81 at 179.

87 Cited in Leonard Levy. The Palladium of Justice: Origins of Trial by Jury. New York: Ivan R. Dee (2000): 86.

88 Supra 77 at 86

89 Supra 77 at 91

90 Lysander Spooner. Trial By Jury. Boston: John P. Jewett and Company (1852): 1.

91 *Sparf v. United States*, 156 US 51 (1895).

92 Supra 90 at 9.

93 Supra 90 at 15.

94 Supra 90 at 16–17.

95 Akhil Reed Amar. The Bill of Rights. New Haven, CT: Yale University Press (1998): 82.

96 Id at 83.

97 Emphasis added.
98 Supra 95 at 105.
99 Supra 95 at 105.
100 Supra 95 at 94.
101 Alexis de Tocqueville. Democracy in America. London: Penguin Classics (2003): 293.
102 Here, I wish to pause for a moment to acknowledge a comment from my dear friend and Yale Law School colleague, Daniel Quintanilla, who raised an important question pertaining to the conservative Tocqueville's endorsement of the jury trial. After all, wasn't Tocqueville a strong proponent of state power? It is important to keep in mind that part and parcel with the ideological construction of *Homo economicus* as a reasonable and rational individual also required a rational positive system of law formulated around a rights regime that would simultaneously empower "the people" and serve to legitimate positive law. In this way, the people have "buy-in"; they have a stake in promoting due process of law since the establishment of predictable market relations is paramount to the capitalist mode of production. By serving as system reproducers, jurors serve the dialectical purpose of both restricting employment of and solidifying collective support for due process of law. Through their service as jury members, jurors are perceived to be cogs in a system-reproducing process that, while it may at times prove unwieldy as when jurors engage in nullification (refuse to indict or convict regardless of the factual basis), the far more system-important function lies in the fulfillment of their role as jurors. Upon the rendering of each guilty verdict, the jury further embeds constitutional due process into the marrow of culture.
103 Cited in Amar, supra note 95, at 93.
104 James Madison, Alexander Hamilton, and John Jay. Federalist Number LXXXIII. London: Penguin Classics (1987): 465. Emphasis added.
105 Supra 82 at 881.
106 Cited in Supra 82 at 906 (Alschuler and Deiss).
107 Supra 82 at 916.
108 Supra 81 at 181.
109 Supra 82 at 917.
110 Michael Freeman. Lloyd's Introduction to Jurisprudence. London: Sweet and Maxwell (2014): 76.
111 John Finnis. Natural Law & Natural Rights. London: Oxford University Press (2011): 86--90.
112 Supra 110 at 77.
113 Supra 110 at 80.
114 Cited in Brian Bix. Jurisprudence. Durham, NC: Carolina Academic Press (2009): 68.
115 Frederick Schauer and Walter Sinnett-Armstrong. The Philosophy of Law: Classic and Contemporary Readings with Commentary. New York: Harcourt Brace (1996): 9.
116 Id at 11.
117 David Brooke. Jurisprudence. London: Routledge (2013): 112.
118 Supra 115 at 13.
119 John Locke. The First and Second Treatises of Government. Pantianos Classics (1689/2020).
120 Id at 78–79
121 John Locke. The First and Second Treatises of Government. Pantianos Classics (1689), CreateSpace Independent Publishing Platform (2019). See Chapter XVIII – Of Tyranny, and Chapter XIX – Of the Dissolution of Government.

122 Of course, this was not realized in the United States until the passage of the Thirteenth and Fourteenth Amendments, and even then, not until the mid-1960s with the passage of the 1964 Civil Rights Act and the 1965 Voting Rights Act. These are themes taken up in subsequent chapters.
123 Dan Edelstein. On the Spirit of Rights. Chicago: University of Chicago Press (2019): 153.
124 Id at 153.
125 Supra 115 at 10
126 Immanuel Kant. Groundwork of the Metaphysics of Morals. London: Cambridge University Press (2012).
127 See William Twining, General Jurisprudence: Understanding Law From a Global Perspective. London: Cambridge University Press (2009): 173–201.
128 Supra 126 at X.
129 Supra 126 at 40.
130 Supra 126 at 43.
131 Supra 126 at 44.
132 John Finnis. Natural Law & Natural Rights. London: Oxford University Press (2011): 121.
133 Id.
134 Id at 160–164.
135 Id at 164.
136 Dan Edelstein. On the Spirit of Rights. Chicago: University of Chicago Press (2019).
137 Id at 80.
138 Id at 82.
139 Id at 83.
140 "We the People of the United States, in Order to form a more perfect Union, establish Justice, insure domestic Tranquility, provide for the common defence, promote the general Welfare, and secure the Blessings of Liberty to ourselves and our Posterity, do ordain and establish this Constitution for the United States of America."
141 Supra 136 at 144–145.
142 Supra 136 at 154.
143 Cited in supra 136 at 154.
144 Bernard Bailyn. The Ideological Origins of the American Revolution. Cambridge, MA: Harvard University Press (2017): 187.
145 Cited in Id at 187.
146 Cited in Id at 188.
147 Supra 136 at 157.
148 Cited in supra 136 at 159.
149 Supra 136 at 167. My emphasis..
150 Supra 144 at 188.
151 Christophe Menke. Critique of Rights. London: Polity Press (2020): 7.
152 Id at 8.
153 Id at 126.
154 https://www.loc.gov/collections/continental-congress-and-constitutional-convention-from-1774-to-1789/articles-and-essays/to-form-a-more-perfect-union/edmund-randolph/
155 Alexander Hamilton in *The Federalist Papers* number 69. James Madison, Alexander Hamilton, and John Jay. *The Federalist Papers*. London: Penguin Classics (1987): 396–397.
156 The previous case precedent was *United States v. Nixon*, 418 US 683 (1974).
157 See Justice Sotomayor, Dissent, *Trump v. United States*, 603 (2024): 30.

References

Albert Alschuler and Andrew Deiss. A Brief History of the Criminal Jury in the United States. 61 *U. of Chicago Law Review*, 3 (1994)

Akhil Reed Amar. *The Bill of Rights*. New Haven, CT: Yale University Press (1998)

Bernard Bailyn. *The Ideological Origins of the American Revolution*. Cambridge, MA: Harvard University Press (2017)

Brian Bix. *Jurisprudence: Theory and Context*. Durham, NC: Carolina Academic Press (2009)

Paul Brest, Sanford Levinson, Jack M. Balkin, Akhil Reed Amar, and Reva B. Siegel (eds.). *Processes of Constitutional Decision Making: Cases and Materials*. New York: Wolters Kluwer (2018): 360–361

David Brooke. *Jurisprudence*. London: Routledge Q&A Press (2013): 117

Erwin Chemerinsky. *The Case Against the Supreme Court*. New York: Penguin (2015)

Emile Durkheim. *The Division of Labor in Society*. New York: Free Press (1933)

Dan Edelstein. *On the Spirit of Rights*. Chicago: University of Chicago Press (2019): 17–18

John Finnis. *Natural Law and Natural Rights*. London: Oxford University Press (2011): 23

Michael Freeman. *Lloyd's Introduction to Jurisprudence*. London: Sweet and Maxwell (2014): 76

Lon Fuller. *The Morality of Law*. New Haven, CT: Yale University Press (1964)

Jurgen Habermas. *Legitimation Crisis*. Thomas McCarthy (trans.). Boston, MA: Beacon Press (1975)

Jeffrey M. Jones. Confidence in U.S. Supreme Court Sinks to Historic Low. *Gallup*. June 23, 2022

Immanuel Kant. *Groundwork of the Metaphysics of Morals*. London: Cambridge University Press (2012)

David Kaplan. *The Most Dangerous Branch: Inside the Supreme Court's Assault on the Constitution*. New York: Crown Press (2018)

Leonard Levy. *The Palladium of Justice*. Chicago: Ivan R. Dee (1999)

Dahlia Lithwick and Mark Joseph Stern. John Roberts Is Winning. The Rest of Us Are Losing. *Slate*. July 3, 2023. https://slate.com/news-and-politics/2023/07/supreme-court-john-roberts-winning-americans-losing.html

John Locke. *The First and Second Treatises of Government*. Pantianos Classics (1689/2020)

Niklas Luhmann. *Law as a Social System*. Klaus A. Ziegert (trans.), Fatima Kastner, Richard Nobles, David Schiff, and Rosamund Ziegert (eds.). London: Oxford University Press (2004)

James Madison, Alexander Hamilton, and John Jay. *Federalist Number LXXXIII*. London: Penguin Classics (1987)

Christophe Menke. *Critique of Rights*. London: Polity Press (2020)

Evgeny Pashukanis. *The General Theory of Law and Marxism*. https://www.marxists.org/archive/pashukanis/1924/law/

Kermit Roosevelt III. *The Nation that Never Was: Reconstructing America's Story*. Chicago, IL: University of Chicago Press (2022)

Max Weber. *Economy and Society*. Guenter Roth and Claus Wittich (eds.). Berkeley, CA: University of California Press (1978): 215–223

Frederick Schauer and Walter Sinnott-Armstrong. *The Philosophy of Law: Classic and Contemporary Readings*. New York: Harcourt – Brace (1996): 13

Frederick Schauer and Walter Sinnett-Armstrong. *The Philosophy of Law: Classic and Contemporary Readings with Commentary*. New York: Harcourt Brace (1996)

Lysander Spooner. *Trial By Jury*. Boston: John P. Jewett and Company (1852)
Alexis de Tocqueville. *Democracy in America*. London: Penguin Classics (2003)
The Yale Law Journal. The Changing Role of the Jury in the Nineteenth Century. 74(1) *The Yale Law Journal*, 171 (1964)
William Twining. *General Jurisprudence: Understanding Law From a Global Perspective*. London: Cambridge University Press (2009)

PART II

5

LAW AND POLITICAL ECONOMY

The Liberty of Contract Doctrine

As we transition to the second part of this book political economy comes to the foreground. Understanding political economy is central to my argument that, as a legal technology implemented for the efficient administration of felony criminal cases, plea bargaining emerged as ideologically consistent with industrial capitalism in the United States. Because of the linear nature of writing books, in this chapter and the next, I will focus almost exclusively upon economics, with attention to governmentality to follow. But please keep in mind that politics and economics are intimately constitutive of each other. That is, capitalism cannot exist without the legislative and judicial branches since each, consistent with its institutional purpose, plays an integral role in the development and promotion of capitalist economic and cultural relations. To begin, I will focus on the evolution of the liberty of contract doctrine as it appears in the United States, beginning in the early 19th century. That doctrine, which contemporary economists claim is long deceased, continues to inform the collective imaginary of neoliberal economists and conservative politicians. But more importantly, it is the liberty of contract doctrine, a doctrine that frames *Homo sapiens* as *Homo economicus*, that establishes the normative ideological frame contextualizing plea bargaining. Having introduced the liberty of contract doctrine as ideologically dominant, I will next present, by way of juxtaposition, Karl Marx's theory of capitalist political, economic, and cultural relations. This is important because Marx envisioned a mode of production and distribution that was premised upon the sanctity of human work and the brevity of our time on the planet.

DOI: 10.4324/9781003385103-7

Supreme Court Opinions and the Liberty of Contract Doctrine

Contemporary scholarship regarding the liberty of contract doctrine suggests that its roots lie in early American constitutional law thought, especially the due process clauses of the Fifth and Fourteenth Amendments.[1] In particular, liberty of contract was considered to be both a substantive due process right associated with the "liberty to work" and contract for employment, as well as a republican attack on feudalist and capitalist preservation of caste and class. The result was what Du Bois referred to as "a new and tremendous dictatorship of capital."[2] For Roscoe Pound, criticism of the liberty of contract doctrine as somehow an instrumental application of elite power to the benefit of the bourgeois capitalists and the judges who provided them with juridical pathways to accrue and maintain wealth and power was only part of the story.[3] Pound interpreted liberty of contract as part of the sociological evolution of the United States as profoundly individualistic, and where its legal system adopted "mechanical" legal reasoning[4] suited to an ever more diverse and expanding population. The liberty of contract doctrine emerges as the confluence of two historical pressures – "the protection of economic liberty and property rights through substantive due process or equivalent constitutional provisions; and second, the limitation of state police powers through the enforcement of certain written and unwritten constitutional rules."[5] In particular as we will see below, was the Supreme Court's interpretation of the Fourteenth Amendment to apply to the protection of private contracts.

Two early 19th-century cases signify a juridical trend away from common law rules toward the liberty of contract – *Palmer v. Mulligan* (1805), and the *Philadelphia Cordwainers Case* of 1806.[6] By the 1820s, contract law had morphed into a legal code that would serve as a precursor to the *Lochner* era Court opinions. That is,

> The role of contract law was not to assure the equity of agreements but simply to enforce only those willed transactions that parties to a contract believed to be to their mutual advantage. The result was a major tendency toward submerging the dominant equitable theory of contract in a conception of contractual obligation based exclusively on express bargains.[7]

By 1842, the Supreme Court of Massachusetts would hold in the case of *Farwell v. Boston*, that the liberty of contract doctrine governed all relationships between an employer and a "fellow servant." The case is notable for giving rise to the "fellow-servant rule," which announced the "assumption of risk doctrine" wherein Chief Justice Shaw presented a new general rule governing employee–employer relationships: "The general rule ... is, that he who engages in the employment of another for the performance of specified duties and services, for compensation, takes upon himself the natural and ordinary risks and perils incident to the performance of such services, and in legal presumption, the compensation is adjusted accordingly."[8] Christopher Tomlins explains what becomes the nub of coded capitalism as manifested by the liberty of contract doctrine.

> From this process there emerged eventually a single paradigmatic legal form, the contract of employment, in which were expressed simultaneous juridical commitments to the liberty of the individual to sell labor to all comers and the right of the buyer of that labor to exercise disciplinary power over its disposal; that is, to continue to assert a property in the commodity – labor power – that had been bought.[9]

Holding consistent with the liberty of contract doctrine, in *Ritchie v. People*[10] the United States Supreme Court struck down an Illinois labor statute that limited the number of hours that women could work in a factory or workshop. The language used by the Court in an opinion written by Justice Magruder lays the narrative foundation for liberty of contract that would later be applied to plea bargaining in *Brady v. United States.*

> Liberty includes the right to acquire property, and that means and includes the right to make and enforce contracts … In this country the legislature has no power to prevent persons who are sui juris from making their own contracts, nor can it interfere with the freedom of contract between the workman and the employer.[11]

The United States Constitution expressly protects the individual right to contract in Article I §10, cl. 1, the "Contract Clause."[12] Early 19th century Supreme Court interpretations of the Tenth Amendment's state police powers were significantly abated when questions pertaining to liberty of contract as expressed by the Contract Clause were at the forefront.[13] Specifically, in *Fletcher v. Peck*[14] Chief Justice Marshall located vested individual rights in either natural law or in "general principles limiting all constitutional government."[15] By the late 19th century, it was clear that the Supreme Court's interpretation of the Fourteenth Amendment provided for liberty of contracts and property ownership by claiming that the Fourteenth Amendment was "economic by design."[16] Eric Foner explains that the Reconstruction Act of 1867, which ultimately led to the passage of the Fourteenth Amendment,

> reflected circumstances of its creation, especially the necessity of finding a program upon which two-thirds of Congress could agree and the Northern electorate would support, and the deeply held beliefs and prejudices that placed limits upon Congressional action. *The free labor ideology* simultaneously inspired efforts to guarantee civil and political

> equality – essential attributes of autonomous citizenship in a competitive society – and *inhibited efforts to provide an economic underpinning for blacks' new freedom.* Indeed, it suggested that once accorded equal rights, the freedmen would find their social level and assume responsibility for their own fate. (My emphasis.)[17]

In his interpretation of the Reconstruction Amendments, Rogers Smith argues that both the Thirteenth and Fourteenth Amendments "must be understood in the context of the 'free labor' ideology of the Republican Party, with its Lockean insistence 'that although the races might not be fully equal in all respects, every human being had a natural right to pursue his trade and reap the fruits of his labor'."[18] As we will see below, it was the *Slaughterhouse Cases* decided in 1873 where the United States Supreme Court makes its first attempt to test the meaning of "free labor" as a civil right.[19]

In an early test of the efficacy of the contract clause, Chief Justice Marshall held in the 1819 case of *Dartmouth College v. Woodward*, that the state of New Hampshire was not permitted to unilaterally modify a private institution's charter to place it under public control.[20] With the Judiciary Act of 1789, Congress produced the rules governing the operation of lower federal courts. Section 34 of the Judiciary Act was referred to as the Rules of Decision Act (RDA).[21] In an 1842 test of the RDA, the United States Supreme Court held in *Swift v. Tyson*,[22] that the RDA did not bind federal courts to the application of state common law. Thus, the Court in *Swift* permitted the federal court to "interpret principles of commercial law as it thought best."[23] The *Swift* case guided the federal trial courts for 96 years (1842–1938),[24] providing corporations engaging in interstate commerce with diversity jurisdiction that, in the hands of federal district courts, frequently ignored state regulatory regimes, thereby protecting corporate interests over those of the citizens of the respective states. In 1873, it was the *Slaughterhouse Cases* that severely limited the application of Tenth Amendment police powers to economic activities, especially with regard to the Tenth Amendment's §1 privileges or immunities protections. Then, in 1895, the Supreme Court addressed the constitutionality of the Tax Act of 1894. In *Pollock v. Farmers' Loan and Trust Co.*[25] the Court held that a federal income tax violated Article I §9 of the Constitution. The Court reasoned that "the Act violated the Constitution since it imposed taxes on personal income derived from real estate investments and personal property such as stocks and bonds; this was a direct taxation scheme, not apportioned properly among the states."[26]

In *Allgeyer v. Louisiana*,[27] the United States Supreme Court held that, "the general right to a contract in relation to his business is part of the liberty of the individual protected by the Fourteenth Amendment." Decided in

1897, *Allgeyer* marks the commencement of the Supreme Court's *Lochner* era cases. In *Allgeyer*, the Supreme Court held that

> The "liberty" mentioned in the [Fourteenth Amendment] means, not only the right of the citizen to be free from the mere physical restraint of his person, as by incarceration, but the term is deemed to embrace the right of the citizen to be free in the enjoyment of all his faculties; to be free to use them in all lawful ways; to live and work where he will; to earn his livelihood by any lawful calling; to pursue any livelihood or avocation, and for that purpose to enter int all contacts which may be proper, necessary and essential to his carrying out to a successful conclusion the purposes above mentioned.

The Court's *Allgeyer* opinion comports with substantive due process where the Due Process Clause "does more than protect against improper procedures that deprive people of life, liberty, or property; it also protects against the substantive infringements of life, liberty, and property quite apart from the procedures the state uses."[28] It is this specific coding of capitalism that would generate one of the nation's most odious of the anti-canon Supreme Court opinions, *Lochner v. New York*.[29] In *Lochner*, the Court upended a unanimously passed New York state statute that sought to regulate the number of hours bakers were required to work during a week. The statute stipulated that bakers were to work no more than 60 hours in a working week, and no more than ten hours per day. Employer Lochner violated the 60-hour maximum work rule. The *Lochner* opinion is notable for a few reasons. First, it was brazen judicial activism in the service of capitalist interests because it reached into legitimately authorized state law to render it unconstitutional in violation of state sovereignty and the police powers guaranteed by the Tenth Amendment.[30] Second, and more to the point I have been making here, the *Lochner* court advanced a juridical norm consistent with Kelsen that constitutionalized the liberty of contract doctrine and the fellow-servant rule, thereby establishing the semiotic construction of a legal code – the code of capitalism – with all of its attendant consequences affecting the wage labor relationship. First, the *Lochner* court proclaimed that,

> We think that there can be no fair doubt that the trade of a baker, in and of itself, is not an unhealthy one to the degree which would authorize the legislature to interfere with the right to labor, and with the right of free contract on the part of the individual, either as employer or employè ... There must be more than the mere fact of the possible existence of some small amount of unhealthiness to warrant legislative interference with liberty.[31]

In its second move, the Court enforces the legal coding of master and servant: "It seems to us that the real object and purpose were simply to regulate the hours of labor between the master and his employès ... in a private business, not dangerous in any degree to morals or in any real and substantial degree, to the health of the employès."[32]

The *Lochner* era would not be upended until the 1937 *West Coast Hotel Co. v. Parrish*[33] opinion, followed one year later by the *United States v. Carolene Products Co.* case.[34] In *West Coast Hotel*, Chief Justice Hughes wrote the majority opinion which overturned both *Lochner* and *Adkins v. Children's Hospital* (discussed below), thereby putting an end to the Court's *Lochner*-era jurisprudence with its emphasis on corporate power and the diminution of states' Tenth Amendment police powers. In his *Adkins* opinion, Chief Justice Hughes writes,

> The exploitation of a class of workers who are in an unequal position with respect to bargaining power and are thus relatively defenseless against the denial of a living wage is not only detrimental to their health and well being but casts a direct burden for their support upon the community ... The community is not bound to provide what is in effect a subsidy for unconscionable employers. The community may direct its law-making power to correct the abuse which springs from their selfish disregard of the public interest.[35]

In other words, capitalists who fail to provide a living wage and safe working conditions in order to squeeze as much profit as possible from exploited workers will not receive the benefit of public assistance as a way to ameliorate resulting social problems. Rather, the states possess sovereign police powers granted to them by the Tenth Amendment, and these police powers may be constitutionally leveled against any action that threatens the health and well-being of the citizens of the states, including interstate and intrastate commerce.

One year later, the Court followed *West Coast Hotel* with its opinion in the *Carolene Products* case. In *Carolene Products*, the Court was forced to consider whether the states and Congress possessed the right to regulate the interstate distribution of food products that were considered unhealthy for human consumption. At issue was the constitutionality of the "Filled Milk Act" passed by Congress in March 1923. Specifically, Congress sought to permit the interstate regulation of the sale of "skimmed milk filled with non-dairy fats" that would make the product *appear like* milk or cream. Writing for a nearly unanimous Court (with Justice Butler writing in concurrence, and only Justice McReynolds dissenting), Justice Harlan Fiske Stone upheld the constitutionality of the Act, arguing that Congress may indeed regulate the interstate distribution of products where it is necessary to promote the public welfare.

Following the 1905 *Lochner* opinion was what Mayer suggests was the second most important of the liberty of contract cases, *Adkins v. Children's Hospital*.[36] I cite *Adkins* because it was Justice Sutherland who rendered the opinion, and it would be Sutherland who, in 1930, would write the *Patton v. United States* opinion, and because Sutherland's opinion in *Adkins* foreshadows his affirmative expression of the unconstitutional conditions doctrine in *Frost & Frost Trucking Co. v. Railroad Commission*.[37] For Sutherland, "liberty of contract was not absolute." He states in *Adkins* that "There is, of course, no such thing as absolute freedom of contract," but within certain constraints, "freedom of contract is the general rule and restraint the exception, and the exercise of legislative authority to abridge it can be justified only by the existence of exceptional circumstances."[38] Three years after *Adkins*, Sutherland's *Frost* opinion articulates just one of those "exceptional circumstances" – the state's presentation of an offer to waive a fundamental right in order to receive some benefit, what has come to be known as the unconstitutional conditions doctrine (presented in Chapter 8).[39] As we see in *Frost*, Sutherland's bounded approach to liberty of contract clashed with his privileging of Enlightenment-inspired individual autonomy, the root of natural law, and the Declaration of Independence. In what is considered one of the clearest statements of the unconstitutional conditions doctrine, Justice Sutherland holds that,

> It would be a palpable incongruity to strike down an act of state legislation which, by words of express divestment, seeks to strip the citizen of rights guaranteed by the federal Constitution, *but to uphold an act by which the same result is accomplished under the guise of a surrender of a right in exchange for a valuable privilege which the state threatens otherwise to withhold* .... If the state may compel the surrender of one constitutional right as a condition of its favor it may, in a like manner, compel a surrender of all. It is inconceivable that guarantees embedded in the Constitution of the United States may thus be manipulated out of existence. (My emphasis.)

I have italicized the portion of Justice Sutherland's opinion that most specifically applies to plea bargaining, but the remainder of that paragraph is most relevant to the argument relating to trial by jury that appeared in the previous chapter. If the state may frame a constitutional right as a commodity held as the sole possession of the subject, that right may be negotiated away "for some valuable privilege." Once established, the practice of rendering a right a privilege becomes commonplace, and the sanctity of a right no longer exists as a categorical imperative.

The trend toward the supremacy of the individual contract over common law commitments to public welfare made its first appearance in the late 18th century. According to Horowitz, "Beginning sometime in the early 1780s and reaching a high point in the first decade of the nineteenth century, American jurists succeeded in dethroning the common law from the unchallenged place it had occupied in the jurisprudence of the revolutionary generation."[40] Tomlins contextualizes the juridical move to the liberty of contract doctrine as part of a new master/servant relationship under capitalism, whereby master is synonymous with employer, and servant with employee. In concluding his argument, Tomlins expresses what is plain on its face:

> Increasingly, [throughout the 19th century] courts justified this outcome through resort to a discourse of labor freedom and liberty of contract. As free persons owning their own capacity to labor, employees who entered into employment signified by that action their assent to be bound by the terms and conditions upon which employment had been offered – terms and conditions that, presumptively, they had been given the opportunity to negotiate.[41]

And while Tomlins is correct as his analysis applied to working-class white immigrant and domestic labor in the North, during Reconstruction in the South freed men and women found it nearly impossible to participate freely with white workers in the wage labor market. This was largely due to three factors identified by Du Bois. First and foremost, the newly emerging industrial class of merchants from the North, what Southerners referred to as "carpetbaggers," were primarily interested in profit maximization regardless of who it was that they would exploit. To that end, Northern capitalists could share with Southern planters the exploitation of both the newly freed 4 million former slaves and poor Southern whites. Ostensibly, then, laissez-faire economics should have generated resounding support for the exploitation of workers regardless of their former status as slaves. That didn't happen.

Second, recognition by poor whites that the planter class (which poor whites had optimistically identified with) was willing to make concessions to newly freed labor raised fears of competition for remedial work. Third, in what must have seemed like a devil's bargain, white Southern laborers were forced to align their allegiances with either the planter class, or with the Northern merchant carpetbaggers with whom they had just fought a Civil War, but who promised a future of industry and commensurate wages. What emerged was a deep-seated fear of an emerging political and economic bloc in the South fueled mostly by Northern investment capital, and the always-present race hatred manifested by poor white laborers.[42]

It was this contingency that the poor whites of all grades feared. It meant to them the reestablishment of that subordination under Negro labor which they had suffered during slavery. They, therefore, interposed by violence to increase the natural antagonism between Southerners of the planter class and Northerners who represented the military dictatorship [i.e., Freedmen's Bureau] as well as capital, and also to increase the fear of the Negroes that the planters might try to reenslave them.[43]

For Du Bois, despite efforts to reform the South, especially with regard to providing education, suffrage, property, and wage labor to newly freed men and women, white planters and poor white wage laborers shared one thing in common – a mutual hatred of former slaves.

> The efforts at reform, therefore, at first widely applauded, one by one began to go down before a new philosophy which represented understanding between the planters and poor whites. This again was not an easy thing for the planters to swallow, but it was accompanied by deference to their social status, by eagerness on the part of the poor whites to check the demands of the Negroes by any means, and by willingness to do the dirty work of the revolution that was coming, with its blood and crass cruelties, its bitter words, upheaval and turmoil. This was the birth and being of the Ku Klux Klan.[44]

One of the most important assessments of the successes and failures of the Freedmen's Bureau, as previously discussed, was produced by Missouri Representative and 13th United States Secretary of the Interior, Carl Schurz. Schurz was commissioned by President Andrew Johnson to travel throughout the South and report back to him about the effects of the Freedmen's Bureau on Reconstruction. Schurz's report signified a scathing assessment of the exploitation and violence directed at freed men and women. Consistent with Tomlins's emphasis upon the master/slave relationship, Schurz provides ample evidence. For example, Schurz cites W.B. Stickney, a Freedmen's Bureau agent from Louisiana, regarding the Reconstruction era attempt to re-enslave black men and women by continuing to claim them as property. Stickney relayed to Schurz the story of a white planter confronted with relinquishing hold over his former slaves: "This boy Calvin has permit to hire to whom he pleases, but I shall hold him as my property until set free by Congress." Schurz follows Stickney's quote with additional evidence documenting *the role of the police* in protecting white Southern control over black people. For Schurz,

> The spirit of the above [Stickney's quote] also made its appearance in another form, in the action of the police board of the parish of Bossier, which was an attempt to revive at once the old slave laws, and to prevent

the freedmen from obtaining employment (away) from their former masters. The gist of the enactment alluded to is contained in the paragraph directing the officers on patrol duty 'to arrest and take up all idle and vagrant persons running at large without employment and carry them before the proper authorities, to be dealt with as the law directs.[45]

In the parish of Bossier, Louisiana, the police board adopted an action directed at the control over black people. The action, which Schurz describes as a way to revive old slave laws and prevent black people from leaving their plantations for wage labor in the towns, included a paragraph that directed police officers "to arrest and take up all idle and vagrant persons running at large without employment and carry them before the proper authorities, to be dealt with as the law directs."[46] But it gets worse. An ordinance passed by the police board of the town of Opelousas, Louisiana, included language that made it impossible for freed men and women to gain employment away from their masters. At issue were Sections 3, 4, and 8 of the Ordinance.

- Section 3 of the ordinance stated that, "No negro or freedman shall be permitted to rent or keep a house within the limits of the town under any circumstances, and any one thus offending shall be ejected and compelled to find an employer or leave the town within twenty-four hours. The lessor or furnisher of the house leased or kept as above shall pay a fine of ten dollars for each offense."
- Section 4 of the ordinance stated that, "No negro or freedman shall reside within the limits of the town of Opelousas who is not in regular service of some white person or former owner."
- Section 8 of the ordinance stated that, "No freedman shall sell, barter or exchange, any articles of merchandise or traffic within the limits of Opelousas without permission in writing from his employer, or the mayor, or president of the board."[47]

Why did this matter? Because despite the ideology of "free labor," freed men and women were confronted with persistent formal and informal obstacles to actually procure work away from their former masters. In fact, Schurz makes it clear that despite the rhetoric, he "found a very few instances of original secessionists also manifesting a willingness to give the free-labor experiment a trial."[48]

The role of the police in assuring the disciplining of freed men and women is, as this book has argued, an important institutional mechanism for the retention of Southern plantation and poor white power. Law enforcement served as an instrument of capitalist exploitation by providing a steady stream of poor, illiterate, and desperate freed men and women to be pursued by Southern capitalists as cheap labor. This occurred as a way to facilitate surety and convict leasing. Surety was a system that disproportionately affected poor unemployed black people in the South. Conviction for violation of vagrancy laws arose from arrests made by police of those assumed to be idle, having no money with them on their person, looking at or speaking to a white woman, or for failing to cross the street to avoid passing white people.[49] Vagrancy laws existed in each of the states and in the District of Columbia and they accounted for thousands of arrests each year. Why were vagrancy laws so popular? Because they provided law enforcement with significant latitude in making arrests.[50] Since police had unlimited discretion to arrest people for violations of loitering or being "suspicious," vagrancy laws provided law enforcement with a mechanism to avoid violating the Fourth Amendment's probable cause requirement for arrest. In addition, "vagrancy laws made it a crime to be certain types of persons ... Where most American laws required people to *do* something criminal before they could be arrested, vagrancy laws emphatically did not."[51] From their inception, surety laws were used to accomplish many different purposes depending upon location: "to force the local poor to work or suffer for their support; to keep out poor or suspicious strangers; to suppress differences that might be dangerous; to stop crimes before they were committed; to keep racial minorities, political troublemakers, and nonconforming rebels at bay."[52] As both a tool for discipline and profit maximization, the surety system signified the confluence of state power (through creation of the criminal code and the use of local police to enforce it), juridical power (quick convictions), and economic power (police arrests feed the system with indigent arrestees who, upon conviction and unable to pay their fines, were subjected to surety where they served as free labor for local merchants and planters).

Since those violating vagrancy statutes were typically destitute, they were unable to pay their fines and were forced to remain in jail. Local manufacturers and plantation owners in need of labor power would descend upon the jails seeking out those destitute criminals, whereupon they would pay their debts and the convicts would be released from jail. Convicts were then required to work for the manufacturer or planter who paid their fines until such time as they had compensated their benefactor for their benevolence. Newly freed men and women provided the nascent manufacturing and agricultural industries with a constant supply of free labor (save for the sum needed to pay the fines), thereby enhancing profit. In *United States v. Reynolds*,[53] the Supreme Court struck down Alabama's criminal surety program. Specifically, "The Alabama Code authorized a person to appear as surety for a defendant convicted of a misdemeanor and pay his fine in exchange for the defendant's entering into an employment contract to repay surety."[54] Following Baker, "The criminal surety system was part of a larger scheme designed to provide white employers with cheap black labor."[55] In his opinion in the *Reynolds* case, Justice Day makes it plain that, as it relates to the cycle of indenture through surety, "the convict is thus kept chained to an ever-turning wheel of servitude to discharge the obligation which he has incurred to his surety." Criminal surety systems were declared unconstitutional under the Thirteenth Amendment's "involuntary servitude" provision. The *Reynolds* case presented the Court with a potentially confounding problem – If surety is a product of a contractual negotiation between the state and private industry to procure the labor power of destitute convicts, should the Court have any role to play? After all, the Constitution encourages and protects at a nearly sacred level the right to engage in the making of contracts. In his analysis of the *Reynolds* opinion and its justification, Benno Schmidt declares:

> The Court was not prepared to cast doubt on the legality of convict leasing, which was also characterized by forced servitude for private masters, often under barbarous conditions. Moreover, there could be nothing wrong with contracts whereby convicts got the money to pay fines and escape imprisonment. Finally, the state's enforcement of the obligations of such contracts by its criminal law undoubtedly increased the opportunities for convicts to make such agreements .... But looked at as a whole, with the distorting effects of racism in the system of law enforcement and the history of black forced labor given their due, the Alabama criminal-surety system stood as a major support of involuntary servitude.[56]

For his part, Justice Day draws the same conclusion in *Reynolds* as Schmidt – Alabama's criminal surety law amounted to indentured servitude in violation of the Thirteenth Amendment.

I find Schmidt's description of the contract-legitimated surety system to be similar to the justification provided by the Supreme Court for the constitutionality of plea bargaining. For example, Schmidt says that, "there could be nothing wrong with contracts whereby convicts got the money to pay fines and escape imprisonment." In other words, the state provides the legal coding (i.e., statutory criminal code) for a system of economic oppression leading to profit maximization that, but for its overtly racist qualities in the South, should comport with the liberty of contract doctrine. In a similar way, one could argue that it is the state's legal coding of plea bargaining that enables the state to offer defendants a benefit (reduced sentence) in exchange for the abdication of their Fifth and Sixth Amendment rights protections. So long as the contract is non-coercive and intelligently entered into, the procedure is constitutional.

Consistent with Goluboff's claim that vagrancy laws were directed at *who people were* and not necessarily *what they did*, Carl Schurz provides a caustic account of the deeply embedded prejudice that constitutes the South, and that will make attempts at Reconstruction difficult at best.

Sounding much like Du Bois, Schurz alerts President Johnson to the challenges confronted by Reconstruction since, "The multitude of [white] people who have no definite ideas about the circumstances under which they live and about the course they have to follow; whose intellects are weak, but whose prejudices and impulses are strong, and who are apt to be carried along by those who know how to appeal to the latter."[57] In fact, Schurz's interviews with educated Southern whites made it clear that freed men and women occupied an intractable paradox:

> If negroes walked away from the plantations, it was conclusive proof of the incorrigible instability of the negro, and the impracticability of free negro labor. If some individual negroes violated the terms of their contract, it proved unanswerably that no negro had, or ever would have, a just conception of the binding force of a contract, and that this system of free negro labor was bound to be a failure.[58]

Schurz concludes by saying that, "A belief, conviction, or prejudice, or whatever you may call it, so widely spread and apparently so deeply rooted as this, that the negro will not work without physical compulsion, is certainly calculated to have a very serious influence upon the conduct of the people entertaining it."[59] Southern planters and merchants understood that following the passage of the Reconstruction Amendments, they could no longer hold black people in bondage. But their rabid prejudice and race hatred led them to establish work environments that often resembled those under slavery. Specifically, Southern employers introduced into the new economic model what Schurz called an element of physical compulsion.

> This was done by simply adhering, as to the treatment of the laborers, as much as possible to the traditions of the old system, even where the relations between employers and laborers had been fixed by contract. The practice of corporal punishment was still continued to a great extent, although, perhaps, not in so regular a manner as it was practiced in times gone by.

Freed men and women who dared to leave their masters to pursue wage work in town "were shot or otherwise severely punished, which was calculated to produce the impression among those remaining with their masters that an attempt to escape from slavery would result in certain destruction."[60] That black people could be viewed as common workers who shared a class position similar to them was a bridge too far for most white people. From his interviews with Southerners, Schurz came to understand that from the perspective of Southern whites, slaves solely existed to produce staple crops like cotton, rice, and sugar *for whites*. In a letter sent to Schurz by the assistant commissioner of the Mississippi Freedmen's Bureau, Colonel Thomas, Thomas makes this point crystal clear:

> The whites esteem the blacks their property by natural right, and, however much they may admit that the relations of masters and slaves have been destroyed by the war and by the President's emancipation proclamation, *they still have an ingrained feeling that the blacks at large belong to the whites at large, and whenever opportunity serves, they treat the colored people just as their profit, caprice or passion may dictate.* (My emphasis.)[61]

Such was the depth of Southern white hatred and prejudice toward black people that no matter what freed men and women attempted to do as it related to exercising their newly won freedom to work at wage labor, short of returning to plantations as property to slave owners, and without the protection offered by the presence of the Freedmen's Bureau,[62] there was no possible way that they could successfully defeat the myriad obstacles put in their place. In fact, "The negro is not only not permitted to be idle [for fear of arrest for vagrancy], but he is positively prohibited from working or carrying on a business himself; he is compelled to be in the 'regular service' of a white man, and if he has no employer he is *compelled* to find one."[63] For Schurz, ordinances like those previously presented amounted to a kind of martial law since they invest "every white man with the power and authority of a police officer as against every black man [and] subjects them to the control even of those individuals who in other communities are thought hardly fit to control themselves."[64]

To summarize, the experiences of Northern white wage laborers were unique relative to their Southern counterparts due largely to the hydraulic effect of the industrial revolution on the one hand, with attempts by the planter class to return to an aristocracy of agriculture on the other. Exploitation of Northern factory labor, which was comprised of domestic white and some black workers, along with a growing influx of European poor immigrants, most especially from Ireland, experienced the "freedom to work" as akin to slavery. In his widely circulated essay, *Cannibals All! Or, Slaves Without Masters*, Virginian and advocate of slavery as an economic system, George Fitzhugh juxtaposed Southern slavery to Northern wage labor. Among his more notable insights was his argument that, "The Negro slaves of the South are the happiest, and, in some sense, the freest people in the world. The children and the aged and infirm work not at all, and yet have all the comforts and necessities of life provided for them."[65] When juxtaposed to what Fitzhugh viewed as the inhumane and exploitative working conditions that appeared with manufacturing wage labor in the North, his point could not be clearer:

> The free laborer must work or starve. He is more of a slave than the Negro because he works longer and harder for less allowance than the slave and has no holiday, because the cares of life with him begin when its labors end. He has no liberty, and not a single right.[66]

Fitzhugh makes clear that under wage labor capitalism, "Free laborers have not a thousandth part of the rights and liberties of Negro slaves. Indeed, they have not a single right or a single liberty, unless it be the right or liberty to die."[67] As it relates to his critique of Northern wage labor capitalism, it's hard to argue with Fitzhugh's logic. Northern wage laborers were subjected to severe working conditions, poor wages, and intense competition from even less well-positioned European immigrants, experiences that would lead to the eventual growth of powerful industrial labor unions. Consistent with the liberty of contract doctrine and its concomitant Supreme Court opinions, white and black wage laborers in the North were precariously left to capitalist merchants to do with as they pleased in a profit-maximizing system reproducing a feeding frenzy. In short, newly freed men and women, according to Fitzhugh, should be careful of what they wish for since their "freedom" from the institution of slavery will lead them to an even worse state of affairs under wage labor capitalism. For Fitzhugh, human bondage signified the only legitimate economic model.

> But, reader, well may you follow the slave trade. It is the only trade worth following, and slaves the only property worth owning. All other is worthless, a mere *caput mortuum* ("dead head"), except insofar as it vests the owner with the power to command the labor of others – to enslave them.

It is clear that the liberty of contract doctrine presented Northern and Southern laborers, especially newly freed slaves, with vastly different experiences. While contemporary legal scholars argue that the liberty of contract doctrine ended with the Supreme Court's opinion in *West Coast Hotel v. Parish*, the semiotic and juridical construction of the liberty of contract doctrine as coded law was by 1937 a well-established normative construct. This is important for my purposes because it is the *norm* established by the legal coding process that paves the way for the negotiation of fundamental rights protections afforded to the criminally accused. It is, in short, the jurisprudential narrative necessary to legitimize plea bargaining as a contractual negotiation where a defendant is "free" to choose between a not-guilty plea and retain constitutional trial protections, or to plead guilty and abdicate their Fifth and Sixth Amendment rights (e.g., *Brady v. United States* and its progeny).

As a superstructural institution intricately bound to dominant cultural, political, and economic interests by way of its system maintenance function, the United States Supreme Court paved the way for both the law of slavery and burgeoning capitalist wage labor.[68] As it should be clear, the Supreme Court advanced a bipolar jurisprudence that assured the maintenance of the Southern slave economy and a cultural commitment to white supremacy from the founding of the nation until the 1954 *Brown v. Board of Education*[69] decision, all the while advancing the principle of liberty of contract that would provide the foundation for the evolution of wage labor capitalism beginning in the early 19th century with the 1819 *Dartmouth College v. Woodward*[70] opinion through to the present day.

The Legal Coding of Capital

Legal and political expressions of the liberty of contract doctrine are semiotically embedded within the institutional legal coding of capitalism.[71] As a legal code, the liberty of contract doctrine establishes normative legal commitments to the preservation of rules, standards, and principles that are in accord with the ideologically powerful expression of human freedom to work for whomever, wherever, and for however long a person chooses. The political, economic, and cultural legitimacy of capitalist social relations manifested in the power of law to coerce actors toward its compliance.[72] For Norbert Elias, "legal forms correspond at all times to the structure of society."[73] Intensification of the division of labor, when coupled with magnification of social integration needs, requires increasing governmentality to facilitate the cultural validity of the law and for written agreements (i.e., a legal code). Legal positivist John Austin's command theory of law stipulates that it is the right and responsibility of the sovereign to determine what law is, to prescribe its proper application, and to assure compliance to it through the coercive power of the state.[74] The sovereign, according to Austin, refers to "a person (or determinate body of persons) who receives habitual obedience from the bulk of the population, but who does not habitually obey any other (earthly) person or institution."[75] It is the hegemonic power of the sovereign (what we would consider the state) to administer punishment to those who violate established legal codes. For Kelsen, law was synonymous with power, but his emphasis was upon the authority to coerce compliance to legal norms. For Kelsen, "Norm is the meaning of any act by which a certain behavior is commanded, permitted, or authorized."[76] Legal norms are conveyed as speech acts meant to enforce behavioral conformity. In a far less sophisticated yet more clearly articulated response to Kelsen, H.L.A. Hart makes plain that all institutional codes (of which coded capitalism is a part) generate the following normative context:

> In any large group general rules, standards and principles must be the main instrument of social control, and not particular directions given to

> each individual separately. If it were not possible to communicate general standards of conduct, which multitudes of individuals could understand, without further direction, as requiring from them certain conduct when occasion arose, nothing that we now recognize as law could exist.[77]

Rhetorical construction of an objective sovereign authority invests the sovereign with the power to *establish* rules, standards, and principles; to *determine* the meaning of those rules, standards, and principles; and the *power to coerce* adherence to them. It is this semiotic function that signifies the linguistic construction of the legal code.

Goodrich identifies two prevalent constructs used by legal theorists to understand legal coding – correlational and institutional.[78] For my purposes, I will focus exclusively on his assessment of institutional legal coding. Specifically,

> The institutional code ... is canonically defined as a system of rules or grammar of norms which, while it may include correlations, is differentiated by virtue firstly of the inferential or functional status of the rules, which inferences or functions produce the consistency or coherence of the system as code ... [It] is a set of social conventions governing and instructing behaviour, issuing imperatives or offering generalised instructions as to how to act... Obedience to the rules of an institutional code indicates a decision to appear faithful to the institution, an act of acceptance whose significance resides both in the general justificatory grounding of the institution and in the more specific interpretation of its rules in the context of their openness, their motivation.[79]

Coded capitalism is a semiotic form of institutional legal coding. The origin of modern capitalism's complex codes guiding global and domestic economic activity can be identified in the mid to late 19th century. This is because trade and commerce became far more expansive and the relationships between economic actors far more complex. Moving from local, small-scale manufacturing and agricultural production and distribution required the adoption of new legal norms that acknowledged increasingly centralized hierarchical power, as well as increasing layers of segmented labor.[80] Under these circumstances, argues Pistor, "a different mode of social ordering becomes necessary, one that is capable of upholding stronger claims even against strangers. States and state law are examples of such institutions, and they have been critical for the rise of capitalism."[81] Economic interactions are facilitated by law, which serves as a "social ordering technology"[82] necessary to protect the interests of actors engaged in trade with strangers by way of the coercive power of the state to punish violations of it. Evidence of the important role played by the state as agents of coded capital can be found beginning in Holland, followed by England, with historical precedent appearing in Genoa, Venice, Spain, and Portugal where "the primitive accumulation of capital that was the basis for manufacturing had been accomplished through the agencies of a 'colonial system, public debts, heavy taxes, protection, commercial wars, etc.' – all the attributes of state structures."[83]

Emerging in the 19th century, and most especially during the Gilded Age, capitalists engaged lawmakers (including the courts) to generate a legal code that would advantage their interests. Legitimating a hegemonic legal code is necessary for the centralization and accumulation of wealth because the

> code confers attributes that greatly enhance the prospects of some assets and their respective owners to amass wealth, relative to others ... Choosing the assets and grafting onto them the legal attributes of priority, durability, universality, and convertibility is tantamount to controlling the levels for the distribution of wealth in society.[84]

The advancement and centralization of economic power primarily in the North required effective governmentality to establish the necessary rules and legal norms that would accompany accumulation and to provide the coercive force necessary to assure allegiance to them. In fact, it was "the rising power of organized wealth and capitalist industry in the North" that most directly threatened to upset political economic power emerging in the West and sputtering in the South where "[M]onopoly profits from investments were increasing, and destined to increase, and their increase depended upon a high protective tariff, the validity of the public debt, and the control of the national banks and currency."[85] Neither the slave trade (which directly benefited Northern capital), nor newly freed men and women, presented the North with the kinds of challenges that would affect the South as Northern industry was seeking to expand in the South where it would find 4 million newly freed wage laborers from which to enhance industrial production, distribution, and ultimately profit. Northern capitalists were far from supportive of the Freedmen's Bureau, for example, since it signified direct government intervention into the labor market, thereby violating the laissez-faire ideology that constituted the liberty of contract doctrine. So while in the North, coded capitalism was directed at promoting suffrage and the "freedom to work" for working-class white men, including immigrant labor largely emigrating from Europe, in the South, coded capitalism facilitated the increasing oppression of freed men and women. For freed men and women, the end of slavery brought about by the Union Civil War victory, and the passage of the Thirteenth, Fourteenth, and Fifteenth Amendments (the Reconstruction Amendments), paradoxically landed them in a far more precarious place than they had occupied under slavery. For as Du Bois emphasizes, "A legal status of freedom without civil rights would mean almost nothing. The answer of the South to a proposal of civil rights was the Black Codes, which established a new status of slavery with a modified slave trade."[86] Growing organized labor dissatisfaction with wages and working conditions in the North was perceived by Northern workers as part of a "growing dictatorship of wealth and corporate control. It made little difference what laws were made as long as their interpretation by the courts and administration was dictated by capital."[87] What organized labor understood was that real power lies in the ability possessed by politicians, lawyers, and the Supreme Court to code the interests of capital into law. However, the political and economic interests that coalesced to promote specific policies were liquid; it was constituted and reconstituted in forms that were representative of interests that emerged and dissolved over time depending upon geopolitical historical factors (e.g., growing Northern finance, technology, manufacturing, and distribution as compared with Southern attempts to maintain plantation aristocracy and some form of slavery). These interests form what is called a power bloc. I will spend more time developing the relevance of the power bloc to our work in Chapter 7. For now, it is important to understand that while historians can identify historically relevant power blocs manifesting during the late 19th century, those power blocs emerged premised upon contingent political, economic, and cultural conditions. For example, in the South, it was planters, carpetbaggers, scalawags, poor whites, and freed men and women who competed for economic power.

Pistor articulates a view held by both Foucault and Jessop regarding the contingent (anti-essentialist) interaction between state and legal actors who signify a power bloc. Specifically, Pistor states that, "States and state law are central to the coding of capital ... Capital and capitalism would not exist without the coercive power of the states."[88] But, and this is her argument for contingency, "[S]tates often do not, in fact they need not, control the legal coding process itself."[89] It is at this point where Pistor nudges up against Jessop's emphasis on state strategic selection as she contends that while state actors need not and do not directly intervene on behalf of capitalist interests, state actors do "provide the legal tools that lawyers use; and they offer their law enforcement apparatus to enforce the capital that lawyers have crafted."[90] Reconstruction-era capitalism signified a free-for-all attempt among the industrial, extraction, farming, and finance sectors of the economy at assuming total control over land and resources, including labor.

> An almost unprecedented scramble for this new power, new wealth and new income ensued. It broke down old standards of wealth distribution, old standards of thrift and honesty. It led to the anarchy of thieves, grafters, and highwaymen. It threatened the orderly processes of production as well as government and morals. ... An empire of rich land, larger than France, Belgium, and Holland together, had been snatched from the

> hands of prospective peasant farmers and given to investors and land speculators. All of the national treasure of coal, oil, copper, gold and iron had been given away for a song to be made the monopolized basis of private fortunes *with perpetual power to tax labor for the right to live and work*. (My emphasis.)[91]

In a similar vein, Thomas Piketty contends that "Inequality is neither economic nor technological; it is ideological and political."[92] What Piketty means is that the roles, rules, and substance of capitalism are artifacts of ideological adherence to temporal and spatial commitments to questions of justice and fairness. Specifically,

> the market and competition, profits and wages, capital and debt, skilled and unskilled workers, natives and aliens, tax havens and competitiveness – none of these things exist as such. All are social and historical constructs, which depend entirely on the legal, fiscal, educational, and political systems that people choose to adopt and the conceptual definitions they choose to work with.[93]

Piketty is acknowledging the historical contingency constituting the legal coding of capital, especially Foucault's emphasis upon law as an *instrument* of power ("that is neither the truth of power, nor its alibi"). His argument, like Pistor's (and Foucault developed in Chapter 7), insists upon the historical autonomy of actors and institutions. The importance of this framing of political, economic, and cultural arrangements is historically analogous to a semi-permeable membrane that both restricts and provides cleavages that enable the manifestation of new ideas about ways of organizing ourselves. For, as Piketty rightly observes, "At every level of development, economic, social, and political systems can be structured in many different ways; property relations can be organized differently; different fiscal and educational regimes are possible; problems of public and private debt can be handled differently."[94] The legal coding of capital that emerges in the United States in the early 19th century originates within an ideological context that Piketty calls "slave society," which he equates with a historical period of extreme inequality premised upon the "quasi-sacrilization of private property in the nineteenth century."[95] The American ideological commitment to the system of slavery grew increasingly profitable and remained relatively stable from 1800 to 1860. Restrictions in cotton production in the French colony of Saint-Domingue in 1790 stimulated interest in the Southern United States cotton production market. According to Piketty, from 1800 to 1860 the number of slaves increased by a factor of four, and cotton output by ten.[96] The recursive relationship between British textile manufacturing and American cotton production was so extensive that just prior to the commencement of the Civil War, Britain was purchasing 75 percent of its cotton from the United States.[97] Why does this matter? Because it was this political, economic, and cultural nexus, contextualized by the ideology of slavery and aided by coded capital, that combined to lead to the commencement of the Industrial Revolution. The sustained growth of the Southern plantation economy, however, would by 1860 begin to confront a juvenescent wage labor economy emerging in the manufacturing sectors of the North. Northern economic power, while more diversified than in the South, parasitically fed upon Southern slavery through a system of bank loans made to Southern plantation owners seeking funds to purchase new slaves. In fact, not only did the commodification of agriculture and technology create new financial instruments, but as Beckert and Rockman establish, "[T]he story of plantation finance ... [added] a second layer of commodities – enslaved human beings – to the nation's financial history."[98] Loans were made to plantation owners with slaves used as collateral. Those funds would then be used to purchase additional land and slaves.[99] So profitable was the cotton production trade that during the late 1830s the most powerful banks in the United States – Barings, Browns, and Rothschilds – each made significant loans to Southern plantations. Beckert and Rockman argue that the practice of implementing lending instruments supporting cotton production enabled it to facilitate trade with Great Britain, France, and Germany.[100] When it came to slavery, there appeared to be few unstained regions of the country. The slave trade grew so profitable that in 1860, "the market value of slaves exceeded 250 percent of the annual income of the Southern states and came close to 100 percent of the annual income of all the states."[101] Moreover, when compared with wage laborers in the North, "the market price of a slave was generally about ten to twelve years of an equivalent free worker's wages."[102] Such was the political, economic, and cultural context of the Antebellum South, which recoiled when confronted with President Lincoln's Emancipation Proclamation, Reconstruction, the Reconstruction Amendments, and the Northern-inspired wage labor movement.

As a participant in the making of contractual relationships, each individual was embodied as an agent of their own circumstance and choosing. As a linguistic and juridical expression of human freedom, liberty of contract possessed, as its highest virtue, its dialectical opposition to prior modes of production under slavery, feudalism, and indentured servitude. Moreover, in the United States, the liberty of contract doctrine was intricately bound up with the manifestation of liberal economic and political theory comprising a constitutional republic wherein normative legal coding provided for the supremacy of contract and protection of private property. The mythological American origin story presents individualism, private rights, civil society, free labor, and a free economy as constitutive of American exceptionalism, a "natural" outgrowth of a people unfettered by the intrusion of an oppressive state.[103]

Law's hegemonic function legitimates state power and authority,[104] especially United States Supreme Court opinions.[105] By doing so, it generates a sense of normativity (what ought to happen) with regard to the principles articulated by statutes and case law. This sense of normativity leaves the purpose behind plea bargaining open to obfuscation. How? By locating the privilege to plea bargain within the language of *Homo economicus* – free choice, i.e., the right to engage in contractual negotiations over one's punishment.[106] This superficially "free" choice is couched in the economic language of liberty of contract and the mandate under a capitalist mode of production for each member of society to negotiate the terms of their own working relationship. In previous work on this subject,[107] I have provided the following assessment of *Homo economicus*.

> Homo economicus – economic man – of classical economic theory is said to possess the following characteristics: "(1) maximizing (optimizing) behavior; (2) the cognitive ability to exercise rational choice; (3) individualistic behavior and independent taste preferences." A less charitable description of homo economicus might frame him as being "cold and calculating, worries only about himself, and pursues whatever course brings him the greatest material advantage." Homo economicus is a single-minded, wealth-maximizing automaton, who does not take into account "morality, ethics, or other people." Important for our purposes, the adoption of the ideological rationalization of human beings as homo economicus leads to confronting juridical problems through the application of cost-benefit analysis, where solutions are framed as incentives and disincentives. The framing of *homme juridique* as homo economicus provides the jurisprudential legitimization for plea bargaining.[108]

In some ways, it is true that the ability to negotiate the conditions of one's own labor and compensation required a larger political and ideological commitment to liberty as expressed through republican government. The two, it seems, historically went hand in hand, especially in the United States. What is not discussed in the context of plea bargaining is the extent to which capitalists and politicians employed law in the service of their own profit-maximizing needs, social control, and expressions of cultural superiority.[109] For W.E.B. Du Bois, the onset of industrial capitalism meant the oppression of all workers regardless of race/ethnicity.

> The new industry had a vision not of work but of wealth; not of planned accomplishment, but of power. It became the most conscienceless, unmoral system of industry which the world has experienced. It went

with ruthless indifference towards waste, death, ugliness and disaster, and yet reared the most stupendous machine for the efficient organization of work which the world has ever seen.[110]

American ideology mystifies the power of the state to regulate private and public relations by "downplay[ing] the more historical and 'artificial' role of collective decision-making, public law, government, and regulation in American political-economic development."[111] Counter to mythological rhetorical expressions of laissez-faire capitalism, for example, 19th-century governmentality was so pervasive, argues Shaw, that "the one common and striking characteristic of this huge collection of new [19th century] statutes is its utter disregard of the laissez-faire principle."[112] The state has at its command the power to create the legal tools that lawyers apply to political and economic regulation and the power necessary to coerce adherence to those regulations. The indeterminate and contested relationship between system reproduction and law must be revealed through historically situated statutory and case law research. Consider the role played by the United States Supreme Court, functioning as a system-reproducing steering mechanism to perpetuate the capitalist mode of production by reference to the liberty of contract doctrine.

While the liberty of contract doctrine was at least initially developed and implemented in the nascent industrial economy of the North, from its founding as a nation the United States coded slavery and subsequent white supremacy into law governing freed men and women in the South. As we have learned, the liberty of contract doctrine manifested in the South during Reconstruction, especially as it related to the abolition of plantation paternalism. According to the doctrine, freed men and women would now be viewed as similarly situated to wage labor workers in the North insofar as their status related to the application of the fellow-servant rule, assumption of risk doctrine, and freedom to contract for work. But as was revealed in the previous section of this chapter, in addition to their new status as wage laborers, freed men and women would confront the vulgarity and indignity of white supremacy as coded into the law of Southern capitalism. It is in this way that the Southern power bloc comprising producers of cotton, food, turpentine, coal, tobacco, textiles, and lumber engineered a system of political, economic, and cultural oppression that relied upon the semiotic construction of a legal code consistent with capitalism's slavery – Jim Crow laws.

In dialectical opposition to the liberty of contract doctrine, we find Marxist economic theory. In the section to follow, I will present a brief overview of Marx's theory of value since it presents a theory of human thriving at odds with the evolution of liberal economics and with natural law's physiocratic emphasis upon individual autonomy. As we will see, this is important because Marx was able to articulate a theory of the economy and the state that exposed the legal coding of capital as an oppressive move that would have dramatic effects well beyond the economic sphere. Moreover, and in keeping with the political economy theme of this book, Marx's theory exposes the intersection of the capitalist mode of production with the need to discipline wage labor to the dictates of profit maximization. This section will provide the context for the substantive deconstruction of contract law as applied to the plea, where beginning during Reconstruction, the plea served as an efficient legal technology for promoting social control over white and black wage laborers in both the North and the South.

Marx's Theory of Value and the Coding of Capital

For the purposes of this section, I will provide a summary assessment of Marx's theory of value largely as interpreted by Martin Hägglund.[113] To be clear, I will not provide a discussion of the interstices of Marx's economic theory per se, as that would take me too far afield of my purpose. Rather, by referencing value theory I have a far simpler goal in mind – acknowledging his urgent defense of the innate spirituality of temporally bounded human life. This, it seems to me, is the philosophical thread animating the core of Marx's work. Following the exposition of the theoretical aspects of Marx's value theory, I apply that theory to the confluence of interlocking capitalist interests[114] with United States Supreme Court jurisprudence as each symbiotically emerges as a power bloc essential to enhancing the hegemonic power of capitalist social relations. Here I will rely in part upon the cogent insights recently offered by Katharina Pistor and her exposition of legally coded capital.[115] In addition to Pistor's work, much of the scholarship diagnosing the capitalist–governmentality–law nexus emerged during the early 20th century as part of a progressive and Legal Realist critique of the institutional role played by the United States Supreme Court as a superstructural institution instrumental in the hegemonic development of the capitalist mode of production, as well as capitalist social relations.

Memento Mori

Approaching life by prioritizing impending death speaks to the urgent spiritual aspect of Marx's emphasis upon "species-being." The concept first appears in the *Economic and Philosophic Manuscripts* of 1844.[116] And while it was not specifically revived in subsequent publications, I contend, with Hägglund, that it signifies a fundamental aspect of what remained of Marx's economic and political work. According to Wartenburg, "Marx makes two distinctive moves in his use of the concept of specific human character or being. First, Marx generalizes 'thought' to 'free conscious activity' as the species characteristic of human beings. Second, he uses this theory as a standard for a radical critique of bourgeois society."[117] Furthermore, the German word that Marx deploys is *Gattungswesen*. This concept has a complex meaning, one that includes not only a very clear reference to mortality (*memento mori*), but also the more familiar sense of *Homo sapiens* as "total" or "genus." A more properly interpreted definition of *Gattungswesen* would therefore be: "generic-being," or "genus-being." For two reasons, this is an important distinction. First, reference to "genus" as opposed to "species" distinguishes Marx's concept from the prevalent 19th-century socio-biology associated with Herbert Spencer.[118] Relatedly, Marx's primary emphasis appears to have been on the latter concept "being," in that a "being" is "a type of thing that can only exist in social or communal situations with others of its type."[119] By constructing *Gattungswesen* in this way, Marx dialectically opposes his analysis to contemporary 19th-century bourgeois atavistic conceptualizations of *Homo economicus*. Finally, Marx's exposition of *Gattungswesen* emphasizes the concept of "essence," the foundational principle constituting his analysis of capitalist alienation. Again, with reference to Wartenburg, "only in virtue of this species character can the human being be seen as the distinctive type of creature which it is."[120] And that the defining feature of Marx's articulation of "species-essence" is that "the distinctively human activity is not thought per se, but rather 'free conscious activity,' that is, labor in accordance with one's own conscious deliberation."[121] Regardless of whether we adopt a more nuanced definition of *Gattungswesen*, one that would later find expression in the work of Habermas, species-being as essence constitutes Marx's conceptualization of the uniqueness of *Homo sapiens* as a collective being capable of conscious deliberation and activity in accordance with its own agency. Recognition of the agentic power of *Homo sapiens* when confronted with oppressive capitalist social relations is what enervates much of the appeal of a Marxist theory of value. Specifically, for Marx, to be fully constituted as essence, human beings must be emancipated from oppressive external conditions imposed upon them so that they are not only free to labor, but that they are free to labor the way that they wish to. Emancipated from coercive political and economic conditions, consciously agentic human beings "would be able to work on the basis of our commitments rather than due to coercion."[122] Actual free labor (*wirklich freie Arbeten*), labor that we direct for reasons intrinsic to ourselves, is the foundation of species-essence for "who we are is inseparable from what we do."[123]

Hägglund commences his analysis of Marxist value theory by contending that all economic systems (slavery, feudal, capitalist, socialist) are premised upon a relationship with time. But unlike Marx, who barely concerns himself with matters of spirituality, Hägglund sees in Marx's work (especially in his writing prior to the *Grundrisse*), a deeply situated sense of spirituality expressed as "actual free labor" that is premised upon the inevitability of death. Recognition of human frailty and inexorable deterioration is what compelled Marx's work and why it can be read as an urgent and always passionate critique of oppressive political and economic relations. In short, our time on Earth is finite. All human beings should be provided with opportunities to enhance their essence, their species-essence, in the absence of coercion. This is because all human life is valuable unto itself without reference to others.

Marx clearly wasn't the first political philosopher to emphasize the realization of human essence as a fundamental principle of rational beings. Isaiah Berlin establishes that from Erasmus to the mid-20th century, the common thread among liberal philosophers was a commitment to the belief that, "To threaten a man with persecution unless he submits to a life in which he exercises no choices of his goals; to block before him every door but one, no matter how noble the prospect upon which it opens, or how benevolent the motives of those who arrange this, is to sin against the truth that is a man, a being with a life of his own to live."[124] Benjamin Constant (1767–1830) moves in this direction, and his concerns equate with those of Marx and his critique of bourgeois liberal democracy. For Constant, "transference by a successful rising of unlimited authority, commonly called sovereignty, from one set of hands to another does not increase liberty, but merely shifts the burden of slavery."[125] He continues, "usually men protested against this or that set of governors as oppressive, when the real cause of oppression lay in the mere fact of the accumulation of power itself … It is not against the arm that one must rail, but against the weapon. Some weights are too heavy for the human hand."[126] Here Constant makes direct reference to surplus *power* and indirectly to hegemony. Finally, it is important to note the extent to which Constant and Marx (and Kant, Mill, Locke, Smith, Rousseau, Condorcet) signify a line of thought celebrating individual liberty in varying ways, and each uniquely expressing with R.H. Tawney (1880–1962) the conviction, "that liberty of the strong, whether their strength is physical or economic, must be restrained."[127] Following Berlin, I raise the point here to emphasize that Tawney's view does not require what Berlin calls "an a priori rule" emanating from a vision or plan directing a new constellation of the social, but rather, stems from a very basic, very human "respect for the principles of justice, or shame at gross inequality of treatment."[128] This is important for my purposes because my prioritizing Marx's value theory as one way to dialectically critique liberalism's ideological commitment to freedom of contract does not also mean that I subscribe to the notion that there will ever be a "final solution," and this book does not advocate for one. Rather, human beings and their institutions will perennially morph over time and space. That is because our expressions of morality are not evolutionary or linear. They are spasmodic over the course of history. As Kant said, "out of the crooked timber of humanity not a straight thing was ever made."[129] What matters most, it appears, is that, "In the end, men choose between ultimate values; they choose as they do because their life and thought are determined by fundamental moral categories and concepts that are, at any rate over large stretches of time and space, and whatever their ultimate origins, a part of their being and thought and sense of their own identity; part of what makes them human."[130] This conviction is what animates Marx's value theory. As I transition now to a more detailed discussion of surplus value and alienation, it will be important to keep these caveats in mind.

Surplus Value, Exploitation, and Alienation in Marx's Thought[131]

Marx's economic theory, especially his theory of value, was solely focused on his critique of the emergence of industrial capitalism. His labor theory of value was predicated on insights generated by David Ricardo.[132] In general, "Marx's theory of value, for example, has been interpreted as an attempt to show that social wealth is always and everywhere created by human labor, and that, in capitalism, labor underlies the nonconscious, "automatic," market-mediated mode of distribution."[133] In his publications of the *Grundrisse* and the *Economic and Philosophic Manuscripts of 1844*, Marx seeks to understand economic exploitation from the perspective of labor because "it demystifies capitalist society, first by revealing labor to be the true source of social wealth, and second, by demonstrating that society rests upon a system of exploitation."[134] In sum, for Marx "[V]alue is a social form that expresses, and is based on, the expenditure of labor time."[135]

In addition to unmasking the generation of surplus value through the transformation of raw materials into commodities possessing use value, Marx also understood that the capitalist mode of industrial production came at the expense of a now fragmented human laborer who experienced their work and their relationship to the products that they produced as alienating. Alienation of the human worker from himself, his work, his coworkers, and the product that he produces is central to Marx's theory.

Surplus Value

The capitalist mode of production is premised upon the exploitation of labor time through the extraction of surplus value.[136] Surplus value is the amount of revenue generated by the labor power of workers over the course of a given period of time.[137] Surplus value is what generates profit, the amount of revenue remaining once factoring in commodity production and distribution costs. And while there was generally no disagreement among 19th-century political economists as to the source of surplus value and subsequent profit, there was, and remains, significant disagreement over how it should be distributed. For Marx, surplus value, like all value, is generated solely by the workers who put their knowledge and production skills to the task of turning raw materials into finished goods for sale as commodities on the market. For their part, capitalists provide the raw materials and facilities necessary for workers to transform those raw materials into commodities. Without the hand of labor put to the task of transforming raw materials into a valuable commodity for sale on the market, it rests as unmolded fodder. It is in this way that it is workers who generate all value, for without their knowledge and skill being applied to raw materials, no value can later be generated by commodities sold on the market. The Marxist labor theory of value establishes that it is workers, and not the "invisible hand of the market," who generate value, and it is for this reason that it is the workers who should reap the benefits of surplus value – profit. Because workers were not privy to the surplus value generated by their labor power, they were victims of exploitation.

Marx's primary insight was to take this analysis of surplus value further than, say, Adam Smith, by exposing what Marx viewed as the hidden relationship that existed between workers and capitalists with regard to claims that could be made toward appropriation of surplus value. Specifically, the wage labor relationship is predicated upon what superficially appears as an equitable contractual relationship between worker and employer. Employers need workers to transform raw materials into commodities for sale on the market. Workers need work in order to survive. The two, it seems, have entered into an equitable contractual bargain wherein employers offer workers what on the surface appears to be compensation for the value generated by the workers during a given period of time, say, over the course of a working day. In simplified form, a worker generates through their labor power enough commodity production during four hours of an eight-hour working day that, once sold on the market, will generate enough surplus value to compensate that worker through money wages. What the worker doesn't know is that through their continued productive work for the remaining four hours of the working day generating production of commodities for sale on the market, they are creating surplus value for the employer beyond that which is necessary for the employer to reproduce employee labor power. It is this amount of surplus value that is considered profit. It is the core of Marx's labor theory of value that the products generated by the worker in the second half of the production day, and that will be sold on the market as commodities, produce surplus value that belongs to the worker since it is the worker who has created the value in that commodity by putting their productive capacities to it. The mystification of the capitalist wage labor relationship hides this aspect of extracted surplus value from the worker by making it appear that the contractual relationship between compensation for work completed is equal to the amount of value generated. This is exploitation.

Alienation

Related to exploitation is Marx's theory of alienation.[138] Understanding alienation is important for my purposes since it provides the substantive materialist evidence for understanding the broader implications of value theory and species-essence. For Marx,

> What requires explanation is not the *unity* of living and active human beings with the natural, inorganic conditions of their metabolism, with nature, and therefore their appropriation of nature; nor is this the result of a historical process. What we must explain is the *separation* of these inorganic conditions of human existence from this active existence, a separation which is only fully completed in the relation between wage labor and capital.[139]

The industrial capitalist mode of production generates four dimensions of alienation: (1) alienation from one's self, (2) alienation from one's coworkers, (3) alienation from the product one produces, and (4) alienation from the process of production. Each aspect of alienation signifies fragmentation of the worker from their species-essence. The wage labor relationship is premised upon coercion and exploitation. As such, the worker is obliged to work under conditions that are not of their own choosing and it does not comport with those commitments most satisfying to species-essence. Capitalist wage labor is the antithesis of purposive activity. Rather, it is activity that, for the sake of survival, confronts us as against our own interests. This was readily apparent to Marx, who, writing in the *Grundrisse* during 1857–1858, makes the following argument:

> Labour no longer appears so much to be included within the production process; rather, *the human being comes to relate more as watchman and regulator to the production process itself* ... He steps to the side of the production process instead of being its chief actor. In this transformation, it is neither the direct human labour he himself performs, nor the time during which he works, but rather the appropriation of his own general productive power, his understanding of nature and his mastery over it by virtue of his presence as a social body – it is, in a word, the development of the *social individual* which appears as the great foundation-stone of production and of wealth.[140]

Since *who* we are cannot be separated from *what* we do, we become alienated from ourselves.

The wage labor system is premised upon intense competition for available work and the compensation that it affords. Since capitalists are at liberty to set wage compensation at any level they deem suitable to maintain their labor force while still generating profit, workers are set against each other as distinct labor units who must compete for scarce resources. Workers willing to work for less will, generally speaking, be more appealing to employers than those who demand more. This dynamic generates a kind of social Darwinist survival of the fittest environment. As such, coworkers are viewed as competition for survival rather than companions confronted with similar structural impediments, thereby *separating us from the collective.*

Under a capitalist mode of production, because workers have little to no say over the products that they produce, and because those products will upon completion become commodities for sale on the market, these products assume a power over the worker who has produced them, thereby alienating the worker from the *product* of their creation.

Finally, workers had no voice with regard to the *process* of production, specifically how products were actually made. This became increasingly important with industrialization and the introduction of factory production and scientific management. Briefly, skilled guildsmen and women working during the period prior to, and for a time during, the evolution of merchant capitalism constituted the entirety of the production process from conception through distribution.[141] They determined what to produce, how to produce it, and how to market their products. Slowly, beginning with the emergence of the English putting-out system in the 17th and 18th centuries, merchant capitalists, many of whom were previously guildsmen, adopted a system of production that employed semi-skilled workers who were only required to complete one task along the continuum leading to a completed product. The putting-out system was typically applied to the textile, clothing, metal goods (nailing and cutlery), watchmaking, hat, wood, and leather industries.[142] But there is also evidence of piece-rate compensation being applied to those industries where work could not be performed in the home. For example, workers signed contracts either individually or in groups in "the coal, tin and copper mines, as well as in carpet and lace mills, ironworks, potteries, building and civil engineering projects, transport, and quarrying."[143]

These semi-skilled workers did not conceive the product, had no knowledge about how to produce the entire product, and had no role to play in its marketing and distribution. They were compensated by the pieces produced (the piece rate) or by subcontract rates. These were the early days of what would later become factory production, the earliest onset of a division of labor premised upon deskilling.[144] For Braverman, as for Marx,

> While all such systems involved the payment of wages by piece rates, or by subcontract rates, it must not be supposed that this in itself was their essential feature. Piece rates in various forms are common to the present day, and represent the conversion of time wages into a form which attempts, with very uneven success, to enlist the worker as a willing accomplice in his or her own exploitation.[145]

Through a practice of piece rate putting out, merchant capitalists introduced alienation of the worker from the process of production. Full-blown industrial capitalism would perfect the practice to the point where singular routinized tasks performed along an assembly line would by the 1980s be replicated by robots (as in the auto manufacturing industry). Separating the worker from the process of production generates alienation.

This brief summary of Marx's value theory, surplus value, and alienation provides the context for juxtaposition to the liberty of contract rationale and opinions emanating from the United States Supreme Court, as well as the application of law to the preservation of capitalist social relations as part of a legal code. What Marx understood was that "the code of capital is a legal code."[146]

In sum, the political and economic power of the United States that emerged during the 19th century was predicated upon slavery, a mode of production that was codified in the United States Constitution (Article IV §2, the Fugitive Slave and the Three-Fifths Clauses), and federal and state law (e.g., The Fugitive Slave Act, Abolition of the Slave Trade Act of 1807, Black Codes, Jim Crow laws, and vagrancy laws). Slavery served the twin purposes of profit maximization and maintenance of white supremacy. The system signified the confluence of political, economic, and cultural power as administered through laws designed to code capital production and accumulation consistent with both Northern and Southern interests.

Central to the manifestation and control of the legal code of capitalism was, and remains, lawyers. This is because lawyers are the ones who largely created the code, and by virtue of that fact, know how to navigate the complex weave of law that has evolved to maintain segmented wealth and the distribution of it. The primary tools applied by lawyers to hierarchical wealth preservation are the legal codes[147] defining the law of trusts, bankruptcy, contracts, and corporate law.[148] By the early 1800s, the United States was already considered a "legal economy." Pistor explains that lawyers continued to become increasingly popular throughout the mid-19th century as they actively engaged in "surveying and conveying land on the Western frontier, coding credit instruments, setting up firms, locating assets of defaulting debtors, or salvaging defunct firms for value."[149] It was and remains the case that the always-evolving code of capital is the exclusive province of the lawyers' preserve.[150] Lawyers code and recode laws to the benefit of wealthy and powerful benefactors. But when it comes to legitimating the legal code as applied to trusts, bankruptcy, contracts, and corporate law, practicing lawyers need to rely upon the power of the courts. Beginning in the earliest days of the republic, the United States Supreme Court demonstrated fealty to, and became part of, the power bloc that ensconced segmented capitalist power.

***

In stark contrast to Marx's value theory, which serves as its dialectical antithesis, with few exceptions at nearly every opportunity, 19th and early 20-century Supreme Court jurisprudence served to preserve the interests of the plantation aristocracy and bourgeois capitalists while surrendering to each the lives and dignity of African slaves and their descendants, and the largely white working poor who clamored for survival in the manufacturing sectors of the North. As a superstructural institution intricately bound to dominant cultural, political, and economic interests by way of its system maintenance function, the United States Supreme Court paved the way for both the law of slavery and burgeoning capitalist wage labor. As it should be clear, the Supreme Court advanced a bipolar jurisprudence that assured the maintenance of the Southern slave economy and a cultural commitment to white supremacy from the founding of the nation until the 1954 Brown v. Board of Education[151] decision (or perhaps more accurately, the passage of the 1965 Voting Rights Act), all the while advancing the principle of liberty of contract that would provide the foundation for the evolution of wage labor capitalism beginning in the early 19th century with the 1819 *Dartmouth College v. Woodward*[152] opinion through to the present day.

Notes

1 David N. Mayer. Substantive Due Process Rediscovered: The Rise and Fall of Liberty of Contract. 60 Mercer L. Rev. 563 (2008): 569. See also David E. Bernstein. *Lochner v. New York*: A Centennial Retrospective. 83 Wash. ULQ. 1469 (2005).

2 W.E.B. Du Bois. Black Reconstruction in America: 1860–1880. New York: The Free Press (1998): 239.

3 Roscoe Pound. Liberty of Contract. The Yale Law Journal, 18, 7, (1909): 454–487.

4 It is important to recall that Roscoe Pound was a sociologist. Pound's reference to "mechanical" jurisprudence is consistent with Durkheim's expression of mechanical and organic solidarity, but Pound inverts Durkheim's application of them. Social systems constituted by mechanical solidarity were essentially pre-industrial, geographically and numerically small, and homogenous groups that could generate shared norms and values with little exogenous threat to them. With the onset of industrial capitalism, however, and increasing divisions of labor and secularization in both Europe and the United States, along with the rapid growth of diverse populations in each location, there needed to be an institutional response to promote national identity and solidarity within the culture. All nation-states are "invented realities" (Berger and Luckmann. The Social Construction of Reality. NY: Anchor (1967)) in that there is nothing "organic" about them. They are constructed through the application of wealth, power, and law where their values are coded into capital. Organic solidarity was less personal than life under mechanical solidarity, but organic solidarity provided reasoned and rational law to guide people toward constructive ends. Durkheim introduced mechanical and organic society in T*he Division of Labor in Society*, published in 1893.

5 Supra 1at 572.

6 Morton Horowitz, The Transformation of American Law, 1780-1860. Cambridge: Harvard University Press.
7 Id at 161–166. Emphasis added.
8 *Farwell v. The Boston and Worchester Railroad Corporation*, 45 Mass. 49 (1847)
9 Christopher L. Tomlins. Law, Labor, and Ideology in the Early American Republic. London: Cambridge University Press (1993): 259–297.
10 40 NE 454 (Ill. 1895). *Ritchie v. People* was decided two years before the Court's *Allgeyer* opinion (1897), and ten years before the *Lochner* opinion (1905).
11 Id at 455.
12 "No State shall enter into any Treaty, Alliance, or Confederation; grant Letters of Marque and Reprisal; coin Money; emit Bills of Credit; make any Thing but gold and silver Coin a Tender in Payment of Debts; pass any Bill of Attainder, ex post facto Law, or Law impairing the Obligation of Contracts, or grant any Title of Nobility."
13 In *Lochner v. New York*, 198 US. 45, 53 (1905), the Supreme Court held that the meaning of police powers assumed by the Tenth Amendment pertained to: "safety, health, morals, and general welfare of the public."
14 10 US (6 Cranch) 87 (1810).
15 Supra 1 at 596.
16 Supra 1 at 611.
17 Eric Foner. Reconstruction: America's Unfinished Revolution – 1863–1877. New York: Harper (1988): 277.
18 Paul Brest, Sandford Levinson, Jack Balkin, Akhil Reed Amar, and Reva Siegel, Processes of Constitutional Decisionmaking: Cases and Materials. New York: Walters Kluwer (2018): 359.
19 Id at 359.
20 17 US 481 (1819).
21 Jack H. Friedenthal, Arthur R. Miller, John E. Sexton & Helen Hershkoff. Civil Procedure: Cases and Materials. Twelfth Edition. St. Paul, MN: West Academic Publishing (2018): 404.
22 41 US (16 Pet.) 1, 10 L.Ed. 865 (1842). *Swift* served as a precedent regarding diversity jurisdiction and the authority of federal over state law until the Supreme Court held in *Erie R. Co. v. Tompkins*, 304 US 64, 58 S.Ct. 817, 82 L.Ed. 1188 (1938), respecting state sovereignty, especially relating to substantive law.
23 Supra 21 at 404.
24 The *Swift* doctrine gave way to the Erie doctrine following the United States Supreme Court's opinion in *Erie v. Tompkins*, 304 US 64 (1938).
25 157 US 429 (1895).
26 https://www.oyez.org/cases/1850-1900/157us429
27 *Allgeyer v. Louisiana*, 165 US 578 (1897)
28 Supra 18 at 471.
29 198 US (1905).
30 "The powers not delegated to the United States by the Constitution, nor prohibited by it to the States, are reserved to the States respectively, or to the people."
31 Supra 13.
32 Supra 13.
33 300 US 379.
34 304 US 144.
35 Supra 18 at 554.
36 261 US 525 (1923).
37 271 US 583, 594 (1926).
38 Sutherland reproduced in Mayer, supra 1 at 624.

39 The unconstitutional conditions doctrine, as expressed by Justice Sutherland in *Frost & Frost Trucking Co. v. Railroad Commission*, 271 US 583 (1926), is the most frequently cited articulation of it. Cited in Paul Brest, Sanford Levinson, Jack Balkin, Akhil Reed Amar, and Reva Siegel, Processes of Constitutional Decision Making: Cases and Materials. New York: Walters Kluwer (2018): 1727. While space limitations prohibit the development of it, it is my argument that plea bargaining is an unconstitutional condition on the right to exercise Sixth Amendment rights.
40 Morton Horowitz, The Transformation of American Law, 1780–1860 (1977): 1–13.
41 Supra 9.
42 Supra 2 at 608–610.
43 Supra 2 at 623.
44 Supra 2 at 623.
45 Carl Schurz. Report on the Condition of the South. 39th Congress, Senate Ex. Doc. 1st Session. No. 2 (1865): 24.
46 Id at 24.
47 Id at 24.
48 Id at 22.
49 For a thorough discussion of the impact of vagrancy laws upon newly freed black people, see Risa Goluboff. *Vagrant Nation*. London: Oxford University Press (2016).
50 Id at 2.
51 Id at 2.
52 Id at 3.
53 235, US 133 (1914).
54 Supra 18 at 483.
55 Ray Stannard Baker cited in Brest et al., supra 18 at 483.
56 Supra 18 at 484.
57 Supra 45 at 6.
58 Supra 45 at 18.
59 Supra 45 at 19.
60 Supra 45 at 19.
61 Supra 45 at 22.
62 The presence of the United States military as facilitators of the Freedmen's Bureau was effectively ended with the United States Supreme Court opinion in *Ex parte Milligan*, 71 US 2 (1866). The absence of the military to protect freed men and women, as well as the newly created institutions of government, exposed free black people to the Black Codes and subsequent Jim Crow laws, and both organized and ad hoc physical violence.
63 Supra 45 at 25.
64 Supra 45 at 25.
65 George Fitzhugh. Cannibals All! Or, Slaves Without Masters. National Humanities Center (1857): 2.
66 Id at 2.
67 Id at 3.
68 In his important book, The Hollow Hope, Gerald N. Rosenberg addresses the conditions under which the United States Supreme Court may serve as an institution advancing social change. The book emphasizes Civil Rights, Women's Rights, Environmental Law, and Same-Sex Marriage. In short, the book's primary focus is upon what would be considered social justice (consistent with Rawls) or progressive movements advancing human dignity and environmental protection. He contends that the Court is constrained in three ways from

acting as a promoter and/or protector of each of these substantive areas: 1) The limited nature of constitutional rights; 2) The lack of judicial independence; and 3) The judiciary's lack of powers of implementation (35). What the book fails to address, however, is how the Court acts in ways that certainly promote "social change," but in ways that (with a few episodic exceptions notable for resisting anti-canon status) are tailored to the preservation of largely white supremacist, patriarchal, imperial, resource-depleting capitalist political and economic conditions. These, of course, are hegemonic – constitutionally and culturally normative – and require no explanation. Social justice and environmental protection, on the other hand, signify outliers requiring creative interpretations of the Commerce Clause and Reconstruction Amendments (Thirteenth, Fourteenth, and Fifteenth). See Gerald N. Rosenberg. The Hollow Hope: Can Courts Bring About Social Change? Chicago: University of Chicago Press (2018).

69 *Brown v. Board of Education of Topeka*, 347 US 483 (1954).

70 *Dartmouth College v. Woodward*, 17 US 481 (1819).

71 Katharina Pistor. The Code of Capital: How Law Creates Wealth and Inequality. Princeton, NJ: Princeton University Press.

72 Marx never developed a complete analysis of law and capitalism, but while serving as an editor of the Rheinische Zeitung, he wrote a series of five articles addressing what he called, "Debate on Law on Thefts of Wood." These articles were published throughout 1842, and they emphasized what could be loosely referred to as a new "coding of capital" to serve the interests of property accumulation.

73 Norbert Elias. The Civilizing Process. London: Blackwell (2000): 230.

74 John Austin. Lecture V. 1832: 117.

75 Id.

76 Cited in Peter Goodrich. Legal Discourse: Studies in Linguistics, Rhetoric and Legal Analysis. London: Macmillan Press (1987): 71.

77 Id at 72.

78 Id at 66.

79 Id at 66–67.

80 I apply the neo-Marxist economic reference to "segmentation" over the noun more commonly used by American economists, "stratification." Segmentation has the benefit of signifying entrenched (segmented) layers of class that are artifacts of political, economic, and cultural power. On the other hand, stratification is used by American economists and sociologists to describe what appears to be an organic distinction among human beings based upon merit. In my view, segmentation more readily captures class immobility and economic oppression.

81 Supra 71 at 17. Emphasis added.

82 Supra 71 at 17.

83 Cedric J. Robinson. *B*lack Marxism: The Making of the Black Radical Tradition. Charlotte, NC: University of North Carolina Press (1983): 58.

84 Supra 71 at 19.

85 Supra 2 at 327.

86 Supra 2 at 329.

87 Supra 2 at 358.

88 Supra 71 at 19.

89 Supra 71 at 19.

90 Supra 71 at 19.

91 Supra 2 at 581.

92 Thomas Piketty. Capital and Ideology. Cambridge, MA: Harvard University Press (2020): 7.
93 Id at 7.
94 Id at 8.
95 Id at 203.
96 Id at 232.
97 Id at 232.
98 Sven Beckert and Seth Rockman. Introduction to Slavery's Capitalism. In Beckert and Rothman (eds) Slavery's Capitalism: A New History of American Economic Development. University of Pennsylvania Press (2018): 17.
99 Id at 17.
100 Id at 19.
101 Supra 92 at 237.
102 Supra 92 at 236.
103 See William J. Novak. The Myth of the "Weak" American State. American Historical Review, 113 (3) (2008): 755.
104 See Max Lerner. The Supreme Court and American Capitalism. 42, Yale L. J. 5 (1933): 668-701; Max Weber, Economy and Society: Volume 1, University of California Press, 1978. See Chapter 3: The Types of Legitimate Domination (p. 212). See also, Edwin Meese's speech to the American Bar Association, July 9, 1985. "But this is not to suggest that the justices are a body of Platonic guardians. Far from it. The Court is what it was understood to be when the Constitution was framed – a political body. The juridical process is, at its most fundamental level, a political process. While not a partisan political process, it is political in the truest sense of that word. It is a process wherein public deliberations occur over what constitutes the common good under the terms of a written constitution."
105 Erwin Chemerinsky. The Case Against the Supreme Court. New York: Penguin (2014); David Kaplan. The Most Dangerous Branch. New York: Crown (2018); Mark Tushnet. Taking The Constitution Away From The Courts. Princeton, NJ: Princeton University Press (1999).
106 *Brady v. United States*, 397 US 742 (1970*); Santobello v. New York*, 404 US 257 (1971).
107 Robert Schehr and Chelsea French. Mental Competency Law and Plea Bargaining: A Neurophenomenological Critique. 79, 3, Albany L. Rev. 1091 (2015/2016).
108 Id at 1165–1166.
109 Consider the Lochner era Supreme Court opinions. *Lochner v. New York*, 198 US 45 (1905).
110 W.E.B. Du Bois. Black Reconstruction in America: 1860–1880. New York: The Free Press (1992) 182.
111 Supra 103.
112 Albert Shaw cited in Novak supra 92 at 753.
113 Martin Hägglund. This Life: Secular Faith and Spiritual Freedom. New York: Pantheon (2019). While I will not present it here in its totality, Hägglund's economic reinterpretation of Marx's Capital is comprehensive. For example, in Chapter 5 ("The Value of Our Finite Time"), he presents the four categories of Marx's economic theory that signify its core components – appearance (price), essence (the measure of value), transhistorical conditions (how we organize our lives into an economy of time), and what Hägglund refers to as the conditions of intelligibility for spiritual life ("the measure of value as your finite lifetime, which renders intelligible the value of all else"). It is this fourth aspect of Marx's

theory of value that serves as Hägglund's primary emphasis, and the one that I wish to emphasize here.

114 John R. Munkirs. The Transformation of American Capitalism: From Competitive Market Structures to Centralized Private Sector Planning. New York: Routledge (1986). Munkirs provides an institutional economic analysis. His argument relating to interlocking directorates mirrors Gramsci's early conceptualization of the power bloc. See also, William Domhoff. Who Rules America: The Triumph of the Corporate Rich. New York: McGraw-Hill Education (2013); Robert Reich. Supercapitalism: The Transformation of Business, Democracy and Everyday Life. New York: Vintage (2007).

115 Katharina Pistor. The Code of Capital: How Law Creates Wealth and Inequality. Princeton, NJ: Princeton University Press (2019).

116 Thomas E. Wartenburg. "Species-Being" and "Human Nature" in Marx. Human Studies, 5 (1982): 77.

117 Id at 79.

118 Herbert Spencer. Social Statics: The Conditions Essential to Human Happiness Specified, and The First of Them Developed. Robert Schalkenbach Foundation (1995).

119 Supra 73 at 79. Here Wartenburg argues that by framing *Homo sapiens* as "beings," Marx is drawing a direct theoretical and philosophical connection to Aristotle's zoon politikon, or "political animal." That is, human beings, by their embeddedness within the common, share a collective commitment to its health and well-being.

120 Supra 116 at 79.

121 Supra 116 at 79.

122 Supra 113 at 214.

123 Supra 113 at 214.

124 Isaiah Berlin. Liberty. Henry Hardy (ed.). London: Oxford University Press, (2002):174.

125 Id at 209.

126 Id at 209.

127 Id at 215.

128 Id at 215.

129 Id at 216.

130 Id at 217.

131 Marx's conventional emphasis was upon productive labor. However, subsequent generations of Marxist economists have sought to develop work that Marx had contemplated in Volume III of Capital but never completed. Specifically, Marx anticipated the capitalist mode of production transitioning to increasing production of financial services, but he did not consider that kind of work to be generative of surplus value. For an attempt to establish the surplus value generated by public and private sector service work, see Simon Marginson. Value Creation in the Production of Services: A Note on Marx. Cambridge Journal of Economics, 22 (1998): 573–585.

132 David Ricardo. The Principles of Political Economy and Taxation. London: Dent (1973).

133 Moishe Postone. Time, Labor, And Social Domination. London: Cambridge (1993): 8.

134 Id at 8.

135 Id at 25.

136 Marx discusses the theory of surplus value in Parts III, IV, and V of Capital. His discussion of the exploitation of labor power takes place in Part III, Chapter IV,

Section 1. Karl Marx. Capital. Vol. 1. Frederick Engels (ed.). New York: New World Paperbacks (1979).

137 For a cogent defense of the accumulation of wealth as a legal virtue, see Richard A. Posner, The Economics of Justice. Cambridge, MA: Harvard University Press (1983): 60–73; 88–99.

138 See Karl Marx. The German Ideology. International Publishing Co. Inc. (2016); Karl Marx. The Economic and Philosophic Manuscripts of 1844. Dover Publications (2007).

139 Karl Marx cited in Bertell Ollman. Alienation: Marx's Conception of Man in Capitalist Society. London: Cambridge University Press (1976): 133.

140 Karl Marx. Grundrisse: Foundations of the Critique of Political Economy. New York: Penguin (1993): 705. First emphasis is mine.

141 See E.P. Thompson, The Making of the English Working Class. London: Vintage (1966), and Herbert Applebaum, The Concept of Work: Ancient, Medieval, and Modern. New York: SUNY Press (1992).

142 Harry Braverman. Labor and Monopoly Capital, Monthly Review Press (1974): 61.

143 Id at 61.

144 See Harry Braverman, Labor and Monopoly Capital, Monthly Review Press (1974).

145 Id at 62–63.

146 Supra 71 at 15.

147 In 1848, the state of New York adopted a comprehensive code of civil procedure named for its primary innovator and advocate, David Dudley Field. By 1938, the Field Code had been adopted by over 30 jurisdictions across the United States, and it served as a precursor to the Federal Rules of Civil Procedure. According to Kellen Richard Funk (2018), the Field Code was notable for "the creation of a lawyer's code, written and enacted by lawyers, and written for and addressed to the trial bar ... As a code, it geared toward easing the burden of practicing lawyers by giving them a single volume to consult rather than the 'vast irregular mass' of case law on pleading. It advanced professional interests most notably by eliminating the public regulation of fees, ushering lawyers into an age of free-market capitalism ... The code gave lawyers effective control over the mode of trial, to the investigation of facts, to the election of remedies and the speed of their enforcement." The Lawyers' Code: The Transformation of American Legal Practice, 1828–1938. PhD Dissertation, Princeton University: (6). See also, Kellen Funk, The Union of Law and Equity: The United States, 1800–1938. In Kellen Funk. Law and Equity: Fusion and Fission. London: Cambridge University (2020): 46–69.

148 Supra 71 at 160.

149 Supra 71 at 174.

150 Supra 147 note 86.

151 *Brown v. Board of Education of Topeka*, 347 U.S. 483 (1954).

152 *Dartmouth College v. Woodward*, 17 U.S. 481 (1819).

References

Herbert Applebaum. *The Concept of Work: Ancient, Medieval, and Modern*. New York: SUNY Press (1992)

Sven Beckert and Seth Rockman. Introduction to Slavery's Capitalism. In S. Beckert and S. Rothman (eds.) *Slavery's Capitalism: A New History of American Economic Development*. Philadelphia: University of Pennsylvania Press (2018)

Sven Beckert and Seth Rockman (eds.). *Slavery's Capitalism: A New History of American Economic Development.* Philadelphia: University of Pennsylvania Press (2018)
Isaiah Berlin. *Liberty.* Henry Hardy (ed.). London: Oxford University Press
David E. Bernstein. Lochner v. New York: A Centennial Retrospective. 83 *Wash. U. L. Q.*, 1469 (2005)
Harry Braverman. *Labor and Monopoly Capital.* New York and London:Monthly Review Press (1974)
Paul Brest, Sandford Levinson, Jack Balkin, Akhil Reed Amar, and Reva Siegel. *Processes of Constitutional Decisionmaking: Cases and Materials.* New York: Walters Kluwer (2018)
Erwin Chemerinsky. *The Case Against the Supreme Court.* New York: Penguin (2014)
William Domhoff. *Who Rules America: The Triumph of the Corporate Rich.* New York: McGraw-Hill Education (2013)
W.E.B. Dubois. *Black Reconstruction in America: 1860–1880.* New York: The Free Press (1992)
W.E.B. Dubois. *Black Reconstruction in America: 1860–1880.* New York: The Free Press (1998)
Norbert Elias. *The Civilizing Process.* London: Blackwell (2000)
George Fitzhugh. *Cannibals All! Or, Slaves Without Masters.* Raleigh, North Carolina: National Humanities Center (1857)
Eric Foner. *Reconstruction: America's Unfinished Revolution – 1863–1877.* New York: Harper (1988)
Jack H. Friedenthal, Arthur R. Miller, John E. Sexton, and Helen Hershkoff. *Civil Procedure: Cases and Materials.* Twelfth Edition. St. Paul, MN: West Academic Publishing (2018)
Kellen Funk. *Law and Equity: Fusion and Fission.* London: Cambridge University (2019)
Risa Goluboff. *Vagrant Nation.* London: Oxford University Press (2016)
Peter Goodrich. *Legal Discourse: Studies in Linguistics, Rhetoric and Legal Analysis.* London: Macmillan Press (1987)
Martin Hägglund. *This Life: Secular Faith and Spiritual Freedom.* New York: Pantheon (2019)
Morton Horowitz. *The Transformation of American Law, 1780–1860.* Cambridge: Harvard University Press (1977)
David Kaplan. *The Most Dangerous Branch.* New York: Crown (2018)
Max Lerner. The Supreme Court and American Capitalism. 42(5) *Yale L. J.*, 668–701 (1933)
Simon Marginson. Value Creation in the Production of Services: A Note on Mark. 22 *Cambridge Journal of Economics*, 573–585 (1998)
Karl Marx. *Capital.* Vol. 1. Frederick Engels (ed.). New York: New World Paperbacks (1979)
Karl Marx. *Grundrisse: Foundations of the Critique of Political Economy.* New York: Penguin (1993)
Karl Marx. *The Economic and Philosophic Manuscripts of 1844.* Garden City, New York: Dover Publications (2007)
Karl Marx. *The German Ideology.* New York, New York: International Publishing Co. Inc (2016)
David N. Mayer. Substantive Due Process Rediscovered: The Rise and Fall of Liberty of Contract. 60(563) *Mercer L. Rev.*, 569 (2008)
John R. Munkirs. *The Transformation of American Capitalism: From Competitive Market Structures to Centralized Private Sector Planning.* New York: Routledge (1986)

William J. Novak. The Myth of the "Weak" American State. 111(3) *American Historical Review* (2008)
Bertell Ollman. *Alienation: Marx's Conception of Man in Capitalist Society.* London: Cambridge University Press (1976)
Thomas Picketty. *Capital and Ideology*. Cambridge, MA: Harvard University Press (2020)
Katharina Pistor. *The Code of Capital: How Law Creates Wealth and Inequality.* Princeton, NJ: Princeton University Press (2019)
Richard A. Posner. *The Economics of Justice*. Cambridge, MA: Harvard University Press (1983)
Moishe Postone. *Time, Labor, and Social Domination*. London: Cambridge (1993)
Roscoe Pound. Liberty of Contract. 18(7) *The Yale Law Journal*, 454–487 (1909)
Robert Reich. *Supercapitalism: The Transformation of Business, Democracy and Everyday Life*. New York: Vintage (2007)
David Ricardo. *The Principles of Political Economy and Taxation*. London: Dent (1973)
Cedric J. Robinson. *Black Marxism: The Making of the Black Radical Tradition.* Charlotte, NC: University of North Carolina Press (1983)
Gerald N. Rosenberg. *The Hollow Hope: Can Courts Bring About Social Change?* Chicago: University of Chicago Press (2018)
Robert Schehr and Chelsea French. Mental Competency Law and Plea Bargaining: A Neurophenomenological Critique. 79(3) *Albany L. Rev.*, 1091 (2015/2016)
Carl Schurz. Report on the Condition of the South. 39th Congress, Senate Ex. Doc. 1st Session. No. 2 (1865)
Herbert Spencer. *Social Statics: The Conditions Essential to Human Happiness Specified, and The First of Them Developed*. Princeton, NJ: Robert Schalkenbach Foundation (1995)
E.P. Thompson. *The Making of the English Working Class*. London: Vintage (1966)
Christopher L. Tomlins. *Law, Labor, and Ideology in the Early American Republic.* London: Cambridge University Press (1993)
Mark Tushnet. *Taking the Constitution Away from the Courts*. Princeton, NJ: Princeton University Press (1999)
Thomas E. Wartenburg. "Species-Being" and "Human Nature" in Marx. 5(2) *Human Studies* 77–95 (1982)
Max Weber. *Economy and Society: Volume 1*. Berkeley: University of California Press (1978)

6

PLEA BARGAINING AS CONTRACT

Autonomy and Efficiency

In the preceding chapter, I introduced the liberty of contract doctrine and the ideological construction of *Homo economicus*. By way of reminder, it is my argument that the constitutionality of plea bargaining is articulated as a product of framing human subjects as "free agents" confronting accusations made by the state of criminal wrongdoing armed with the power to negotiate the terms of a contract that will benefit both the state and the accused. The power of the state to enter into contractual negotiations regarding specific charges and a proposed sentence has, since the 1970 *Brady v. United States* opinion, been legitimated through the juridical coding of capitalism. The specific juridic code applied to plea bargaining first required the centuries-long proliferation of an ideological commitment to essentializing individual autonomy. As I demonstrated in Chapter 5, this occurred as part of a larger historical transformation in the mode of production in the United States, one that positioned each individual as the master of their own destiny – *Homo economicus*. The "free labor" ideology that emerged during the mid-19th century demonstrated both a philosophical commitment to privileging human agency and an ideological justification for the pursuit of political, economic, and cultural self-interest. Serving as the Archimedean core, Article I §10, cl. 1, also known as the "Contract Clause" of the United States Constitution, stipulates the following:

> No state shall enter into any Treaty, Alliance, or Confederation; grant Letters of Marque and Reprisal; coin Money; emit Bills of Credit; make any Thing but gold and silver Coin a Tender in Payment of Debts; pass any

DOI: 10.4324/9781003385103-8

> Bill of Attainder, ex post facto Law, *or Law impairing the Obligations of Contracts*, or grant any Title of Nobility. (My emphasis.)[1]

As I sought to demonstrate in Chapter 5, the United States Supreme Court further developed the essentializing power constituting the individual right to contract through its 19th and early 20th-century common law opinions. It was this important juridical and cultural emphasis upon *Homo sapiens* as *Homo economicus* that provided the hegemonic context necessary to argue, as it did in *Brady v. United States* and the other relevant 1970s plea cases discussed in Chapter 1, that an indicted felony criminal defendant may, if they choose (autonomy), abdicate their constitutionally protected Fifth and Sixth Amendment trial rights in exchange for a sentencing reduction. As Chapter 4 made clear, the right to trial by jury was, until the mid-19th century, viewed as a vital instrument of the judiciary, one that would serve as a public check upon executive and legislative power. But for ease of prosecution, certainty of outcome, and efficient use of scarce resources, plea bargains emerged as an artifact of powerful state actors – including lawyers working in concert with captains of industry – to isolate and segment the mass of Americans who, like today, largely operate outside the corridors of power. Once successfully framed within the discourse of *Homo economicus*, Americans were susceptible to being selectively preyed upon by political, economic, and cultural forces that isolated and separated them from each other, thereby discursively negating what had historically been life lived in common. In sum, each American is perceived as an agent of their own making, separated from their community. Through the process of valorizing the making and protection of contracts in Article I §10 of the Constitution and through Supreme Court case law, combined with the successful ideological construction of *Homo sapiens* as *Homo economicus*, the legislative, executive, and judicial branches have at their disposal the structural legitimacy necessary to construct a legal code (i.e., Federal Rule 11) in such a way that the right to trial by jury has all but disappeared.

In this chapter, I will briefly return to the liberty of contract doctrine to explore the two principal ideological and political assumptions guiding it: individual autonomy and efficiency. Next, I will discuss the application of conventional contract law to plea bargaining by exploring concerns relating to improperly obtained assent. Finally, I will introduce my argument that plea bargaining signifies the confluence of conventional contract law with contracts of adhesion.

Liberty of Contract: Autonomy and Efficiency

The liberty of contract doctrine was and remains constituted by two prevailing principles: 1) individual autonomy (liberty), and 2) efficiency. As I will demonstrate, justifications for plea bargaining that rest upon individual autonomy fail in two important ways. First, the notion of the free-thinking, free-acting, reasonable rational actor possessing free will is a myth. Second, granting the existence of an autonomous individual as was and continues to be the hegemonically rhetorical standard, plea bargaining still fails by constitutional standards. I give primacy to the former argument, and I juxtapose the latter one to demonstrate what I perceive to be a misapplication of constitutional law.

Autonomy

Generally, from a moral and political philosophy perspective, we can view autonomy as being comprised of two conditions – competency and authenticity.[2] Competency refers to "various capacities for rational thought, self-control, freedom from debilitating pathologies, [and] systematic self-deception ... Authenticity conditions often include the capacity to reflect upon and endorse (or identify with) one's desires, [and] values."[3] Consistent with *Homo economicus*, "Autonomy is the source of all obligations, whether moral or non-moral, since it is the capacity to impose upon ourselves, by virtue of our practical identities, obligations to act."[4] Viewing individuals as rational economic maximizers is the premise of the Coase theorem, the nucleus of the law and economics school of thought.[5] Generally, the Coase theorem posits individuals as rational cost calculators driven by utility maximization. Moreover, "in virtually all economic accounts ... the individual is the fundamental unit of economic behavior ... The interaction of rational individuals, each maximizing his or her own self-interest, tends toward market 'equilibrium' or steady state that will not change in the absence of outside forces."[6] Since markets are solely produced through the interaction of self-interested individuals, there is no need to consider politics, law, or culture as exogenous to them and influential over them.

As it pertains to plea bargaining, Coase's theorem suggests that "when parties are free to bargain *costlessly* they will succeed in reaching efficient outcomes regardless of the initial allocations of legal rights" (my emphasis).[7] Law may be implicated in restoring system equilibrium under circumstances producing "transaction costs."[8] Coase was primarily concerned with acknowledging that every decision produces unanticipated collateral effects. This is especially important as it pertains to my argument in this book since, as Coase makes clear in his conclusion,

> It would clearly be desirable if the only actions performed were those in which what was gained was worth more than what was lost. But in choosing between social arrangements within the context of which individual decisions are made, we have to bear in mind that a change in the existing

> system which will lead to an improvement in some decisions may well lead to worsening of others.[9]

Of course, in the plea bargaining context, transaction costs are transparent and costly. They may be experienced through the assertion of the right to trial where, upon conviction, a defendant may be sentenced to a lengthy prison term. Or perhaps transaction costs associated with the plea might entail relinquishing access to government-funded housing, child care, or the opportunity for employment. Most egregiously, the adoption of felony criminal plea procedures with its emphasis on negotiated contracts between a powerful representative of the government and a powerless defendant, along with procedural rules barring access to impeachment evidence known to the prosecutor (*Ruiz*) while requiring abdication of Fifth and Sixth Amendment rights, signifies the ultimate in transaction costs – the creation of a criminal procedure technology that presents as a threat to democracy. Why?

Through the legal coding of capitalism, and consistent with Justice Harlan's contentions in *Hopt* and *Thompson* that rights may not be taken away, nor given away (i.e., through waiver of the Fifth and Sixth Amendment to plead), Coase's theorem and its emphasis upon an autopoietic economic system of self-interested individual utility maximizers leads to a broader system-wide diminution of juridical rights protections. If the state may engage in "trading" rights for a benefit (the *commodification* of rights), cherry-picking rights protections from theoretically atomized individuals, then the right no longer possesses the cultural, institutional, or constitutional authority to protect people from the coercive power of the state. Following Coase's theorem, so long as transaction costs are kept to a minimum, and so long as there is "mutuality of benefit" (e.g., the state gains a conviction, the defendant receives downward departure on sentencing), the accused who confronts the state is a "free agent" possessing the "right" and "ability" to "knowingly" and "voluntarily" negotiate the charges against them, and the subsequent punishment, but only after abdicating their rights protections. While I contend that this construction is mythological as applied to economics, it is perhaps not quite as dangerous to liberty as when it is applied to plea bargaining.

Liberalism's contribution to political philosophy and autonomy was fundamental to the adoption of the liberty of contract doctrine and the "freedom" to negotiate the terms of one's work. Inherent in the liberty of contract doctrine is individual autonomy as a prerequisite to forging the contracts integral to private law where "mutual recognition or the equality of persons is the necessary condition for the correlation of rights and obligations in the private legal relationship."[10] But autonomy is also integral to a commitment to the *social contract* upon which liberal democracy would be formed. Important for my purposes, "liberalism refers generally to that approach to political power and social justice that determines principles of right (justice) prior to, and largely independent of, determination of conceptions of the good."[11] Liberal conceptualization of autonomy is integral to *Homo economicus* since it "implies the ability to reflect wholly on oneself to accept or reject one's values, connections, and self-defining features, and change such elements of one's life at will."[12] At bottom is the belief that individuals possess rights "by virtue of their having some "property" (moral autonomy, human dignity) that constitutes them as bearers of rights."[13] As such, "Law and political decisions are binding to the degree to which they respect individual rights"[14] since they signify expression of individual autonomy.

In sum, to be autonomous as envisioned by liberal theorists of the Enlightenment period, or as we continue to hear from juridical actors today, is to assume that *Homo sapiens* possesses an objective awareness of self and others to such an extent that a "reasonable man" will be able to properly comprehend and act in accordance with published law.[15] Consistent with this narrative, and with the exception of those who are mentally compromised, violation of the law is a *choice* made by a reasonable rational actor who calculated the costs and benefits of their actions and *chose* the illegal path. Arguing from within the narrative of liberalism and moral philosophy, ascribing autonomy to a defendant confronted with plea bargaining demonstrates species respect for the individuality constituting *Homo sapiens*. That is, providing a defendant with an option regarding their punishment for charged crimes signifies acknowledgment that each of us has the capacity to make "reasonable" decisions premised upon our objective assessment of the circumstances we are confronting. It is precisely this kind of justification for the plea that was provided by the Court in *Brady* and its progeny. So long as there is a "mutuality of benefit" accruing to the state and to the defendant, and so long as the defendant has the *voluntary choice* to plead guilty or not guilty, then the system preserves both the integrity of individual autonomy and system efficiency. Such is the accepted wisdom of legal scholars and practitioners, but for the reasons I present below, it is wrong.

Many years ago, while developing my ideas regarding the constitutionality of the plea, I had an email exchange with Harvard Law Professor Lawrence Tribe. Professor Tribe had read a short early draft of my work, and while he agreed with me that there were problems regarding plea procedure, he was not willing to concede my argument that plea bargaining is per se unconstitutional. Specifically, Professor Tribe said,

> I should say, however, that I don't agree with you that the very notion of waiver of fundamental rights is somehow oxymoronic or otherwise unacceptable ... I believe that the autonomy and independent agency of supposedly free individuals ordinarily presupposes that they should be

able to "trade" otherwise fundamental rights in exchange for benefits they desire more.[16]

Professor Tribe's emphasis upon individual autonomy is the normative legal position, especially as it pertains to plea bargaining. However, his position, like that of the legal profession more generally, and the Supreme Court most specifically, is simply at odds with what we know about how *Homo sapiens* comes to an awareness of subjective identity. As I established in Chapter 5, notions of "freedom," "liberty," and "autonomy" constitute the foundation of the liberty of contract doctrine, a doctrine that posits each person as a reasonable and rational individual fully capable of engaging in all social relationships as a "free agent." At bottom, there is a Kantian presumption of free will.[17] But as more than a century's worth of Sociology,[18] Psychology,[19] Anthropology,[20] Neuropsychology,[21] and more recently Neurophenomenology[22] establishes, *Homo sapiens* are politically, economically, and culturally embedded subjects constituted by their respective brains and experiences. That means that no person has the capacity to "step outside" of themselves in order to perceive the "world as it is." This is because: a) there is no "world as it is," an objective reality signifying an overdetermined essentialism available to all who are able to reason, and b) subjects limited as they are by their own physiology and cultural experiences (especially language)[23] will always filter new information through their political, economic, and cultural lenses. Moreover, each brain is a snowflake,[24] unique in its composition and its capacity for processing information. Each brain symbiotically processes information consistent with its cultural embeddedness, making the question of "choice" and autonomy suspect. After all, "[t]he complex interactions of genes and environment mean that all citizens—equal before the law—possess different perspectives, dissimilar personalities, and varied capacities for decision-making. The unique patterns of neurobiology inside each of our heads cannot qualify as choices; these are the cards we're dealt."[25] Events and experiences occurring outside a subject's field of influence will not stimulate consciousness leading to action or inaction in the same way that they would for those who are more familiar with them. Three brief examples will suffice to establish the point: 1) those who followed and continue to follow the autocratic white supremacy of former president, Donald Trump; 2) those who follow and believe in QAnon conspiracies; and 3) those Russians who believe Vladimir Putin's "deNazification" rhetoric is a legitimate justification for war with Ukraine. Limited as we are by our political, economic, and cultural experiences, including the quality of information we receive, our relative fear over the state of the country and our families, and the precariousness of our lives, what is real and true will always be a contested terrain of competing values and ideas, not something that lives objectively "outside" of us. As it pertains to neuropsychology, a subject far too complex to develop here, we know that for reasons associated with species preservation, the *Homo sapiens* brain defaults to the "fixation of belief" in original positions adopted by it.[26] *Homo sapiens*, then, is constituted by a complex and ongoing intersection of political, economic, cultural, and neuropsychological factors that make any argument for "free will" theoretically and empirically anachronistic.[27]

In previous work deconstructing the knowing and voluntary prongs of Federal Rule 11, I have emphasized the power of neurophenomenology to provide a far more thorough assessment of constituted subjects.[28] Specifically, "It [neurophenomenology] seeks a comprehensive understanding of human identity construction and consciousness through integration of the natural and social sciences, and phenomenology."[29] Consider the following assessment of neurophenomenology to embedded notions of autonomy, especially as manifested in plea bargaining.

> What appears to be common among neurophenomenologists, and that is especially significant as it pertains to our concerns with mental competency and plea bargaining, is recognition that cognition and consciousness is a far more dynamic and nuanced process than what the courts have generally understood. Common among neurophenomenologists is the assumption that, "[c]onscious experience is not located in a specific part of the brain, nor can it be identified in terms of special neural structures. It is an emergent property of a particular cognitive process—the formation of transient functional clusters of neurons." For Varela, "each conscious experience is based on a specific cell assembly, in which many different neural activities—associated with sensory perception, emotions, memory, bodily movements, etc.—are unified into a transient but coherent ensemble of oscillating neurons." Consciousness thereby manifests as the confluence of a dynamic and emergent process combining neurological networks with subjective environmental experiences.[30]

Much more could be said with regard to the neurophenomenological critique of free will and the rational actor model that has constituted the criminal legal system since the Enlightenment. However, suffice it to say that the evidence exists from within the social sciences, neuroscience, and phenomenology that human subjects are anything but "autonomous," "reasonable," and "rational actors" confronting the state.[31]

So why is it that the criminal legal system continues to cling to an outmoded and simplistic framing of human consciousness? Because presumptions of "individual autonomy" serve as a hegemonic rhetorical device necessary for both the coding of capital (e.g., freedom to work and to contract) and for state-sanctioned governmentality through the application of law (control over subject behavior, especially punishment).

To contend, as Professor Tribe, the legal community, and certain state actors do, that Americans are autonomous actors each capable of confronting the state on equitable grounds in order to bargain for advantage is, when confronted with neurophenomenology, a cynical straw man argument useful for justifying the exercise of power over criminal defendants confronting the police power of the state.

I indicated in the opening paragraph of this chapter that there were two reasons for rejecting the Court's justification for the plea – individual autonomy was the first. The second pertains to the positive right to a criminal trial by jury expressed in Article III §2 and the Sixth Amendment. Assuming for the moment that *Homo sapiens* is a species capable of "individual autonomy," I find the argument for the constitutionality of plea bargaining still fails to convince. As discussed in Chapter 4, Article III §2 and the Sixth Amendment were crafted precisely to *protect liberal notions of individual autonomy* against an overpowering judging and punishing state. That is, just as Justice Harlan explained in *Hopt* and *Thompson*, as well as the constitutional protections afforded by the Fourth, Fifth, Sixth, Eighth, Thirteenth, Fourteenth, and Fifteenth Amendments, presuppose an *autonomous actor* confronted by the police and prosecutorial power of the state. With the exception of the Sixth Amendment, those protections were largely assumed to be negative rights that limited how far the state could go to intrude upon *individual* (autonomous) liberty. To summarize, while I contend consistent with the published neurophenomenological scholarship that no *Homo sapiens* is an island unto itself, rather that each is constituted by its neurological soundness and cultural embeddedness, even if I were to concede the autonomous actor argument consistent with the Constitution, Bill of Rights, and Reconstruction Amendments, it is clear that the dignity of the subject confronted with state authority is embedded in each.

Law and Efficiency

Classical and neoliberal economists fetishize efficiency, especially as it affects the accumulation of wealth. But is it always best to be efficient? Should efficiency be a subjective quality, a systemic quality, or both? What does it mean to be "efficient?" Synonyms include: "well organized," "methodical," "systematic," "logical," "coherent," "well regulated," "orderly," "streamlined," "effective," "labor-saving," "cost-effective," and "energy-saving." To be efficient according to any of the synonyms listed above would facially appear to be a good thing, especially from a systems perspective since what is most valued is utility maximization. As we read in Chapter 5, the putting-out system, which compensated semi-skilled workers on a piece-rate basis, was an initial move to a more efficient process of production, one that narrowly tailored the required skill set to a few repetitive acts enabling merchants to generate a predictable product in specified increments of time, and at as low a cost as possible. As the Industrial Revolution developed first in England and then in the United States, the factory system came to replace putting out since it made it far more efficient for merchants to gather workers in one location under the merchant's supervisory authority than it was to travel the countryside delivering raw materials, retrieving them, and passing them along to the next semi-skilled worker in a different location. Wealth maximization, it seemed, was premised upon an efficiently operating mode of production. As Chapters 1 and 5 make clear, essentializing wealth maximization consistent with the liberty of contract doctrine appeared to be the *modus operandi* of the United States Supreme Court, as well as the lower federal district and circuit courts, especially during the late 19th and early 20th centuries (what is referred to as the *Lochner* era). It is Professor Posner's contention that the common law, with its judge-made rules, is a far superior mechanism for establishing efficiency than the legislative process.[32] He goes so far as to suggest that, "My point is not that positive economic analysis, and in particular the efficiency hypothesis, is the only valid application of economics to law, but, to repeat, that it is a mode of analysis that must be taken seriously by anyone interested in understanding our still largely judge-made legal system." And more nakedly transparent, Posner's fondness for common law rules over legislative regulation of markets stems from his belief that "within the limits of administrative feasibility, the law brings the economic system closer to producing the results that effective competition – a free market operating without significant externality, monopoly, or information problems – would produce."[33] In short, Posner prefers judge-made law over legislation because judges can unilaterally act to secure the legal codes necessary to the proliferation of wealth, whereas a democratic legislative body may raise serious concerns over negative externalities like those generated by the New York legislature in the *Lochner* case (e.g., pollution, unemployment, public health, leisure, working conditions). In the law and economics literature, efficiency is normatively viewed from the perspective of power.

Utility maximization means generating the greatest happiness and the least pain for most of the people, most of the time. What matters most are the consequences of acts, not whether they were *intrinsically* "good or bad." If one acts in ways that produce overall unhappiness, then the system must respond to return to a state of equilibrium. It is here where Bentham articulated his proportional theory of punishment.[34] For Bentham, the utility calculus was both judicious and fraught. It was judicious in that, if properly administered through law, political economic systems would generate the greatest good for the greatest number by maintaining overall system stability. All animals seek avoidance of pain. Our social systems should be engineered to that aim.

However, Bentham was prescient in his awareness of the always contingent, always constituted subject who will not always act consistently with utilitarian pain avoidance. Consistent with neurophenomenology, people are shaped by their experiences and their brains to such an extent that they may not always be aware of, or capable of understanding, optimal conditions, and they will often act in ways that are not in their own best interests. It follows that, rather than as *individualistic* rational actor models would have it, people are *subjects* who act the way they do for complicated multivariate spatiotemporal and neurophenomenological reasons, constituted as they are by cultural capital and habitus,[35] and their luck in the genetic lottery. Following Bentham's model, Durkheim emphasized that with the slowly unraveling grip of religion over modern political, economic, and cultural organization, it was law, our modern secular religion, that would provide the guardrails necessary to coax people toward the culturally preferred utility-maximizing system maintenance behavior.

For Americans socialized within a culture steeped in pragmatism and committed to the efficiency of Archimedes ("The shortest distance between two points is a straight line"), we should not be surprised to find that a legal system that comports with the concept of efficiency is one to be sought after and preserved. We are, after all, the children of William James:

> Pragmatism asks its usual question. "Grant an idea or belief to be true," it says, "what concrete difference will its being true make in anyone's actual life? How will the truth be realized? What experiences will be different from those which would obtain if the belief were false? What, in short, is the truth's cash-value in experiential terms?"[36]

James's pragmatism is consequentialist in orientation in that what is moral is what benefits the public interest, i.e., that which produces the greatest happiness. But in the hands of Max Horkheimer, pragmatism appears as an ideological extension of industrial capitalism and the factory mode of production:

> Pragmatism, in trying to turn experimental physics into a prototype of all science and to model all spheres of intellectual life after the techniques of the laboratory, is the counterpart of modern industrialism, for which the factory is the prototype of human existence, and which models all branches of culture after production on the conveyor belt.[37]

Horkheimer's interpretation of pragmatism as juxtaposed to American manufacturing resonates with my emphasis on rhetorical expressions of efficiency as somehow liberatory, or in the field of criminal procedure and plea bargaining, somehow just. The dominant cultural efficiency narrative is a *master narrative* in the Lacanian sense since it hegemonically signifies benign public understanding and manufactured consent justified by the list of synonyms provided above, but it is enforced through the legal coding of capital and the preservation of dominant cultural authority through the application of its strategic relational power to enhance system stability (e.g., Posner, Jessop). It is the power hiding unseen through the rhetorical veil that is revealed to be "surplus power" functioning beneath its surface-level justification as a system reproducing steering mechanism necessary to maintain political, economic, and cultural control.

The Coase theorem in law and economics (discussed in detail below) finds its closest sociological companion in functionalist theory. Functionalist theory shares much in common with the 19th-century work of Herbert Spencer.[38] Spencer was a biologist and sociologist (what sociology refers to as a socio-biologist) who was heavily influenced by Darwin's Theory of Evolution – survival of the fittest. Like the natural environment, social systems, according to Spencer, operate consistent with the laws of nature in that they constantly seek structural equilibrium where the optimal condition is system "efficiency." Consider the human body. The external "structure" of the body, what we see when we look in a mirror, is constituted by the 78 organs (e.g., heart, liver, kidneys, etc.) pulsing within it. So long as the organs are functionally operable, the system is in equilibrium. But as soon as one or more of these vital organs fails us, our bodily system is in disequilibrium and must be repaired as near to its original state as possible. Sometimes that means removing the defective organ. Sometimes the system will self-correct and heal. But most often we need a little help from a doctor to assist the body back to normalcy (i.e., strategic relational system reform). Most important is that the bodily system returns to a state of health (equilibrium).

As with the human body, social systems function smoothly when each of the primary "organs" necessary for its survival operates to the benefit of the social structure. If dysfunction appears in any one of the institutions (organs), then state actors must act through their power of governmentality (discussed in Chapter 7) to tweak that institution through reform measures that will bring the system back to normalcy (this could include statute, case law, and/or executive order). Spencer's theory was later developed by French sociologist, Emile Durkheim, where it finds its most coherent and valuable expression in *The Division of Labor in Society*.[39] Simply put, each institution within a society plays a necessary and vital role in preserving that society's equilibrium. Primary institutions include the media, religion, politics, economics, education, family, and law. Each of these institutions is constitutive of the systemic whole. That is, each in its own way is responsible for system maintenance and reproduction as its primary "function." At bottom, functionalist theory seeks the most "efficient" pursuit of societal outputs cognizant of significant differences in individual aptitudes. The functionalist theory of stratification, for example, most famously promoted by Davis and Moore,[40] suggests that just as in nature, some of us will not be able to compete at the same levels of excellence as others. That isn't a bad thing so long as each of us knows our respective role to play as system reproducers. For example, few of us possess the capacity for high-level mathematics, science, philosophy, medicine, and the like. Cultures should be designed to promote the cultural significance of those professions by providing greater status and wealth to those possessing them. But it is equally true that we will always need someone to literally pick up the garbage. Marginal working-class and gig workers have a significant role to play in reproducing system equilibrium because their responsibility for maintaining sanitary communities and moving goods and services is of utmost importance to achieving system-wide survival through continuous profit maximization (efficiency). The concept of stratification suggests, then, that while none of us possesses the same quantum of intellectual, physical, or artistic ability, each of us has an important role to play in system maintenance and reproduction. Because we are possessing of greater or lesser aptitudes, stratification should not only be permissible but encouraged as a way to compensate those with skill to a greater degree than those without, while stimulating within-group competition to attain ever higher levels of system-desired skills. Following the functionalist model, then, what is efficient is what is good for system reproduction so long as the system maintains equilibrium.[41]

Law and Economics

Beginning in the mid to late 19th century, the discipline of economics increasingly gained status as a social science. Among its more commonplace applications, economics was applied to the administration of law as a means of achieving greater efficiency. Two important historical events emerged to position economics as a powerful force for influencing jurisprudence. The first was the discovery and application of high-order mathematics to social problems, followed by the growth of economics as a profession. In 1885, for example, the American Economics Association was founded.[42] There are two recognized historical moments characterizing the law and economics movement: the first appeared with the turn of the 20th century Progressive movement, and the second arrived in roughly 1970 following the publication a decade earlier of Ronald Coase's article, *The Problem of Social Cost*.[43]

The Progressive era law and economics movement was premised upon ameliorating the negative effects of capitalism through policies directed at the redistribution of wealth. Prior to the emergence of the Progressive law and economics era, the United States and England were each guided by classical economic assumptions regarding the near-sacred nature of laissez-faire capitalism with its free market mandate. Classical economists argued that there should be no state regulation of economic relationships since regulation would insert an external artificial stimulus into the organic functioning of the market that would inevitably disrupt trade by artificially affecting wages, working conditions, and product quality assurance, each of which would severely impact profit maximization and the autonomy of business merchants and laborers to encounter each other in the free market. It was the "invisible hand" of the market that would perennially reshape the economy in ways that would produce the greatest national wealth and health, and any intrusion upon market relationships by the state would invariably muck up the works. As we saw in Chapter 5, the United States Supreme Court's *Allgeyer* and *Lochner* opinions fell within classical economic theory, one that was instrumental in promoting the liberty of contract doctrine. The Court's *Allgeyer* opinion clearly aligns its ideological justification for liberty of contract in the Fourteenth Amendment, and in so doing articulates a position regarding the framework through which to determine wages and working conditions that was premised upon subjective as opposed to objective value preferences. This is important because the Court positioned itself in opposition to Progressive era legal scholars through its privileging of individualization – *Homo economicus*. Progressive law and economics scholars, on the other hand, applied their scientific assessment of inequality and capitalist oppression to objective measures of each. That is, rather than viewing *Homo sapiens* as atomized subjects who succeed or fail based upon their own skill and effort, Progressive law and economics scholars applied their critical lens to objective measures of structurally induced poverty that applied to an entire *class* of people. Rather than focusing upon individual decision-making, they emphasized how classes of people in the United States were subjected to dehumanizing, alienating, and exploitative work and life in civil society.[44] For sociologist and legal scholar Roscoe Pound, "liberty of contract represented the judicial triumph of the subjective, individualistic doctrine of welfare over the 'social' or objective doctrine."[45]

Legal scholars of the Progressive era applied the theory of *marginal utility* to the accumulation of wealth. The argument was simple enough. For the wealthy, the accumulation of an additional dollar will generate only "marginal utility" since a dollar added to hundreds of thousands or millions of dollars already procured will not significantly enhance their quality of life. However, for the poor, every additional dollar accumulated does significantly enhance their quality of life, and in so doing, the overall health of the national economy. According to marginal utility theory, "the transfer of dollars from the millionaire to the pauper would continue to improve total welfare until the millionaire and the pauper had the same amount of marginal utility for the next dollar."[46] The redistributive nature of Progressive marginal utility theory led to its practitioners being referred to as the material welfare school of economics. The material welfare school was influential from the turn of the 20th century until 1930.[47] Hovenkamp states that the material welfare school influenced the jurisprudence of tort law, family law, environmental law, criminal law, and civil rights law.[48] They supported the application of marginal utility economics to a vast array of policies and practices meant to counteract the well-known detritus generated by the capitalist mode of production, including "minimum wage laws, graduated income taxes, subsidized public education, welfare payments to the poor, taxes on monopoly profits, and other devices by which the relatively wealthy were required to finance the provision of goods and services to the relatively impoverished. Health and safety regulation could also be justified as taxes on wealthy producers for the benefit of poorer consumers."[49] With its attention to the degradation of human life generated through oppressive living and working conditions, the material welfare school of economics responded with policies that, in my opinion, seem consistent with those recommended by the physiocrats discussed previously. The physiocrats, you may recall, were foremost in promoting the natural law ideology of individual autonomy consistent with the application of property and the right to freely labor. They were also well aware of the abject suffering of the laboring poor and argued for policies that would ameliorate it. The Progressive era material welfare school applied marginal utility to a set of policies designed to protect the poor and vulnerable through the redistribution of wealth.

Richard T. Ely was a progressive law and economics scholar writing in the early to mid-20th century. He was, like many of his predecessors, heavily influenced by the German Historical School of economics. I mention Ely because his analysis is both historical and structural in nature, and because of his analysis of contracts. In 1914, Ely published his two-volume *Property and Contract in Their Relations to the Distribution of Wealth*. An institutionalist economist by training, Ely "argued that the distribution of wealth in society was a product of *previously created legal rules*, not merely that of the natural laws of economics" (my emphasis).[50] That is, no "invisible hand" drove economic prosperity. Rather, individual wealth was established and maintained through a series of legal codes (recall Katharina Pistor and the coding of capital) produced by those with access to power. Important for my purposes is Ely's concern with contract law. Ely insists that

> unregulated bargaining enhances power that already exists and creates increasingly greater economic inequality. The law of contract tends to preserve advantages once secured, because the inequalities of disadvantages under which one party may labor will express themselves in contract. And as contract tends to preserve advantages secured, so it continues disadvantages – contract tends to keep the existing conditions of things, or to allow existing currents to flow on.[51]

As applied to plea bargaining, Ely's expression of the power vested in the progenitor of contracts (i.e., a prosecutor), and the sempiternal application of plea procedure as a contractual bargain, signify a self-contained autopoietic process that over time constructs its own internal logic. Importantly, to the extent that there is no substantive systemic oversight of prosecutorial authority in the context of the plea (recall Federal Rule 11), the process shares similarities with Ely's larger concern over "unregulated bargaining." In addition, Ely's contention that it is the contract as legal technology that facilitates the perpetuation of the inequalities and disadvantages that exist between the author of a contract (a prosecutor) and its recipient (a defendant) is precisely the point that I am making in this chapter. What prosecutors achieve through the application of contract law to plea negotiations is: a) normalizing the hierarchical authority of the state in the person of the prosecutor, b) legitimating the application of contract law to criminal procedure, c) promoting *Homo economicus,* the atomized rational individual confronting the state, d) efficiency and ease of conviction, and e) autopoietic normalization of the plea process. The practical result of the normalization of the application of contract law to plea bargains is, as Ely suggests the "preservation of advantages secured" for the powerful, while contracts continue to promote disadvantages for the powerless since they tend to perpetuate the "condition of things." In sum, for Ely it is contract as legal technology that serves to perpetuate unequal bargaining. This point will become clearer as I discuss contracts of adhesion below.

Beginning in 1970 and continuing throughout the decade, neoclassical (or neoliberal) economics began to take hold with its primary emphasis on a reinterpretation of common law (judge-made law) to emphasize efficiency, where the common law was considered more desirable than legislation for promoting individual wealth and societal well-being. Neoliberal economists considered common law superior to legislation for two reasons. First, "common law is designed to give effect to private bargains with minimum active interference from the state" because the "invisible hand" of the market was a more efficient mechanism for determining resource allocations. Second, "common law rules tend to become precedential only to the extent that they are efficient – i.e., through an evolutionary process, more efficient rules are upheld while less efficient ones are overruled."[52]

What I find compelling is the emerging confluence of neoliberal economics during the 1970s with the United States Supreme Court opinions relating to plea bargaining. As I emphasized in Chapter 1, a brief review of the Court's 1970s plea jurisprudence makes it clear that the Court's majority had been influenced by an enervated liberty of contract doctrine that emerged largely in response to the publication of Coase's 1960 article. As applied to the plea, the Court's language speaks specifically to procedural efficiency by framing criminal defendants as atomized individuals subject to the power of government through the office of the prosecutor. The historical timing of the Court's plea jurisprudence with an emergent neoliberal law and economy movement cannot be overlooked.

There are two prevailing theories applied to questions of efficiency and that are normative within law and economics – the Pareto efficiency principle and the Kaldor–Hicks efficiency principle.

The Pareto efficiency principle (which ultimately leads to the development of the Coase theorem) stipulates that "a policy is efficient if there is no alternative policy that makes someone better off without making anyone worse off (what Coase referred to as 'transaction costs')."[53] The ultimate Pareto achievement is equilibrium, the balancing of interests. In order for a policy to be Pareto efficient, "a state policy may be said to increase welfare only if at least one person subjectively perceived that he benefitted and no one subjectively perceived that she was injured."[54]

In the 1930s, marginal utility theory met with severe opposition from ordinal economics. Rather than emphasizing class as an independent variable affecting all manner of human behavior, ordinal economics assessed individual preferences for, say, commodity purchases, by ranking them on an ordinal scale. Ordinal efficiency analysis most commonly appears in the form of the Kaldor-Hicks efficiency principle. Nicholas Kaldor and John R. Hicks conceived an efficiency principle that would embellish upon Pareto efficiency. The Kaldor–Hicks efficiency principle posits that the most efficient policy is the one that *people are most willing to pay for.*[55] That is, a law or procedure is Kaldor–Hicks efficient, not when relationships are in equipoise as with Pareto efficiency, but rather when the beneficiaries of an agreement "*are able to compensate the losers fully for their losses and still have something left over*" (my emphasis).[56] Axiomatic of contractual negotiations, Kaldor–Hicks efficiency acknowledges that there will be "winners" and "losers." This is most likely to be true under circumstances where contracts of adhesion (discussed below) are in play since a clear power imbalance exists between the author of the negotiation and those to whom the terms of the contract will be applied.

Plea bargaining is Kaldor–Hicks efficient. It is my argument that to the extent the question of efficiency is paramount for legal scholars and members of the judiciary who defend the contractual nature of plea bargaining, it is the Kaldor–Hicks efficiency principle that most clearly encapsulates the post-indictment plea agreement between a prosecutor and a defendant. Unlike Pareto efficiency, which tolerates a unit of improvement for one subject so long as, in accruing that unit of improvement, no other subject is harmed, the criminal legal process may be considered Kaldor–Hicks efficient when one subject receives a unit of improvement at the expense of the other subject, but the other subject is compensated for their loss. As applied to the administration of justice through plea bargaining, prosecutors "win" by gaining an admission of guilt from a defendant who must also abdicate their Fifth and Sixth Amendment rights (i.e., their losses), while those defendants are "compensated" for their loss (abdication of Fifth and Sixth Amendment rights) through receipt of charge and sentencing reductions. So while the plea process fails to produce *equitable* contractual outcomes, it is Kaldor–Hicks efficient since it satisfies the needs of the state (a unit of improvement) while simultaneously compensating defendants for their decision to forego trial.

In summary, the law and economics movement in the United States has a fascinating and bipolar history. Initially forming in response to the deleterious effects of capitalism, early material welfare school economists applying marginal utility theory turned to the state for regulation of industrial practices. The influence of the material welfare school began to wane in the 1930s, and by the 1970s the United States was firmly in the grip of neoliberal economic theory – a return to classical economics with its emphasis on deregulation of industry and the free labor liberty of contract language that generated *Homo economicus*. The 1970s economic turn emerged at precisely the same moment as the plea bargaining cases presented in Chapter 1 were decided by the United States Supreme Court. The Kaldor–Hicks efficiency principle provided the theoretical and juridical justification for a constitutionally protected form of due process – plea bargaining – substantively codified through a legal code of capitalism – Rule 11.

Plea Bargaining and Improperly Obtained Assent

The final step in our economic critique of plea bargaining leads us directly to its justification by the Supreme Court in *Brady* – the application of a juridically distorted law of contracts to plea bargaining. Since the Court has found justification for the plea in contract law, it seems only reasonable that the law of contracts should equally apply to plea bargains to determine whether they are constitutionally permissible. This section will focus exclusively on the *deficits* arising from the application of contract law to pleas, with particular emphasis placed on improperly obtained assent.[57] I will focus exclusively on misrepresentation, duress, undue influence, and unconscionability. The reason for this emphasis is consistent with the law of contracts and *improperly obtained assent* where, "each of the promisors [defendants] ... manifested their assent to contract and were competent to do so. Nonetheless, their assent was alleged to have been induced by conduct on the part of the promisee [prosecutors] that undermines the normal significance of a manifestation of consent."[58] As I will demonstrate, the structure of plea bargaining as a contract is such that it is infected by four manifestations of deficit that would, under private law, render the contracts to be in violation of constitutional law.

Misrepresentation

According to the Restatement (Second) of Contracts §159, misrepresentation "is an assertion that is not in accordance with the facts."[59] Furthermore, §162 stipulates the following:

(1) A misrepresentation is fraudulent if the maker intends his assertion to induce a party to manifest his assent and the maker
  a. knows or believes that the assertion is not in accord with the facts, or
  b. does not have the confidence that he states or implies in the truth of the assertion, or
  c. knows that he does not have the basis that he states or implies for the assertion.
(2) A misrepresentation is material if it would be likely to induce a reasonable person to manifest his assent, or if the maker knows that it would be likely to induce the recipient to do so.[60]

Police only share case information directly with prosecutors. The typical plea case file will include a police crime scene report, a presentencing report, and possibly, though rarely, post hoc witness interviews. Three practices signify case misrepresentation: 1) withheld material impeachment information, 2) charge stacking, and 3) an actual factual basis upon which to conclude the truth of events as asserted by the state. Each of these three practices is fraught with misrepresentation as defined by §162.

In *United States v. Ruiz*[61] a unanimous Supreme Court held that the United States Constitution does not require prosecutors to share material impeachment evidence with criminal defendants prior to entering plea negotiations. The justification for the opinion, written by Justice Breyer, pivots on the defendant's waiver of non-jurisdictional defects that accompanies the guilty plea (as discussed in the first part of this chapter), as well as the burden that would be placed upon the state to conduct an investigation prior to entering into plea negotiations.[62] What this means is that prosecutors who relied upon confidential informants and other witnesses providing information leading to the subsequent arrest and indictment of a defendant are not required to share the identities of those informants and witnesses with the defendant for possible impeachment.[63] That means that there is no way for the defendant to know a) who bore witness against them, b) their ability to confront that witness (Sixth Amendment waiver), or c) even know the substance of the information shared with prosecutors. What is as yet unknown is whether the *Ruiz* opinion equally applies to withheld exculpatory evidence that would at trial be guided by *Brady v. Maryland*[64] and its progeny. In those states with open discovery laws, inculpatory and exculpatory evidence should be shared as a routine matter. But even in those states, how would we know? Prosecutorial control over all information relating to the case puts the defense at a serious disadvantage regarding discovery. Defendants will not be afforded the time or resources to conduct a pre-plea investigation, resulting in asymmetrical control over and dissemination of information.

Charge stacking is the practice of intentionally overcharging criminal defendants with violations of criminal law to induce a downward charge and sentence bargain.[65] Typically, these are charges that the state has no intention of pursuing as part of its case in chief were the case to go to trial since the existing evidence would be too thin to gain a conviction. Threatened but superfluous charges are used as bargaining chips held by the state and presented to defendants by prosecutors as an indication of "good-faith" negotiations over optimal benefits. With little knowledge of the evidence that actually exists within the state's file, the absence of resources (including time) to properly investigate the case, and the probability of a conviction at trial generating a far greater sentence than that offered by the plea (the trial tax), the state is guilty of misrepresentation.

Finally, Federal Rule 11 provides no guidance for determining the quantum of evidence constituting the "factual basis" necessary to convict by way of a guilty plea. Syllogistically, it must be true that since guilty pleas are the immediate byproduct of indictments, and since the standard of proof necessary for a grand jury to indict is probable cause, we must assume that the quantum of evidence necessary to meet the "factual basis" criteria to convict by way of the plea is probable cause. Probable cause is the second lowest standard of proof. This is, of course, quite reasonable since no case investigation has taken place to generate a more robust accounting of alleged criminal activity. With no case investigation, neither the prosecutor nor the defense attorney has much information pertaining to factually accurate accounts of allegedly criminal events. The question, then, is whether the probable cause standard generates enough of a factual basis to meet constitutional muster. With one-sided adversarial control over negligible case evidence, and no mandate to share exculpatory material impeachment evidence with the defense (and likely any other exculpatory *Brady* material), by what standard should we be assured that prosecutors are engaging in truthful plea negotiations? In sum, how does the defendant prove a negative? When exposed to actual plea practice, Federal Rule 11's "factual basis" standard is legal sophistry, and as a result, criminal defendants are subjected to systemic information asymmetry generative of misrepresentation.

Duress

Plea bargains are "negotiated" under conditions of duress. And while the noun "duress" is not one that most of us use in daily interaction, its meaning is well known to all lay people. Simply, duress means: "threats," "violence," "constraints," or other action brought to bear on someone to do something against their will or better judgment. The lay definition of duress provides context for the Restatement (Second) of Contracts. While the Restatement (Second) of Contracts speaks specifically to physical duress, basing my argument on my previously published work on neurophenomenology, I would add *psycho-emotional* duress as well. Specifically, "the paradigm defense to contract is that of physical duress. It seems obvious that one's 'consent' to contract is not binding if it was obtained by the use or threatened use of force."[66] Barnett and Oman cite Lord Coke's expression of the conditions manifesting physical duress, and they include: "1. for fear of losse of life, 2. of losse of member, 3. of mayhem, and 4. of imprisonment."[67] In §175 of the Restatement (Second) of Contracts, the definition of duress includes the following:

> (1) If a party's manifestation of assent is induced by an improper threat by the other party that leaves the victim no reasonable alternative, the contract is voidable by the victim.[68]

In §176, the Restatement (Second) of Contracts identifies "When a threat is improper."[69] Among the list of actions that render a contract void, and that would apply to plea bargaining, is:

- What is threatened is a criminal prosecution.
- What is threatened is the use of the civil process and the threat is made in bad faith.
- The threat is a breach of duty of good faith and fair dealing under a contract with the recipient.
- A threat is improper if the resulting exchange is not on fair terms, and
  - (a) The threatened act would harm the recipient and would not significantly benefit the party making the threat.
  - (c) What is threatened is otherwise a use of power for illegitimate ends.

The ways in which defendants confronted with the plea are exposed to duress include: 1) the trial tax (excessive sentence if convicted at trial), 2) charge stacking, 3) minimal case investigation (if any), 4) no procedural access to impeachment evidence (*Ruiz*), and 5) threatening a defendant with increased punishment if the prosecutor's plea offer is rejected and the defendant is convicted at trial (see *Brady* and *Bordenkircher*).

Undue Influence

Undue influence puts prosecutorial pressure front and center during plea negotiations. An expression of undue influence as applied to the law of contracts appears in the 1868 case *Hall v. Hall*:

> To make a good contract a man must be a free agent. Pressure of whatever sort which overpowers the will without convincing the judgment is a species of restraint under which no valid contract can be made. *Importunity or threats, if carried to the degree in which the free play of a man's will is overborne, constitute undue influence, although no force is used or threatened.* A party may be led but not driven, and his acts must be the offspring of his own volition and not in accord with someone else's.[70]

Barnett and Oman clarify the meaning of the *Hall* opinion by stressing that

> undue influence involves the use of excessive pressure to persuade one vulnerable to such pressure, pressure applied by a dominant subject to a servient object. In combination, the elements of undue susceptibility in the servient person and excessive pressure by the dominating person make the latter's influence undue, for it results in the apparent will of the servient person being in fact the will of the dominant person.[71]

Under the Federal Rules of Criminal Procedure Rule 11, plea bargains are entirely the province of prosecutors who determine a) whether to charge, b) whether to plea, c) the conditions of the plea, and d) the proposed sentence. This process unfolds premised upon indictment by grand jury where the standard for indictment is probable cause. And while it may be said that the Sixth Amendment right to counsel should abate concerns of undue influence, the scholarship surrounding assistance of counsel in plea cases suggests that for a host of economic and pragmatic professional culture reasons, defense attorneys in no way serve to ameliorate the power imbalance constituting plea negotiations.

For reasons previously stated, defendant *Homo sapiens* is presented with a Faustian bargain: a) plead *not guilty* and exercise the right to trial where, if convicted, the sentencing ranges are draconian (trial tax), b) *threaten* to plead not guilty and be pressured by prosecutors and/or judges to reconsider the guilty plea offer or risk the maximum sentence if convicted at trial (which may include execution – *Brady* and *Bordenkircher*), c) confront charge stacking (overcharging cases, which confuses the plea negotiation by introducing duress), d) withholding impeachment evidence (*Ruiz*), and e) withholding other non-jurisdictional defects known to the prosecutor but not to the defendant (e.g., *Brady v. Maryland* material).

Finally, Rule 11's prohibition on judicial oversight relating to the substance of the plea deal means that the prosecutor, and only the prosecutor, has the power to administer the plea process. Because plea deals are arranged in private, based upon an admittedly thin police crime scene report and a presentencing report (Why conduct an investigation at this point in the process when an admission of guilt makes it unnecessary?), and without judicial review of the substance of the charges and the "factual basis" necessary to establish whether the appropriate charges have been brought and guilt has been properly established, working a plea conviction case on appeal is nearly impossible to do. That means that once codified, the plea deal will likely stand without any attack upon substantive or procedural defects. In this context, the plea should be voided as an improperly obtained assent since "negotiations" took place under circumstances of undue prosecutor influence.

Unconscionability

The last of the concerns to be raised relative to improperly obtained assent to contract is unconscionability. To be an unconscionable act means an act that is "wrong" or "excessive." In the language of contract law, unconscionability means

> an absence of meaningful choice on the part of one of the parties together with contract terms which are unreasonably favorable to the other party ... In many cases the meaningfulness of the choice is negated by a gross inequality of bargaining power. The manner in which the contract was entered is also a relevant consideration. Did each party to the contract, considering his obvious education or lack of it, have a reasonable opportunity to understand the terms of the contract[?] ... But when a party of little bargaining power, and hence little real choice, signs a commercially unreasonable contract with little or no knowledge of its terms, it is hardly likely that his consent, or even an objective manifestation of his consent, was ever given to all the terms.[72]

In order to prevail on a charge of unconscionability, a defendant has available §2-302 of the Sales Contracts: The Uniform Commercial Code, and §208 of the Restatement (Second) of Contracts. §2-302 provides for court consideration of the substantive contractual agreement to determine whether unconscionability existed, and if so, whether it tainted the contract. The Restatement (Second) of Contracts, §208, applies nearly identical language, voiding any contract, or part of a contract, where unconscionability has been uncovered.

Two problems are immediately noticeable when attempting to apply unconscionability in the context of plea bargaining as a contract. First, Rule 11 expressly forbids judicial participation in, or review of, substantive plea negotiations and agreements (judges affirm the knowing and voluntary prongs during the plea colloquy, and they issue the sentence). Second, considering the absence of judicial oversight, coupled with Supreme Court precedent forbidding defense access to impeachment evidence (and possibly other exculpatory *Brady v. Maryland* material) known to the prosecutor during plea negotiations (*Ruiz*), charge stacking, and threats of harsher punishment if convicted at trial, we are left with a negotiation procedure that bears the hallmark of unconscionability but without any apparent statutory or common law remedy. In sum, the private law of contracts provides far greater judicial oversight and legal remedies for unconscionably procured agreements, but it does so because judges have the authority to scrutinize the terms and conditions generating the agreement for fairness.

Unlike the prosaic defense of the proof beyond a reasonable doubt standard expressed in *Winship*, *Brady*, with its emphasis upon contract law, ushered in constitutional protection for a bastardization of both criminal procedure and contract law since plea bargaining as a contract gives rise to improperly obtained assent.

Contracts of Adhesion

In this final section of the chapter, I would like to explore what I think may be a hybrid application of contract law to plea bargaining. While it superficially appears to be a *conventional* contractual negotiation between two parties where concerns relating to misrepresentation, duress, undue influence, and unconscionability as related to the plea context are paramount, the plea bargaining context also resembles *contracts of adhesion*. Contracts of adhesion are typically entered into by two or more *private* parties negotiating a deal. To the extent that contracts of adhesion are guided by private and not public law, they do not automatically appear to apply to plea bargain contracts negotiated between criminal defendants and the government. In 1983, Professor of Law at Harvard Law School Todd Rakoff published what is considered now to be the standard articulation of contracts of adhesion.[73] For Rakoff, there are seven characteristics defining contracts of adhesion:

1. The document whose legal validity is at issue is a printed form that contains many terms and clearly purports to be a contract.
2. The form has been drafted by, or on behalf of, one party to the transaction.
3. The drafting party participates in numerous transactions of the type represented by the form and enters into these transactions as a matter of routine.
4. The form is presented to the adhering party with the representation that, except perhaps for a few identified items (such as the price term), the drafting party will enter into the transaction only in terms contained in the document. This representation may be explicit or may be implicit in the situation, but it is understood by the adherent.

5. After the parties have dickered over whatever terms are open to bargaining, the document is signed by the adherent.
6. The adhering party enters into few transactions of the type represented by the form – few, at least, in comparison to the drafting party.
7. The principal obligation of the adhering party in the transaction considered as a whole is the payment of money.[74]

What should be most apparent from Rakoff's list of adhesion contract characteristics is the fact that, in the plea bargaining context, it is the prosecutor who, constituted by points 1–4 listed above, holds absolute power over "adherents" or criminal defendants. It is point 7, "payment of money," that only slightly deviates from the felony plea bargaining situation. That is, depending upon the seriousness of the charge, some felony criminal defendants may be able to bargain with prosecutors such that their punishment will be *financial remuneration* provided to victims and/or the state. In that way, criminal defendants confronting a plea offer are similarly situated to those private parties prosecuted for violating adhesion contracts. More often than not, however, in the criminal context, fines and fees are combined with some kind of probation tail requiring a commitment to avoid criminal activity or confront serious jail or prison time.

Contracts of adhesion are offered in a "take it or leave it" format. That is, in the private law context, a contract's forms and terms have already been determined by corporate attorneys and are used to establish boilerplate language that applies to all who wish to engage with the party offering the service. Adherents, those who pursue the good or service being offered by the private seller, are confronted with a contract that includes the "small print" necessary to establish the legal authority and responsibility accruing to each party to the agreement. It is my argument that, but for a few structural differences, plea bargaining represents a hybrid juridical procedure guided by both conventional contract law and contracts of adhesion.[75]

Let us return for a moment to the plea bargaining process. Let us also be reminded of the fact that it is the legislature that determines which behaviors will be considered "criminal" violations of law. Those behaviors are clearly articulated and appear as part of each state's criminal code. In addition, states' legislatures are equally responsible for establishing the sentencing ranges that apply to convictions of each type of criminal violation. For example, in my home state of Arizona, the legislature has created three classes relating to the crime of robbery: Robbery, Aggravated Robbery, and Armed Robbery.[76] A subject convicted of Robbery (a Class 4 felony) and who has no priors will be sentenced to between 1 and 3.75 years in prison. A subject with one prior conviction will confront a sentencing range of between 2.25 and 7.5 years. For Aggravated Robbery (a Class 3 felony), a subject with no priors may be sentenced to between 2 and 8.75 years in prison, while a subject with one prior will be subjected to between 3.5 and 16.25 years in prison. Finally, for Armed Robbery (a Class 2 "dangerous" felony), a subject with no priors is confronted with a prospective sentence of between 7 and 21 years in prison, while a subject with one prior "dangerous" conviction will be sentenced to between 14 and 28 years in prison. The sentencing ranges provide prosecutors with the ability to focus their sentencing recommendations upon the known facts of the case, with the more serious facts (and the presence of prior convictions) pushing prosecutors to the higher end of the sentencing range. Regardless, there is still a discreet range, a non-negotiable framework, that is presented to the adherent felony defendant in what is a "take it or leave it" context. At the local level, institutional practices may become ensconced over time and with regard to specific county attorneys and their preferences for punishing certain types of crimes (say sexual assault or drug dealing) consistent with their community's standards and expectations. Still operating within the charge and sentencing guidelines, those local practices may deviate relative to other counties in each state, but there will still emerge a specific set of patterns and practices premised upon the legislatively enacted law that produces a structured procedure for negotiating plea agreements.

At issue when confronting plea bargains as negotiated contracts is an academic and judicial concern over the application of monopoly power.[77] Readers will recall from Chapter 1 that plea bargaining is premised upon Federal Rule 11 and accompanying case law. Federal Rule 11 requires judges to establish in open court as part of a plea colloquy that the defendant has entered the plea agreement without coercion by establishing that the defendant understands the charges they are facing and the rights they are relinquishing (knowing and intelligent), and that they are voluntarily entering into the agreement (voluntariness). As I have previously demonstrated in Chapter 1, both the knowing and voluntary prongs characterizing plea bargaining are empty signifiers requiring far greater scholarly and juridical understanding. Given the monopoly power constituting prosecutors in the plea context, and the fact that it is unlikely that the defendant will be fully aware of the nature of the terms of the contract, plea bargains as adhesion contracts raise the specter of executive force to the level of concern that I have reserved for it in this book. What is known to prosecutors is that most defendants will not understand the terms and conditions of their proposed charges and sentence. In fact, argues Rakoff, "the adhering party is in practice unlikely to have read the standard terms before signing the document and is unlikely to have understood them if he has read them."[78] More important, prosecutors know this as well. As the drafter of the proposed plea deal, "In all probability the drafting party, too, knows this fact about adherents' behavior."[79] For Rakoff, it is this aspect of contracts of adhesion – form clauses and the monopoly power of prosecutors – that raises questions about their enforceability. And while the law and terminology used in the private law context may not be properly or easily applied to the public law context, in the case of *Williams v. Walker-Thomas Furniture Co.*,[80] Judge Wright's explication of the unconscionability of adhesion contracts applies to the plea bargaining case.

> Ordinarily, one who signs an agreement without full knowledge of its terms might be held to assume the risk that he has entered a one-sided bargain. But when a party of little bargaining power, and hence little real choice, signs a commercially unreasonable contract with little or no knowledge of its terms, it is hardly likely that his consent, or even an objective manifestation of his consent, was ever given to all terms.[81]

Of course, our concern in this book is for the felony plea bargain and not a "*commercially* unreasonable contract," but with this one exception, Justice Wright's remark in *Williams* directly applies to the plea. Questions relating to the probity of applying adhesion contracts to pleas include whether there is a public interest at stake, or whether "one party to the transaction had 'superior bargaining power'."[82] In his work addressing adhesion contracts, Kessler contends that they most often appear when there are significant power imbalances between the offering party and the adherent. Specifically,

> Standard contracts are typically used by enterprises with strong bargaining power. The weaker party, in need of the goods or services, is frequently not in a position to shop around for better terms, either because the author of the standard contract has a monopoly (natural or artificial) or because all competitors use the same clauses. His contractual intention is but a subjection more or less voluntary to terms dictated by the stronger party, terms whose consequences are often understood only in a vague way, if at all. Thus, standardized contracts are frequently contracts of adhesion.[83]

Once again, it bears repeating that plea bargains take place as part of *public law*. Contracts of adhesion are typically considered ubiquitous in the *private law* context. But it is my argument that, with very few substantive exceptions, plea bargaining is a contract of adhesion. Unlike a person who engages in negotiation over the purchase of a new automobile where they will be confronted with the terms of an adhesion contract and may shop those terms to other competitors in the automobile market, criminal defendants are not free to disengage from unfavorable plea negotiations by requesting to negotiate with a different and perhaps more amiable prosecutor. Rather, criminal defendants "get what they get." All power to determine whether to charge, what to charge, what to sentence, and whether to negotiate lies solely within the purview of prosecutorial discretion. Kessler's assessment of the lawfulness of adhesion contracts, then, "lies in their being employed to exert monopolistic, or at least oligopolistic, power."[84]

Consistent with a Weberian analysis of contracts of adhesion is attention to the bureaucratic organization of firms and institutions toward the use of form documents. As a way to promote efficiency and consistency, form documents facilitate coordination among departments; eliminate linguistic confusion through the use of familiar terms; make efficient use of expensive managerial and legal talent; provide for supervisory evaluation of administrative actions; and help to solidify the organization's internal power structure.[85] Consistent with the argument that I made in Chapter 5 regarding *Homo economicus* and the liberty of contract doctrine, each of which was ideologically deployed to the capitalist cause of framing all people as "free to labor," in a similar way Rakoff suggests that "The consumer's experience of modern commercial life is one not of freedom in the full sense posited by traditional contract law [i.e., liberty of contract], but rather one of submission to organizational domination, leavened by the ability to choose the organization by which he will be dominated."[86] Here, Rakoff makes precisely the same connection to political economy and domination that I have argued for throughout. That is, the ideological construct of "free labor" really only means the "freedom" to choose one's oppressor. In the private law context discussed by Rakoff, that would mean the "choice" between commercial vendors. In the public law context, framing criminal defendants as atomized individuals who are confronting the power of the state alone to "negotiate" the terms of their case falls squarely within the narrative construction of *Homo economicus* and the liberty of contract doctrine as applied to contract law. That being so, each of the concerns raised relating to power and information imbalances as attaching to adhesion contracts are equally present in the plea bargaining case. I conclude this section by arguing, consistent with Rakoff, that adhesion contracts, like those I have suggested are applied to the plea bargaining context, are unenforceable.

> Once placed in its proper context as a matter primarily implicating the ordering of power and freedom in our society, the general rule that contracts of adhesion are presumptively enforceable cannot be upheld. The inevitable infringement of adherents' individual freedom that results from the rule leads one to suggest that form terms should never be enforced.[87]

There are two important principles raising serious concerns about continued reliance upon adhesion contracts for plea bargains. The first concern is infringement upon the freedom of the adhering parties. The second concern emerges from the first. For Rakoff,

> The danger of upholding *the authoritarian relationship between the drafting party and the adherent* is a danger different in kind from the risk that the terms of the transaction, overall, represent *an unfair exchange of values*, and is less likely to be cured by competition. Indeed, there is a very real possibility that drafting parties will attempt to capitalize on any legal toleration of form contracting. (My emphasis.)[88]

As we saw in Chapter 1, the United States Supreme Court has firmly established the constitutionality of criminal felony plea bargaining premised upon the right of each autonomous defendant to bargain away their Fifth and Sixth Amendment rights protections in pursuit of a charge and sentence reduction. So long as the plea procedure meets Rule 11 and case law guidelines establishing the factual basis, knowing and intelligent, and voluntary prongs, the resulting agreement, the bargain, will be considered structurally sound and constitutional. The legal frame presented to the defendant will manifest as "form contracting" since, while there will be some room for charge negotiation depending upon a host of factors generated by offices of probation and provided to the court for review prior to issuing sentence, the substance of the frame has already been established by local county attorney office priorities and the legislature in each state.

"*It's Good To Be Inefficient.*" At the root of the justification for plea bargaining is that it is an extremely efficient way for the courts to manage overwhelming caseloads. As we have seen, plea cases are disposed of post indictment without the resource pressure imposed by trials. Operating in a normatively procedural way, prosecutors, defense attorneys, judges, and defendants participate in an adjudication procedure that finds its origins in the economics of efficiency where primary emphasis is placed upon maximizing utility through the vehicle of time management and resource scarcity. The model is predicated upon the factory system and its utilitarian application of rigid managerial oversight, predictability of outcome, preservation of scarce resources, and reproduction of system stability. All are ostensibly laudable goals insofar as power and control are concerned, as well as a kind of system stability emerging from the cultural satisfaction resulting from the conviction of a defendant for crimes committed against the community.

But what if I argue that sometimes the most efficacious way is not the most efficient one? Consider the process of knowledge production. There is, in my experience, simply no substitute for the discipline and hard work necessary to deeply learn a subject. Reading, writing, and arguing constitute an often chaotic, non-linear process that moves through fits and starts without necessarily producing anything resembling knowledge production. Every adult knows that their youth-inspired life plans were so much fantasy since life resembles bumper pool – we direct our actions toward a specific set of goals when we are suddenly confronted with an obstacle requiring us to switch gears and move in a different direction. We do this throughout our lives often without realizing it until we are much older and can look back at the crooked path we've taken. This experience is captured by the Yiddish expression, "*Der mensch tracht, Un Gott lacht.*" Man plans, and God laughs.

At most universities in the United States, students are provided with structural inducements to graduate in the most efficient way possible. This can mean that students are guaranteed that their tuition will not increase throughout their four-year pursuit of a baccalaureate degree as long as they are making progress toward completion. Of course, changing one's mind regarding their major area of study, especially if they are a few years into its completion, is clearly not efficient since the student is "wasting their time" and "wasting their money." Or it may mean that promising undergraduate students can start a graduate degree while still working toward the completion of their undergraduate degree. In some situations, students are so motivated to graduate that they routinely register for the maximum credit hours permitted (at our institution, it would be 19 credit hours per semester or six courses). Isn't it a good thing if a student can graduate a semester early? Universities are replete with procedures like these meant to enhance the efficient completion of a four-year degree, including the requirement that academic departments produce "career-ready" curricula meant to prepare students for post-baccalaureate employment. Such initiatives devalue the Humanities and Social Sciences since they tend not to be directed at producing specific skills translatable to the contemporary labor market (as if any academic discipline can accurately predict labor market needs five or more years in advance). What efficiency means in each case is the completion of the degree in as short a time as possible, at the lowest price possible, and with skills that are immediately translatable to the labor market. Or consider the now-nationwide university and college commitment to no longer hiring tenure-track PhD faculty, relying instead upon non-tenure-track year-to-year contracts. It is certainly efficient from the perspective of the university as a corporate entity since it provides annual flexibility with regard to resources allocated for instruction. If the market crashes, as it did in 2008, and again in March 2020 with the arrival of COVID-19, having the flexibility to fire non-tenure-track faculty improves institutional fiscal health and flexibility. But what the move to non-tenured faculty also does is produce less institutional commitment from those faculty, less direct engagement with their academic discipline, and less published research, not to mention working under the constant threat of dismissal and being relatively deprived of any institutional power (this is especially relevant for non-white, female, and non-binary academics).

In short, the most efficient (i.e., linear) path is an ideological construct that assumes perfect knowledge about alternatives and the ability to control all externalities that may intercede upon our plans. Life is messy precisely because it is constituted by an infinite number of subjective and objective variables replicated over seven billion people on the planet. But perhaps the most important reason for human beings to confront the neoliberal demand for efficiency is that it fails to attend to the human need to manage time in ways that are determined entirely by them, and for the purpose of realizing their species essence. Sometimes people do organize their lives in as efficient a way as possible given externalities. And sometimes, as with experiences that take place in civil society where people live most of their lives, efficiency is unlikely to prevail. A traditional lover of baseball has no concern with efficiency. Prior to the 2023 season, baseball had no time limitations. A game would last as long as it was necessary to determine a winner. Consistent with a more efficient management of time, Major League Baseball introduced pitching and hitting time clocks to reduce the amount of time per game. Prior to the changes, a typical game would last roughly three hours. Cricket is an even less efficient game, lasting on average seven and a half hours per day for five days. What is special for those of us who love baseball or cricket is the opportunity to relax into a game. Baseball moves at a quicker pace than it used to, but it still provides ample time for casual conversation and contemplation of the action on the field. In each game it is time that is privileged most. As I discussed in the previous chapter, all *Homo sapiens* must grapple with impending death. As far as we know, *Homo sapiens* is the only species that is aware of mortality. In short, our time on Earth is the most precious gift we have. And while it may be argued that spending our time efficiently is consistent with *memento mori*, what it typically amounts to in a capitalist society is frantic multitasking in order to stay alive.

***

In this chapter, I have deconstructed the language of contracts as applied by the United States Supreme Court to plea bargaining to demonstrate that the criminal legal fetishization of individual autonomy and efficiency, as contextualized within the liberty of contract doctrine, serves state interests in governmentality toward enhanced social control. Through the application of social science, neuroscience, and neurophenomenology, I sought to demonstrate the woeful inadequacy of the concept of "autonomy" ("free will") to properly justify either pleas or contracts (whether public or private). Finally, since the Court introduced the private law of contracts (and not merely by analogy) to the adjudication of felony criminal indictments, it only seems appropriate that the conditions under which plea bargains are procured should be scrutinized consistent with the law of contracts and improperly obtained assent. In each of the areas of misrepresentation, duress, undue influence, and unconscionability, there are serious concerns relating to the procurement of plea bargains that, under private law and statute, would void those bargains. However, to facilitate assessment of the totality of circumstances leading to a plea agreement, we need a more thorough record of discovery and far greater judicial review of substantive inculpatory and exculpatory evidence.

Finally, basing my argument on the preceding information, it is my contention that plea bargaining violates the unconstitutional conditions doctrine (Chapter 8) and that it leads to the commodification of rights protections.

Through the application of Foucault's emphasis upon governmentality as efficiency, and his analysis of law as but one institution existing among others available to facilitate the realization of dominant cultural power, in the next chapter I present, as Marx did before me with regard to *surplus value* (see Chapter 5), the *surplus power* that exists whenever law is imposed upon a set of political, economic, or cultural conditions. Specifically, the law systemically presents as a detached apolitical and objective superstructural institution[89] responsible for enhancing the likelihood of liberal democracy.[90] However, as with surplus value, surplus power as expressed through law signifies the hidden expression of dominant cultural capitalist interests and values.[91] The law's rhetorical expression of "efficiency" in private, administrative, and public law serves as surplus power, a seemingly benign yet hegemonic expression of dominant cultural interests. As explained by Grewal and Purdy, "[I]n practice, neoliberal policies are *always* distributive decisions, yet ones in which distributive choices get couched in the neutral-sounding language of efficiency, liberty, and responsibility, or the pragmatic language of 'what works'."[92] Efficiency manifests as a core principle in neoliberal capitalist states through hegemonic expression of

> the view that strong property rights and private contracting rights are the best means to increase overall welfare, with the sole justification for political intervention being to "correct market failures." The second premise is another version of market fundamentalism, *based on the belief that strong property rights best protect the equal freedom and dignity of individuals*, so that a commercial social order governed by the market is the most decent society that is possible to achieve.[93]

In the spirit of unmasking (Mannheim), Grewal and Purdy's application of political economic critique to neoliberal expressions of efficiency exposes the surplus power operating through ideology and hegemonically constructed legal narratives. Specifically, here Grewal and Purdy conclude by making a point similar to my own,

> The way a series of constitutional doctrines have coalesced around a vision of personal liberty that centers on individual choice in spending,

> consumption, and self-expression, *in disregard of the legally constituted structural setting in which these choices take place.* In this kind of analysis, the concept of neoliberalism ties together the operational effects and ideological predicates of a series of judgments that work in different doctrinal areas, such as free speech, *equal protection, and substantive due process* .... Neoliberal constitutional doctrines have recently extended market-modeled liberty into areas of law where other versions of liberty have previously been important.[94]

Having established the liberty of contract doctrine in Chapter 5, and then having applied contract law to the plea here in Chapter 6, we are left with one final substantive analysis that will complete our political economic critique of the plea – governmentality. Neither economic markets, nor the construction of *Homo economicus*, nor the creation of slavery could appear absent the theoretically, conceptually, and empirically central role played by the state and civil society.

Notes

1 The Constitution of the United States.
2 John Christman. Autonomy in Moral and Political Philosophy. Stanford Encyclopedia of Philosophy (2020).
3 Id at 4.
4 Id at 6.
5 R.H. Coase. The Problem of Social Cost. J. L. and Econ. 3 (1960): 1–44.
6 Lauren B. Edelman and Robin Stryker. A Sociological Approach to Law and the Economy. In The Handbook of Economic Sociology. Neil J. Smelser and Richard Swedberg (eds). Princeton, NJ: Princeton University Press (2005): 527.
7 Id at 528.
8 See the work of Bob Jessop cited supra 3. Application of Jessop's strategic relational analysis captures this dynamic of state administrative and regulatory power, whereby select state agencies and/or institutions (e.g., the courts, Congress, and the executive branch) have the power to identify the source of system disequilibrium and make changes necessary to return the system to equilibrium. This is a perennially dynamic and contingent dialectical process.
9 Supra 5 at 44.
10 Christophe Menke. Critique of Rights. London: Polity Press (2020): 21.
11 Supra 2 at 10.
12 Supra 2 at 11.
13 Jean Cohen and Andrew Arato. Civil Society and Political Theory. Cambridge, MA: MIT Press (1992): 8.
14 Id at 8–9.
15 Consider Jeremy Bentham's "felicity calculus," the seven-stage process by which reasonable people calculate costs. In Westley C. Mitchell, Bentham's Felicific Calculus. Political Science Quarterly, 3 (2) (1918): 161–183.
16 Correspondence with Prof. Lawrence Tribe, July 2, 2012.
17 Robert Johnson and Adam Cureton. Kant's Moral Philosophy. The Stanford Encyclopedia of Philosophy (Spring 2022) https://plato.stanford.edu/entries/kant-moral/. It is important to note that even Kant understood that the concept

of "free will" was bounded. Johnson and Cureton emphasize this point with reference to Kant's Critique of Pure Reason, where Kant makes it clear that, "we have no rational basis for *believing* our wills to be free. This would involve, he argues, attributing a property to our wills that they would have to have as 'things in themselves' apart from the causally determined world of appearances. Of such things, he insists, we can have no knowledge." This is precisely the point that I make below in the following section of this Article. Subjects cannot "step outside of themselves" to consider and adopt "objective" or "essential" reality and, by doing so, adjust their wills in accordance with that reality. Interpretations of reality are contingent upon each subject's neurophenomenological comprehension of the world as they engage with it.

18 The discipline of Sociology is premised upon the theory of the constituted subject culturally embedded in preexisting social, political, economic, and cultural relationships. Please see, for example Pierre Bourdieu. Distinction: A Social Critique of the Judgement of Taste. Richard Nice, trans., Cambridge, MA: Harvard University Press. See in particular Bourdieu's articulation of cultural capital and habitus; E.P. Thompson. The Making of the English Working Class. New York: Open Road Media (2016); Jay MacLeod. Ain't No Makin' It: Aspirations and Attainment in a Low-Income Neighborhood. London: Routledge (2018).

19 Joshua W. Buckholtz & René Marois, *The Roots of Modern Justice: Cognitive and Neural Foundations of Social Norms and Their Enforcement*, 15 Nature Neuroscience 655, 656 (2012); Fritjof Capra, the Hidden Connections: Integrating the Biological, Cognitive, and Social Dimensions of Life into A Science of Sustainability 46 (2002); Adrian Raine, The Anatomy of Violence: The Biological Roots of Crime 312, 313 (2013); Nancy J. Burke et al., *Theorizing Social Context: Rethinking Behavioral Theory*, 36 Health Educ. Behav. 55, 56, 61 (2009); Gerd Gigerenzer & Wolfgang Gaissmaier, *Heuristic Decision Making*, 62 Ann. Rev. Psychol. 451, 462 (2011; Herbert A. Simon, *Invariants of Human Behavior*, 41 Ann. Rev. Psychol; Jeffrey J. Rachlinski, *Gains, Losses, and the Psychology of Litigation*, 70 S. Cal. L. Rev. 113, 128 (1996); Jeremy A. Blumenthal, *Law and the Emotions: The Problems of Affective Forecasting*, 80 Ind. L.J. 155, 206 (2005); Marcel Zeelenberg & Rik Pieters, *A Theory of Regret Regulation 1.0*, 17 J. Consumer Psychol. 3, 11–14 (2007); Richard Birke, *Reconciling Loss Aversion and Guilty Pleas*, 1999 Utah L. Rev. 205, 209, 244–45; Russell B. Korobkin & Thomas S. Ulen, *Law and Behavioral Science: Removing the Rationality Assumption from Law and Economics*, 88 Calif. L. Rev. 1051, 1055 (2000); Chris Guthrie, *A New Social Scientific Assessment of Law and Human Behavior:*
Prospect Theory, Risk Preference, and the Law, 97 NW. U. L. Rev. 1115, 1116 (2003); Chris Guthrie, *Better Settle Than Sorry: The Regret Aversion Theory of Litigation Behavior*, 1999 U. Ill. L. Rev. 43, 52; Christine Jolls et al., *A Behavioral Approach to Law and Economics*, 50 Stan. L. Rev. 1471, 1477 (1998).

20 See, for example Bronislaw Malinowski. Magic, Science, and Religion And Other Essays. London: McCormick Press (2014); Clifford Geertz. Interpretation of Cultures. New York: Basic Books (2017).

21 Adrian Raine, The Anatomy of Violence: The Biological Roots of Crime 312, 313 (2013); Fritjof Capra, The Hidden Connections: Integrating the Biological, Cognitive, and Social Dimensions of Life into A Science of Sustainability 46 (2002).; Joshua W. Buckholtz & René Marois, *The Roots of Modern Justice: Cognitive and Neural Foundations of Social Norms and Their Enforcement*, 15 Nature Neuroscience 655, 656 (2012); Bruce H. Lipton, The Biology of Belief: Unleashing the Power of Consciousness, Matter & Miracles 103 (2008); D. Michael Bitz & Jean Seipp Bitz, Comment, *Incompetence in the Brain Injured*

Individual, 12 St. Thomas L. Rev. 205, 235, 238 n.237 (1999); James H. Fallon, *The Relationship Between Brain Development, Cognitive Functioning, and Accountability Under the Law: Neuroanatomical Background to Understanding the Brain of the Young Psychopath*, 3 Ohio St. J. Crim. L. 341, 350 (2006); Antoine Bechara et al., *Emotion, Decision Making and the Orbitofrontal Cortex*, 10 Cerebral Cortex 295, 300, 301 (2000); Max Planck-Gesellschaft, *Decision-Making May Be Surprisingly Unconscious Activity*, Sci. Daily (Apr. 15, 2008); Benjamin Libet et al., *Time of Conscious Intention to Act in Relation to Onset of Cerebral Activity (Readiness-Potential): The Unconscious Initiation of a Freely Voluntary Act*, 106 Brain 623, 624 (1983); William M. Hedgcock et al., *A Magnetoencephalography Study of Choice Bias*, 202 Experimental Brain Res. 121, 126 (2010); Richard E. Redding, *The Brain-Disordered Defendant: Neuroscience and Legal Insanity in the Twenty-First Century*, 56 AM. U. L. Rev. 51, 59–60 tbl.1 (2006); *See* Stephen Morse, *Neuroscience and the Future of Personhood and Responsibility*, in Law And Neuroscience 123, 123 (2014); See Owen D. Jones & Timothy H. Goldsmith, *Law and Behavioral Biology*, 105 Colum. L. Rev. 405, 466 (2005); Stephen J. Morse, *Uncontrollable Urges and Irrational People*, 88 Va. L. Rev. 1025, 1036, 1037 (2002); Rick Hanson & Richard Mendius, Buddha's Brain: The Practical Neuroscience of Happiness, Love & Wisdom 25 (2009).

22 The leading scholar in the field of neurophenomenology is Francisco Varela. See his coauthored book, The Embodied Mind: Cognitive Science and Human Experience. Boston, MA: MIT Press (2017). See also Michael Beaton et al., Editorial, *Neurophenomenology–A Special Issue*, 8 Constructivist Found. 265, 265 (2013); C. G. Jung, Synchronicity: An Acausal Connecting Principle 139, 141 (R. F. C. Hull trans., 1972); Robert Garfield McInerney, *Oz Never Did Give Nothing to the ... Scarecrow: Neurophenomenology and Critical Pedagogy*, 4 Phenomenology & Prac. 68, 70 (2010).

23 Jurgen Habermas. Theory of Communicative Action. London: Beacon Press (1985), Ludwig Wittgenstein. Tractatus Logico-Philosophicus. NY: Cosmo (2007).

24 David Eagleman. The Brain: The Story of You. London: Vintage Press (2017).

25 David Eagleman, The Brain on Trial, Atlantic, July/August, 2011 at 116.

26 In the final substantive chapter of my book, Convictions Without Truth: The Incompatibility of Science and Law (Routledge Press, May 2022), I develop this argument consistent with the literature addressing neuropsychology and cognitive psychology. Briefly, it appears that the preservation of fixed beliefs has a physiological origin in different regions of the brain. Among those that have been identified are: the precuneus, the inferior parietal cortex, the medial prefrontal cortex, the orbitofrontal cortex (OFC), the dorsolateral prefrontal cortex (DLPFC), the insular cortex, the amygdala, and the left and right inferior gyrus.

27 Sam Harris. Free Will. London: Free Press (2012).

28 Robert Schehr and Chelsea French. Mental Competency Law and Plea Bargaining: A Neurophenomenological Critique. 79, 3, Alb. L. Rev. 1091 (2016).

29 Id at 1138.

30 Id at 1140.

31 For a fascinating argument consistent with mine, but which is focused upon cognitive psychology and the fact that *Homo sapiens* are not utility maximizers, see Daniel Kahneman. Thinking, Fast and Slow. New York: Farrar, Straus and Giroux (2013).

32 Richard A. Posner. Some Uses and Abuses of Economics in Law. 46 U. of Chicago. L. Rev. (1979): 288.

33 Id at 289.

34 See James E. Crimmins. Jeremy Bentham. The Stanford Encyclopedia of Philosophy (Winter 2021). https://plato.stanford.edu/cgi-bin/encyclopedia/archinfo.cgi?entry=bentham
35 Pierre Bourdieu. Distinction: A Social Critique of the Judgement of Taste. Cambridge, MA: Harvard University Press (1984); Pierre Bourdieu. Language & Symbolic Power. Cambridge, MA: Harvard University Press (1999).
36 https://www.azquotes.com/quote/366381?ref=pragmatism
37 https://www.azquotes.com/quote/1119588
38 Herbert Spencer. Social Statics: Or, The Conditions Essential To Happiness Specified. Moscow: Dodo Press (2009).
39 Emile Durkheim. The Division of Labor in Society. London: Free Press (2014).
40 Kingsley Davis and Wilbert Moore. Some Principles of Stratification. American Sociological Review, Apr. 1945, 10 (2): 242–249.
41 Related to structural functionalism in sociology is rational choice theory. Space limitations prohibit a thorough account of the rich and insightful applications of rational choice to all manner of political, economic, and cultural activities including criminal law and criminal procedure. See James Coleman and Thomas Farraro, Rational Choice Theory: Advocacy and Critique. NY: Sage (1992).
42 Herbert Hovenkamp. The First Great Law and Economics Movement. 42 Stan. L. Rev. 4 (1990): 996.
43 R. H. Coase. The Problem of Social Cost. J. of L. and Econ. 3 (1960).
44 Perhaps the iconic example of Progressive Era reporting is Upton Sinclair's The Jungle. CreateSpace Independent Publishing Platform (2019).
45 Supra 42 at 1013.
46 Supra 42 at 1001.
47 Supra 42 at 1001.
48 Supra 42 at 1051. I would add labor law to this list.
49 Supra 42 at 1002.
50 Supra 42 at 1022.
51 Ely cited in Hovenkamp, supra, 42 at 1023.
52 Supra 42 at 1015.
53 Zachary Liscow, Is Efficiency Biased? U Chi L. R., 85, 7 (2018): 9.
54 Supra 42 at 1037.
55 See Richard Posner. The Economics of Justice. Cambridge, MA: Harvard University Press (1983).
56 Supra 42 at 1037.
57 Randy Barnett and Nathan Oman. Contracts: Cases and Doctrine. New York: Walters Kluwer (2017): 961–1064.
58 Id at 961.
59 Id at 967.
60 Id.
61 536 US 622 (2002).
62 Id (Ruiz).
63 Federal Rules of Evidence, Rules 607, 608, and 609 would ordinarily cover witness impeachment.
64 373 US 83 (1963).
65 https://harvardcrcl.org/use-the-rules-of-criminal-procedure-to-limit-prosecutors-power/
66 Supra 57 at 976.
67 Supra 57 at 976.
68 Supra 57 at 988.
69 Supra 57 at 988.
70 Supra 57 at 992. Emphasis added.

71 Supra 57 at 992.
72 Supra 57 at 1005.
73 Todd Rakoff. Contracts of Adhesion: An Essay in Reconstruction. 96 Harv. L. Rev. 6 (1983): 1173–1284.
74 Id at 1177.
75 It is here that one could object to my argument by pointing to the assignment of counsel for the defendant in a plea bargain as a significant constitutional protection seriously eroding my analogy. For the reasons discussed in Chapter 1 pertaining to the serious institutional obstacles confronting criminal defense attorneys, I disagree.
76 https://www.findlaw.com/state/arizona-law/arizona-robbery-laws.html
77 Supra 73 at 1178.
78 Supra 73 at 1179.
79 Supra 73 at 1179.
80 350 F.2d 445 (DC Cir. 1965).
81 Id at 449.
82 Supra 73 at 1193.
83 Cited in Rakoff at 1218.
84 Supra 73 at 1218.
85 Supra 73 at 1223.
86 Supra 73 at 1229.
87 Supra 73 at 1242.
88 Supra 73 at 1247.
89 Karl Marx and Friedrich Engels. The German Ideology. New York: International Publishers (1984).
90 "Judges and Justices are servants of the law, not the other way around. Judges are like umpires. Umpires don't make the rules, they apply them. The role of an umpire and a judge is critical. They make sure everybody plays by the rules, but it is a limited role. Nobody ever went to a ballgame to see the umpire." Chief Justice John Roberts's statement during his nomination hearing before the Senate Judiciary Committee. September 29, 2005.
91 See Louis Powell's, Attack on American Free Enterprise System: Confidential Memorandum submitted to Eugene B. Sydnor, Jr., August 23, 1971. ("Under our constitutional system, especially with an activist-minded Supreme Court, the judiciary may be the most important instrument for social, economic, and political change" (26).)
92 David Singh Grewal and Jedediah Purdy. Introduction: Law and Neoliberalism. 77, Law and Contemporary Problems (2014): 18.
93 Id at 6. Emphasis added.
94 Id at 15. Emphasis added.

References

Randy Barnett and Nathan Oman. *Contracts: Cases and Doctrine.* New York: Walters Kluwer (2017): 961–1064

Michael Beaton et al. Editorial, *Neurophenomenology–A Special Issue.* 8 *Constructivist Found.*, 265, 265 (2013)

Antoine Bechara et al. Emotion, Decision Making and the Orbitofrontal Cortex. 10 *Cerebral Cortex*, 295, 300, 301 (2000)

Richard Birke. Reconciling Loss Aversion and Guilty Pleas. 205 *Utah L. Rev.*, 209 244–245 (1999)

D. Michael Bitz and Jean Seipp Bitz. Comment, *Incompetence in the Brain Injured Individual.* 12 *St. Thomas L. Rev.*, 205, 235, 238 n.237 (1999)

Jeremy A. Blumenthal. Law and the Emotions: The Problems of Affective Forecasting. 80 *IND. L.J.*, 155, 206 (2005)
Pierre Bourdieu. *Distinction: A Social Critique of the Judgement of Taste*. Richard Nice (trans.). Cambridge, MA: Harvard University Press (1984)
Pierre Bourdieu. *Language & Symbolic Power*. Cambridge, MA: Polity Press (1999)
Joshua W. Buckholtz and René Marois. The Roots of Modern Justice: Cognitive and Neural Foundations of Social Norms and Their Enforcement. 15 *Nature Neuroscience*, 655, 656 (2012)
Nancy J. Burke et al. Theorizing Social Context: Rethinking Behavioral Theory. 36 *Health Educ. Behav.*, 55, 56, 61 (2009)
Fritjof Capra. *The Hidden Connections: Integrating the Biological, Cognitive, and Social Dimensions of Life into a Science of Sustainability*. New York: Doubleday 46 (2002)
John Christman. *Autonomy in Moral and Political Philosophy*. Stanford Encyclopedia of Philosophy (2020)
R. H. Coase. The Problem of Social Cost. 3 *J. of L. and Econ.*, 1–44 (1960)
Jean Cohen and Andrew Arato. *Civil Society and Political Theory*. Cambridge, MA: MIT Press (1992)
James Coleman and Thomas Farraro. *Rational Choice Theory: Advocacy and Critique*. Newbury Park: Sage (1992)
James E. Crimmins. Jeremy Bentham. The Stanford Encyclopedia of Philosophy (Winter 2021). https://plato.stanford.edu/cgi-bin/encyclopedia/archinfo.cgi?entry=bentham
Kingsley Davis and Wilbert Moore. Some Principles of Stratification. 10(2) *American Sociological Review*, 242–249 (April 1945)
Emile Durkheim. *The Division of Labor in Society*. London: Free Press (2014)
David Eagleman. *The Brain: The Story of You*. London: Vintage Press (2017)
David Eagleman. The Brain on Trial. *Atlantic* (July/August, 2011)
Lauren B. Edelman and Robin Stryker. A Sociological Approach to Law and the Economy. In Neil J. Smelser and Richard Swedberg (eds.) *The Handbook of Economic Sociology*. Princeton, NJ: Princeton University Press (2005): 527
James H. Fallon. The Relationship Between Brain Development, Cognitive Functioning, and Accountability Under the Law: Neuroanatomical Background to Understanding the Brain of the Young Psychopath. 3 *Ohio St. J. Crim. L.*, 341, 350 (2006)
Clifford Geertz. *Interpretation of Cultures*. New York: Basic Books (2017)
Gerd Gigerenzer and Wolfgang Gaissmaier. Heuristic Decision Making. 62 *Ann. Rev. Psychol.*, 451, 462 (2011)
David Singh Grewal and Jedediah Purdy. Introduction: Law and Neoliberalism. 77 *Law and Contemporary Problems,* 18 (2014)
Chris Guthrie. A New Social Scientific Assessment of Law and Human Behavior: Prospect Theory, Risk Preference, and the Law. 97 *NW. U. L. Rev.*, 1115, 1116 (2003)
Chris Guthrie. Better Settle Than Sorry: The Regret Aversion Theory of Litigation Behavior. 43 *U. ILL. L. Rev.*, 52 (1999)
Jurgen Habermas. *Theory of Communicative Action*. London: Beacon Press (1985)
Rick Hanson and Richard Mendius. *Buddha's Brain: The Practical Neuroscience of Happiness, Love & Wisdom*. Oakland, CA: New Harbinger 25 (2009)
William M. Hedgcock et al. A Magnetoencephalography Study of Choice Bias. 202 *Experimental Brain Res.*, 121, 126 (2010)
Herbert Hovenkamp. The First Great Law and Economics Movement. 42(4) *Stan. L. Rev.*, 996 (1990)

Robert Johnson and Adam Cureton. *Kant's Moral Philosophy*. The Stanford Encyclopedia of Philosophy (Spring 2022). https://plato.stanford.edu/entries/kant-moral/

Christine Jolls et al. A Behavioral Approach to Law and Economics. 50 *Stan. L. Rev.*, 1471, 1477 (1998)

Owen D. Jones and Timothy H. Goldsmith. Law and Behavioral Biology. 105 *Colum. L. Rev.*, 405, 466 (2005)

C. G. Jung. *Synchronicity an Acausal Connecting Principle*. 139, 141 R. F. C. Hull (trans.). Princeton: Princeton University Press (1972)

Daniel Kahneman. *Thinking, Fast and Slow*. New York: Farrar, Straus and Giroux (2013)

Russell B. Korobkin and Thomas S. Ulen. Law and Behavioral Science: Removing the Rationality Assumption from Law and Economics. 88 *Calif. L. Rev.*, 1051, 1055 (2000)

Benjamin Libet et al. Time of Conscious Intention to Act in Relation to Onset of Cerebral Activity (Readiness-Potential): The Unconscious Initiation of a Freely Voluntary Act. 106 *Brain* 623, 624 (1983)

Bruce H. Lipton. *The Biology of Belief: Unleashing the Power of Consciousness, Matter & Miracles*. New York: Hay House Inc., 103 (2008)

Jay MacLeod. *Ain't No Makin' It: Aspirations and Attainment in a Low-Income Neighborhood*. London: Routledge (2018)

Bronislaw Malinowski. *Magic, Science, and Religion and Other Essays*. London: McCormick Press (2014)

Karl Marx and Fredrich Engels. *The German Ideology*. New York: International Publishers (1984)

Robert Garfield McInerney. Oz Never Did Give Nothing to the . . . Scarecrow: Neurophenomenology and Critical Pedagogy. 4 *Phenomenology & Prac.*, 68, 70 (2010)

Christophe Menke. *Critique of Rights*. London: Polity Press (2020)

Westley C. Mitchell. Bentham's Felicific Calculus. 3(2) *Political Science Quarterly*, 161–183 (1918)

Stephen Morse. Neuroscience and the Future of Personhood and Responsibility. *Law and Neuroscience*, 123, 123 (2014)

Stephen J. Morse. Uncontrollable Urges and Irrational People. 88 *VA. L. Rev.*, 1025, 1036, 1037 (2002)

Max Planck-Gesellschaft. Decision-Making May Be Surprisingly Unconscious Activity. *Sci. Daily* (April 15, 2008)

Richard A. Posner. Some Uses and Abuses of Economics in Law. 46 *U of Chicago. L. Rev.*, 288 (1979)

Richard Posner. *The Economics of Justice*. Cambridge, MA: Harvard University Press (1983)

Jeffrey J. Rachlinski. Gains, Losses, and the Psychology of Litigation. 70 *S. Cal. L. Rev.*, 113, 128 (1996)

Todd Rakoff. Contracts of Adhesion: An Essay in Reconstruction. 96(6) *Harv. L. Rev.*, 1173–1284 (1983)

Adrian Raine. *The Anatomy of Violence: The Biological Roots of Crime*. New York: Pantheon Books 312, 313 (2013)

Richard E. Redding. The Brain-Disordered Defendant: Neuroscience and Legal Insanity in the Twenty-First Century. 56 *AM. U. L. Rev.*, 51, 59–60 tbl.1 (2006)

Robert Schehr. *Convictions Without Truth: The Incompatibility of Science and Law*. London: Routledge Press (May 2022)

Robert Schehr and Chelsea French. Mental Competency Law and Plea Bargaining: A Neurophenomenological Critique. 79(3) *Alb. L. Rev.*, 1091 (2016)

Herbert A. Simon. Invariants of Human Behavior. 41 *Ann. Rev. Psychol.* (1990)
Upton Sinclair. *The Jungle*. CreateSpace Independent Publishing Platform (2019)
Herbert Spencer. *Social Statics: Or, The Conditions Essential To Happiness Specified*. Moscow: Dodo Press (2009)
E.P. Thompson. *The Making of the English Working Class*. New York: Open Road Media (2016)
Francisco Varela. *The Embodied Mind: Cognitive Science and Human Experience*. Boston, MA: MIT Press (2017)
Ludwig Wittgenstein. *Tractatus Logico Philosophicus*. New York: Cosmo (2007)
Marcel Zeelenberg and Rik Pieters. A Theory of Regret Regulation 1.0. 17(3) *J. Consumer Psychol.*, 11–14 (2007)

7

GOVERNMENTALITY, THE STATE, AND CIVIL SOCIETY

In Chapters 5 and 6, I introduced the economics of plea bargaining. As I indicated in the Introduction to Chapter 5, the nature of writing books requires the presentation of substantive material in an artificially linear and stochastic process. But if it were possible to present substantive material in a multidimensional format, such as what one might find with three-dimensional concept mapping, the politics of governmentality would *coexist* in a recursive and constitutive way with any discussion of economics. This is because the economic system cannot function without intervention by the state and the judiciary. This chapter focuses on the contingent institutional and structural role played by state actors to reproduce dominant cultural, political, and economic relationships.

This chapter will require the reader to commit to a complex presentation of governmentality, the state, and civil society-lifeworld. The reader will be exposed to the following important context: 1) understanding how the intersectionality of politics, economics, and culture produces and reproduces the spatio-temporal dominance of power blocs; 2) understanding the always fluid, never sedimented complex of interests producing power blocs, each vying for political, economic, and cultural superiority in a discursive milieu that reproduces dominant cultural norms and values; 3) understanding that power contains both positive and negative (i.e., repressive) elements; 4) understanding that the development and manifestation of "the state" has occurred over millennia and produced regionally unique spatio-temporal forms; 5) understanding that "governmentality" and "the state" are grammatically and practically disparate since "governmentality" refers to a *process*, while "the state" refers to a *system-reproducing steering institution*; "governmentality" is a verb, and the "state" is a noun; and 6) understanding

DOI: 10.4324/9781003385103-9

that theoretical models that occlude the inclusion of civil society-lifeworld neglect perhaps the most vital location of lived experience.

In the sections that follow, I will begin with a discussion of Michel Foucault's articulation of governmentality, the *process* that facilitates the implementation of state power. Once established, I move to locate the act of governmentality within an analysis of state theory, especially as presented by Bob Jessop. Missing from nearly all liberal and even neo-Marxist political economic accounts of the state and economy, but most especially in the neotenic law and political economy scholarship, is the conceptualization of civil society-lifeworld. I have combined references to *civil society* with *lifeworld* as the two concepts are useful despite having emerged from discrete origins. In particular, my analysis of civil society is indebted to the brilliant treatise on the subject written by Jean Cohen and Andrew Arato. Reference to "lifeworld" originates with Jurgen Habermas. When combined, as Cohen and Arato do, an understanding of the primacy of civil society-lifeworld as a nutrient-rich cultural synapsis situated between the state and the economy and conceived as the locus of life lived in association comes into view. The diagram below signifies a simplified recursive relationship existing between the state, civil society-lifeworld, and the economy where the effects of governmentality administered by state actors,[1] and the economic circumstances existing at specific times and in specific locations, are mediated by our experiences living in civil society-lifeworld. Essential to this diagram are feedback loops that intersect each of the units of analysis (state, civil society-lifeworld, economy) such that overdetermined linear path diagrams popular in the social sciences and ostensibly depicting "cause and effect" are too static to capture the sempiternal nature of institutional and subject interactions.

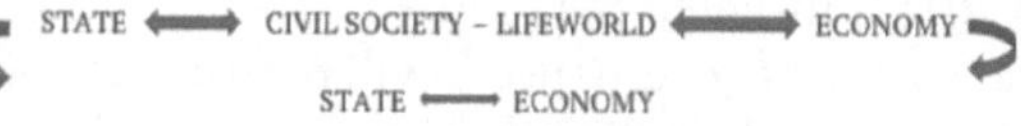

Why is this important to our concern with the constitutionality and practice of plea bargaining? As will be clear below, law functions as an institution *within* civil society-lifeworld. As such, civil society-lifeworld serves as the location for the ideological formation of adherence to law, as well as the administration of police power necessary to enforce it.

Governmentality

In a series of lectures delivered to the Collège De France,[2] Michel Foucault articulated an approach to the study of power and the state that liberated the concept from reified neo-Marxist debates over whether the state was constituted by "interests" *instrumental* to the proliferation of liberal capitalism, or whether the state signified the institutional site of *structural* imperatives necessary for the proliferation of the capitalist mode of production. Instrumentalist theorists tended to emphasize the specific people and groups that held access to and wielded real power and were significantly influenced by analysts such as C. Wright Mills and Robert Dahl. Structuralist theorists, by way of contrast, tended to emphasize system "needs," that is, the structural requirements necessary for the continued functioning of the capitalist system. The actual people or groups that might be privileged at a particular time and in a specific space were generally interchangeable since it was the pragmatic functioning of the system and *maintenance* of the system's smooth functioning that socialized people and groups to system demands. The so-called "instrumentalist" v. "structuralist" debate that took place in the 1970s amongst New Left scholars signified a rigorous yet often superficial and artificially polarizing accounting of the works of Ralph Miliband ("instrumentalist") and Nicos Poulantzas ("structuralist"). In the Foreword to Ralph Miliband's pathbreaking book, *The State in Capitalist Society*,[3] Leo Panitch contends, and I agree, that the artificial distinction that arose in scholarly argument pitting Miliband against Poulantzas misses the central point of agreement in their respective missions: "which was to provide a nuanced counterpoint to the notion that the modern state in the West had freed itself from the determining power of capital, rather than, to the contrary, having become an ever more integral element in modern capitalism's development and reproduction."[4] What neither Miliband nor Poulantzas was able to capture, however, was the day-to-day lived experience of state actors engaged in routinized practices meant to reproduce system stability (at both the system and sub-system levels) within civil society-lifeworld through the implementation of law and policy meant to "manage" contingent relationships. So complex is the practice of governing that Jessop (2022) invented the phrase "contingent necessity" to signify the heterarchical nature of governance (I will return to the conceptualization of the state as heterarchy below). What Jessop means by contingent necessity is that "the concrete actualization of events results from the *interaction* of diverse causal tendencies and countertendencies."[5] As applied to the language of chaos theory in quantum physics, micrological perturbations (i.e., tiny vibrations) produce certain but unanticipated consequences at the macro level. With the volatility emblematic of the collision of conflicting interests and values, something's going to happen, but we just don't know what. It is the purpose of governance to minimize the chaotic noise indicative of a multiplicity of interests privileging diverse values. Without perfect information, "Contingent necessity also implies an unbounded surplus of (unmanageable, often mutually exclusive) future possibilities, thereby ensuring that the world is an 'open' structure'"[6] rather than a determinative one. It is the function of governance to reduce the "surplus of future possibilities and its resulting social complexity."[7] As governance may be seen as the art of controlled chaos, governance is always directed at really existing material life, of life lived in civil society-lifeworld. Following Marx, what manifests in our respective lives as the "real-concrete is the complex synthesis of multiple determinations."[8] That is, it is nearly impossible to refer to cause and effect when considering policies and practices since those emergent policies and practices arise from contested polyvalent discourse. The purpose of governance, then, may be "interpreted as one way to self-reflexively transform unstructured (because infinite) into structured (because simplified) complexity based on appropriate social imaginaries [i.e., ideology] and coordination procedures."[9]

Perhaps it is most prudent to commence with Foucault's definition of governmentality, which he indicates shares the following three qualities. First, governmentality refers to "the ensemble formed by institutions, procedures, analyses and reflections, calculations, and tactics that allow the exercise of this very specific, albeit very complex, power that has the population as its target, political economy as its major form of knowledge, and apparatuses of security as its essential technical instrument."[10] The emergence of "government" as the locus of a type of force that generates the development of "a series of specific government apparatuses (*appareils*) on the one hand, [and, on the other] to the development of a series of knowledges (*savoirs*),"[11] forms the second quality of governmentality. Finally, and consistent with Foucault's genealogical approach to historical analysis, he locates the origin of governmentality as the movement away from what he refers to as "the state of justice in the Middle Ages," to the administrative state emerging in the 15th and 16th centuries. But what does it mean to "govern"? What is the etymology of the word?

The English word, *govern*, finds its roots first in the Greek word, *kubernan*, which means, "to steer," followed by the Latin word, *gubernare*, which adopts the Greek emphasis upon "steering" but adds "to rule." The French word, *gouverner*, means "to govern," but *gouverner* contains within it at least two possible meanings. First, according to Foucault, "we find the purely material, physical, and spatial meaning, of to direct, move forward, or even to move forward oneself on a track, a road."[12] To govern also refers to "supporting," "providing for," and "giving a means of subsistence to" one's family.[13] So, in the first sense of the French word *gouverner* we are presented with acts meant to provide subsistence, care, and forward movement. But there is a second sense in which *gouverner* refers to the morally complex act of *governing a person*. By Foucault's account, gouverner may refer to "the spiritual government of souls," or to "impose a regimen" (as with physicians who "govern" the patient), or finally to "conduct in the specifically moral sense of the term: a daughter who was of 'bad government,' that is to say, whose conduct was bad."[14] From his etymological account of the semiotics of government, Foucault is able to historically situate the origin of specific modes of government that were motivated by spatio-temporally unique circumstances.

In his genealogical accounting, Foucault identifies three unique modes of governing responding in time and space to the relationship between leaders and the led. Starting in Egypt, Assyria, and Mesopotamia, a pastoral model of government arose premised upon the metaphorical figure of the shepherd guarding its flock. Importantly, the *pêtre* or pastor (*pasteur*) signified the conduit between God and "the people" with the pastor as shepherd heeding God's call to protect them. As signified, pastoral government, then, was exclusively focused upon care for people and not, as Foucault reminds us, territory. For example, the traditional Hebrew reference to pastoral government facilitated by the shepherd is "essentially exercised over a multiplicity in movement."[15] Pastoral power was directed at doing good. For Foucault, pastoral power is "defined by its beneficence; its only *raison d'être* is doing good, and in order to do good. In fact, the essential objective of pastoral power is the salvation (*salut*) of the flock."[16] The pastoral mode of government, a government largely of souls, begins to fade during the 15th and 16th centuries largely due to a proliferation of cultural upheaval. Paramount was the emergence in the 16th century of the Protestant Reformation, a social movement that fragmented the previous dominance of the Catholic Church in Europe, and that had significant impact upon politics and culture. Foucault contends that the dynamism that captures the West during the 15th and 16th centuries, and that ultimately destabilizes pastoral power, arose as "insurrections of conduct." Over the course of the 15th and 16th centuries, insurrections of conduct grew in frequency and intensity, so much so that "feudal structures, and … the forms of power connected to them [were ill-equipped] to cope with these struggles and put an end to them."[17] Beginning in the 16th century, then, ecclesiastical authority gives way to the government of conduct. This is a new manifestation of governmental power that is directed at both public and private conduct (though that distinction was not prevalent at the time), what appears for the first time as government as "political," announces the 16th century as "the age of forms of conducting, directing, and government."[18] Foucault demonstrates that from 1580 to 1660, a new episteme of the sovereign emerges founded upon logic and mathematics where the sovereign is no longer the governor of souls, or the conduit to God. Rather, during this period of transition, the sovereign is now solely responsible for "governing."

> At the end of the sixteenth century, the emergence of the specificity of the level and form of government is expressed by the new problematization of what was called the *res publica*, the public domain or state (*la chose public*). The sovereign is required to do more than purely and simply exercise his sovereignty.[19]

What "governing" meant, what it evolved into, was referred to as *raison d'Etat*, the "reason" of state.[20] Following the Italian theorist, Botero, governing as *raison d'Etat* refers to "the knowledge of the appropriate means for founding, preserving, and expanding ... domination [over peoples]."[21] For him, "*raison d'Etat* [is] the type of rationality that will allow the maintenance and preservation of the state once it has been founded, in its daily functioning, in its everday management."[22] The practice of politics as we contemporaries might recognize it appears in the latter 16th and 17th centuries. In France, for example, it was Louis XIV who first propagated a system of government premised upon *raison d'Etat*. For Foucault, it was Louis XIV who first understood the symbiosis existing between sovereignty and government.

What is Raison d'Etat*?*

The two concepts requiring precise explication are "reason" and "state." That is, what is meant by "reason," and what, precisely, is the "state"? For historical bearings, Foucault draws upon the early 17th-century works of Francis Bacon, Giovanni Antonio Palazzo, and Bogislaw Philipp von Chemnitz. From their collected works, Foucault presents the meaning of "reason."

> Subjectively, reason is a certain power of the soul that enables it to know the truth of things, that is to say, precisely that bond, that integrity of the different parts of that constitutes a thing. Reason is therefore a means of knowledge, but it is also something that allows the will to adjust itself to what it knows, that is to say, to adjust itself to the very essence of things.[23]

Adhering closely to the work of Palazzo, Foucault presents the "state" in the following way:

> A state is a domain, *dominium*. Second, he [Palazzo] says it is a jurisdiction, a set of laws, rules, and customs, if you like, something like what we call ... an institution, a set of institutions. Third, he says ... "state" is a condition of life, that is to say, a kind of individual status, or profession: the state of magistrate, or the state of celibacy, or the religious state. And finally, fourth, the "state," he says, is something that renders things, if not completely immobile ... in any case this state is a quality that means that the thing remains what it is.[24]

Foucault's next move is to apply the conceptualization of "reason" and "state" to their manifestation in a republic. Specifically,

> A republic is first of all a domain, a territory. It is then a milieu of jurisdiction, a set of laws, rules, and customs. If it is not one state, the republic is at least a set of states in the sense of individuals defined by their status. And finally, a republic is a certain stability of these three preceding things, domain, jurisdiction, and institution or the status of individuals.[25]

Having defined both "reason" and "state," we are prepared to provide a working definition of *raison d'Etat*. It is Foucault's contention that by the early 17th century, a new mode of governing emerged to displace its pastoral predecessor. *Raison d'Etat* manifests in both the objective and subjective sense of "reason" discussed above. For Foucault, the *objective* manifestation of *raison d'Etat* as applied to the "state" refers to "that which is necessary and sufficient for the republic to preserve its integrity."[26] Here, Foucault refers to geopolitical territory (i.e., land and water) and the perceived need to defend it. As *subjectively* applied, *raison d'Etat* embodies "a certain political consideration that is necessary in all public matters, councils and plans, which must strive solely for the preservation, expansion, and felicity of the state, and for which we must employ the most ready and swift means."[27]

The emergence of government by *raison d'Etat* signified a major transition away from its pastoral ancestor, specifically in the way that Western Europeans conceived of the administration of power. For Foucault, and premised upon his reading of the 17th-century philosophers, *raison d'Etat* possessed four discrete advantages over the pastoral model. First, stricken was any reference to a natural order of things, divine law, or any external force beyond the state itself. Second, *raison d'Etat* is grounded upon a commitment to the generation and proliferation of knowledge. That is, it was the accumulation of what Durkheim called "social facts" that was the essence of *raison d'Etat* and its source of power. All manner of demographic information, for example, was necessary to accumulate and centralize within the institution of the state as a practical means for the administration of state power. Finally, Foucault suggests that the emergence of the state as *raison d'Etat* is an intentionally conservative move, one that was intended to preserve in times of turmoil a fundamental set of norms, rules, and laws "necessary and sufficient for the state to exist and maintain itself in its integrity, in the event of it being damaged."[28] It is during the 17th century that the neotenic science of statistics emerges. This is important because a sovereign ruler would need to have knowledge about all manner of "things" necessary for the administration of its land and people. Such knowledge included more than law or scripture. Rather,

> Etymologically, statistics is knowledge of the state, of the forces and resources that characterize a state at a given moment. For example, there is knowledge of the population, the measure of its quantity, mortality,

> natality; reckoning of the different categories of individuals in a state and of their wealth; assessment of the potential wealth available to the state, mines, and forests, etcetera; assessment of the wealth in circulation, of the balance of trade, and measure of the effects of taxes and duties.[29]

Most important for Foucault is that as the 17th century wears on, characterized by the governing of *raison d'Etat*, there is a transition away from sovereign knowledge and the application solely of the laws, and toward a growing interest in and awareness of the *population* more generally. In addition to the necessity of possessing such knowledge as the substance of what constitutes the state and its people, and that is required to properly, smoothly, and consistently administer to the republic, detailed knowledge about the daily lives of the population was used to manipulate public opinion. As a mode of political technology and equipped with detailed knowledge of their habitus and cultural capital, *raison d'Etat* established the institutional infrastructure necessary to propagate all manner of ideological manipulation of the population. It appears that in order for a sovereign governing by *raison d'Etat* to maintain and expand its power in relation to the population, it was necessary for it to "act on the conscience of the people." Doing so was not necessarily considered an intentional attempt to mislead the people, as in the case of false consciousness, but rather, to act "in such a way that their [the public] opinion is modified, of course, and along with their opinion their way of doing things, their way of acting, their behavior as economic subjects and as political subjects."[30] *Raison d'Etat* is the rationalization of the state through the application of law and statistics. For Foucault, the more contemporarily familiar manifestation of the state emerges coincident with *raison d'Etat.*

I will spend more time developing state theory below, but here I wish to announce Foucault's articulation of the role of the state as it emerges in the 17th and 18th centuries as a product of *raison d'Etat.* And to be clear, unlike his Marxist counterparts, Foucault spent relatively little time lecturing or writing about the "state" per se. Rather, his focus was upon the *processes* and *effects* of governance as manifested by state actors. Still, in order to make his way to the articulation of governance, some attention to the state as an institution was necessary. First, the state appears as the locus for the intelligibility of a new mode of government premised upon reason. Second, the state appears as the necessary institutional outgrowth of an art of government premised upon *raison d'Etat.* As its institutional vehicle, the state manifests governmental reason as *raison d'Etat* through its focused attention to "necessity," where "it is the function of intelligibility of the state in relation to reality, and it is that which makes it rational, necessary, to govern."[31] For Palazzo, inspirational to Foucault, the state's modus operandi as *raison d'Etat* was to provide for "peace, the rule of living at rest, the perfection of things."[32] By strictly adhering to *raison d'Etat*, the state was assured of keeping to its bearings, especially when it was necessary to maintain moral public order or to protect from internal and/or external forces of opposition. This became especially relevant as nation-states collided on the fields of political, economic, and cultural battle. For as Foucault was keen to acknowledge, each discrete state was burdened by the inevitability of external competition, where "[T]hey seek to assert themselves in a space of commercial competition and domination, in a space of monetary circulation, colonial conquest, and control of the seas."[33] Recognition of what was becoming a global competition for geographic, economic, and political power was, for example, among the most daunting challenges confronting the framers of the American Constitution. In the debates surrounding the adoption of the newly formed Constitution in 1787, federalists were emphatic that a strong centralized national government capable of imposing taxes, raising a standing army, and developing a navy that could provide domestic protection as well as protection of trade routes, was imperative to the success of the United States.[34] Replacing dynastic rivalry leading to endless war, the emergence of *raison d'Etat* inaugurated a new relationship between states, one that was premised upon economic competition rather than violent confrontation. What emerges, according to Foucault, is a new global relationship among states that was premised on the application of a dynamic type of force. Here we begin to unveil a vital historical moment, one that introduces a multiplicity of "interests" each vying for access to, and control over, state power. As we will see, this emphasis upon the multiplicity of forces competing for state power provides a historical foundation for the theoretical contributions to state theory made by Bob Jessop and discussed below. Specifically, interests apply force both internal and external to the state as a way to facilitate changes to (or preservation of) prevailing laws. For Foucault, "[T]he real problem of this new governmental rationality is not therefore just the preservation of the state within a general order so much as the preservation of the relation of forces; it is the preservation, maintenance, or development of a dynamic of forces."[35] Following Gramsci, whom we'll meet below, those subjects possessing "interests" will at times congeal in convivial ad hoc transactional relationships directed at achieving a similar end. These associations of interests Gramsci referred to as a *power bloc*. Following Foucault, it is the purpose of the state under *raison d'Etat* to properly manage competing power blocs as they apply political, economic, and cultural *force* toward the achievement of their specific interests.

In order for the state to properly manage competing interests, it was imperative for it to develop what Foucault refers to as a "mechanism of security," of which two were paramount – military-diplomacy and police. With regard to the former, and as I indicated was a prevailing concern for the American federalist framers, the United States and all states now confronting global competition for land, natural resources, trade routes, labor, and the like would have to develop a form of martial power that "will limit the mobility, ambition, growth, and reinforcement of all other states as much as possible."[36] In summary, in order for all states to flourish, it would be necessary for there to exist an internally sophisticated *raison d'Etat* capable of preventing and/or responding to external threats, while simultaneously seeking regional balancing of strategic state interests. This occurred in Europe during the middle of the 17th century when numerous treaties were entered into between competing European states. Consistent with *jus gentium*, a unity of disparate states, it was during the early stages of the 17th century that European theorists began to advance the idea of a "society of nations," one that is peacefully maintained primarily through the mutual respect of all sovereign states. While resort to war was always an available option, it was to the art of diplomacy that these early states turned.

Equally as important as the maintenance of security arising from external state competitors was domestic order. Available to the state as a domestic technology enabling the maintenance of security and social order was the *police*.

In a previous chapter, I mentioned the awkward resonance the application of the word "police" to any action unrelated to crime prevention puts upon our contemporary ears. But during the 17th and 18th centuries, reference to police power signified a broad set of responsibilities that went far beyond our contemporary application of the concept. As imagined by our predecessors in Europe and in the United States, the language of police powers applied to those state responsibilities that were viewed as the exclusive province of state actors who were responsible for the health and well-being of its citizens.

The Tenth Amendment to the United States Constitution is constituted by "police powers." The Tenth Amendment's sparse language belies the historicity at play when advancing state police powers. The Tenth Amendment simply states:

> The powers not delegated to the United States by the Constitution, nor prohibited by it to the States, are reserved to the States respectively, or to the people.[37]

Writing for the majority in the *Slaughterhouse Cases* (1873), Justice Miller defined police powers in the following way:

> This power is, and must be from its very nature, incapable of any very exact definition or limitation. Upon it depends the security of social order, the life and health of the citizen, the comfort of an existence in a thickly populated community, the enjoyment of private and social life, and the

> beneficial use of property. It extends ... to the protection of the lives, limbs, health, comfort, and quiet of all persons, and the protection of all property within the State, ... and persons and property are subjected to all kinds of restraints and burdens in order to secure the general comfort, health, and prosperity of the State.[38]

Following Justice Miller's explication in the *Slaughterhouse Cases*, state police powers amount to securing the general comfort, health, and prosperity of the state. Police powers were to be used to ensure the security of the social order such that the citizens of each state would realize life, health, and comfort through the exercise of private property. Our late 19th-century understanding of police powers, as expressed by Justice Miller, finds its origin in the 17th and 18th centuries in Europe.

Foucault situates the origin of the more expansive definition of police powers in the 16th century, where reference to "police" commonly appeared alongside "republic" as if the two were synonymous. In fact, the etymology of the verb "police" originates in the 15th century with the Latin word *politia*, which means "citizenship" or "government." But it was during the 17th century that a different meaning of police emerged, one that is more familiar to our contemporary understanding.

> From the seventeenth century "police" begins to refer to the set of means by which the state's forces can be increased while preserving the state in good order. In other words, police will be the calculation and technique that will make it possible to establish a mobile, yet stable and controllable relationship between the state's internal order and the development of its forces.[39]

In general, then, policing was responsible for enhancing the quality of life in the state through order maintenance and the overt manifestation of state force.

In order for policing to be effective, that is, for each state to maintain internal order and the "good use of its forces," state actors needed access to detailed information about the habitus and cultural capital constituting its inhabitants. The Latin word for statistics, *statisticum collegium*, is a noun and it referred to the "council of state." Likewise, the Italian word *statista* refers to a "statesman" or a "politician." Moving closer to our 17th-century understanding of the word, in Germany in 1749 a book was published called *Statistik*. That book addressed both demographic and economic data about the state.[40] The *science* of statistics dates to the 17th century with the publication in 1662 of John Graunt's *Natural and Political Observations Made upon the Bills of Mortality*. In that book, Graunt "estimated the population of London in 1662 as 384,000 using records on the number of funerals per year, the death rate, and average family size."[41] Still, earlier attempts at statistical inference can be located in Athens in the fifth century BC.[42]

The gathering of statistical information was necessary for each state to be able to maintain its population in equilibrium. Among the points of emphasis for state actors were:

> The population, the army, the natural resources, the production, the commerce, and the monetary circulation – all the elements that are in fact provided by the science, or domain of knowledge, statistics, which is founded and developed at this time. How can one establish statistics? It can be established precisely by police, for police itself, as the art of developing forces, presupposes that each state exactly identifies its possibilities, its virtualities. Police makes statistics necessary, but police also makes statistics possible.[43]

Referring to "police" and "statistics" as "technological assemblages," Foucault concludes that "statistics is the state's knowledge of the state, understood as the state's knowledge both of itself and also of other states."[44] In both France and Germany, *police* emerges as the *science of government.* Following the 17th-century work of French philosopher Turquet de Mayerne, agents of police were necessary to maintain "a particular practice of modesty, charity, loyalty, industry, and domestic order."[45] De Mayerne emphasized the important role police played in maintaining public morality and loyalty to the state. But, as Foucault reminds us, police must "equally be concerned with wealth and household management, that is to say, *with the way in which people conduct themselves with regard to their wealth, their way of working, and consuming* [my emphasis]. He is therefore concerned with the mixture of morality and work."[46] This is a point worth ruminating over as it begins to signal the coming role of law enforcement in the 19th century as a microcosm of police, especially as law enforcement played a role in disciplining the working class and unemployed. Why?

Prior to the 16th and 17th centuries, the state's policing concern was primarily with regard to one's status, virtue, or intrinsic qualities. Subjects were expected to be obedient, virtuous, and hardworking. With the onset of statistics and the state's need to maintain equilibrium through system steering (i.e., governance), a new emphasis was placed upon the management of the "population" as a whole. With specific reference to policing, what begins to matter most is what people *do*, that is, we begin to see a specific state interest in *occupations*. Important for our purposes, "the objective of police is therefore control of and responsibility for men's activity insofar as this activity constitutes a differential element in the development of the state's forces."[47] Perhaps the most detailed assessment of the police function in the 18th century was written by Nicolas Delamare. In three volumes,

Delamare identifies 13 domains occupying the attention of police: religion, morals, health and subsistence, public peace, the care of buildings, squares, and highways, the sciences and the liberal arts, commerce, manufacture and the mechanical arts, servants and laborers, the theater and games, and the care and discipline of the poor.[48]

The reader will recall that as the early 19th century unfolded, there was considerable police concern in both the northern and southern United States with vagrancy. Consistent with Delamare's recitation of police functions, concern over the maintenance and promotion of health included preventing subsistence scarcity, limiting the presence of beggars, and controlling vagrancy. The economic aspect of police included regulating the manufacture, distribution, and consumption of products produced for the market. Notably, the police function not only focused upon the circulation of goods and services but also of workers. This will later become a significant part of the police function in the 19th century – helping to establish the circulation of workers to their greatest productive ends.

The emergence of police as the disciplinary arm of the state can be found as early as the 15th century when a mounted constabulary known in France as the *maréchaussée* (military police) served royal power and the public interest by hunting down and punishing violence, delinquency, crime, theft, and murder.[49] So intricately intertwined with politics, economics, and culture, the presence of police was vital to the emergence of mercantilism from the 16th to the 18th centuries. At bottom was a concern to preserve economic *competition* amongst European states as a substitute for wars of aggression. As an economic system, mercantilism "identifies commerce as the essential instrument and fundamental weapon in this intra-European competition that must take place in the form of equilibrium."[50] In each country of Europe, mercantilism required the largest population possible, that every person be put to work, that every worker be paid the lowest wage possible, and that the price of domestic goods remain as low as possible in order to penetrate export markets.[51] It is with the onset of mercantilism that the disciplinary police function begins to coalesce with manufacturing, distribution, and consumption of goods. This relationship will come to full flower in the 19th century as industrial capitalism accentuates and focuses narrowly upon the accumulation of profit while shedding the historically relevant disciplinary functions it had previously served. To initiate the move away from characterization of the state as responsible for the happiness of the totality of its people, it was the physiocrats, whom we have previously met, who signify a powerful interest bloc. Specifically, the physiocrats reject the caretaker role of the state, opting instead for a vision of the state that advances specific interests. First, the physiocrats reintroduce the importance of land, especially agriculture, as the primary concern of the state. Second, physiocrats were concerned with too much population growth since that would tend to lower wages and reduce the incentive for work. The final policy proposal introduced by physiocrats included unfettered economic competition at both domestic and international levels. That is, rather than viewing the state as a mediator amongst competing interests to maintain system equilibrium, physiocrats argued for the removal of bureaucratic obstacles to penetrating markets at home and abroad. Foucault succinctly summarizes physiocratic influence upon state utility by concluding: "The state is envisioned as the *regulator of interests* and no longer as the transcendent and synthetic principle of the transformation of the happiness of each into the happiness of all" (my emphasis).[52] In short, as interpreted by the physiocrats, *raison d'Etat* manifested as principally a concern with economics.

The influence of the 18th-century physiocrats cannot be underestimated. *Raison d'Etat* emerged alongside the science of statistics. Concerns relating to public health and happiness, documented through neotenic population data collection, transitioned under physiocratic influence to the privileging of statistical analysis to promote all manner of state efficiency. A new mode of "scientific rationality" was necessary to generate two separate spheres of influence. First, the new scientific rationality was not concerned with the "art of government" as had been the case during the 17th century. Rather, scientific knowledge increasingly became associated with economics, while the application of scientific data to the population as a whole took on new purposes. Here, Foucault contends that "population appears as a both specific and relative reality: it is relative to wages, to the possibilities of work, and to prices."[53] But perhaps most important is the onset of a powerful economic doctrine, one that is popularized by Adam Smith as "laissez-faire," which argues for the proliferation of the organicity, the naturalness of the population and its interests. The emerging *raison d'Etat*, therefore, must attend to the population in all of its naturalness as a way to thinly regulate through governmentality all manner of public issues (e.g., public health, demography). The role of the state will be circumscribed to "steer" or to "govern" the population consistent with a philosophical commitment to *Homo economicus*. Consistent with Smith's invisible hand, at bottom was a respect for and a concern to protect individual autonomy, especially as it was expressed through the procurement and protection of private property. Consistent with natural law, Smith's articulation of laissez-faire stipulated that the least possible state regulatory intrusion into domestic and international economic relationships signified not only the most efficient mode of production and circulation of goods but it did so by framing the emergence of *Homo economicus* as the greatest expression of individual liberty. During the 18th and early 19th centuries, changes taking place in the sphere of political economy radically altered traditional notions of policing in keeping with their now more conventional practice.

Transitioning away from *raison d'Etat*, the systemic role of the police as a source for all manner of public health maintenance was narrowed to one that required law enforcement. Once the naturalness of the pursuit of self-interest as articulated through laissez-faire ideology had successfully penetrated dominant cultural institutional mandates, the state, with its associated police powers, would become increasingly limited in its regulatory function. No longer would policing be applied to ameliorating all manner of political, economic, and cultural marginalization. For Foucault, it is during this period of transition that the noun *police*, and the verb, *policing*, take on purely regulatory meanings, as the role of police will increasingly be to limit public disorder. As for the state and its responsibility for governmentality, Foucault contends that "We can construct the genealogy of the modern state and its different apparatuses on the basis of a history of governmental reason. Society, economy, population, security, and freedom are the elements of the new governmentality whose forms we can still recognize in its contemporary modifications."[54]

Summarizing Governmentality

I contend that governmentality is the functional manifestation of ideology (what Jessop refers to as "imaginaries") and power. It is the expression of dominant cultural interests as revealed through the administrative and regulatory power of the state.[55] The reproduction of capitalist social relations requires an administrative and regulatory system that consciously seeks to maintain system stability. That this is so is by no means to support dogmatic essentialist claims purporting to establish omniscient and homogeneous state actors who move in tandem to generate set outcomes. Rather, the state as a locus of governmentality is a contested terrain of powerful public and private interests that constitute multiple power blocs, each vying for regulatory and administrative supremacy insofar as their colloquial interests are concerned. Ideology provides the intellectual framing constituting institutional motives and preferred outcomes. It is the ideology of liberal democracy that provides the semiotic material necessary for the legal coding of capitalism. Consequently, facilitators of the administrative and regulatory state, as well as capitalists operating within prevailing domestic and global economic systems, must consciously commit to the norms constituting liberalism and capitalism. It is through the hegemonic transference of liberal ideology that this commitment is first obtained. But it is through regulatory and administrative governmentality that this commitment is realized, and by which management of forever fragmented political, economic, and cultural relations amongst disparate power blocs is managed going forward. This is because, "Law is neither the truth of power nor its alibi. It is an instrument of power which is at once complex and partial. The form of law with its effects of prohibition needs to be resituated among a number of other, non-juridical mechanisms."[56]

Perhaps the most comprehensive analysis of efficiency and law can be found in Max Weber's identification of the history of forms of law and legal thought. Most important was Weber's identification of four typologies that captured the role of law in different social systems. For Weber, the four types of law included formal rationality (the system adopted by advanced capitalist states like the United States of America), formal irrationality, substantive rationality, and substantive irrationality. A formal-rational system like the one adopted by the United States is constituted by syllogistic, deductive, positive law. At bottom was a professionalized system of rules of conduct carried out by a system of professional bureaucratic agents with specific skills necessary to perform those roles, and to which people would surrender their liberty due to general acceptance in the logical rationality of the rule, as well as its consistent and unbiased application. For Weber

> An order will be called law if it is externally guaranteed by the probability that coercion (physical or psychological), to bring about conformity or avenge violation, will be applied by a staff of people holding themselves specially ready for that purpose.[57]

Weber clearly understood that formal-rational law (i.e., positive law) was intrinsic to the legal coding of capital since it was an expression of utilitarianism, profit maximization, the ethic of individual responsibility, and *Homo economicus*. It was the purpose of law in capitalist states to facilitate the creation of a bureaucratic system of rules that enabled the efficient administration of economic and political relationships where "the modern capitalist enterprise rests primarily on calculation and presupposes a legal and administrative system, whose functioning can be rationally predicted by virtue of its fixed general norms."[58] Efficiency in this context accrues from actions taken by professional system actors to provide for juridically created market predictability and stability necessary to enhance capitalist profit maximization and preservation of power. Weber's extraordinary work addressing the technology of control manifesting from legal-rational bureaucratic institutions forms the foundation for any discussion of efficiency since bureaucracies were ostensibly established with efficiency as a primary objective.

While in many ways his analysis adopts Weberian insights, Foucault's emphasis is upon bio-power. Governmental rationality as expressed through Foucault suggests a mode of regulation that specifically focuses upon rational and pragmatic acts meant to solve problems, in a word, *efficiency*. In this way,

> Rationalities are thus practical rather than theoretical or discursive entities. They are forged in the business of problem solving and attempting to make things work. Consequently, they manifest in a logic of practice, rather than of analysis, and tend to bear the hallmarks of the institutional settings out of which they emerge.[59]

It is precisely this kind of governmental rationality that helps to explain the application of plea bargaining as a procedural technology designed for the express purpose of rendering convictions more *efficient* by way of expediency and the centralized power of prosecutors. Consistent with the liberty of contract doctrine discussed in Chapters 5 and 6, Garland contends that *economic rationality* seeks similarly to uncover the "increasing reliance upon an analytical language of risks and rewards, rationality, choice, probability, targeting, and the demand and supply of opportunities,"[60] as expressions of state-based governmentality contextualized within an ideology of liberalism.

It is this "analytical language" that constitutes legal coding consistent with the hegemonic project of capitalism and that appears in the rhetoric of plea bargaining as rational choice premised upon liberty of contract. For Foucault, the art of governmentality emerged consistent with liberalism's attempt to distinguish the role of the state from excessive government, a government of oppression. To that end, governmentality "is one that seeks to identify these different styles of thought, their conditions and formation, the principles and knowledges that they borrow from and generate, the practices that they consist of, how they are carried out, their contestations and alliances with other arts of governing."[61] The contested nature of governmentality in Foucault's work at once expresses a dialectical synchronicity amongst the governed whereby "the governed are, variously, members of a flock to be nurtured or culled, juridical subjects whose conduct is to be limited by law, individuals to be disciplined, or, indeed, people to be freed."[62] In his own words, Foucault presents the idea of governmentality to mean:

> By this word "governmentality" I mean three things. First, by "governmentality" I understand the ensemble formed by institutions, procedures, analyses and reflections, calculations, and tactics that allow the exercise of this very specific, albeit very complex, power that has the population as its target, political economy as its major form of knowledge, and apparatuses of security as its essential technical instrument. Second, by "governmentality" I understand the tendency, the line of force, that for a long time, and through the West, has constantly led towards pre-eminence over all other types of power – sovereignty, discipline, and so on – of the type of power that we can call 'government' and which has led to the development of a series of specific governmental apparatuses (appareils) on the one hand, [and on the other] to the development of a series of knowledges

> (savoirs). Finally, by "governmentality" I think we should understand the process, or rather, the result of the process by which the state of justice in the Middle Ages became the administrative state in the fifteenth and sixteenth centuries and was gradually "governmentalized."[63]

The state's role in governmentality is to operate alongside other technologies of system maintenance and coercion, but without representing a single nodal point of power. Foucault's governmentality runs parallel to Bob Jessop's construction of strategic-relational power.[64]

The ideological and hegemonic ubiquity of the liberty of contract doctrine, with its emphasis upon individualism, autonomy, and systemic efficiency, provided the narrative framing necessary for the Supreme Court to justify the waiver of the constitutional right to trial by jury as an affirmation of individual freedom to choose one's punishment.

Agents of governmentality have available to them at any one time a host of what Louis Althusser called ideological state apparatuses (ISAs).[65] ISAs play an integral role in all political and economic systems, not just capitalist ones. The role of ISAs is to ensure the viability and longevity of existing modes of production. Althusser's expression of ISAs builds upon Marx's base–superstructure metaphor. For Marx, the economic base of all societies is constituted by the mode of production. The mode of production includes the means and social relations of production. Facilitating the reproduction of the mode of production is the superstructure, which for Marx included two separate but related prongs – the governmentality–law prong and the ideology prong. Althusser's contribution to enhancing the complexity of Marx's model was to emphasize additional institutions existing within the superstructure that were viewed as coincident with the reproduction of the mode of production and political power. These, Althusser referred to as ISAs. Althusser's set of ISAs includes religion, education, family, law, politics, trade unions, media, and culture.[66] Each of these institutions operates consistent with prevailing ideology to advance the economic base regardless of the mode of production. What makes ISAs effective as system reproducers is that they operate consistent with hegemonic ideology, an ideology that has found general compliance from those to whom it is applied. However, ISAs may also act in repressive ways to achieve repressive state ends. This conflagration of what at times may be contested interests between ISAs and the state, argues Althusser, is mediated by ideology such that it "ensures (sometimes a teeth-gritting) 'harmony' between the repressive State apparatus and the Ideological State Apparatuses, and between the different State Ideological Apparatuses."[67]

Finally, while Althusser rests his analysis upon the reproductive power of education, it is my intention here to emphasize the reproductive power of law as ISA, where law may be called upon in the interest of system reproduction by dominant cultural power blocs that confront the state with fragmentation and instability, threatening the means and social relations of production, thereby negatively affecting economic and political stability. Foucault equally draws upon this line of thinking but with a specific emphasis upon bio-power. For him,

> the figures who articulated eighteenth-century liberalism were bearers of a hybrid form of expertise: they were grounded in both political economy and public law. Foucault proposed that this duality constituted proof of liberalism's twofold practical nature: liberal governmentality imposed a principle of limitation on the jurisdiction of the state that derived from the truth-telling, "veridiction," of the market [what Piketty refers to as the "quasi-sacrilization of private property"].[68]

Here, Foucault is referencing the semiotic coding of capital in law, a point that I take up below.

The State

In this brief presentation of state theory, it is important to remember that it is the legislatures of each state government that possess the constitutional authority to name behavior as a crime and to legally establish the sentencing ranges accompanying conviction for those crimes. It is the state, through its governmentality function, that regulates and administers the code of capitalism.

For Scott, state-based attempts to effectuate enhancements to politics, economics, and culture, which were driven by social engineering, tended to produce four "pernicious" elements: (1) the administrative ordering of nature and society, (2) high-modernist ideology, (3) the appearance of an authoritarian state, and (4) a "prostrate civil society unable to resist authoritarian plans."[69] Scott contends that the arrival of high modernist ideology presented "a strong, one might even say musclebound, version of the self-confidence about scientific and technical progress, the expansion of production, the growing satisfaction of human needs, the mastery of nature (including human nature), and, above all, the rational design of social order commensurate with the scientific understanding of natural laws."[70] Scott joins Foucault, Jessop, and Katarina Pistor (whose theory of coded capital was presented in Chapter 5) when he argues that "high modernism was about 'interests' as well as faith. Its carriers, even when they were capitalist entrepreneurs, required state action to realize their plans ... In most cases, they were powerful officials and heads of state."[71] Those "interests" that tended to be most influential regarding high modern social policy were "planners, engineers, architects, scientists, and technicians," whose skills and status it celebrated as the designers of the new order."[72] As Foucault had also noticed, while "interests" were articulated across the political spectrum, those with the greatest influence were those most interested in the kind of social engineering that affected people's "work habits, living patterns, moral conduct, and world views."[73] The *authoritarian state* appears as the most efficacious institutional vehicle to implement political, economic, and cultural transformations consistent with high modernism, since by definition there will be no institutionally acceptable way to contest its power. Finally, the emergence of the authoritarian state as *raison d'Etat*, was made possible due to a moribund civil society. Most of us live our lives in the civil society-lifeworld. That is, it is civil society-lifeworld that serves as a dialectical buffer against state power. It is the location of our voluntary associations (e.g., religious worship and membership, coaching youth sports, engagement with the arts, and the like) that provides us with *thick* cultural experiences heavily embedded in local norms. State intrusion upon civil society typically occurs during periods of political, economic, and/or cultural unrest. As Scott makes clear, "war, revolution, and economic collapse often radically weaken civil society as we make the populace more receptive to new dispensation."[74] (I will briefly take up the subject of civil society below.) Additional insights provided by Scott's analysis of the state include the state's role in establishing uniform weights and measures,[75] simplification and standardization of measurement,[76] designing cities to maximize social control,[77] establishing surnames,[78] establishing an official language,[79] and creating traffic patterns.[80] The manner in which each of these institutional practices was established and facilitated is the purpose of Professor Bob Jessop's state theory.

Beginning with his 1990 publication, *State Theory: Putting Capitalist States in their Place*,[81] to be followed in 2016 by *The State: Past, Present, Future*,[82] Jessop has demonstrated theoretical and conceptual sophistication beyond what most who write in the area of state theory have been able to match. The main reason for this is that like Foucault, Jessop conceptualizes the state as the locus of contested interests facilitating the administration and regulation of politics, economics, and culture. At the center of Jessop's state theory is an emphasis on contingency. In opposition to what he refers to as "reified state theory," Jessop contends that

> The challenge for social scientists is to demystify the state, to unmask it radically, to prove that the state as a substantial, unitary entity does not "always already" exist. This opens space to study efforts by state personnel and others to impose some provisional, temporary, and unstable unity on the actually existing state system and to create relative coherence across official policies in diverse areas of action.[83]

I commence my presentation of Bob Jessop's work on state theory with his expression of what he means by the "state" as a construct. Jessop identifies six interrelated characteristics of the state:

> (1) The exercise of state power (2) as an institutionally and discursively mediated condensation (a reflection and refraction) (3) of a changing balance of forces, (4) which seeks to influence the forms, purposes, and content of the polity, politics, and policy (5) in specific conjunctures, marked by a variable mix of opportunities and constraints, (6) themselves linked to the wider natural and social environment.[84]

The most apt description of the state as presented by Jessop is that it is the site of a contingent set of relationships among diverse interests vying for political, economic, and cultural power. As a site of contested power, the state does not exist in "majestic isolation," but rather, it is embedded within broader sets of social relations (especially, as Jessop points out, the economic and legal systems). Specifically,

> Whatever the degree of the state's autonomy from other orders, the exercise and impact of state power (or, better, state powers) are activated through changing sets of politicians and state officials located in specific parts of the state apparatus, in specific conjunctures, and reflect the prevailing balance of forces, as it obtains beyond as well as within the state.[85]

Jessop frames his understanding of the state in part on the work of Foucault, Tim Mitchell, Antonio Gramsci, and Michael Mann. On the issue of "state effects," Jessop cites Foucault as providing perhaps the most radical assessment:

> it is likely that if the state is what it is today, it is precisely thanks to this governmentality that is at the same time both external and internal to the state, since it is the tactics of government that allow the continual definition of what should or should not fall within the state's domain, what is public and what private, what is and what is not within the state's competence, and so on. So, if you like, the survival and limits of the state should be understood on the basis of the general tactics of governmentality.[86]

Gramsci was perhaps the first Western state theorist to articulate a contingency model, one that was premised upon the acknowledgment of competing interests that he called "power blocs" and "hegemonic blocs." A power bloc is a "durable alliance among dominant classes and class fractions that structures the politics of power and defines the 'art of the possible' on the political scene ... Its durability is grounded in a viable mode of growth and in a solid presence in the wider system."[87] By way of contrast, yet intimately related, a hegemonic bloc "is a broader ensemble of national popular forces mobilized behind a specific hegemonic project." A hegemonic project "reflects the historical unity of ruling classes, supporting classes, mass movements, and intellectuals. It depends on a durable alliance organized by a class (or class faction) that has proved itself capable of exercising political, intellectual, and moral leadership over the dominant classes and popular forces alike."[88] For Gramsci, the state signified a "complex social relation that articulates state and nonstate institutions and practices around particular economic, political, and societal projects and strategies. He emphasized the centrality of private institutions, organizations, and movements in state power, the formation of political alliances, and the disorganization of subaltern forces."[89]

Finally, Michael Mann articulated a vision of the state's governance capacities as consistent with "capitalist, military, theocratic, or democratic according to the balance of forces, especially as these affect the state ensemble and its exercise of power."[90] Inspired by Mann, Jessop presents the following definition of the state:

> The core of the state apparatus comprises a relatively unified ensemble of socially embedded, socially regularized, and strategically selective institutions and organizations [*Staatsgewelt*] whose socially accepted function is to define and enforce collectively binding decisions on the members of a society [*Staatsvolk*] in a given territorial area [*Staatsgebeit*] in the name of the common interest or general will of an imagined political community identified with that territory [*Staatsidee*].[91]

Jessop's state theory was heavily influenced by Nicos Poulantzas and by Foucault.[92] It was Poulantzas, drawing upon Marx, Gramsci, and others, who made the initial move toward the conceptualization of the state as a "social relation." Specifically, Poulantzas (as cited by Jessop) contends that rather than being a passive assemblage of regulatory agents, the state is "like 'capital,' it is ... a relationship of forces, or more precisely the material condensation of such a relationship among classes and class fractions, such as this is expressed within the State in a necessary specific form."[93]

Drawing closely upon Poulantzas, but with the contingency expressed in Foucault's governmentality, Jessop's novel creation of the theory of the strategic relation approach (SRA) "widens its [theory of the state] focus, so as to capture not just the state apparatus but the exercise and effects of state power as a contingent expression of a changing balance of forces that seek to advance their respective interests inside, through, and against the state system."[94] The SRA envisions a new specification of the relationship between structure and agency in relational terms. Specifically, "The changing balance of forces is mediated institutionally, discursively, and through governmental technologies. It is conditioned by the specific institutional structures and procedures of the state apparatus as embedded in wider political system and environing societal relations."[95] What, then, generates state effects? For Jessop, it is "the interaction of the structurally inscribed strategic selectivity of the state system and competing forces with diverse strategies."[96] The system-wide dynamic that Jessop describes has clear roots in Hegelian dialectics, where the collision of competing interests will produce certain but unanticipated state effects (outcomes). For example, "changes in the identities, interests, resources, goals, strategies, and tactics of particular forces also modify the emergent constraints and opportunities associated with particular structures."[97] In a word, contingency. From this space of systemic dynamism emerge three recurring state strategies: *economic strategies; state projects*; and *hegemonic visions*, each of which "involve specific articulations of elements drawn from wider technological, economic, juridico-political, and social imaginaries, and their success depends on complementarities with the deeper structure and logics of a given social formation and its insertion into the world market, interstate system, and world society."[98]

According to his students, Bertramsen, Frolund Thomsen, and Torfing, "Jessop reformulates the structure-agency relationship as the complex dialectic between the structural conditioning of action and the structurally transformative role of strategies pursued by different social agents."[99] With due recognition and privileging of spatial and temporal flux, Jessop's SRA analysis provides the context for what will manifest as actions by state actors possessing the power, access, and knowledge necessary to facilitate the demands placed upon the state by power blocs seeking expressions of its interests through the exercise of state actions.

> [T]he SRA emphasizes that the biased composition of constraints and opportunities can only be understood in relation to specific strategies pursued by specific forces in order to advance specific interests over a given time horizon in terms of a specific set of other forces, each advancing its interests through specific strategies.[100]

Important, too, is the more obvious point that as an institution, all that is functionally available to state actors is the manipulation of the levers of power. Jessop identifies three strategic modalities through which strategies affect the balance of power amongst the state, economy, and society – hegemonic projects, accumulation strategies, and state strategies.[101] It is in that way, Jessop contends, that all power consists of "state-strategic selection," the ability of state actors to determine where to place their thumbs on different levers of institutional state power to facilitate outcomes. So, to understand the implementation of specific administrative and regulatory policies requires sensitivity to the historical moment and the power blocs arranged within it. Here, Jessop suggests the following:

> (1) The state's historical and formal constitution as a complex institutional ensemble, with a spatiotemporally specific pattern of 'strategic-selectivity' that reflects and modifies the balance of forces; (2) the historical and substantive organization and configuration of political forces in specific conjunctures and their strategies, including their capacity to reflect on and respond to the strategic selectivity is inscribed in the state apparatus as a whole; and (3) the interaction of these forces, on this strategically selective terrain or at a distance from it, as they pursue immediate goals or seek to alter the balance of forces or. To transform the state and its basic strategic selectivities.

In sum, Jessop's SRA theory includes the power of strategic selection over the levers of strategic state power. For example, for Jessop, "a *state strategy* [is] a [emergent] pattern of intervention in the economy which: (a) favors the course of an accumulation strategy and the flow of material benefits to the requisite social base; and (b) constructs forms of representation that systematically favor the access of key sectors and social groups to sites of political and economic power."[102] The resulting effect is the stabilization of a hegemonic project. It is that power, always contested, that under spatiotemporal conditions provides the substantive context for governmentality. As I hope will become clear as we proceed, it is this agentic power of state actors that facilitates the creation of the tools necessary for lawyers to introduce and code capital, and to provide the enforcement mechanisms necessary to facilitate it.

The final leg of the stool yet to be developed is civil society. When combined with an analysis of governmentality and the state, civil society-lifeworld constitutes the lived experiences of people in society. It is to a brief introduction to civil society-lifeworld that we now turn.

Civil Society-Lifeworld

Most of us experience our lives in community, in local culture. We are nestled among our neighbors, work and schoolmates, friends, and lovers. We eat at our local restaurants, worship at our neighborhood mosques, churches, and synagogues, walk in our parks, and shop in our local stores. We take pride in our administration of city and county government as it seeks to provide the greatest good for the greatest number. We share complex discursive codes (i.e., language and symbols) that, in some ways, may distinguish us from those living outside of our community. In short, we live our lives *thickly steeped in culture*. The distinction between "thick" and "thin" cultural experiences references the work of anthropologist Clifford Geertz.[103] Embellishing the work of Habermas and Wittgenstein, Geertz refers to the construct, "culture," as "interworked systems of construable signs (what, ignoring provincial usages, I would call symbols). Culture is not a power, something to which social events, behaviors, institutions, or processes can be casually attributed; it is a context, something within which they can be intelligibly – that is, thickly – described."[104] To more fully understand what it means to be steeped in one's local culture:

> Behavior must be attended to, and with some exactness, because it is through the flow of behavior – or, more precisely, social action – that cultural forms find articulation. They find it as well, of course, in various sorts of artifacts, and various states of consciousness; but these draw their meaning from the role they play (Wittgenstein would say their "use") in an ongoing pattern of life, not from any intrinsic relationships they bear to one another.[105]

In my estimation, one of the most common lacunae in the Law and Political Economy literature is the lack of attention to civil society-lifeworld. In this final part of Chapter 7, I will only briefly introduce the constructs – civil society and lifeworld – to lay a foundation for future work to be conducted in this area. As my introduction to this section suggests, civil society-lifeworld signifies the rich, symbolically complex, and hermeneutically distinct cultural context within which each of us comes to have a *thick* moral and pragmatic sense of who we are relative to those both within and outside of our cultural milieu. My intellectual guides through the explication of civil society-lifeworld are Jean Cohen and Andrew Arato, Bob Jessop, Jürgen Habermas, and Jeffrey Alexander.

At this point, readers may scratch their heads wondering, after having developed theories of both governmentality and the state, why a discussion of civil society is necessary. Let's establish a few preliminary points. First, *as a regulative institution, the criminal legal system is structurally located within civil society.* That is, the criminal legal system is structurally set apart from both the political and economic (though neither of those could exist without law). Second, and most important for our purposes, *it is within civil society that people make demands upon their government.* As Alexander contends, and I agree,

> To maintain democracy and to achieve justice it is often necessary for the civil to "invade" non-civil spheres, to demand certain kinds of reforms, and to monitor them through regulation in turn. In modern times, aggrieved parties have demanded justice by pointing angrily to what they come to see as destructive intrusions into the civil realm, [what Cohen and Arato, following Gransci, refer to as the "third realm"] intrusions whose demands they construct as particularistic and self-serving.[106]

Much as Tocqueville had done, Alexander argues that in democratic societies, civil society trumps the political and economic realms since it is in civil society that subjects make system demands to enhance the quality of life for both the community and the individual. This being true, and with due recognition that the criminal legal system is located within civil society, *it is within civil society that the people may make demands upon legislatures, as well as state judges, defense attorneys, and prosecutors, to dramatically restrict the application of the plea bargain to criminal cases.* So for Alexander, "The aspiration toward which democratic law aims is a civil society. In fact, to the degree that the civil sphere gains authority and independence, obedience to law is not seen as subservience to authority, whether administrative or communal, but as commitment to rules that allow solidarity and autonomy."[107] But perhaps as it is most relevant to our purposes, it is Alexander's contention that,

> To the degree that societies are democratic, law can crystallize the seemingly oxymoronic commitment to individuality and collectivity that defines the sphere of civil life ... It can, at the same time, restrict the scope of individuality by prohibiting individuals from injuring fellow members of the civil sphere, whether by cheating, lying, or by threatening them with physical force.[108]

Agreed. As applied to our concern over the ubiquity of plea bargaining, it is within the civil sphere that the discursive interaction between subjects and the criminal legal system takes place, and where the demands for truthful convictions generated by a truly transparent procedure that affords the criminally accused a pathway to case adjudication that preserves (and enhances) due process protections while eliminating the "trial tax" manifest. Moreover, it is within civil society, and with the intention of making our democracy more *civil*, as in more *moral*, that questions first addressed in Chapter 1 relating to plea bargaining and the lack of procedural transparency, non-existent oversight of prosecutorial power, ineffective criminal defense resources, the lack of discovery, the invalidity of the knowing and voluntary prongs, the inherent coercion leading defendants to the plea through threats of harsher punishment if convicted at trial (trial tax), viewing plea bargains as contracts, and the ongoing free-wheeling legislative effects upon the criminal legal system take place. My emphasis on *moral law* is a clear reference to natural law philosophy.

As the reader is by now well aware, plea bargaining has been discursively framed by the United States Supreme Court as a matter of contract law. Viewed as a tool for cultural cohesiveness, contract law is promoted as a way to enhance democratic liberty by binding contracting parties to terms relating to a voluntarily agreed-upon set of commitments. In theory, binding contracts enhance liberty by restricting the actions of contracting parties to the legally sanctioned terms of the contract, thereby promoting order. Contract law is administered within civil society through the civil legal system, and it serves as a regulatory technology integrating civil society with the economic and political systems. At bottom, the liberty of contract had as its most authoritative claim the elevation of the autonomous status of all people. As we have seen, the paradox of physiocratic assertions of natural law was to lay bare the subject as *Homo economicus*; a free thinking, freely acting, reasonable, and rational actor. As *Homo economicus*, each individual was solely responsible for their actions. In short, "The law is a system of moral regulation that *discursively constructs autonomy*, punishes actors so constructed if they deviate too sharply from this ideal, and allows an escape valve if they seem not to be capable of autonomy at all (my emphasis)."[109] Since it is contract law that serves as the vehicle for the constitutionality of plea bargaining, and since contract law is administered in civil society, and since (consistent with Habermas) civil society is constituted through its subject discursivity, civil society, then, must become the systemic locus of a social movement leading to plea bargaining's eventual demise.

In *Civil Society and Political Theory*,[110] Cohen and Arato make an extraordinary contribution to the theory of civil society. In this compendium, inspired by Critical Theory, the authors demonstrate their intellectual acuity by deftly navigating the complex theoretical work of Hannah Arendt, Carl Schmitt, Reinhart Koselleck, Jürgen Habermas, Michel Foucault, and Niklas Luhmann, among others. Moreover, in nearly 600 pages, Cohen and Arato provide an archeological recounting of the origin and development of the construct of civil society.

Among the most pressing issues leading to the revitalization of civil society in the West was

> the conception of self-limitation, the idea of civil society as comprised of social movements as well as a set of institutions, the orientation to civil society as a new terrain of democratization, the influence of civil society on political and economic society, and finally an understanding that the liberation of civil society is not necessarily identical with the creation of bourgeois society but rather involves a choice between a plurality of types of civil society.[111]

Following Tocqueville, civil society is the locus of democratization and democratic institution building. As such, in a rights-based liberal democratic society, civil society signifies the milieu in which subjects come to understand and debate all matters of political, economic, and cultural importance – including law – through their discursive lens as rights-bearing people.

Cohen and Arato's pluralist conceptualization of civil society as representing the "third realm," a space that is both of, and not of, the political and economic realms, emphasizes "a highly articulated civil society with cross-cutting cleavages, overlapping memberships of groups, and social mobility [that] is the presupposition for a stable democratic polity, a guarantee against permanent domination by any one group and against the emergence of fundamentalist mass movements and antidemocratic ideologies."[112] As their conceptualization of civil society makes clear, Cohen and Arato view the democratization of the third realm – the family, associational life, and the public sphere – as vital to maintaining the vibrancy of political parties and institutions. For Jessop, "civil society comprises a heterogeneous set of institutional orders and a pluralistic set of agents, many of which are operationally autonomous and resistant to control from outside."[113] Jessop cites Habermas's view that civil society is a "contested space ... for representatives of very different types of interests, norms, and values. It serves both as a horizon of action for strategies to secure the dominance of a given institutional order, and as *a reservoir of antagonistic 'instincts' (rooted in other identities) and social resources for resisting such colonization* (my emphasis)."[114]

Life in civil society signifies a dialectical relationship to the economy. Neither is civil society completely separate from economic activity, nor does economic activity come to essentialize life in civil society. Rather, it is civil society that enables us to buffer economic imperatives and effects. This is the view taken by Gramsci. For him, civil society was considered to be a "realm of political, cultural, legal, and public life that occupied an intermediate zone between economic relations and political power."[115] Consider the private right to property. It is Cohen and Arato's contention that private property as experienced within civil society blunts the magnitude of the liberal zero-sum game constitutive of *Homo economicus*. How?

> Only if one construes property to be not simply a key right but the core of the conception of rights – only, that is, if one places the philosophy of possessive individualism at the heart of one's conception of civil society and then reduces civil to bourgeois society – does the rights thesis come to be defined in this way. If, however, one develops a more complex model of civil society, recognizing that it has public and associational components as well as individual, private ones, and if, in addition, one sees that the idea of moral autonomy does not presuppose possessive individualism, then the rights thesis begins to look a bit different.[116]

Civil society, then, signifies the location of "autonomous (freed from state control) *communicative interactions* of individuals with one another in the public and private spheres of civil society, as well as a new relation of individuals to the public and the political spheres of society and state."[117] The rights associated with our First Amendment freedom of speech and assembly are what positively constitute liberty in civil society. Actors living in civil society will appropriate these positive rights to "collectively debate issues of common concern, act in concern, assert new rights, and exercise influence on political (and potentially economic) society."[118] Finally, and this is the most important aspect of civil society as it relates to my purposes in this book, the third realm is the locus of our collective deliberation over all manner of political, economic, and cultural matters. For Cohen and Arato, civil society represents the "terrain upon which we learn how to compromise, take reflective distance from our own perspective so as to entertain others, learn to value difference, recognize or create anew what we have in common, *and come to see which dimensions of our traditions are worth preserving and which ought to be abandoned or changed* (my emphasis)."[119] Similarly, Keane refers to civil society as, "the realm of social activities, a realm that includes privately owned, market directed, voluntarily run, and friendship-based organizations and phenomena."[120]

In sum, it is through our positioning within civil society that we are able to contemplate, critique, and reimagine the ways in which we organize ourselves and our institutions. *Inasmuch as the criminal legal system is located there, it is through civil society that we commence our deconstruction of plea bargaining.*

In parallel fashion to Cohen and Arato and Jessop, Habermas, following sociologist Talcott Parsons, develops a discursive theory of the *lifeworld* that shares many of the characteristics of civil society. For Habermas, "lifeworld refers to the reservoir of implicitly known traditions, the background assumptions that are embedded in language and culture and drawn upon by individuals in everyday life … Thus, individuals can neither step out of their lifeworld nor bring it into question as a whole."[121] What Habermas was keen to reveal was the complex process of interpellation that takes place within a lifeworld that provides the context "of what is to be said, discussed, addressed in a situation … The lifeworld is the intuitively present, in this sense familiar and transparent, and at the same time vast and incalculable web of presuppositions that have to be satisfied if an actual utterance is to be at all meaningful, that is, valid *or* invalid."[122]

The justification for including in this chapter a section addressing civil society should be clear. If fundamental changes are to be made with regard to plea bargaining, arguments and actions associated with those changes will take place in civil society, where associations of concerned citizens earnestly engage with legislators, prosecutors, judges, and defense attorneys to discern the most efficacious (though not necessarily most efficient) way to adjudicate criminal cases.

***

Arguing from the perspective of political economy requires deconstruction of the economic and political systems. In Chapters 5 and 6, readers were introduced to the liberty of contract doctrine and contract law, respectively. In this chapter, I have provided the political context necessary to understand the role played by state actors engaged in the act of governmentality who, aided by ideological state apparatuses facilitating the ideological manipulation of civil society-lifeworld, seek to provide the political and economic equilibrium necessary for the facilitation of domestic and international economic development. When coupled, the substantive content of Chapters 5, 6, and 7 provides the theoretical context for understanding the political economy of plea bargaining. Premised as it was upon the ideological construction of the economically autonomous *Homo economicus*, first mercantilism and then industrial capitalism prepared the way for the individuation, alienation, and exploitation of workers. This was accomplished both through state statute and case law. The former signifies the central focus of this chapter, namely, the administration of state power premised upon influential power blocs to establish the most efficient means to procure profit while maintaining control over civil society-lifeworld. As I have demonstrated, the evolving role of police led to a specific emphasis on law enforcement, especially in relation to vagrancy.

Subject autonomy. Efficiency. Order maintenance. Social control. Each of these system imperatives emerged in the United States to create a perfect storm leading to the eventual creation of a legal technology – plea bargaining. And it is within civil society-lifeworld where subjects find the discursive tools necessary to buffer the effects of the state and economy, and where any attempts to reform our current criminal legal system will take place.

Notes

1 In this chapter, when I refer to "the state," or "state," unless otherwise indicated, I am referring to nation-states.

2 Foucault's lectures were sponsored by the Collège de France and were to provide him with the opportunity to explore subjects relating to his ongoing research. In the 1977–1978 and the 1978–1979 college terms, Foucault lectured on two subjects. In his 1977–1978 lectures, which were eventually assembled and published as Security, Territory, Population (New York: Picador, 2007), Foucault first addressed what he means by the concept of "governmentality." Foucault invented the neologism "governmentality" to emphasize the processes and effects generated by state administrators. In fact, Foucault would later regret the title he chose for the 1977–1978 lectures, proposing instead to have called the book Governmentality. The following year, Foucault would address what would become perhaps his most important and mature rendering of power. In his 1978–1979 lectures, Foucault introduced the concept of "biopolitics." The series of lectures was later published under the title The Birth of Biopolitics (New York: Picador, 2008). In it, Foucault moves beyond his well-established articulation of micro-power, the kind of power that intrudes upon the bodies of

subjects in order to repress and dominate. Those ideas were most closely associated with his books Discipline and Punish: The Birth of the Prison (New York: Vintage, 1979), and The History of Sexuality: An Introduction, Volume 1 (New York: Vintage, 1978, 1990). In The Birth of Biopolitics, Foucault raises his level of analysis to include technologies of power existing at the macro-level, the kind of power that enables institutions to proliferate within social structures.

3 Ralph Miliband. The State in Capitalist Society. Pontypool, Wales: Merlin Press (2009).
4 Leo Panich in Miliband. Id at xxiii.
5 Bob Jessop. Putting Civil Society in its Place. Bristol, England: Policy Press (2022): 37.
6 Id.
7 Id.
8 Cited in Jessop, Id at 38.
9 Id at 39.
10 Michel Foucault. Security, Territory, Population. New York: Picador (2007): 108.
11 Id.
12 Supra 10 at 121.
13 Supra 10 at 121.
14 Supra 10 at 121.
15 Supra 10 at 125.
16 Supra 10 at 126.
17 Supra 10 at 228.
18 Supra 10 at 231.
19 Supra 10 at 236.
20 Reference to "reason of state" infers the principles upon which state power rested, its reason and logic, and under what circumstances that power could be enervated.
21 Supra 10 at 238.
22 Supra 10 at 238.
23 Supra 10 at 256.
24 Supra 10 at 256.
25 Supra 10 at 256–257.
26 Supra 10 at 257.
27 Chemnitz cited in Supra 10 at 257.
28 Supra 10 at 258.
29 Supra 10 at 274.
30 Supra 10 at 275.
31 Supra 10 at 287.
32 Cited in supra 10 at 287.
33 Supra 10 at 291.
34 Michael Klarman. The Framer's Coup: The Making of the United States Constitution. London: Oxford University Press (2019): 330–335.
35 Supra 10 at 296.
36 Supra 10 at 296.
37 The Constitution of the United States of America.
38 Cited in Paul Brest, Sanford Levinson, Jack Balkin, Akhil Reed Amar, and Reva Siegel. Processes of Constitutional Decision Making: Cases and Materials. New York: Wolters Kluwer (2018): 361.
39 Supra 9 at 313.
40 https://homepage.divms.uiowa.edu/~dzimmer/alphaseminar/Statistics-history.pdf

41 https://homepage.divms.uiowa.edu/~dzimmer/alphaseminar/Statistics-history.pdf
42 https://homepage.divms.uiowa.edu/~dzimmer/alphaseminar/Statistics-history.pdf
43 Supra 10 at 315.
44 Supra 10 at 315.
45 Cited in Supra 10 at 319.
46 Supra 10 at 321.
47 Supra 10 at 322.
48 Delamare cited in Supra 10 at 334.
49 Supra 10 at 336.
50 Supra 10 at 337.
51 Supra 10 at 337.
52 Supra 10 at 346.
53 Supra 10 at 351.
54 Supra 10 at 354.
55 Max Weber. Economy and Society. Berkeley, CA: University of California Press (1978); Sabeel Rahman. Reconstructing the Administrative State in an Era of Economic and Democratic Crisis. 131 Harv. L. Rev. 671 (2018); Abeel Rahman and Jocelyn Simonson. The Institutional Design of Community Control. 108 Cal. L. Rev. 679 (2020).
56 Michel Foucault. Power/Knowledge: Selected Interviews & Other Writings 1972–1977. Colin Gordon (Ed.) New York: Pantheon (1980): 141.
57 Supra 55 at 34.
58 Supra 55 at 1394. This is what Pound referred to as "mechanical jurisprudence."
59 David Garland. 'Governmentality' And the Problem of Crime: Foucault, Criminology, Sociology. Theoretical Criminology, 1(2) (1997): 184.
60 Id at 185.
61 Nikolas Rose, Pat O'Malley, and Mariana Valverde. Governmentality. Ann .Rev. Law. Soc. Sci., 2, (2006): 84.
62 Id at 85.
63 Foucault, cited in Ben Golder and Peter Fitzpatrick, Foucault's Law. London: Routledge Press (2009): 33.
64 Bob Jessop. The State: Past, Present, Future. London: Polity Press (2016): 52–90.
65 Louis Althusser. Ideology and Ideological State Apparatuses: Notes Toward an Investigation. In Andy Blunden (Trans.) Lenin and Philosophy and Other Essays. Monthly Review Press (1971).
66 Id.
67 Id.
68 Stephanie L. Mudge. Leftism Reinvented: Western Parties From Socialism to Neoliberalism. Cambridge, MA: Harvard University Press (2018): 12.
69 James Scott. Seeing Like a State. New Haven, CT: Yale University Press (1998): 4–5.
70 Id.
71 Id.
72 Id at 5.
73 Id.
74 Id.
75 Id at 24.
76 Id at 30–32.
77 Id at 54–2.
78 Id at 64–71.

79 Id at 72.
80 Id at 73.
81 University Park, PA: University of Pennsylvania Press.
82 London: Polity Press.
83 Supra 64 at 18.
84 Supra 64 at 53.
85 Supra 64 at 20.
86 Supra 64 at 47.
87 Supra 64 at 72–73.
88 Supra 64 at 73.
89 Supra 64 at 47–48.
90 Supra 64 at 42.
91 Supra 64 at 49.
92 Jessop's students, Bertramsen, Frolund Thomsen, and Torfing (1991) criticize Poulantzas's economic determinism as taking the notion of state autonomy too far. They then apply Jessop's strategic relation model to state theory as a "middle-range concept" (109). Rene B. Bertramsen, Jens Peter Frolund Thomsen, and Jacob Torfing. State, Economy, and Society. London: Unwin-Hyman (1991).
93 Supra 64 at 54.
94 Supra 64 at 54.
95 Supra 64 at 54.
96 Supra 64 at 54.
97 Supra 64 at 55.
98 Supra 64 at 58–59.
99 Supra 92 at 109.
100 Supra 64 at 55.
101 Supra 92 at 109.
102 Supra 92 at 113.
103 Clifford Geertz. The Interpretation of Cultures. New York: Basic Books (1973). See also, Michael Walzer. Thick and Thin: Moral Argument at Home and Abroad. South Bend, IN: Notre Dame University Publishing (1994).
104 Id at 14.
105 Id at 17.
106 Jeffrey Alexander. The Civil Sphere. London: Oxford University Press (2006): 34.
107 Id at 152.
108 Id at 153.
109 Id at 179.
110 Jean L. Cohen and Andrew Arato. Civil Society and Political Theory. Cambridge, MA: MIT Press (1992).
111 Id at 16.
112 Id at 18.
113 Bob Jessop. Putting Civil Society in its Place. Bristol: Policy Press (2022): 2.
114 Id at 3.
115 Jeffrey Alexander. The Civil Sphere. London: Oxford University Press (2006): 28.
116 Supra 110 at 22.
117 Supra 110 at 22.
118 Supra 110 at 23.
119 Supra 110 at 23.
120 John Keane cited in Jeffrey Alexander. The Civil Sphere. London: Oxford University Press (2006): 29.

121 Supra 110 at 428.
122 Jurgen Habermas. The Theory of Communicative Action. Volume II. Thomas McCarthy (Trans.) London: Beacon Press (1987): 131.

References

Jeffrey Alexander. *The Civil Sphere*. London: Oxford University Press (2006)

Louis Althusser. Ideology and Ideological State Apparatuses: Notes Toward an Investigation. In Andy Blunden (trans.) *Lenin and Philosophy and Other Essays*. Monthly Review Press (1971)

Rene B. Bertramsen, Jens Peter Frolund Thomsen, and Jacob Torfing. *State, Economy, and Society*. London: Unwin-Hyman (1991)

Paul Brest, Sanford Levinson, Jack Balkin, Akhil Reed Amar, and Reva Siegel. *Processes of Constitutional Decision Making: Cases and Materials*. New York: Wolters Kluwer (2018)

Jean L. Cohen and Andrew Arato. *Civil Society and Political Theory*. Cambridge, MA: MIT Press (1992)

Michel Foucault. *Discipline and Punish: The Birth of the Prison*. New York: Vintage (1979)

Michel Foucault. *Power/Knowledge: Selected Interviews & Other Writings 1972–1977*. Colin Gordon (ed.). New York: Pantheon (1980)

Michel Foucault. *Security, Territory, Population*. New York: Picador (2007)

Michel Foucault. *The Birth of Biopolitics*. New York: Picador (2008)

Michel Foucault. *The History of Sexuality: An Introduction, Volume 1*. New York: Vintage (1978, 1990)

David Garland. 'Governmentality' And the Problem of Crime: Foucault, Criminology, Sociology. 1(2) *Theoretical Criminology*, 184 (1997)

Clifford Geertz. *The Interpretation of Cultures*. New York: Basic Books (1973). See also, Michael Walzer. *Thick and Thin: Moral Argument at Home and Abroad*. South Bend, IN: Notre Dame University Publishing (1994)

Ben Golder and Peter Fitzpatrick. *Foucault's Law*. London: Routledge Press (2009)

Jurgen Habermas. *The Theory of Communicative Action. Volume II*. Thomas McCarthy (trans.). London: Beacon Press (1987)

Bob Jessop. *Putting Civil Society in its Place*. Bristol: Policy Press (2022)

Bob Jessop. *The State: Past, Present, Future*. London: Polity Press (2016): 52–90

Michael Klarman. *The Framer's Coup: The Making of the United States Constitution*. London: Oxford (2019)

Ralph Miliband. *The State in Capitalist Society*. Pontypool, Wales: Merlin Press (2009)

Stephanie L. Mudge. *Leftism Reinvented: Western Parties From Socialism to Neoliberalism*. Cambridge, MA: Harvard University Press (2018): 12

Sabeel Rahman. Reconstructing the Administrative State in an Era of Economic and Democratic Crisis. 131 *H. L. Rev.*, 671 (2018)

Abeel Rahman and Jocelyn Simonson. The Institutional Design of Community Control. 108 *Cal. L. Rev.*, 679 (2020)

Nikolas Rose, Pat O'Malley, and Mariana Valverde. Governmentality. 2 *Ann. Rev. Law. Soc. Sci.*, 84 (2006)

James Scott. *Seeing Like a State*. New Haven, CT: Yale University Press (1998)

Max Weber. *Economy and Society*. Berkeley, CA: University of California Press (1978)

8

PLEA BARGAINING AND THE UNCONSTITUTIONAL CONDITIONS DOCTRINE

In this chapter, I will introduce the unconstitutional conditions doctrine and apply it to plea bargaining. Part of my plan is to provide readers with some case law to aid in establishing the efficacy of the doctrine as it has been applied by previous incarnations of the United States Supreme Court. But as I discuss below, the existence of case law precedent provides little comfort when making my argument enshrouded by the current configuration of the Court. Before commencing the unconstitutional conditions doctrine discussion in earnest, I feel there may be a need for a brief reality check.

It is generally true that courts of appeal in the United States of America, especially the United States Supreme Court, will, when considering questions relating to constitutional law, rely upon three types of historical evidence – legislative history, statutory language, and case law precedent. The latter, which is referred to by the Latin phrase *stare decisis* ("to stand by things decided"), is considered a bedrock principle of law. The reason that *stare decisis* is so important is that, in order for a society to smoothly and predictably function, the law must be consistent over time. Regardless of whether one is considering the application of civil, criminal, or administrative and regulatory law, orchestrating the heterogeneous interests of more than 333 million people toward the promotion of a common culture requires, among other things, a social technology (*stare decisis*) grounded in our English ancestry. So, when a question relating to the constitutionality of a particular statute arises before the United States Supreme Court, the Court will be expected to consider the holding and principle articulated in all prior opinions it has rendered related to the matter in question. (Because all cases are somewhat unique in their factual bases, it would be extremely rare to find a precedent case that was precisely on point.) Generally speaking, in the

DOI: 10.4324/9781003385103-10

interest of system stability, which engenders continuity through adherence to the Court's prior opinions, the Court will, at a minimum, take into consideration its prior holdings before entering judgment in a more contemporary case. Well, at least that used to be how the United States Supreme Court operated. As I indicated in the introduction to Chapter 4, the most recent incarnation of the Court, with a 6–3 conservative majority,[1] has shown no fealty to precedent, especially when considering equal protection and due process originating in the Fourteenth Amendment.[2] This appears in its most dramatic and controversial form through the Supreme Court's controversial application of the "shadow docket" to all manner of private and public law.[3]

What Is the Unconstitutional Conditions Doctrine?

Put succinctly, the unconstitutional conditions doctrine stands for the principle that the federal government may not condition the receipt of a government benefit upon the relinquishment of constitutional rights. More simply, it would be impermissible for the federal government to say to low-income Americans receiving food support through the federally funded Supplemental Nutrition Assistance Program (SNAP) that, in order to receive that support, they would have to vote for the political party in power. By doing so, the government has created an unconstitutional condition (usurping the right to vote one's conscience as established by the Fourteenth, Fifteenth, Seventeenth, Nineteenth, and Twenty-Sixth Amendments to the Constitution) on the receipt of a benefit (government-subsidized food). Important, the doctrine "reflects the triumph of the view that government may not do indirectly what it may not do directly over the view that the greater power to deny a benefit includes the lesser power to impose a condition on its receipt."[4] According to Sullivan, legal "commentators have overwhelmingly supported the doctrine's basic premises." And it is clear from the case law that the United States Supreme Court has as well.[5] For Hale, the government may

> induce me to contract to forego the liberty to these acts [actions that the government may not imprison me for doing]; and after making a valid contract I have relinquished *pro tanto* my constitutional right, even in the stricter sense of the term; for, by enforcing the contract against me, the state may now forbid me by direct sanctions to do those things which it could not so forbid in the absence of the contract.[6]

Sharp-eyed readers may be able to discern here, and in the following statement from Professor Hale, the context for plea bargaining:

> What we are principally concerned with, however, is whether, and in what circumstances, a government (state or federal) may use one power

> that is normally valid in order to induce a person to forego the exercise of what is admittedly a "constitutional right."[7]

Criminal defendants presented with the "option" to plea bargain are confronted with just this predicament. Prosecutors use their prosecutorial authority (*normally valid authority*) to induce abdication of a defendant's Fifth and Sixth Amendment rights (*forego the exercise of a constitutional right*).

Why is this important? As I demonstrate, beginning in the latter part of the 19th century, the United States Supreme Court has considered unconstitutional conditions relating to international trade.[8] In the 20th century, the Court held in *United States v. Butler*[9] that The Agricultural Production Act of 1933, which required farmers to reduce their productive acreage in exchange for federal support, created an unconstitutional condition. At issue for the Court was whether Congress had exceeded its regulatory authority by creating an unconstitutional condition (reduce productive acreage) on the receipt of a benefit (access to federal agricultural loan support). Writing for the majority in *Butler*, Justice Roberts conveys the following biting criticism:

> The Government asserts that whatever might be said against the validity of the plan if compulsory, it is constitutionally sound because the end is accomplished by *voluntary cooperation*. There are two sufficient answers to the contention. *The regulation is not in fact voluntary*. The farmer, of course, may refuse to comply, but the price of such a refusal is the loss of all benefits. The amount offered is intended to be sufficient to exert pressure on him to agree to the proposed regulation. *The power to confer or withhold unlimited benefits is the power to coerce or destroy*. (My emphasis.)[10]

Butler remains good law.[11] At a minimum, the *Butler* Court addressed two issues paramount to my critique of plea bargaining: 1) the voluntariness component and 2) the concern that the "power to confer or withhold unlimited benefits is the power to coerce or to destroy." By way of reminder, Federal Rule 11 of the Rules of Criminal Procedure mandates that plea bargains only be entered into if they are knowing/intelligent and voluntary (i.e., absent coercion). As I have demonstrated in this book and elsewhere, the structural conditions imposed upon a criminal defendant confronting a plea presume that the defendant confronts the state as *Homo economicus* – the free-thinking, freely acting, reasonable, and rational individual who, as an autonomous agent, is "free" to "negotiate" criminal charges and eventual sentences. *Homo economicus* aside, let's return for a moment to Justice Roberts's opinion in *Butler*. What the *Butler* majority was keen to understand and operationalize by way of its holding was that the implementation of state and federal due process is enshrouded in the power first established by the state, soon to be followed by subsequent legal coding to legitimate that power (see Chapters 5 and 7). As an ideological state apparatus (Althusser), the criminal legal system rhetorically genuflects to American ideological commitments to the pursuit of liberty, individuality, and autonomy, in short, to *Homo economicus*. However, it was the *Butler* court, and numerous subsequent courts, that penetrated the ideological veneer that presented the relationship between subjects of the state and those operating as state actors as existing on an equal plane. The resulting opinion rendered by Justice Roberts exposed the ideologically motivated fog that rhetorically situates subjects as contractual equals to the power of the state. To conclude, the Supreme Court's holding in *Butler* identifies both the absence of voluntariness and the manifestation of state coercion as generating an unconstitutional condition on a benefit.

While the United States Supreme Court in *Butler* clearly identifies the presence of an unconstitutional condition on a benefit (the right to travel, the right to commerce, etc.), it was the Court's opinion in the 1821 case *Townsend v. Townsend*[12] that sounded early alarm bells. At issue was an attempt by the Tennessee legislature to issue paper money as legal tender.[13] The condition in *Townsend* was that plaintiffs in a civil judgment would have to wait for two years before being compensated unless the plaintiff accepted the award in the form of paper money. In deciding against the state of Tennessee, the Tennessee Supreme Court held that the condition was unconstitutional: "By such inventions every constitutional right may in succession be bartered away. Constitutional rights are vested, unexchangeable, and unalienable. They belong to posterity as well as to the present generation. We may use and enjoy, but not transfer them; and every such condition is utterly void."[14]

The Court once again addresses unconstitutional conditions in the 1867 case *Cummings v. Missouri.*[15] In the *Cummings* case, the Court was confronted with a priest who had been denied the right to practice his ministry because he refused to recite a loyalty oath. The Court held that loyalty oaths were illegal because they were intended as punishment for past disloyalty. Like the Court before it, and those that came after, the *Cummings* Court held that the state *may not* accomplish a goal through conditions placed upon constitutional rights (i.e., restrictions upon speech and the right to work) that, as the Tennessee Supreme Court had stated in its *Townsend* opinion, are "vested, unexchangeable, and unalienable." For its part, the *Cummings* Court announced that,

> The legal result must be the same, for *what cannot be done directly cannot be done indirectly*. The Constitution deals with substance, not

> shadows. Its inhibition was levelled at the thing, not the name. It intended that the rights of the citizen should be secure against deprivation for past conduct by legislative enactment, under any form, however disguised. (My emphasis.)[16]

In his analysis of the origin of the unconstitutional conditions doctrine, Maurice Merrill argues that "the story begins with the efforts put forth by many states to prevent foreign corporations doing business within their boundaries from resorting to the federal courts."[17] Those states attempting to extract concessions from foreign corporations in exchange for doing business in their state raised the specter of an unconstitutional condition generating a restraint upon trade. *Subject-matter jurisdiction* was of prime concern. In a federalist system, both federal and state law may address a specific civil action. To determine which court has the authority to hear cases, the courts are guided by federal and state statutes and case law directing their subject-matter jurisdiction. This is an extremely complex area of civil procedure law, and not something that can thoroughly be presented here. What is important to understand for our purposes is that matters of subject-matter jurisdiction, when combined with *diversity of citizenship* designations, provide a Gordian knot of legal pathways that both enable and restrict, corporations (foreign and domestic) from removing cases automatically to federal court where they are more likely to receive genial treatment.[18]

Another important case appearing in the United States and that raised the unconstitutional conditions doctrine from within civil procedure was *Insurance Co. v. Morse*.[19] For Merrill, despite the fact that the United States Supreme Court never uses the phrase, "the case seems clearly to be the fountainhead of the doctrine which now goes by that name [unconstitutional conditions]."[20] At issue in this 1874 case was a Wisconsin statute passed in 1870 which forbade any foreign corporation doing business in the state from seeking a change in venue from state to federal courts.[21] State courts possess "general jurisdiction." That means state courts can hear all manner of violations of civil and criminal law. States like Wisconsin, seeking to compel foreign corporations to adhere to and be held accountable by state law, attempted through statute to forbid foreign corporations from attempting to "forum shop" for the most "friendly" federal court in which to hear its claims since doing so would enable corporations to evade state law. The Court held in *Insurance Co. v. Morse* that the Wisconsin statute violated the Constitution of the United States by creating an unconstitutional condition.

> 1st. The Constitution of the United States secures to citizens of another state than that in which suit is brought an absolute right to remove their

cases into the federal court upon compliance with the terms of the Act of 1789.

2nd. The statute of Wisconsin is an obstruction to this right, is repugnant to the Constitution of the United States and the laws in pursuance thereof, and is illegal and void.

3rd. The agreement of the insurance company derives no support from an unconstitutional statute and is void, as it would be had no such statute been passed.[22]

Justice Hunt made plain in *Morse* that "a man cannot barter away his life, his freedom, or his constitutional rights."[23]

The clearest early 20th century articulation of the unconstitutional conditions doctrine appeared in *Frost & Frost Trucking Co. v. Railroad Commission.*[24] The *Frost* opinion was authored by conservative Supreme Court Justice George Sutherland (who would later famously author the holding in the previously presented precursor to plea bargaining law, *Patton v. United States*, in 1930). At issue in the *Frost* case was a California law that predicated the use of public roads by a trucking company on limiting charges that the trucking company may impose upon its customers. The condition? You may use public roads in California, but only if you charge your customers less for your services. In striking down the statute, Justice Sutherland and the majority of the Supreme Court held that the California Railroad Commission's actions amounted to an unconstitutional condition on a benefit. To be sure, the opinion, which appears within the context of the Liberty of Contract doctrine and the *Lochner* era cases, presents the Court with a Tenth Amendment state police power being invoked by the state of California to minimize fees charged by trucking companies to state residents. Was the condition imposed upon *Frost* an unconstitutional condition because it violated the economic liberties established by the Commerce Clause and all related *Lochner* era opinions? Most certainly. But despite its liberal economic Lochnerian taint, the reason for invoking the *Frost* opinion is Justice Sutherland's full-throated explication of the unconstitutional conditions doctrine.

> *It would be a palpable incongruity to strike down an act of state legislation which, by words of express divestment, seeks to strip the citizen of rights guaranteed by the federal Constitution, but to uphold an act by which the same result is accomplished under the guise of a surrender of a right in exchange for a valuable privilege which the state threatens otherwise to withhold.*
>
> *It is not necessary to challenge the proposition that, as a general rule, the state, having power to deny as a privilege altogether, may grant it upon such conditions as it sees fit to impose; but the power of the state*

> *in that respect is not unlimited, and one of the limitations is that it may not impose conditions which require the relinquishment of constitutional rights.*
>
> *If the state may compel the surrender of one constitutional right as a condition of its favor, it may, in a like manner, compel a surrender of all.* (My emphasis.)[25]

Justice Sutherland's aggressive defense of constitutional rights when confronted with state or federal attempts to commodify them by extorting concessions for benefits finds its clearest expression in this passage from the *Frost* opinion:

> There is involved in the inquiry not a single power, but two distinct powers. One of these, the power to prohibit the use of the public highways in proper cases, the state possesses; and the other, the power to compel a private carrier to assume against his will the duties and burdens of a common carrier, the state does not possess. It is clear that any attempt to exert the latter, separately and substantively, must fall before the paramount authority of the Constitution. May it stand in the conditional form in which it is here made? If so, constitutional guarantees, so carefully safeguarded against direct assault, are open to destruction by the indirect, but no less effective, process of requiring a surrender, which, *though in form voluntary, in fact lacks none of the elements of compulsion.* Having regard to form alone, *the act here is an offer to the private carrier of a privilege, which the state may grant or deny, upon a condition which the carrier is free to accept or reject. In reality, the carrier is given no choice, except a choice between the rock and the whirlpool – an option to forego a privilege which may be vital to his livelihood or submit to a requirement which may constitution an intolerable burden.* (My emphasis.)[26]

The *Frost* opinion signifies acknowledgment that "If government must provide a benefit *unconditionally*, it may not offer that benefit *conditionally* regardless of the content of the condition."[27] Accepting this statement as true, it might be useful here to return to my historical account of the right to trial by jury in the United States (Chapter 4). First, the right to a trial by a jury of one's peers was established in each of the American colonies and appeared in their colonial constitutions. Second, the right to a trial by jury was, alongside the right to religious worship, among the first rights agreed to by all members participating in the 1787 Constitutional Convention. Third, the right to a trial by jury appears in Article III, § 2 of the United States Constitution, and in the Fifth (grand jury), Sixth, and Seventh Amendments. To sum up, *a trial by jury is something that the state must provide unconditionally as it appears as an inalienable right.* As such, and consistent with the statement above, *the state may not condition a right that must be provided unconditionally on the offer of a benefit for the abdication of that right.* And why is this true? Because as Justice Sutherland explained in his *Frost* opinion, "If the state may compel the surrender of one constitutional right as a condition of its favor, it may, in a like manner, compel a surrender of all." The state may not impose conditions upon the assertion of an inalienable right. The right to a jury trial is an inalienable right. To impose a condition on the assertion of that right (abdication of a defendant's Fifth and Sixth Amendment rights) invokes an unconstitutional condition.

This same conclusion may be drawn from a critical analysis of Justice Holmes's "greater-lesser power" doctrine.[28] Briefly, if the government possesses the greater power to *offer* a benefit, it equally possesses the lesser power to *condition* that benefit. If, as with Justice Holmes, attention is primarily directed toward the consequences of the agreement, permitting the state to condition a benefit (i.e., the right to trial by jury) on perceived outcomes should actually generate stricter scrutiny of those conditions, not less. More precisely, "it translates into the claim that an impact on constitutional rights is sufficient to invalidate an allocation."[29] Countering Holmes, Professor Kreimer concludes that "the government that encourages nonexercise of constitutional rights by using allocational sanctions may be quite as dangerous as the government that 'attempts to impose its will by force of law.'"[30] Precisely. In fact, Kreimer, citing work from Appleton, Fried, and Berlin, makes the claim that since positive rights signify a claim to a shared cultural good, and negative rights stipulate restrictions upon government intrusion into our lives, "a withholding of benefits may be a violation of both negative and positive rights." Article III, §2 and the Sixth Amendment to the Constitution of the United States announce a positive right. That is, it is a right that extends to those who are accused of violating criminal law. It is a right that, with the Fourteenth Amendment, seeks to afford the accused both due process and equal protection of the law. In short, the Sixth Amendment is a positive right that provides some balance of power, a firewall if you will, between the executive branch of the state, with its sole possession over sanctioned violence, and the American people.

Perhaps the most important question as it relates to unconstitutional conditions is whether any of our rights are *inalienable.* One might argue that by definition a right, as opposed to a privilege, is inalienable; it cannot be taken away from us by the state. If we accept, as I do, that the rights expressed in Article III §2 and the Sixth and Seventh Amendments, each establishing the right to a jury trial in criminal and civil cases respectively, are inalienable and cannot be taken from us by any state authority, is there any way that the state's allocation of a benefit in the form of a charge and sentencing bargain (a plea) may be constitutional? The simple answer is no. It may not. When the state attempts to deviate from constitutionally inalienable rights protections by way of an inducement to plea rather than go to trial, "the allocation at issue does not reduce constitutional liberties, it [the charge and sentence bargain] may still be constitutionally unacceptable *if the right involved is inalienable.* The inalienability of a constitutional right turns on both the context of this offer and the nature of the right" (my emphasis).[31] This is important. Let's say that, in its wisdom the state decides to provide criminal defendants with procedural "benefits" that at first blush expand the options available to that defendant when considering both the charges being leveled against them and the possible sentencing range. Let's also agree that the state's benevolence is driven by ideological acceptance of *Homo economicus*. That is, as a way to honor the *individual* autonomy of the accused, the state provides the accused with a menu of procedural options from which to *choose*. Here, like in Holmes's "greater-lesser" doctrine, the state has the power to *confer* those benefits and as such equally possesses the power to *condition* those procedural benefits in ways it chooses.

The question that arises from this scenario is whether, by providing a criminal defendant with procedural options, it actually enhances their liberty. It is my argument that it does not. In fact, following Kreimer, "if, without taking into account potential recipients' exercise of their constitutional rights, that same government would *provide* the benefit, *the conditional allocation is not an offer that expands options, but rather is a threat that contracts the right-holder's scope of autonomy* (my emphasis)."[32] As applied to plea bargaining, this statement takes some unpacking as it facially appears oxymoronic. After all, how can it be that the availability of greater procedural "liberty" to determine one's future as provided by the state through its option to plea bargain actually constrains subject action? Let us return for a moment to criminal procedure.

Please recall that in most jurisdictions in the United States, the first procedural step toward advancing a conviction in a criminal case requires prosecutors to present evidence before a grand jury in order to elicit an indictment (a true bill). For a grand jury to indict a criminal defendant, the jurors must be convinced that there is *probable cause* that: a) a crime was committed, and b) the defendant is the most likely offender (by way of reminder, probable cause is the second lowest standard of proof, appearing just above reasonable suspicion). Immediately upon indictment, a criminal defendant is presented with a procedural fork in the road – plead not guilty and assert their right to trial or enter into plea bargaining with the prosecutor. So far, so good. Plea bargaining appears as a "legal technology" created by statute and subsequent case law, manifesting one "option" for criminal defendants regarding charges and an associated sentence. If only it were that simple.

Ideologically operating within the liberal economic context generating *Homo economicus*, respect for individual autonomy mandates that criminal defendants be presented as atomized rights-bearing people who are legally positioned in a state of equity in relation to prosecutors. After all, each individual possesses the right to trial, and most likely the privilege to negotiate a plea bargain. This procedural "option" is offered at the behest of the executive branch and superficially appears to honor subject autonomy as partners to a bargain that each would find mutually beneficial. Or so the story goes.

As previously presented, criminal defendants do not encounter plea bargaining as *tabula rasa*, unmoored from neurophenomenological or procedural noise (e.g., thorough case investigation, discovery restrictions, prior convictions). Rather, as I have endeavored to establish, criminal defendants are nearly powerless when confronted by a prosecutor with a post-indictment plea bargain. The plea offer confronts the most structurally foreboding threat to defendants when a positive assertion of their Sixth Amendment right to trial meets a threatened trial tax (*Brady v. United States* and *Bordenkircher v. Hayes* are good examples). In what I believe to be an intentionally crafted autopoietic system-reproducing legal coding of social control, the state and the courts have constructed a Rube Goldberg simulacrum of procedural fairness and equity. In reality, the state's presentation of procedural "options" to an indicted criminal defendant is a manifestation of *surplus power,* indicative of Foucault's articulation of governmentality presented in the previous chapter. The so-called procedural option to plea bargain, when considered within the Gordian knot constituting the criminal legal system, turns out to be just so much bait-and-switch. The constitutional due process protections afforded to the accused are all still intact should a defendant decide to exercise their right to trial. However, with the prevailing threat of excessive punishment if convicted at trial, *the additional "option" to plea bargain actually narrows, rather than expands a defendant's options.* As applied to Professor Kreimer's assertion, it is in this way that plea bargaining "contracts the right-holder's scope of autonomy." Consider this hypothetical problem relating to the constitutional right to free speech. The federal government is conducting an experiment that requires 100 subjects to not speak for two days. Should the participant subjects break their silence during the two-day respite, they will see their taxes increase by $200.00.[33] Here, as with plea bargaining, the assertion of the constitutional right to speak will, if acted upon, generate a negative consequence that will cost participants $200.00. This is an unconstitutional condition. This is a hypothetical example of the trial tax confronting nearly all criminal defendants who are considering asserting their constitutional right to trial. You may assert the right, but there will be a price to pay. For our hypothetical subject, the price for asserting the right to speak is $200.00. For criminal defendants, the price for asserting the right to trial may be an excessive prison sentence and financial compensation.

It may be useful here to briefly address the distinction between an *offer* as an inducement to act in a certain way and a *threat* that would accomplish the same. For Simons, "a 'threat' is more troublesome than the 'offer' because it is presumptively unfair for government to make citizens worse off, even to serve a legitimate interest, when citizens have neither contributed to the problem they have been 'drafted' to correct nor received a reciprocal benefit."[34] My concern as it applies to plea bargaining is the threat of enhanced punishment if a defendant chooses to assert their right to trial and is found guilty. This is the trial tax. As the plea case law makes clear (Chapter 1), the Supreme Court has found that a criminal defendant confronted with the threat of harsher punishment if convicted at trial in order to induce them to plea bargain has in no way been "coerced" into the plea. Instead, because the Court has framed plea jurisprudence in the context of contract law, each defendant is presented with a set of "options" that they may, or may not, assert. But *plea bargaining presents legal scholars with a unique circumstance where both the threat and the offer are coercive.* For Simons, "a 'threat' is a government proposal to make the citizen worse off than she would otherwise be if she refuses to accept an objectionable condition [trial tax], while an 'offer' is a proposal to make her better off than she would otherwise be if she accepts the condition."[35] *For our purposes, both threat and offer must be viewed in tandem.* The offer may make the defendant better off, but the offer is presented in the context of a threatened trial tax. In other words, as with all things dialectical, there are two sides to this coin – the velvet glove and the iron fist.

This is precisely the circumstance that Justice Sutherland in *Frost* referred to as being *stuck between a rock and a whirlpool.* The executive branch of the state has procured for itself unfettered authority to serve as judge and jury in felony criminal cases, and it has done so through the vehicle of coded law. Consider the following.

In an important footnote, Professor Kreimer cites Lyons's far more critical assertion that resonates with Justice Harlan's vigilant critique of unconstitutional conditions. Specifically, it is Lyons's assertion, as it is mine, that conditions placed upon a right by the state signify the usurpation by the state of those birthright protections. This isn't supposed to happen. As the Fourteenth Amendment makes perfectly clear, rights to life, liberty, and property are the sole possession of the rights-holder as a member of a larger rights-based community. Lyons cautions that conditions on benefits (such as we find in plea bargaining) are outward expressions of an all too powerful state and judiciary, an ensemble of institutions that over time have accrued to themselves the power to define and deliver public goods, including rights. The fear is that when the state or the courts are permitted to claim authority over constitutional rights by restricting their use to their own purposes, they may couple that power with the offer of some conditioned benefit, thereby appearing to return the right to the people *in piecemeal fashion.* Lyons puts it this way: "The importance of this condition is that a clever tyrant would take away people's rights wholesale, in one stunning coup, and then dribble them back retail, as conditional privileges."[36] Reference to "retail" signifies rights as commodities that may be exchanged as if we are discussing hogs or motorcycles. As I have demonstrated, the commodification of the criminal legal system manifests in the charge and sentencing bargain. And just like Justice Harlan before him, Lyons's claim that a "tyrant" may appropriate all rights, and then return them to the people "retail" as a way to provide them with "options," is precisely my concern in this book. Rights only matter when they matter. We only need them when we need them. But when we need them, we need to know that we will be able to assert them in their most robust form. But what if the state can canvass the American people to see which rights they would be willing to forego in exchange for some state-sanctioned benefit? Assuming that some proportion of Americans would take the state up on its offer, the constitutional right will be so diluted as to cease to have any collective power. At that point, the right becomes a "right." Scare quotes intended.

The circumstance described above signifies the current situation regarding plea bargaining. The state, as manifested through executive branch power, possesses total control over the commodification of the criminal legal system. Where the right to trial by jury was considered to be inseparable from democratic government, the executive branch of the state, and the judiciary, have successfully conspired to deter criminal (and civil) defendants from asserting it.[37] Consider the following hypothetical problem. The United States government would like to know how dedicated to religious observance the American public is. A representative sample of American citizens is offered $20,000.00 *not to attend religious services.*[38] Does this offer meet constitutional muster? No. In this hypothetical problem, American citizens are being paid *not to assert* a constitutional right (First Amendment).

Now, let's apply the underlying principle being asserted in the religious observance hypothetical to plea bargaining. The United States government would like to test the fealty of American citizens to Article III §2 of the Constitution, and the Sixth Amendment. In the hypothetical problem, a representative sample of American citizens presented as criminal defendants was offered a significant downward departure from the maximum sentence if convicted at trial. In this hypothetical, a criminal defendant confronting a 25-year prison sentence if convicted at trial will only receive a ten-year prison sentence if they plead guilty. Does the executive branch's offer of a sentencing departure if the defendant chooses plea bargaining over assertion of the right to trial present an unconstitutional condition? Yes. There is little daylight separating the previous two hypotheticals. Whether one is offered financial remuneration ($20,000.00), or a significant reduction of a prison sentence (ten years rather than 25), the state's motivation is the same – to deter the assertion of a constitutional right by offering an attractive benefit.

The final point that I wish to raise in relation to unconstitutional conditions and plea bargaining pertains to the question of the waivability of rights. I have previously dedicated space to this question, so I will not belabor it here.[39] Still, it is important to consider the conditions under which the courts have held that an accused may waive their constitutional rights; generally speaking, there are three: 1) the right must be waivable, 2) the right must be alienable, and 3) it must be permissible for the state to procure the waiver of the right.[40]

It is my contention that through its adoption of plea bargaining, the criminal legal system has facilitated a threat to our democracy. This is because rights do not exist solely to promote the interests of *Homo economicus*. Rather, rights signify a community compact, a collective commitment to a way of living together under the social contract. Solely framing plea bargaining as a matter of efficient criminal procedure belies the more important political, economic, and cultural effect that the plea has upon our common commitment to each other. Relatedly, Simons argues that American citizens should not even be put to the choice between a constitutional right and a benefit since that process itself raises the specter of unconstitutional conditions.[41]

***

Case by case, prosecutors, defense attorneys, and judges participate in the facilitation of a legally coded technology of power that commodifies constitutional rights in the name of efficient and certain criminal case conviction to the point where, following death by a thousand cuts (or more aptly, millions of cuts), the right exists solely as a hollowed-out shell more analogous to the Wizard of Oz than to the United States Constitution and its positive rights-producing Amendments.

The result is the ever-growing usurpation of constitutional power and the use of force by the executive branch of the state. With no substantive judicial oversight, and no systemic check or balance, the criminal legal system's normative adoption of plea bargaining in the United States has morphed into a threat to the American people as power and force are systemically concentrated among the ensemble of legislators, judges, prosecutors, and defense attorneys, each of whom participate in securing to the state the authority it desires to maintain social control.

Notes

1 The conservative members of the United States Supreme Court include Chief Justice John Roberts, and Justices Clarence Thomas, Samuel Alito, Neil

Gorsuch, Brett Kavanaugh, and Amy Coney Barrett. The liberal Justices are Sonia Sotomayor, Elena Kagan, and Ketanji Brown Jackson.

2 For recent examples see *Dobbs v. Jackson Women's Health Organization*, 597 US (2022), and *Students for Fair Admissions, Inc. v. President and Fellows of Harvard College*, 600 US (2023). The *Dobbs* opinion upset 50 years of precedent established in 1973 by *Roe v. Wade* and affirmed in 1992 in *Planned Parenthood of Southeastern Pennsylvania v. Casey*, recognizing a woman's right to bodily integrity. In *Students for Fair Admissions*, the Court upset 46 years of precedent finding that universities *may not* consider a student's race/ethnicity as a variable in university admission decisions. This case struck at the heart of affirmative action necessary to diversify student populations. As did the *Dobbs* opinion, *Students for Fair Admissions* overturned one precedent-establishing case, *Regents of the University of California v. Bakke* (1978), and an additional case affirming *Bakke*, *Grutter v. Bollinger* (2003). What is the result? Instability. Unpredictability. No longer a matter of equal protection under law, women in the United States now must rely upon the wisdom of their state legislatures to determine whether and under what conditions they possess bodily integrity. With *Dobbs*, the Court upended reproductive freedom. In *Students for Fair Admissions*, the Court upset nearly 50 years of affirmative action that, as *Grutter* established, had been beneficial not only to colleges and universities as institutions, but to the culture as a whole.

3 Stephen Vladeck. The Shadow Docket: How the Supreme Court Uses Stealth Rulings to Amass Power and Undermine the Republic. New York: Basic Books (2023).

4 Kathleen M. Sullivan. Unconstitutional Conditions. 102, 7, Harv. L. Rev. 1413 (1989): 1415.

5 Id.

6 Robert Hale. Unconstitutional Conditions and Constitutional Rights. 35 Col. L. Rev. 3, 321 (1935): 321.

7 Id at 325.

8 See Maurice H. Merrill. Unconstitutional Conditions. U Penn. L. Rev. May, 1929.

9 297 US 1 (1936).

10 Cited in Paul Brest, Sanford Levinson, Jack M. Balkin, Akhil Reed Amar, and Reva B. Siegel. Processes of Constitutional Decisionmaking: Cases and Materials. New York: Wolters Kluwer (2018): 600.

11 In *South Dakota v. Adams*, 506 F. Supp. 50 (1980), the federal district court cited *Butler* to hold that all government restrictions upon the receipt of a benefit must be grounded in the general welfare of the people.

12 7 Tenn. (Peck) 1 (1821).

13 Seth Kreimer, Allocational Sanctions: The Problem of Negative Rights in a Positive State, 132 U. Penn. L. Rev. 1293 (1984): 1302.

14 Id.

15 71 US (4 Wall.) 277 (1867).

16 Id at 325.

17 Maurice H. Merrill, Unconstitutional Conditions. U. Penn. L. Rev. 879 (May 1929): 879.

18 See Chapters 2, 4, 5, and 6 in Jack H. Friedenthal, Arthur R. Miller, John E. Sexton & Helen Hershkoff. Civil Procedure: Cases and Materials. St. Paul, MN: West Academic Publishing (2018).

19 20 Wall. 445, 447 (US 1874).

20 Supra 8 at 880.

21 A statute of Wisconsin passed in 1870 enacts as follows:

"It shall not be lawful for any fire insurance company, association, or partnership, incorporated by or organized under the laws of any other state of the United States or any foreign government for any of the purposes specified in this act directly or indirectly to take risks or transact any business of insurance in this state unless possessed of the amount of actual capital required of similar companies formed under the provisions of this act, and any such company desiring to transact any such business as aforesaid by any agent or agents in this state shall first appoint an attorney in this state on whom process of law can be served containing *an agreement that such company will not remove the suit for trial into the United States circuit court or federal courts, and file in the office of the secretary of state a written instrument, duly signed and sealed, certifying such appointment, which shall continue until another attorney be substituted.*" https://supreme.justia.com/cases/federal/us/87/445/

22 Supra 19 at 87.
23 Cited in Hale, Supra 6 at 326.
24 271 U.S. 583 (1926).
25 Supra 10 at 1727.
26 Supra 8 at 889.
27 Supra 4 at 1423.
28 *Western Union Tel. Co. v. Kansas*, 216 US 1, 53 (1910) (Justice Holmes dissenting). In a case relating to whether the Massachusetts legislature had the right to restrict speaking permits on the Boston Commons, Justice Holmes wrote in dissent: "For the Legislature absolutely or conditionally to forbid public speaking on a highway or public park is no more an infringement of the rights of a member of the public than for the owner of a private house to forbid it in his house ... [T] he Legislature may end the right of the public to enter upon the public place by putting an end to the dedication to public uses. So it may take the lesser step of limiting the public use to certain purposes."
29 Seth F. Kreimer. Allocational Sanctions: The Problem of Negative Rights in a Positive State. 1413 Faculty Scholarship at Penn Law, 1293 (1984): 1313.
30 Id at 1319. Here, Kreimer cites the Supreme Court opinion in *Maher v. Roe*, 432 US 464 (1977).
31 Id at 1352.
32 Id at 1372.
33 Kenneth Simons. Offers, Threats, and Unconstitutional Conditions. 26, San Diego L. Rev. 289 (1989): 291.
34 Id at 291.
35 Id at 291.
36 Supra 29 at 1372, n. 294, at 1372.
37 The verb, conspired, refers to the Supreme Court's *Brady* opinion being used as the foundation for the United States Congress's composition of Federal Rule 11, with the Court vigorously affirming its *Brady* opinion upon subsequent legal challenges.
38 Supra 33 at 296.
39 Robert Schehr. The Emperor's New Clothes: Intellectual Dishonesty and the Unconstitutionality of Plea Bargaining. 2, Tex. A&M L. Rev. 385 (2015).
40 Supra 29 at 1386.
41 Supra 33 at 297.

References

Paul Brest, Sanford Levinson, Jack M. Balkin, Akhil Reed Amar, and Reva B. Siegel. *Processes of Constitutional Decisionmaking: Cases and Materials*. New York: Wolters Kluwer (2018)

Jack H. Friedenthal, Arthur R. Miller, John E. Sexton, and Helen Hershkoff. *Civil Procedure: Cases and Materials.* St. Paul, MN: West Academic Publishing (2018)
Robert Hale. Unconstitutional Conditions and Constitutional Rights. 35(3) *Col. L. Rev.*, 321 (1935)
Seth Kreimer. Allocational Sanctions: The Problem of Negative Rights in a Positive State. 132 *U. Penn. L. Rev.*, 1293 (1984)
Maurice H. Merrill. Unconstitutional Conditions. 77 *U Penn. L. Rev.*, 879 (May, 1929)
Robert Schehr. The Emperor's New Clothes: Intellectual Dishonesty and the Unconstitutionality of Plea Bargaining. 2 *Tex. A&M L. Rev.*, 385 (2015)
Kenneth Simons. Offers, Threats, and Unconstitutional Conditions. 26 *San Diego L. Rev.*, 289 (1989)
Kathleen M. Sullivan. Unconstitutional Conditions. 102(7) *Harv. L. Rev.*, 1413 (1989)
Stephen Vladeck. *The Shadow Docket: How the Supreme Court Uses Stealth Rulings to Amass Power and Undermine the Republic.* New York: Basic Books (2023)

9

CONCLUSION

The United States of America resolves nearly all of its felony criminal cases by way of plea bargaining. Increasingly, across the globe, nation states have commenced experimentation with plea bargaining along the lines of the United States, and for the same reasons – efficiency, predictability of outcome, and cost-savings.[1] As should be obvious at this point, I think that this is a negative trend in the wrong direction.

In this book, I have argued that the plea emerged in the United States alongside growing industrialization, that it was an outgrowth of equity and conciliation model courts, the professionalization and increasing influence of lawyers, and the need to maintain social control over marginal populations in both the North and the South. I have presented evidence that the historical reference to police powers was narrowed in the middle of the 19th century with the increasing influence of the state and its facilitation of the growth of industrialization and the influence of corporate power.

The most important claim that I make in this book is that plea bargaining is a threat to democracy. This is admittedly "pants on fire" language that could be dismissed as so much hyperbole. After all, how can one lone criminal procedure pose a threat to the institutional legitimacy of the entire nation?

The United States of America is populated by 333 million people. Data gathered from the 2020 census indicates that the United States is comprised of nearly 1,500 ethnic groups, including 30 detailed and four regional Hispanic origin groups, 270 detailed race groups, 1,187 American Indians and Alaska Natives (AIAN) tribes and villages, and 24 regional race groups.[2] The US land mass encompasses 3,532,316 square miles. There are approximately 43 languages spoken in the United States. By far the most common

DOI: 10.4324/9781003385103-11

language spoken in the home is English, followed in descending order by Spanish, Chinese, Tagalog, Vietnamese, Arabic, French, Korean, Russian, Portuguese, Haitian Creole, Hindi, German, Polish, Italian, Urdu, Persian, Telugu, Japanese, Gujarati, Bengali, Tamil, Punjabi, Thai, Serbo-Croatian, Armenian, Greek, Hmong, Hebrew, Khmer, Navajo, Indo-European languages, West African languages, Afro-Asiatic languages, West Germanic languages, Austronesian languages, other Asian languages, other Indic languages, Ukrainian and Slavic languages, Central, Eastern and Southern African languages, Dravidian languages, native languages of North America.[3]

One of the most important 19th-century sociological questions was posed by French sociologist Emile Durkheim. Unlike his predecessor Karl Marx, who focused his attention on the conflict that was inherent in the capitalist mode of production, Durkheim asked a far more complex and interesting question: "How is society possible?" It is true that conflict of all kinds is a simple matter of dialectical human engagement. But how is it that despite our differences, we are still able to carry on in somewhat predictable ways? How is it that, for the most part, each of us each day awakens to a largely orderly and predictable set of experiences that will unfold at school or at work or on our days off? For Durkheim, concern flowed from the fact that during and after the Enlightenment period occurring in the West (1715–1789), people were moving away from organized religion as providing a moral compass for social behavior, and toward the language of individual rights under *Homo economicus*. For Durkheim, it was the introduction of law as the prevailing organizing principle in industrial societies that would provide the necessary ideological legal-rational glue to hold diverse populations together as an organized whole. Of course, as we have seen, while the application of law to social behavior will have the effect of altering that behavior, the question then becomes, "Who has the power and authority to code and to wield the law?" This was the purpose of Max Weber's analysis of power and authority.

Now put to the contemporary United States, the language of law must coordinate the actions of 333 million people speaking 43 languages, from just under 1,500 ethnic groups living in a geographic region that encompasses 3,532,316 square miles. There are many ways that cultures seek to indoctrinate their people to a wider sense of connectivity with those who are similarly situated ethnically and geographically. Education is one of the primary institutions responsible for transmitting cultural values, as are the media, religion, politics, economics, and law. This was the insight offered by Luis Althusser's articulation of ideological state apparatuses (ISAs). It is ISAs in all cultures that provide the people with the knowledge of their cultural capital and habitus, including language, necessary to live in that culture. As I indicated in Chapter 7, among the list of ISAs existing at any one time to affect dominant cultural values, I selected law. That is, and consistent with Althusser, it is the function of law to maintain system stability and reproducibility. One law, in the case of the United States driven by the Constitution, the Bill of Rights, and all subsequent Amendments and case law, blankets one of the most diverse assemblages of *Homo sapiens* that has ever existed on the planet. No matter our ethnic backgrounds or the languages that we speak, each of us understands that we have access to the courts of law ostensibly serving as a neutral arbiter of disputes, whether criminal or civil, and that law serves as an Archimedean point of all disputes and interests, thereby stabilizing the previously unstable by returning us to system equilibrium. By way of analogy, consider the insight offered by chaos theory. While there exists vibrant energy at the local level (think cultural differences in music, food, language, religious practice, etc.), at the level of social structure that localized energy smooths out to form a somewhat ossified patterned set of cultural practices that inevitably generates system stability. System stability, it will be recalled, is necessary for any culture to survive, most especially political and economic stability as it manifests in international trade and geopolitical relations between nation-states. Law is the language that has been adopted by nearly all cultures to establish predictability and reliability in domestic and international relations.

The trial by jury accomplished many important goals necessary for the establishment of a constitutional democracy. First and foremost among them was to provide a procedural mechanism that would enable common people to determine matters of law and fact when questions of criminal guilt were raised.

Criminal procedure during the Middle Ages was a fairly simplistic affair. The accused was forced into swearing an oath – *oath de veritate dicenda* – to tell the truth to all interrogatories. The purpose of the oath was to induce confessions. Under canon law, the oath was viewed as the most perfect or complete proof of guilt. Oaths were banned in 1725 as they were considered too unreliable. In addition to the sworn oath, an accused was not permitted to know the charges against them or who bore witness against them.

As applied to contemporary plea bargaining, the accused is confronted with an "oath" of sorts, in that they must assert their guilt before a prosecutor and a judge. In addition, as with criminal procedure in the Middle Ages, defendants confronting a plea have no right to know who bore witness against them (*United States v. Ruiz*). But at least contemporary defendants will know the charges against them, right? As I presented in Chapter 1, sort of. When prosecutors engage in charge stacking, meaning they accumulate as many charges as they can possibly squeeze from the known facts regardless of whether they can prove those charges beyond a reasonable doubt at trial, they engage in a practice of "hiding the ball" that was common in European ecclesiastical courts. Opposite from the experience of our European ancestors who were not informed of the charges they faced, currently in the United States defendants *are overwhelmed with too many charges*. The result, however, is the same: decisional ambiguity generated by the legitimate representative of state power – the prosecutor.

The reasons for supporting plea bargaining are circular. As I argued in this book, it is legislatures in each of the states that control the naming of behavior as criminal and who erect sentencing ranges for each category of crime. So, why are there "too many cases" to prosecute? Because legislatures tend to add to the list of criminal behaviors rather than reducing them. The hydraulic effect is to require more arrests from police and more cases to consider for adjudication by prosecutors. The cycle is now complete. Prosecutors, defense attorneys, and judges will each be positioned to rightfully claim that there are simply too many cases before them and not enough trial-related resources for each case to realize its constitutional promise. This statement is both true and not true. It is true that the sheer quantity of cases will increase over time as legislatures add more crimes requiring adjudication. It is also true that the additional cases will place significant pressure upon criminal legal system actors and resources. However, in two important ways, it is not true. First, prosecutors should adhere to the American Bar Association guidelines regarding plea bargaining.[4] Second, as I established in Chapter 7, legislatures signify the power of the state through governmentality and they should act in a way that decriminalizes non-violent crimes, especially those relating to marijuana possession and distribution, which across the United States account for a significant proportion of felony convictions. In addition, as I presented in Chapter 5, legislatures engage in the "coding of capital" through their construction of draconian sentencing ranges. In order to generate a rupture in the circular argument that justifies plea bargaining, subjects acting within the civil society-lifeworld must organize a power bloc to pressure legislatures to significantly reduce mandatory maximum sentences. With mandatory maximum sentences reduced to a more reasonable amount of incarceration (say 15 years for homicide), the criminally accused will no longer be required to confront the coercive trial tax when considering whether to assert their right to trial.

It is my contention that once the trial tax is removed from consideration, the United States may return to a greater sense of democratic due process. In so doing, criminal defendants will be able to realize their constitutional rights protections under the Fourth, Fifth, Sixth, Eighth, and Fourteenth Amendments. In addition to the obvious equal protection and due process rights that are fully activated, each case will include a check on executive branch power by the person of the judge. Our system of procedural checks and balances at trial is by no means perfect. However, turning the Constitution and the Bill of Rights on their respective heads and eschewing them for the efficiency and predictability of contract-inspired plea bargaining has generated a role within the criminal legal system for prosecutors that places them squarely within the ambit of the Star Chamber. No more transparency. No more objection to coerced confessions. No more thorough discovery of case facts. No more procedural right to know who is making a claim against you, or whether there is any material impeachment evidence. No real investigation. And perhaps most important of all, *there exists no institutional check on the executive power of the prosecutor to serve as judge and jury.*

Contemporary defendants are exposed to a model of the criminal legal system premised upon the factory production line, where efficiency and predictability of outcomes are generated through routinized institutional autopoiesis. The plea is the norm. It has emerged over the course of the last two centuries to contaminate the democratic administration of justice like a slow-boiled frog. Incrementally, over time, and not without support from the afflicted, as can be expected from a hegemonic force, Americans have become participants in the creation of what Weber referred to as their own "iron cage."

In the case of plea bargaining and incarceration, Weber's warning is both literal and figurative as the plea has accomplished both its social control and profit-maximizing functions. With regard to the latter, while we no longer exist in a world that is dominated by industrial capitalism, *carceral capitalism* has emerged to perpetuate continued profit maximization through mass or hyper-incarceration.[5] With formal indentured servitude, surety systems, and vagrancy laws no longer providing nascent capitalism with a steady stream of marginal and impoverished bodies to exploit for profit, the political economy of the criminal legal system transitioned to criminal incarceration as an emerging profit-maximizing enterprise.[6]

For Zatz, "racialized mass incarceration enables new forms of economic exploitation that simultaneously operate outside conventional forms of socioeconomic regulation even while being integrated into conventional markets."[7] With the ease of conviction constitutive of plea bargaining, criminal legal system actors serving as agents of governmentality, wittingly or not, provide contemporary capitalist enterprises associated with the preservation and perpetuation of hyper-incarceration as a means to capital growth. This efficient institutional technology facilitates the needs of capital by providing a predictable flow of bodies (recall Foucault and his emphasis upon bio-power) that, under the twin powers of governmentality and economics, realizes the nation-state's interest in social control, all the while greasing the criminal legal system assembly line necessary to the facilitation of profit maximization characteristic of a necrotic stage of neoliberalism.

Notes

1 Gabriele Paolini, Elena Hantorowicz-Reznichenko, and Stefan Voigt. Plea Bargaining Procedures Worldwide: Drivers of Introduction and Use. Institute of Law and Economics Working Papers, 75 (October 2023). https://www.econstor.eu/bitstream/10419/279472/1/ile-wp-2023-75.pdf

2 Alli Coritz, Jessica E. Pena, Paul Jacobs, Brittany Rico, Joyce Key Hahn, Ricardo Henrique Lowe, Jr. Census Bureau Releases 2020 Census Population for more than 200 New Detailed Race and Ethnic Groups. https://www.census.gov/library/stories/2023/09/2020-census-dhc-a-race-overview.html
3 https://en.wikipedia.org/wiki/Languages_of_the_United_States
4 The American Bar Association Criminal Justice Section 2023, Plea Bargain Task Force Report, dated August 2023. https://www.americanbar.org/content/dam/aba/directories/policy/annual-2023/502-annual-2023.pdf
5 See Jackie Wang. Carceral Capitalism. Massachusetts: MIT Press (2018).
6 See, for example, Noah Zatz. Get to Work or Go to Jail: State Violence and the Racialized Production of Precarious Work, 45 *Law & Social Inquiry* 304 (2020), and Noah Zatz. The Carceral Labor Continuum: Beyond the Prison Labor/Free Labor Divide, in *Labor and Punishment: Work In and Out of Prison* (edited by Erin Hatton, University of California Press, 2021).
7 Id at 213. Get to Work or Go to Jail.

References

Alli Coritz, Jessica E. Pena, Paul Jacobs, Brittany Rico, Joyce Key Hahn, and Ricardo Henrique Lowe, Jr. Census Bureau Releases 2020 Census Population for More than 200 New Detailed Race and Ethnic Groups. https://www.census.gov/library/stories/2023/09/2020-census-dhc-a-race-overview.html

Gabriele Paolini, Elena Hantorowicz-Reznichenko, and Stefan Voigt. Plea Bargaining Procedures Worldwide: Drivers of Introduction and Use. Institute of Law and Economics Working Papers, 75 (October 2023)

Task Force Report, dated August 2023. https://www.americanbar.org/content/dam/aba/directories/policy/annual-2023/502-annual-2023.pdf

The American Bar Association Criminal Justice Section 2023, Plea Bargain

Jackie Wang. *Carceral Capitalism.* Massachusetts: MIT Press (2018)

Noah Zatz. Get To Work or Go To Jail: State Violence and the Racialized Production of Precarious Work. 45 *Law & Social Inquiry,* 304 (2020)

Noah Zatz. The Carceral Labor Continuum: Beyond the Prison Labor/Free Labor Divide. In Erin Hatton (ed.) *Labor and Punishment: Work In and Out of Prison.* Berkeley: University of California Press (2021)

INDEX